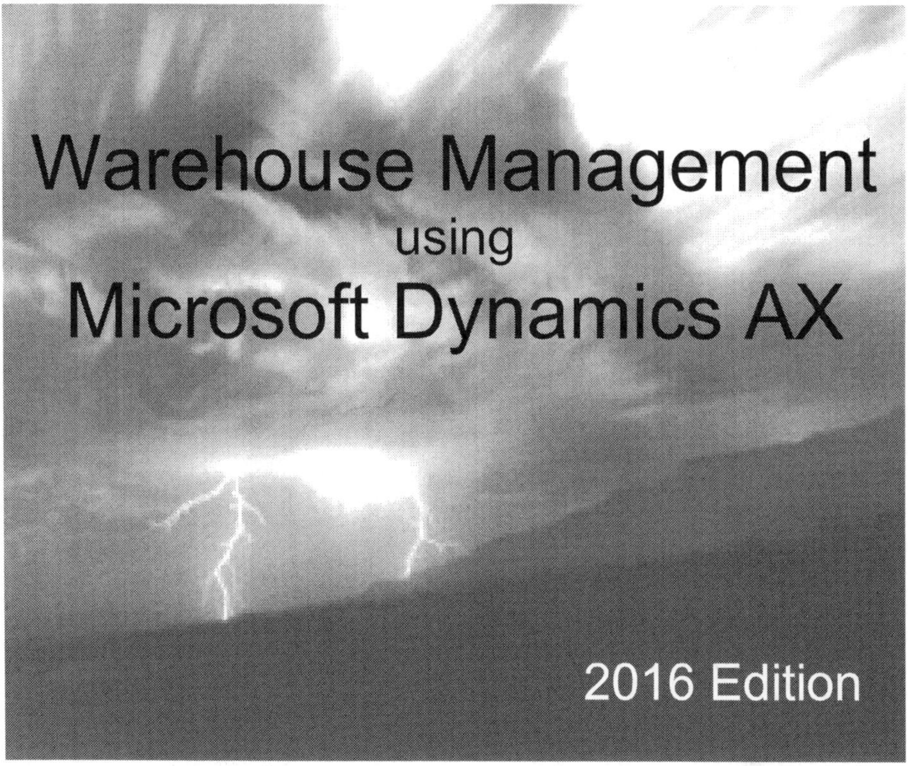
Warehouse Management
using
Microsoft Dynamics AX
2016 Edition

Other Books by Scott Hamilton

Process Manufacturing Using Microsoft Dynamics AX: 2016 Edition, Visions Inc. (2016)

Supply Chain Management Using Microsoft Dynamics AX: 2016 Edition, Visions Inc. (2016)

Warehouse Management Using Microsoft Dynamics AX 2012 R3, Visions Inc. (2015)

Discrete Manufacturing Using Microsoft Dynamics AX 2012, Visions Inc. (2012)

Food Products Manufacturing Using Microsoft Dynamics AX 2012, Visions Inc. (2012)

Managing Process Manufacturing Using Microsoft Dynamics AX 2009, Visions Inc. (2010)

Managing Wholesale Distribution Using Microsoft Dynamics AX 2009, privately published (2010)

Managing Lean Manufacturing Using Microsoft Dynamics AX 2009, Visions Inc. (2010)

Managing Your Supply Chain Using Microsoft Dynamics AX 2009, Printing Arts (2009)

Managing Your Supply Chain Using Microsoft Dynamics AX 4.0, Printing Arts (2007)

Managing Your Supply Chain Using Microsoft Axapta 3.0, McGraw-Hill (2004)

Managing Your Supply Chain Using Microsoft Navision, McGraw-Hill (2004)

Maximizing Your ERP System, McGraw-Hill (2003)

Managing Information: How Information Systems Impact Organizational Strategy (with Gordon B. Davis), Business One Irwin (1993)

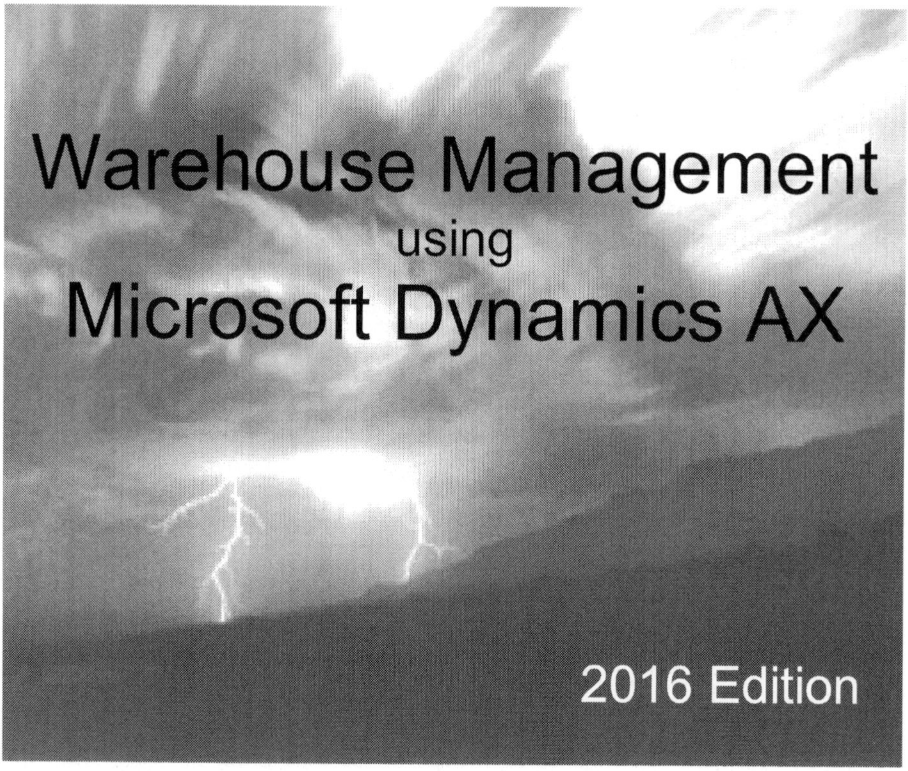

Scott Hamilton, Ph.D.

Print ISBN 978-0-9884976-8-9
eBook ISBN 978-0-9884976-7-2

The front cover photo depicts a lightning storm over Death Valley in California, and was taken by the nationally-recognized photographer Doug Peck (www.douglaspeckphotography.com).

Contents

Advanced WMS Approach

Common Foundation

Preface

The target audience for *Warehouse Management using Microsoft Dynamics AX: 2016 Edition* consists of those individuals involved with inventory and warehouse management within a manufacturing or distribution business. The book contents cover two major options currently available for using AX. One option can be labeled "Dynamics AX 2012", and the book focuses on the business logic within the most recent version of AX 2012 R3 which includes the advanced warehouse management capabilities. The other option represents a new release that can be labeled the "new Dynamics AX", with functionality based on the proven business logic of AX 2012 R3. The two options provide the same warehouse management functionality with some slight differences, so that the book contents apply to both options.

The warehouse management capabilities within AX can be broadly grouped into a basic approach and an advanced approach, and the book describes both approaches. The book also provides a broader perspective of supply chain management (SCM), and covers the related aspects of transportation management and quality management. It acts as a companion book for the 2016 Editions of my books about SCM in discrete and process manufacturing/ distribution businesses, which simply summarized the warehouse management capabilities.

A previous edition of the book covered warehouse management using the AX 2012 R3 version. Other previous books covered just the basic approach to warehouse management in the context of supply chain management using AX 3.0, AX 4.0, AX 2009 and AX 2012.

A trail guide and topographic maps provide essential information when exploring any unknown territory. They identify the most important features of the landscape and provide insights about key considerations and trail variations. Similar essentials apply to those exploring the use of an ERP system to run their business. As a trail guide, this book identifies the most important features of the embedded conceptual models and business processes related to warehouse management using AX, and provides insights about key considerations and variations. The same major topographical features apply to AX 2012 R3 and the new Dynamics AX.

Many people helped in completing this book. They included Deb Skoog, Elise Kling Marty and Sandra Krzyzaniak in preparing the book, and many others that contributed insights during the months of prior research.

The book reflects my interpretation of how to use Microsoft Dynamics AX 2012 R3. Errors of omission and commission, and any misunderstandings, are hopefully minimized.[1] Corrections and suggestions are welcome, as well as additional case study examples. Please send to **ScottHamiltonPhD@aol.com**.

Each day of writing was started with the following prayer:

> Creator of all things, give me a sharp sense of understanding, a retentive memory, and the ability to grasp things correctly and fundamentally. Grant me the talent of being exact in my explanations, and the ability to express myself with thoroughness and charm. Point out the beginning, direct the progress, and help in the completion.

This book and its previous edition would not have been possible without the support from my wife Cindy during the many months of prior research and writing. The book is dedicated to Cindy.

[1] The book is for information purposes only. The author, publisher and Microsoft make no warranties, expressed or implied, in the presentation of information.

Chapter 1

Introduction

A primary challenge for many manufacturing and distribution firms involves effective implementation and use of an ERP system for managing their operations and supply chain, especially the integrated warehouse management capabilities. Learning the capabilities of your ERP software package provides a foundation for effective usage, and re-thinking previous ways of doing business. This book focuses on how Microsoft Dynamics AX supports warehouse management.

The warehouse management capabilities within AX can be broadly grouped into a basic approach and an advanced approach, and the book describes both approaches. The explanation of both approaches includes the larger context of supply chain management (SCM) as well as the related aspects of transportation management and quality management. This book and its detailed explanations act as a companion for the 2016 Editions of my books about SCM in discrete and process manufacturing/distribution businesses, which simply summarized the warehouse management capabilities within AX.

The book contents cover two major options currently available for using AX. One option can be labeled "Dynamics AX 2012", and the book focuses on the business logic within the most recent version of AX 2012 R3 which includes the advanced warehouse management capabilities. The other option represents a new release that can be labeled the "new Dynamics AX", with functionality based on the proven business logic of AX 2012 R3. The two options provide the same warehouse management functionality with some slight differences, so that the book contents apply to both options. The book identifies the slight differences such as the variations in user experience and the workspace capabilities. Beneath these changes in look and feel, the two options share the same embedded conceptual models and business processes.

The targeted reader includes those individuals implementing or considering Dynamics AX as their ERP system, as well as those providing consulting assistance. This chapter starts with suggestions for the targeted reader, and describes the organization of book topics, the prior research and the scope of the book topics. It highlights the use of business process modeling (BPM) diagrams as a learning tool, and a baseline model of operations that simplifies the learning process. These considerations are reflected in the following sections within this chapter.

1. Suggestions for the Targeted Reader
2. Organization of Book Chapters
3. Reasons for Reading the Book
4. Prior Research and Scope of Book Topics
5. Terminology Used in the Book
6. Variations in the User Experience and the Use of Workspaces
7. Business Process Modeling (BPM) Diagrams as Learning Tools
8. Baseline Model of Operations
9. Baseline Model of Operations in the Process Industries
10. Summary of Case Studies

1.1 Suggestions for the Targeted Reader

The targeted reader primarily consists of those individuals responsible for warehouse management at manufacturing and distribution firms. In particular, it is intended to assist professionals implementing or considering Dynamics AX as their ERP system as well as those providing consulting assistance.

The book contents have been segmented to support several categories of targeted readers, so that you can focus on just the relevant chapters for your learning objectives. The various learning objectives are summarized in Figure 1.1 and described below. The suggestions reflect the organization of book chapters into two groupings about the basic versus advanced approach to warehouse management, so it may be helpful to view this information first (Figure 1.2). The underlined words in Figure 1.1 indicate the key differentiator for the learning objective. The last two learning objectives apply to knowledgeable AX users.

Learn the Advanced WMS Approach to Warehouse Management You can focus on just the chapters covering the advanced approach and out-of-the-box mobile device transactions (Chapters 2 and 4, and 13 through 23). These chapters provide a linear sequence of explanation and consist of approximately 200 pages. They build on the chapters covering foundation information about items, batch/serial numbers, and quality management (Chapters 24 through 26).

Figure 1.1 Typical Learning Objectives about Warehouse Management using AX

	Learning Objective	Estimated Pages
	Advanced WMS Approach to warehouse management	200
	Basic Approach to warehouse management	130
	Business Processes related to warehouse management	
	Warehouse management for a Distribution operation	
	Warehouse management for a Manufacturing operation	45
	Integration with Supply Chain Management	
	Integration with Quality Management	20-40
	Integration with Transportation Management	20
For AX Veterans	Incrementally Learn the Advanced WMS Approach	160
For AX Veterans	Confirm/Extend knowledge of the Basic Approach to warehouse management	

Some readers will face a significant learning curve about the extensive functionality, its underlying conceptual models, and the details of designing/using mobile device transactions -- especially those unfamiliar with advanced WMS capabilities in other systems. The advanced approach is reflected in the AX user documentation topics about "features in the warehouse management module".

Learn the Basic Approach to Warehouse Management You can focus on just the chapters covering the basic approach (Chapters 2 through 12). These chapters provide a linear sequence of explanation and consist of approximately 130 pages. They build on the chapters covering foundation information about items, batch/serial numbers, and quality management (Chapters 24 through 26). The basic approach does not include out-of-the box mobile device transactions.

Those unfamiliar with AX will likely face a comparatively shorter learning curve about the simpler functionality and its underlying conceptual models. An incremental learning curve would also apply to those using a third-party application for the mobile device transactions. The basic approach is reflected in the AX user documentation topics about "features in the inventory management module".

Learn Common Foundations for the Basic or Advanced Approach You can read just the chapters focusing on the common functionality related to inventory status, item definition, batch/serial tracking and quality management (Chapter 4 and Chapters 24 through 26). The two approaches share a high degree of common functionality.

Learn both the Basic and Advanced Approaches The choice of an advanced versus basic approach to warehouse management can be warehouse-specific. You can use the advanced approach at some warehouses and the basic approach at other warehouses, especially off-site warehouses representing a subcontractor or remote location. The two approaches share a high degree of common functionality, as summarized in Appendix A.

Learn both approaches for a Selected Business Process You can review both approaches for just a single type of warehouse transaction. This includes an in-depth comparison of the approaches for sales order picking/shipping (Appendix C), and each chapter for the advanced approach includes a section comparing the two approaches. The analysis identifies the comparable steps for a simple yet typical business process.

Learn the Business Processes related to Warehouse Management Each chapter about a warehouse management transaction starts with a simple yet typical business process. A Business Process Modeling (BPM) diagram illustrates the process and identifies the key steps and role responsibilities. Subsequent sections identify the key constructs and their related life cycles, the reversing transactions, and the major variations of the business process. The major variations often involve an in-depth explanation and the same explanatory approach -- with a BPM diagram and the identification of key constructs, life cycles and reversing transactions. The BPM diagrams primarily serve as a learning tool for incremental learning of complex functionality, as described in a subsequent section (Section 1.7).

The business processes for warehouse management (and the larger context of supply chain management) should reflect the new business models embedded within standard AX. Until the project implementation team has a basic understanding of these system capabilities, it is difficult to leverage AX for their business processes except for just asking that the system must do what their current system does today.

Learn Warehouse Management for a Distribution Operation You can focus on the chapters related to purchase orders, sales orders and transfer orders, and skip the chapters related to production orders and the production-related topics within the foundation chapters.

Learn Warehouse Management for a Manufacturing Operation You can focus on the chapters related to production orders and subcontracted production, either for the basic approach (Chapters 9-11) or advanced approach to warehouse management (Chapters 19-21). The explanation consists of approximately 45 pages for either approach. You might also review the production-related topics within the foundation chapters, and other relevant topics as sales orders and purchase orders.

Learn Warehouse Management for Discrete or Process Industries You can focus on each chapter's section about major variations related to each industry, as well as the industry-specific case studies. In addition, the explanation of a baseline model of operations covers discrete and process manufacturing/distribution (Sections 1.7 and 1.8).

The unique requirements in discrete and process industries are supported by standard AX capabilities. Example products representing a discrete industry range from industrial equipment and automotive components to aerospace and electronics. Process industry examples range from food products and beverages to chemicals, powders and polymer molded products. Warehouse management in these two industries often involves unique requirements. Each chapter about a warehouse transaction highlights these unique aspects in the section about major variations.

Many of the unique AX capabilities for manufacturing firms in each industry are differentiated by the approach for defining product structure. A company involved in discrete manufacturing will typically employ a bill of material (BOM) approach to define product structure, and the associated production orders for coordinating warehouse activities. A company involved in process manufacturing will typically employ a formula approach to define product structure, and the associated batch orders for coordinating warehouse activities. Some companies employ a mix of both approaches to product structure. Warehouse management for these two types of manufacturing often involves unique requirements. Each chapter about production highlights these unique aspects in the section about major variations.

Learn Integration of Warehouse Management and Supply Chain Management The broader context of a supply chain management (SCM) perspective is embedded throughout the book. Effective use of AX for supply chain management makes life easier for warehouse management. Examples include realistic ship dates for sales orders, supply orders driven by S&OP game plans, appropriate lead times related to receiving/inspection activities or picking/shipping activities, near-term stability in production schedules, and a manageable level of expediting. This learning objective served as a primary motivator for writing this book.

Learn Integration with Quality Management You can focus on the chapter for quality management (Chapter 25) consisting of 20 pages. A related topic often involves batch number tracking (Chapter 26), and each chapter's section about major variations includes topics about integrating quality management.

Learn Integration with Transportation Management You can focus on the two chapters related to transportation management. One chapter covers the basics of transportation (Chapter 12). Another chapter covers the incremental functionality related to advanced transportation management (Chapter 23). The total learning consists of approximately 20 pages.

Incrementally Learn the Advanced WMS Approach A knowledgeable AX user can focus on just the chapters that provide incremental learning of the Advanced WMS approach (Chapters 2, 4 and 13-26). The total incremental learning consists of approximately 160 pages.

The Advanced WMS functionality represents a dramatic change from previous AX versions, especially for the warehouse processes related to sales orders, transfer orders, purchase orders and production orders. Many people face a significant learning curve about the extensive functionality, its underlying conceptual models, and the details of designing/using mobile device transactions. The learning curve tends to be more difficult for those unfamiliar with advanced WMS capabilities in other systems. The functionality is reflected in the AX user documentation topics about "features in the warehouse management module".

Confirm/Extend Knowledge of the Basic Approach to Warehouse Management A knowledgeable AX user can focus on just the chapters covering the basic approach in order to confirm/extend their knowledge (Chapters 2-12 and 24-26). The basic approach primarily represents functionality within previous versions of Dynamics AX. In the jargon of AX, it represents the "old WMS I" functionality for managing inventory. The book does not cover the "old WMS II" functionality, and this was deprecated in the new Dynamics AX.

Knowledgeable AX users will already be familiar with most aspects of the basic approach. However, there are slight changes and several additional capabilities for the basic approach, such as support for wave picking and calculating space utilization for a non-WMS warehouse. This previous functionality is reflected in the AX user documentation topics about "features in the inventory management module".

The topics and chapters about the basic approach essentially represent a check list for assessing your current level of AX knowledge about warehouse management and its integration with supply chain management and quality management. Hence, it can help quantity your learning curve about unfamiliar topics.

1.2 Organization of Book Chapters

The organization of book chapters reflects two groupings about the basic versus advanced approach to warehouse management. This segmentation reflects the substantially different conceptual models and business processes for each approach. It also supports several categories of targeted readers described in the previous section.

The common starting point of "Strategic Options for Warehouse Management" and the chapters about common functionality (in Chapters 4 and 24-26) apply to both groupings. Figure 1.2 illustrates this segmentation of book chapters, and indicates the common chapters via grey shading. The figure also identifies the unique chapters for advanced warehouse management about work orders (Chapter 14), the additional cycle counting options (Chapter 22), and the integration with advanced transportation management (Chapter 23).

Figure 1.2 Organization of Book Chapters

Chapter	Basic Warehouse Management	Advanced Warehouse Management	Chapter
3	Fundamentals & Basic Transactions	Fundamentals & Basic Transactions	13
4	Significance of Inventory Status	Significance of Inventory Status	4
		Overview of Work Orders	14
5	Purchase Order Receiving	Purchase Order Receiving	15
6	Sales Order Picking/Shipping	Sales Order Picking/Shipping	16
7	Transfer Order Picking/Shipping	Transfer Order Picking/Shipping	17
8	Transfer Order Receiving	Transfer Order Receiving	18
9	Production Order Picking	Production Order Picking	19
10	Production Order Receiving	Production Order Receiving	20
11	Subcontracted Production	Subcontracted Production	21
		Additional Cycle Counting Options	22
12	Basics of Transportation	Integration with Transportation Mgt	23
24 to 26	Common Foundation about Items, Batch/Serial Numbers & Quality Mgt	Common Foundation about Items, Batch/Serial Numbers & Quality Mgt	24 to 26

1.3 Reasons for Reading the Book

Firms involved with a system selection process may be considering Dynamics AX as a candidate package and this book can help evaluate system fit and needed customizations, provide a vision of an integrated system, and reduce selection risks. The book can help businesses involved in implementing and using AX by accelerating the learning process, suggesting prescriptive business processes, reducing implementation time and costs, and reducing user resistance to change. It suggests changes that can improve system usage and revitalize a wayward implementation. For those providing AX consulting services, this book can accelerate the learning process, expand the scope of knowledge, and improve situational fluency. In particular, it can help those with previous AX experience learn the additional capabilities within AX. Figure 1.3 summarizes these reasons for reading the book.

Figure 1.3 Reasons for Reading the Book

		Manufacturing or Distribution Firm	Consultant or Solution Provider
Overall Goal		Improve firm performance through effective warehouse management systems	Improve customer service through increased knowledge of AX
System Implementation Life Cycle	System Selection	Evaluate system fit and needed customizations Provide vision of an integrated system Reduce selection risk	Accelerate learning process Gain knowledge of new functionality Reduce new employee ramp-up time Improve situational fluency Improve training and consulting efforts Prescribe business businesses Support gap/fit analyses Improve customization efforts
	Implementation	Accelerate learning process of new system Suggest prescriptive business processes Take advantage of new business models rather than just replicate previous system Provide ideas for best practices Reduce implementation costs , time and risks Reduce user resistance to change	
	On-Going Operation	Suggest changes to improve system usage Revitalize a wayward implementation	

1.4 Prior Research and Scope of Book Topics

The book focuses on warehouse management in manufacturing and distribution businesses using AX 2012 R3 or the new Dynamics AX, and this focus guided the prior research and the scope of book topics.

Prior Research Several steps of prior research were undertaken to understand the warehouse management requirements of manufacturers/distributors, and the AX functionality to support those requirements. With respect to the warehouse management functionality within AX 2012 R3, these steps included participation in prerelease and post-release training classes, webinars, and conference sessions;

reviews of the existing training materials, e-learning lessons, user documentation and sales demo materials; discussions with users, development personnel, and field consultants; and hands-on testing for thousands of use cases that reflected common requirements. With few exceptions, only those capabilities personally tested and proven were included in the book contents. The same approach was also undertaken for my previous books about Dynamics AX. The discussions with experienced field consultants helped identify the dominant business practices at current users. On-going opportunities to consult with current users have supplemented this understanding.

The prior research concerning the new Dynamics AX has been following similar steps. This included participation in pre-release webinars and conferences, discussions with leading experts and Microsoft team members, reading the currently available information, and hands-on testing. The book contents reflect my prior research up until the beginning of the year 2016.

The prior research about warehouse management within the larger context of supply chain management included my consulting and teaching experiences with manufacturing and distribution firms across the past three decades. These experiences included responses to numerous RFPs (requests for proposal) for an ERP system, face-to-face consulting engagements with several hundred firms, and teaching executive seminars, APICS certification classes, MBA courses, and user group sessions. My understanding of the AX capabilities for the basic approach to warehouse management have been shaped by 10+ years of field experience with previous AX versions, whereas my understanding of the advanced WMS approach only reflects 2 years of field experience. There are many aspects of warehouse management – both technical and managerial – that fall outside the book's scope and my current level of expertise/experience to explain them.

Scope of Book Topics The book topics focus on warehouse management and its larger context of supply chain management, and the selection of book topics was shaped by several factors. First, the selected topics reflect my 80/20 rule about relevance of AX software functionality to support warehouse management. Second, several topics were excluded because they could not be personally tested and proven within the budgeted time. Third, some topics were summarized or excluded because of book length considerations, as illustrated below.

- *Non-Stock Items.* The book focuses on trade goods, and does not cover the warehouse management aspects of purchase orders or sales orders for non-stock items. One exception involves the purchase of a subcontracted service, as described in the chapters about subcontracted production (Chapters 11 and 21).

- *Advanced Transportation Management.* The book summarizes the incrementally unique capabilities for advanced transportation management, and the integration points with the advanced approach to warehouse management.

- *Retail Operations.* The book does not address any of the specialized AX functionality for retail operations, such as the use of warehouses to represent stores.

- *Detailed Design of Mobile Device Transactions.* The detailed design can simplify the end-user experience for handling every possible situation. While some aspects of mobile device transactions are explained, the topic largely falls outside the scope of the book and my expertise. The technical aspects of mobile devices also fall outside the book's scope.

- *Catch Weight Items.* The use of catch weight item functionality is only supported in the basic approach to warehouse management; it is not yet supported in the advanced approach. The topic is not included in this book.

- *Item Identification based on Variant Codes.* This topic is briefly summarized within the book (Section 24.4), but the book focuses on the use of item numbers. The use of variant codes in all warehouse transactions was not completed tested in time for book publication.

- *Warehouse Management using the "old WMS II" capabilities.* An alternative approach to warehouse management – labeled the "old WMS II" approach – was not included in the analysis because it will be discontinued by Microsoft. It also represents a mutually exclusive approach because of license key issues.

- *General Ledger, Payables and Receivables.* Various warehouse transactions impact each of these areas, but the topics largely fall outside the scope of the book and my expertise.

The book length considerations precluded screen shots.[1] Other important topics of system development and usage were also excluded, such as security, alerts, business intelligence, and the customization capabilities within the AX development environment.

---

[1] One argument against screen shot examples is that most users tailor the standard screens, and the displayed information is also affected by license key activation.

Contributions to the AX Body of Knowledge The body of knowledge related to Microsoft Dynamics AX consists of several levels and components. The foundation level consists of the software, documentation and training materials provided by Microsoft, and augmented by access to other sources and to Microsoft's technical libraries. Additional contributions to the AX body of knowledge build on this foundation, and many different blogs and articles have contributed to my understanding. In terms of the book's contributions, I have attempted to explain the warehouse management capabilities using a variety of learning tools (such as BPM diagrams) and explanatory approaches to simplify and accelerate the learning process for others. The book provides a supply chain management perspective to warehouse management, as well as the integration points with quality and transportation management, especially for manufacturing and distribution firms.

1.5 Terminology Used in the Book

The terminology associated with many aspects of warehouse management can vary widely between companies and software packages. It is often difficult to clearly understand the meaning of a term -- such as inventory status, reservation, picking list, work order, license plate or a shipment -- without a lengthy discussion about its significance. This book describes the significance of these terms within AX as well as other terms and key constructs for warehouse management. The significance of a given term can differ between the basic and advanced approaches to warehouse management.

As much as possible, this book consistently uses the same terminology to describe the conceptual models and software functionality within AX. In most cases, the book's terminology reflects the names of forms, tabs, fields, and buttons of the AX software, but it sometimes reflects alternative phrasing to clarify understanding.

One difficulty in terminology stems from the book's attempt to explain two different options for using AX consisting of the new Dynamics AX and AX 2012 R3. The embedded conceptual models and business processes within the two options are fundamentally the same for warehouse management topics, but there are slight changes in AX terminology. As one example, the "ship complete" policy for a sales order line has been changed to the "prevent partial delivery" policy to more accurately indicate its purpose. A comprehensive list of terminology changes was not available prior to book publication. For consistency purposes, the book employs the terminology within AX 2012 R3 rather than mixing terms from the two options.

Other difficulties in terminology stem from the AX design. One example involves the AX approach to enterprise- and company-level information about an item, where the identifier is called a product number and item number respectively. Another example involves manufactured items, and the differences between production orders (for a BOM item) or batch orders (for a Formula item), and kanban orders in a lean manufacturing scenario. The book focuses on production orders, and identifies the major variations for batch orders.

One other terminology issue concerns the different options for warehouse management within AX, where the two major options represent different conceptual models. Several terms have been used to identify the different options, as described at the beginning the next chapter (Section 2.1). For simplicity's sake, the two major options are termed the basic approach and advanced approach to warehouse management.

1.6 Variations in the User Experience and the use of Workspaces

This book focuses on the embedded conceptual models and business processes within standard AX. The user experience and navigational details may differ -- whether using customized forms, workspaces, web-based applications, or hand-held devices -- but the embedded conceptual models and business processes still apply. This section briefly summarizes the variations in user experience and the use of workspaces.

Variations of the User Experience The standard menu structure and user-defined favorites provide commonly used approaches for navigation. When using the new Dynamics AX, the links within workspaces provide another approach for navigating to commonly used tasks. An additional approach – termed "search for a page" – enables you to specify the desired topic, review a list of applicable forms, and then navigate to a selected form.

Use of Workspaces Workspaces represent one variation in the user experience when using the new Dynamics AX. [2] Workspaces provide an aggregation of tasks related to a specific role. Many of the currently available workspaces provide summarized information with drill-down to details, and they

[2] The workspace functionality replaces several capabilities in AX 2012 R3 such as role-centered pages. The role-centered pages were built on the deprecated Enterprise Portal capabilities which have been replaced by the new web client platform. The new platform supports the use of workspaces and the related definition of workspace patterns to support different devices.

provide links for navigating to commonly used tasks. Several workspaces are related to inventory and warehouse management, as described in the following points.

Cost Administration Workspace This workspace includes links to key reports/inquiries about inventory accounting, such as inventory value statements, inventory aging, standard cost transactions, and calculation of ABC classifications.

Cost Analysis Workspace This workspace summarizes inventory turns and inventory accuracy (with drill down to those items with low turns or accuracy) as well as inventory value (with segmentation by item group and also total inventory value over time). The links provide access to key reports/inquiries about inventory accounting, such as inventory value statements, inventory aging, and calculation of ABC classifications.

Outbound Work Planning Workspace This workspace summarizes several aspects of the Advanced WMS approach to sales order picking/shipping as well as transfer order picking/shipping. For example, you can perform the periodic task for automatic release of sales orders or transfer orders. The links provide access to related information such as shipments, waves and work.

Much of the information applies to the use of wave picking. For a selected warehouse, the workspace identifies shipments not on a wave, and shipment waves that have not been processed or released. It also identifies the open picking work for released waves. If needed, you can manually create a new wave and then manually add selected shipments to the wave.

Some of the information applies to the use of replenishment of picking lines, and it identifies the open replenishment work for the selected warehouse. You can also perform the periodic task to create replenishment work via the replenishment calculations or the load demand replenishment calculations.

Outbound Work Monitoring Workspace This workspace summarizes several aspects of the Advanced WMS approach to replenishment of picking lines. For a selected warehouse, it identifies the active replenishment work for shipment waves and the unreleased replenishment work. The links provide access to other types of work orders (such as cycle count work, sales order picking work, transfer order picking work, and inventory movement work), and to information about the shipments (or loads) at a packing station.

1.7 Business Process Modeling (BPM) diagrams as a Learning Tool

One of the book's primary objectives consists of learning the embedded conceptual models and business processes within standard AX. In many implementations, these business processes can help the project team gain an overall understanding of system usage and each team member's roles, enabling them to envision new business practices and the real need for customizations. The business processes can be documented using Business Process Modeling (BPM) diagrams.

In this book, BPM diagrams are primarily used as a learning tool, especially for the chapters about order-related transactions. For example, each chapter starts with a BPM diagram illustrating a simple yet typical business process. It provides the basis for understanding the underlying conceptual models within AX, including key constructs, their life cycles, and reversing transactions. It also provides the baseline for explaining major variations to the process, which represents a "+1" approach to teaching and learning. An additional BPM diagram often applies to each major variation, and they all build on the "basic process" described at the chapter beginning. The explanation of a major variation often employs the same explanatory approach – illustrated by a typical process and a description of the key constructs, their life cycles and the reversing transactions. Stated another way, if you understand the "basic process", you can more easily learn the major variations supported by standard AX.

These business processes are described in terms of the end-user experience with standard AX forms and out-of-the-box mobile device transactions. The navigational details of the end-user experience may differ -- whether using customized forms or variations of mobile device transactions -- but the business processes must still conform to the embedded conceptual models within AX.

My BPM diagrams do not adhere exactly to the standards, and they employ a limited number of symbols to keep things simple. For example, three symbols are used to denote "And", "Or" and "Any, None, or All". A fourth symbol for an "Event" indicates an automatic action within AX, which helps explain some of the behind-the-scenes functionality. The BPM diagrams indicate a sub-process using a bold border.

1.8 Baseline Model of Operations

A baseline model of operations represents the common use of Dynamics AX and the dominant business practices within manufacturing and distribution firms. It provides a foundation for simplified explanations about how to use Dynamics AX to manage the business, and for explaining variations to the baseline model. In summary, the baseline model focuses on a single AX company with one or more AX sites (and their related AX warehouses) with standard products identified by an item number. Inventory is tracked by site, warehouse and bin location, with inventory replenishment logic at the site/warehouse level. Sales prices and purchase prices are typically companywide, although they can optionally reflect site-specific prices. Each manufactured item requires bill of material information, with optional definition of routing data. Further explanation of the baseline model of operations is provided below.

- *Single company and AX instance.* The baseline model consists of a single company using a single AX instance. Some scenarios involve multiple companies within one instance and possible partitioning of these companies within the database.

- *Multiple inventory locations identified by an AX site and warehouse.* Each physical location is identified by an AX site and an associated value for a "site" financial dimension. The site-specific financial dimension supports financial reports by site. In addition, each AX site has at least one AX warehouse, although additional AX warehouses may be necessary to support in-transit inventory (on transfer orders) or some other purpose. Each AX warehouse has one or more bin locations, although use of bin locations is not mandatory. The definition and use of warehouse locations differ significantly between the basic and advanced approach to warehouse management, as described in the fundamentals for each approach (Chapters 3 and 13).

- *Multiple business units within one company identified by an AX financial dimension.* In many cases, different items represent different lines of business that require financial reports by business unit. The business units are identified as different values for the "business unit" financial dimension. The appropriate value of this financial dimension is assigned to the relevant items, thereby supporting financial reports by business unit.

- *Material items identified by item number.* Material items are identified by an item number. In some cases, an item may be identified by an item number and one or more additional fields termed variant codes (Section 24.4). However, these cases fall outside the baseline model of operations and are not covered in the book.

- *Bill of material for a manufactured item.* A bill of material (BOM) defines the product structure for a manufactured item. In many cases, the product structure can be define by a formula (especially in process manufacturing), and these scenarios are explained as variations to the baseline model.

- *Routing information for a manufactured item.* Routing information can be optionally defined for a manufactured item, where routings also require the definition of resources, resource groups and master operations. The routing information involves special considerations for modeling subcontracted production.

- *Standard or actual costing for items.* Each material item must be assigned an inventory valuation method reflecting a standard cost or actual cost method. With standard costing, a costing version must be defined for standard costs, and each material item must have an item cost record for each site with inventory.

- *Inventory replenishment logic applies to the AX site and warehouse.* Replenishment logic is defined in an item's coverage planning data by site/warehouse.

- *Batch/serial numbers for material items.* The use of batch and/or serial numbers is treated as a variation to the baseline model. It is covered as a separate chapter (Chapter 25) and in each chapter's section about major variations to the business process.

- *Standard roles within Dynamics AX* The baseline model employs the standard roles within Dynamics AX to support role-based security. You assign users to these standard roles, and the predefined privileges for each role may be adjusted. For example, the privileges for the purchasing agent role include maintenance of purchase orders and vendor information. The standard roles are also reflected in business process diagrams throughout the book that illustrate typical business processes.

1.9 Baseline Model of Operations in the Process Industries

An explanation of using Dynamics AX in the process industries was provided in the companion book "Process Manufacturing using Microsoft Dynamics AX: 2016 Edition". A baseline model of operations in the process industries is largely the same as the previously-described explanation. Key differences include the formula approach to defining product structure for a manufactured item (rather than the BOM approach), and the critical importance of batch-controlled material and quality management considerations.

These key differences would change some aspects of the book's explanatory approach. For example, the book's explanation of a basic process for purchase order receiving currently focuses on normal material, and receipts of batch-controlled material (and related testing requirements) are identified as a major variation. This emphasis would be reversed for most scenarios in the process industries. As another example, the explanation of production orders would be changed to reflect the primary use of batch orders. The explanatory approach is not meant to minimize these key differences by treating them as a variation. Numerous case studies relevant to the process industries are included in the book.

1.10 Summary of Case Studies

Case studies illustrate how the AX software functionality applies to many different warehouse management scenarios. Some of these cases represent strategic options (as described in the next chapter) and others simply illustrate the use of AX to solve a business problem. Each chapter includes case studies applicable to the topic, and a complete list of case studies is provided at the end of the book.

Chapter 2

Strategic Options for Warehouse Management

Warehouse management represents a critical part of supply chain management for firms involved in manufacturing and distribution. Microsoft Dynamics AX offers users a range of options for warehouse management capabilities. The options can be broadly grouped into a basic approach and an advanced approach, and the choice of an approach can be warehouse specific. For example, a company may use the advanced approach at some warehouses and the basic approach at other warehouses. The two approaches share a high degree of common functionality, but the advanced approach has a much broader amount of functionality and supports out-of-the-box mobile device transactions. Both approaches can optionally take advantage of the capabilities related to Inventory Status.

For some firms, the key question involves "which option is best for my operation." Some may have already made this decision. The reader can then skip this chapter and go to the relevant chapters supporting their learning objectives. For those trying to make the decision, several guidelines can be considered and there are several ways to compare the two approaches. A related question often involves "what are the strategic options for starting with basic capabilities and evolving into more advanced capabilities." The flexibility to evolve can be considered within each of the two major approaches and from one approach to the other. Multiple case studies will be used to illustrate evolving strategies about starting simple and growing in sophistication. These considerations are reflected in the following sections within the chapter.

1. Major Options for Warehouse Management
2. Significance of the Inventory Status
3. Guidelines for Choosing the Basic vs Advanced Approach
4. Strategic Options and Summary of Case Studies

5. Evolving Strategies for Strategic Options
6. Details of Case Studies
7. Comparing Approaches

2.1 Major Options for Warehouse Management

The various warehouse management options have been called many different names, but they boil down to two major options.[1] For simplicity's sake, one major option can be termed the "Basic Inventory approach" or the "basic approach" for short. The second major option can be termed the "Advanced WMS approach" or the "advanced approach" for short. We will use the shortened terms moving forward.

The two major options are differentiated by a warehouse policy and an item-related policy about "use warehouse management processes." The advanced approach only applies to warehouse transactions for a WMS-enabled item at a WMS-enabled warehouse, whereas the basic approach applies to the other combinations of these two policies. Figure 2.1 summarizes these key policies and the two major options for warehouse management (identified as Option #1 and #2). It also identifies the terminology about items and warehouses, such as a WMS-enabled item, a WMS-enabled warehouse, and a non-WMS warehouse.

The two major options are also reflected in the AX user documentation, which differentiates various topics as applicable to "features in the warehouse management module" versus "features in the inventory management module." However, the two major options share a high degree of common functionality, as summarized in Appendix A. The basic approach has some unique constructs and functionality as does the advanced approach.

For those already familiar with previous AX versions, you already know most of the functionality associated with the basic approach based on your experience with the historical "WMS I" capabilities. However, the release of AX 2012 R3 introduced some new capabilities and eliminated some of the old capabilities in the basic approach.

[1] When using AX 2012 R3, the two major options reflect the license key for the "Warehouse and Transportation Management" capabilities, and disabling an alternative but mutually exclusive approach. That is, you disable the feature set for the "Warehouse Management II" functionality.

Figure 2.1 Major Options for Warehouse Management

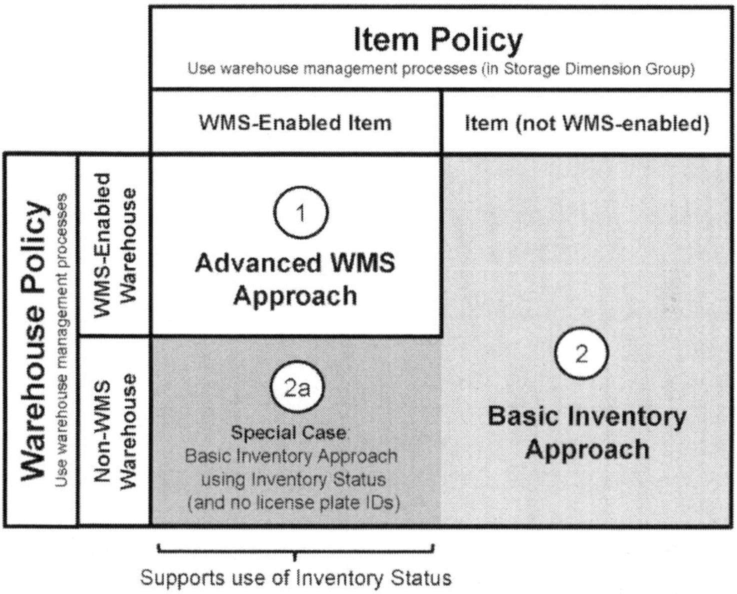

2.2 *Significance of the Inventory Status*

A special case of the Basic Inventory approach—identified as Option #2a in Figure 2.1—can take advantage of the capabilities related to Inventory Status. The Inventory Status capabilities only apply to WMS-enabled items. License plates can also apply to WMS-enabled items, but only for transactions at WMS-enabled warehouses. License plate information does not apply for transactions at a non-WMS warehouse.

Inventory Status has a broad range of potential uses, and its capabilities are largely determined by user-defined values. At its simplest, a single value can be used for Inventory Status so that it provides no additional capabilities.

Most scenarios employ multiple user-defined values to support requirements for quality, warehousing, and other areas of the business. For example, one value typically indicates good inventory, such as a value of *Available* or *Good*. One or more values can be defined and designated as blocked in order to prevent usage of inventory with the assigned value. Examples of these user-defined values include *Blocked* or *Damaged*. Master scheduling logic treats this "blocked" inventory as non-nettable.

The user-defined values can indicate needed action when assigned to existing inventory. Examples include *Needs-Inspection, Needs-Rework, Return-to-Vendor,* and *To-Be-Scrapped.* You typically place the inventory in a related location at the same time, such as moving it to a special location when assigning the value *To-Be-Scrapped.* In the context of these example values, the assigned value indicates the need for a corresponding action to create a quality order, rework order, purchase order return, or an inventory adjustment.

The inspection requirements for a purchased item can be identified by the Inventory Status capabilities, thereby providing an alternative to the use of Quality Associations. For example, the value of *Needs-Inspection* (or its equivalent) can be assigned to an item and a supplying vendor so that the value is automatically inherited by a purchase order line and communicated to receiving clerks at the time of reporting arrival.

The user-defined values can also indicate the grade or condition of inventory, which may or may not affect sales or purchase prices. Examples include *Off-Spec, Refurbished* or *Used.*

A value for Inventory Status must be assigned to orders, typically with a value of *Good* or its equivalent in most scenarios. It can be changed during the receiving process for purchased or manufactured items (or for RMA receipts), such as changing the value from *Good* to *Needs-Inspection.* It can also be changed by quality orders, such as automatically changing the value to *Needs-Rework* or *To-be-Scrapped* when validation failure occurs. In a similar fashion, passing the validation can automatically update the value to *Good.* The value for existing inventory can also be changed when needed. A subsequent chapter provides further explanation about the significance of Inventory Status (Chapter 4).

2.3 Guidelines for Choosing the Basic vs Advanced Approach

As a general guideline, the advanced approach typically applies to those warehouses that require tracking of palletized inventory (identified by license plate IDs), more sophisticated capabilities to support warehouse/transportation requirements, and out-of-the-box functionality for mobile devices—especially when warehouse users need guidance about finding or placing inventory. However, the advanced approach also supports scenarios that do not employ license plate tracking in their inventory locations, and the use of license plate IDs (for internal system purposes) is largely hidden from end users. The more sophisticated capabilities to support variations of warehouse/transportation requirements are sometimes a deciding factor for choosing the advanced approach.

The basic approach typically applies to a warehouse (or company) that does not have sophisticated requirements for sales order picking/shipping, and does not require tracking of palletized inventory. Inventory within the warehouse is typically tracked by piece or each rather than by pallet. In addition, the basic approach does not support out-of-the box mobile device transactions. If needed, third-party applications supporting mobile device transactions can be used with the basic approach. The basic approach supports simple, order-based picking for sales orders and transfer orders, and also supports the wave-picking concept for these orders.

As an additional consideration, the amount of functionality within the advanced approach is approximately twice as much as the basic approach, and often requires a longer and more costly implementation. A subsequent section provides some metrics about the comparative amount of functionality for each approach, and also illustrates the comparative level of complexity within each of the underlying conceptual models (Section 2.7).

2.4 Strategic Options and Illustrative Case Studies

The strategic options for warehouse management go beyond the choice of one approach or the other. For example, the choice of an approach can be warehouse specific. In addition, a key question often involves "what are the strategic options for starting with basic capabilities and evolving into more advanced capabilities." The flexibility to evolve can be considered within each of the two major approaches, and from one approach to the other.

As an explanatory approach, it is easiest to consider the various strategic options in terms of illustrative case studies. Illustrative case studies are summarized in Figure 2.2, and are explained further in a subsequent section (Section 2.6). The numbered case studies are superimposed on the previous diagram about major options, and the arrows indicate the applicable option. These do not necessarily reflect an exhaustive list of strategic options.

Figure 2.2 Strategic Options for Warehouse Management

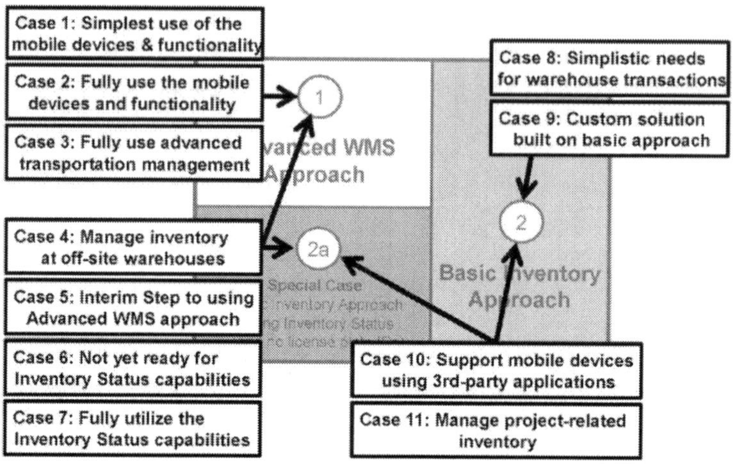

2.5 Evolving Strategies for Strategic Options

An evolving strategy can help reduce the complexity and cost of the initial phase of an ERP implementation. The flexibility to evolve can be considered within each of the two major approaches as well as from one approach to the other. As one example of an evolving strategy within the Advanced WMS approach, a given warehouse may start with the simplest use of mobile device transactions and the advanced functionality (Case 1), and then evolve to fully utilize them (Case 2) and to fully use the advanced transportation management capabilities (Case 3).

As an example for the Basic Inventory approach, a given warehouse may start without using the Inventory Status capabilities (Case 6) and then evolve to fully utilize the capabilities (Case 7). A given warehouse may also start with the basic approach as an interim step to the advanced approach (Case 5). Even when the primary warehouses employ the advanced approach, the basic approach is typically required for managing inventory at off-site warehouses such as subcontractors or remote locations (Case 4).

A firm with simplistic needs for warehouse management can start with out-of-the-box functionality in the basic approach (Case 8), selectively develop custom solutions built on the basic approach (Case 9), and implement mobile device transactions via 3rd-party applications (Case 10).

2.6 Details of Case Studies

Illustrative case studies about the strategic options for warehouse management were summarized in Figure 2.2. This section provides more detail about each case study.

Case 1: Simplest Use of the Mobile Device Transactions and Advanced WMS Functionality The implementation project team at a manufacturer/distributor wanted to implement the Advanced WMS approach as simply as possible, evolving into more sophisticated usage as needed. They considered several options for simplified usage at their main warehouses, including the following.

- *Minimum scope for advanced functionality.* The minimum scope can start with just the basic inventory transactions, the basic processes for handling purchase receipts, and the order-based picking for sales orders and transfer orders. It does not need to include the many aspects of more advanced functionality, such as load planning, manual packing or replenishment of picking locations.

- *Minimum scope for using mobile device transactions.* The minimum scope can start with just the mobile device transactions for the above-mentioned basic inventory transactions and basic business processes. The related putaway transactions for receipts of purchases and transfers can be user directed. The logic for suggested putaway locations can be added later. The detailed design of interacting with the mobile devices can reflect simplistic out-of-the-box capabilities.

- *Minimal tracking of inventory by license plate IDs.* The minimum scope can start with minimal tracking of license plate IDs. Minimal tracking reflects the use of inventory locations designated as "not license plate controlled," and the related use of putaway transactions into these locations. The minimal tracking can apply to selected locations (such as production floorstock) or to almost every location.

- *Minimum scope for advanced transportation capabilities.* The minimum scope can start without using the incremental capabilities for advanced transportation management. These capabilities can be phased in at a later date.

- *Basic use of Inventory Status.* The minimum scope can start with just two values of *Available* and *Blocked.* Additional values and their impact on business processes can be phased in at a later date.

Case 2: Fully Use the Mobile Device Transactions and Advanced WMS Functionality A manufacturing/distribution company fully utilized the mobile device transactions and the functionality within the Advanced WMS approach. The mobile device transactions were used at every possible step in each business process, and the detailed design of interacting with the mobile device was tailored to their operation and warehouse personnel. They were not yet ready for any of the advanced transportation management capabilities.

Case 3: Fully Use the Advanced Transportation Management Capabilities A manufacturing/distribution company used the Advanced WMS approach at their key warehouses to identify and manage outbound loads (for sales orders and transfer orders) and inbound loads (for purchase orders), and used this load information for transportation management purposes. This included the assignment of rates and routes to inbound and outbound loads, the scheduling and reporting of transportation appointments for inbound and outbound docks, and performing freight entry and reconciliation.

Case 4: Manage Inventory at Off-site Warehouses A manufacturer/distributor employed the Advanced WMS functionality and mobile device transactions at their main warehouse. However, they also needed to track inventory and report transactions at their off-site warehouses that represented subcontractors and remote locations. They used simple inventory transactions for many situations, such as reporting purchase order receipts of supplied material at a subcontractor, or transfer order receipts at a remote warehouse. In some situations, they selectively employed capabilities within the Basic Inventory approach, such as generating picking lists for all sales order shipments from a subcontractor or remote warehouse.

Case 5: Interim Step to Using Advanced WMS Approach A manufacturer/distributor was implementing AX with a two-phased approach for warehouse management. For Phase 1, they employed the simpler Basic Inventory approach, which would serve as an interim step before implementing the Advanced WMS approach. More specifically, they defined items as WMS-enabled and initially defined non-WMS warehouses and their locations. For Phase 2, they would define another set of WMS-enabled warehouses with the exact same location identifiers. When cutting over to Phase 2, the inventory in their previous warehouses will be transferred to the corresponding WMS-enabled warehouse and location. In addition, the demands and supply orders would be updated to reflect the change to WMS-enabled warehouses.

Case 6: Not Yet Ready for Inventory Status Capabilities A manufacturing/distribution company was implementing AX in a short time frame, and did not want any additional complexities that would delay the cutover. In terms of using different values of an Inventory Status, they were not quite ready to think through the potential impacts on all business processes. They defined just two values for Inventory Status of *Available* and *Blocked*. The value of *Available* was assigned as the default for all possible transactions. They planned to revisit the use of Inventory Status after the initial cutover.

Case 7: Fully Utilize the Inventory Status Capabilities A manufacturing/distribution company identified multiple values for the Inventory Status in order to support requirements for quality, warehousing, and sales. The use of Inventory Status was fully integrated into the business processes for receiving purchase orders and production output (especially the use of quality orders). The values indicating needed action provided the basis for performing follow-up actions. Different sales pricing was defined for off-spec material.

Case 8: Simplistic Needs for Warehouse Transactions A manufacturing and distribution company had simplistic needs for warehouse transactions. They implemented the Basic Inventory approach at the various warehouses since they did not require the additional functionality within the Advanced WMS approach. In addition, they were happy with screen-based approaches for entering warehouse transactions, and did not yet perceive a need for data collection via mobile devices.

Case 9: Custom Solution Built on Basic Approach A manufacturing and distribution company had simplistic needs for warehouse transactions, and were implementing the Basic Inventory approach because they did not require the additional functionality within the advanced approach. For example, they employed order-based picking for sales orders and transfer orders, and used the Picking Workbench to support their wave-picking requirements. A few requirements were being addressed by customizations—such as a customization to support staging/loading steps prior to sales order shipment.

Case 10: Support Mobile Devices Using 3rd-Party Applications A manufacturing and distribution company was implementing the Basic Inventory approach at the various warehouses since they did not require the additional functionality within the Advanced WMS approach. This meant they could not use the out-of-the-box mobile device transactions, so they employed a third-party solution for these data collection purposes.[2] The solution supported all variations

---

[2] The rfSmart capabilities support mobile device transactions for the Basic Inventory approach, and also provide enhancements for using the mobile device transactions within the Advanced WMS approach. See www.rfSmart.com for more information..

of transactions within the basic approach, and provided a simpler user interface for the mobile device transactions (relative to the out-of-the-box mobile device transactions).

Case 11: Manage Project-Related Inventory A project-oriented business implemented the simpler Basic Inventory approach because they did not require the additional functionality within the Advanced WMS approach. In addition, many of their project-related transactions (such as receipts for project purchase orders and reporting item usage for projects) were not supported by the mobile device transactions within the advanced approach. They are considering a third-party application for supporting their mobile device transactions.

2.7 Comparing Approaches

The two approaches to warehouse management can be compared in several different ways. In the context of strategic options, the level of complexity in each approach may sway the choice of an option. The comparative level of complexity can be considered from several angles, including (1) the comparative amount of functionality, (2) the comparative complexity in the underlying conceptual models, and (3) the comparative complexity of reservation logic. In summary, the basic approach is simpler for the first two metrics, and the advanced approach is simpler for the third metric.

Comparative Amount of Functionality The amount of functionality associated with an ERP package typically correlates with complexity and many related factors, such as cost, duration, and required expertise to implement the ERP package. It is difficult to measure the complexity of an ERP package let alone the amount of functionality. A page count analysis of the book's explanations about each approach provides one metric.[3]

In summary, the advanced approach has approximately twice the aggregate functionality as the basic approach, and its variations for supporting sales order picking/shipping have three times the aggregate functionality. These metrics are described in Appendix B. This makes a strong argument for those leaning toward the basic approach.

The analysis indicates a high degree of common functionality as summarized in Appendix A. However, each approach has significantly different amounts of unique functionality. The unique functionality in one approach does not apply to

---

[3] A detailed explanation of the page count analysis is provided in Appendix B, and the common functionality is summarized in Appendix A.

the other approach. More significantly, the amount of applicable functionality for a given company depends on the choice of a strategic option. For example, the strategic option may reflect an evolving strategy of starting with basic capabilities.

Comparative Complexity in the Underlying Conceptual Models The different conceptual models within the two approaches reflect different levels of complexity, but also the ability to model business process variations. As already noted, it is difficult to measure the complexity of an ERP package. However, it can be illustrated by an apples-to-apples comparison of the two approaches for various business processes related to orders. The analysis includes the comparable steps in the business process, a comparison of the key constructs and their life cycles, and the number of major variations supported by the approach. Appendix C provides a detailed example of this apples-to-apples comparison about the sales order picking/shipping process, but each chapter about order-related transactions includes a section with a similar analysis.

In summary, the basic approach is typically simpler in terms of comparable steps for the exact same business process, and substantially simpler in terms of the number of constructs and related life cycles. It also provides a simpler transaction history that does not involve the many additional work order transactions of the advanced approach. The simpler transaction history is also apparent when viewing batch number tracking information. As a simpler approach, it supported far fewer variations in business processes related to picking/shipping of sales orders and transfer orders.

Comparative Complexity in Terms of Reservation Logic Reservation logic is often one of the more complex aspects of an ERP system, and its significance differs widely between software packages and companies. In the case of AX, the significance and use of reservation logic differs significantly between the basic and advanced approaches to warehouse management.

Reservation logic within the basic approach has been widely and successfully employed across many companies using previous versions of AX. It can support several variations of reservation logic, including First-In-First-Out (FIFO) reservations related to scheduled receipts, and First-Expired-First-Out (FEFO) reservations for batch-controlled items with shelf life considerations. However, some case studies have reported complexities in using this logic, especially when detailed reservations need to be changed.

In contrast, the reservation logic within the advanced approach (based on the concept of a reservation hierarchy assigned to each item) seems to avoid these problems because of its simpler logic. The advanced approach does involve some additional complexity in defining setup information for mobile device transactions, where additional policies must be defined in comparison to the basic approach. One example involves the additional "batch-enabled" policy (and its related strategy) to support reservations for sales order picking of batch-controlled items.

In summary, in comparison to the basic approach, the advanced approach provides a simpler and more effective model for supporting reservation logic.

2.8 Executive Summary

The various warehouse management options for Dynamics AX have had many different names, but they boil down to two major options . For simplicity's sake, one major option can be termed the "Basic Inventory approach" or the "basic approach" for short. Most of the functionality within the basic approach reflects previous versions of AX (and the old "WMS I" functionality), but the newer AX versions introduced some new capabilities and eliminated some others. The second major option can be termed the "Advanced WMS approach" or the "advanced approach" for short. This chapter reviewed the two approaches, including a special case for the basic approach that takes advantage of the Inventory Status capabilities. It provided some guidelines about choosing an approach as well as some comparisons of the two approaches. More importantly, it identified various strategic options—including evolving strategies to start simple and grow in sophistication—and provided illustrative case studies for each option.

Chapter 3

Fundamentals of the Basic Inventory Approach

Several fundamentals of the Basic Inventory approach provide the foundation for explaining business processes in subsequent chapters. These fundamentals include the key setup information such as the definition of warehouse locations and the item-related policies for warehouse management. They include basic inventory transactions such as transfers and adjustments. Related topics include calculations of space utilization.

The proper starting point typically involves the key setup information, but this extended explanation is postponed until later in the chapter. These considerations are reflected in the following sections within the chapter..

1. Summary of Warehouse-Related Transactions
2. Basic Inventory Transactions
3. Define a Non-WMS Warehouse and its Locations
4. Define Item-Related Policies for Warehouse Management
5. Calculate Space Utilization for a Non-WMS Warehouse

3.1 Summary of Warehouse-Related Transactions

The explanation of the warehouse management approach is organized around warehouse-related transactions. These are summarized in Figure 3.1. Each type of transaction is covered in subsequent chapters in terms of an example business process. The figure identifies the section numbers describing each business process.

Figure 3.1 Examples of Warehouse-Related Transactions

Type of Transaction		Example Process
Basic Inventory Transactions	Inventory Transfer (Movement)	Section 3.2
	Inventory Adjustment - Out	
	Inventory Adjustment - In	
	Quantity Adjustment (Count)	
	Cycle Count	
Quality	Change Inventory Status	
Purchase Order	Purchase Order Arrival	Section 5.1
	Purchase Order Return	Section 5.9
Sales Order	Sales Order Picking/Shipping	Section 6.1
	RMA Arrival	
Transfer Order	Transfer Order Picking/Shipping	Section 7.1
	Transfer Order Arrival	Section 8.1
Production Order	Production Order Picking	Section 9.2
	Production Order Receiving	Section 10.1

An equivalent summary is provided for the Advanced WMS approach (Section 13.1) so that you can easily compare the two approaches in terms of warehouse-related transactions.

Other types of inventory transactions are not considered because of book length considerations. Examples include transactions for projects and service orders, retail-specific transactions related to stores, and kanban transactions for lean manufacturing. The inventory transactions related to quarantine orders—such as scrap and putaway—are covered in the quality management chapter (Section 26.6).

3.2 Basic Inventory Transactions

The basic inventory transactions include transfers, adjustments, and cycle counts. These basic transactions and some related inquiries/analyses are summarized in Figure 3.2, which provides an organizing focus for further explanation.

Figure 3.2 Summary of Basic Inventory Transactions

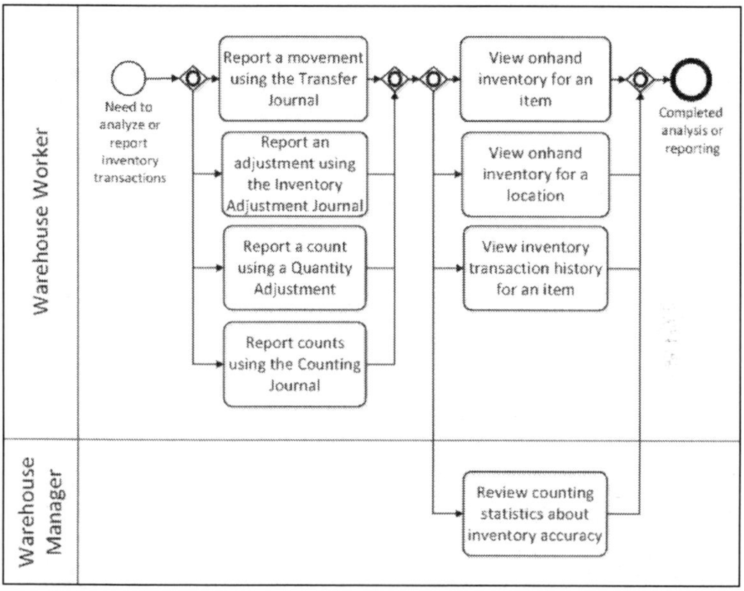

Report Movements Using the Transfer Journal Inventory movements between locations can be recorded in a transfer journal. Each transfer journal has a system-assigned identifier, and consists of a header and journal line items. Each line minimally identifies an item, quantity, and the old and new locations (identified by site, warehouse and bin). The relevant batch and/or serial number may also need to be identified. The transfer quantity is expressed as a negative, and always reflects the item's inventory UM. The transfer entries can be maintained and printed prior to posting the journal. The status for a Transfer consists of a checkbox labeled Posted, which indicates whether it is open or posted.

A transfer journal typically reflects an immediate transfer of material without a requirement for tracking in transit inventory. For example, a transfer journal may be used to move material between locations in two adjacent warehouses. Transfer orders should be used when in-transit inventory must be tracked. Subsequent chapters explain the picking/shipping and receiving transactions for transfer orders.

An inventory transfer journal can support the transfer of one variant of an item to another variant, as well as transferring one batch number to another batch number—much like you would transfer inventory from one location to another. Subsequent chapters describe the use of variants for item identification (Section

24.4) and the use of batch-controlled items (Section 25.3). A transfer journal also provides an alternative approach for merging different batches of an item (Section 25.6).

Case 12: Transfers Between Adjacent Warehouses

The warehouse manager at a manufacturing company with two adjacent warehouses (within the same AX site) employed transfer journals for moving inventory between the warehouses. A Transfer Journal was initially created and populated with the items and quantities to be moved. The printed version provided a picking list (and turnaround document) for warehouse workers at the originating warehouse, and they entered the actual results for the "from warehouse" on the journal lines. After the material was received, warehouse workers entered the results for the "to warehouse," and posted the transfer journal.

In this scenario, the transfer journals were created by firming planned transfer orders. This reflects a site-specific policy to "use transfer journals for movements within the site," since both warehouses are within the same AX site. It also reflects the item's coverage policies about the warehouse source for planned transfer orders. Firming will still create actual transfer orders between warehouses in different AX sites.

Report Adjustments Using the Inventory Adjustment Journal Inventory adjustments can serve a variety of purposes, such as loading initial inventory balances, reporting inventory corrections, and reporting scrap. Adjustments can be recorded using either the Inventory Adjustment Journal or the Movement Journal. The Inventory Adjustment Journal employs a predefined G/L account number for an item's inventory adjustments, whereas a Movement Journal forces you to specify this offsetting G/L account number. Otherwise, these two types of journals are the same in all other respects. Further explanation focuses on just the Inventory Adjustment Journal.

Each Inventory Adjustment journal has a system-assigned identifier, and consists of a header and journal line items. Each line minimally identifies an item, quantity, and location (identified by site, warehouse and bin). The relevant batch and/or serial number may also need to be identified. Items with an actual costing method require an additional entry about the item's unit cost and possible charges. The quantity can be positive or negative, and always reflects the item's inventory UM. The adjustment entries can be maintained and printed prior to posting the journal. The status for an Inventory Adjustment Journal consists of a checkbox labeled Posted, which indicates whether it is open or posted.

Adjustments to an item's inventory quantity can also be recorded using two other approaches described in the next two subsections

Report Counts Using Quantity Adjustments A quantity adjustment is different than using an inventory adjustment journal, and more closely resembles the use of a counting journal. A quantity adjustment can be initiated from on-hand inquiries about an item's inventory or a location's inventory, where you access the Counting form. In either case, you can adjust the quantity for existing inventory or create a new entry to add inventory. Accepting the quantity adjustment(s) will update the inventory and generate a counting history record. You can subsequently view an inquiry of these counting history records, which are not assigned a counting journal number.

Report Counts Using the Counting Journal A Counting Journal can be used to support cycle counting or physical inventories. Performing a physical inventory count helps ensure valid financial reporting of inventory value. Cycle counting can accomplish the same objective. Each Counting Journal has a system-assigned identifier, and consists of a header and journal line items. Each line minimally identifies an item, quantity, and location (identified by site, warehouse, and bin). The relevant batch and/or serial number may also need to be identified. The status for a Counting Journal consists of a checkbox labeled Posted, which indicates whether it is open or posted.

You can manually or automatically create the journal lines identifying the items to be counted, print the journal as a turnaround document, and then record the counted quantity or the adjustment quantity for each journal line. Posting a counting journal updates the inventory balances. This represents a two-step counting process: one step to identify items in the counting journal, and a second step to post the journal. A companywide policy (embedded in the Inventory and Warehouse Management Parameters form) optionally prevents inventory transactions during the counting process.

- *Create Line Items within a Counting Journal.* Automatic creation of journal lines can be based on one or more factors, such as a specified warehouse, a selected range of item numbers or item groups, or the item's cycle counting approach. An item's cycle counting approach (embedded within the Counting Group assigned to an item) typically reflects a periodic interval expressed in calendar days. In this case, you specify a "not counted since" date as the basis for automatically creating journal lines. A further refinement can eliminate any items with no inventory transactions since the last count. Alternatively, the approach can reflect a condition such as on-hand inventory reaching zero or the item's minimum quantity, since this approach minimizes the time and effort for performing a physical count.

- *Control Group Method for Cycle Counting.* Some companies employ a control group method in cycle counting, where the same items are counted every day to immediately identify the sources of error. Copying the journal lines from a previous counting journal into the new journal supports the control group method.

- *Tag Counting Journal for Physical Inventories.* Some companies employ tags (with pre-assigned numbers) to conduct a physical inventory, typically with handwritten count information about the quantity and location. A separate tag counting journal can be used to record the tag numbers, tag status (used, voided or missing), and the count information, and then analyze missing tag numbers. This tag counting journal represents an approach to tag control. Posting it results in the creation of a counting journal (with journal lines for used tags), which must be posted to update inventory balances.

- *View Counting History Records.* You can subsequently view an inquiry of counting history records, which include the identifier of the counting journal.

View Counting Statistics about Inventory Accuracy The warehouse manager can view the Counting Statistics report about the inventory accuracy percentage over a specified date range. The percentage reflects the number of cycle count transactions with a discrepancy divided by the total number of cycle count transactions. The selection criteria for the report typically specify a date range (about counting dates) and summarize the inventory accuracy information by warehouse.

View On-Hand Inventory and Transaction History You can view standardized inquiries about inventory by item or location as well as view transaction history.

3.3 Define a Non-WMS Warehouse and its Locations

Each warehouse has a unique identifier and must be assigned to a site. You designate a non-WMS warehouse by not enabling the *Use Warehouse Management Processes* policy for the warehouse. This policy works in conjunction with a similar item-related policy for determining whether the Basic Inventory approach will be used, as previously described for the major options for warehouse management (Section 2.1). Other warehouse-related information includes its associated bin locations and warehouse type.

Define the Aisles within a Warehouse One or more aisles within a non-WMS warehouse must be defined prior to defining bin locations, because each bin location must be assigned to an aisle.

Define Bin Locations within a Warehouse The identifier for a bin location often reflects its coordinates (consisting of an aisle, rack, shelf level and/or bin), but it can reflect another purpose. The identifier can be manually assigned, or automatically created for specified ranges of aisle, rack, shelf, and bin numbers. You can also copy bin locations from another warehouse. You can print a barcoded label for each bin location.

A bin must be designated with a location type. These predefined location types include a bulk location, an inbound dock, an outbound dock, and a picking location. However, the location type has no significance within the Basic Inventory approach to warehouse management, so that a single location type (such as bulk location) can be assigned to all bin locations.

An item may always be stored in the same bin location. You designate this "fixed location" by assigning it to the item's default bin locations within a warehouse—one for receipts and one for issues.

As optional information, you can specify the maximum weight and volume for a bin location capacity. This provides reference information for comparing bin capacity to the weight/volume of items placed in the bin location. It can also be used to calculate space utilization for a non-WMS warehouse, as described in a subsequent section (Section 3.6).

Warehouse Types A normal warehouse is designated with a warehouse type of main. Another type of warehouse is needed to support transfer orders, and yet another type is needed to support quarantine orders.

- *Transit Warehouse.* The use of transfer orders requires the definition of a transit warehouse and its assignment to a main warehouse. A transit warehouse has a separate identifier, a warehouse type of transit, and at least one bin location that acts as a default. A typical value for this bin location is "InTransit." You need a minimum of one transit warehouse per site, which can be assigned to each main warehouse within the site. Alternatively, a transit warehouse can be defined for each main warehouse that acts as a ship-from location for transfer orders. The different transit warehouses provide more granular visibility of intransit inventory related to transfer orders. Subsequent chapters provide further explanation of transfer order transactions in the Basic Inventory Approach (Chapters 7 and 8) and in the Advanced WMS approach (Chapters 17 and 18).

- *Quarantine Warehouse.* The use of quarantine orders requires the definition of a quarantine warehouse and its assignment to a main warehouse. A quarantine warehouse has a separate identifier, a warehouse type of quarantine, and its own bin locations. Most situations will employ one quarantine warehouse for each normal warehouse. A minimalist approach would employ one quarantine warehouse per site. A subsequent chapter about quality management provides further explanation about quarantine orders (Section 26.6), which only apply to the Basic Inventory approach.

Warehouse-Related Policies A warehouse can have a default bin location that applies to all receipts, and a second default bin location that applies to all issues. These bin locations serve as a default when item-specific defaults are not specified. These default bin locations for a warehouse should only be specified when a single bin location makes sense, such as a single default bin location for a transit warehouse. Two other policies are critical for master scheduling logic.

- *Calendar.* A warehouse should have a specified calendar of working hours.

- *Nettable vs Non-Nettable Inventory.* Most warehouses will contain nettable inventory. A warehouse can be designated as non-nettable (via the manual planning flag) so that supplies are ignored by master scheduling logic.

3.4 Define Item-Related Policies for Warehouse Management

Several item-related policies must be defined in order to support the Basic Inventory approach to warehouse management. Many of these policies also apply to the Advanced WMS approach. Hence, it is easier to explain the policies just once in subsequent chapters about common information and simply summarize the topics here. For each topic, the summary identifies the relevant section for an extended explanation.

- *Policies within the Storage Dimension Group.* The policies within a Storage Dimension Group identify a WMS-enabled item and also define the applicability of information about site, warehouse, and bin location (Section 24.10).

- *Policies within the Tracking Dimension Group.* The policies within a Tracking Dimension Group identify the need for tracking serial numbers or batch numbers for an item (Sections 25.1 and 25.3).

- *Unit of Measure (UM) Considerations.* An item can have multiple units of measure and unique UM conversion factors (Section 24.4).

- *Negative Inventory Policies.* The policies determine whether negative inventory will be allowed for an item (Section 24.6).

- *Fixed Location for an Item.* Sometimes an item is always stored in the same bin location. You designate this "fixed location" by assigning it to the item's default bin locations within a warehouse—one for receipts and one for issues.

3.5 Calculate Space Utilization for a Non-WMS Warehouse

The calculation of space utilization and its associated report provide an aggregate indicator of over- and under-loaded utilization of warehouse capacity, expressed in daily increments over a user-defined time horizon. The space utilization can reflect weight or volume, and the daily increments (expressed as a percentage) provide trending information. This information can highlight intermittent or extended periods of over- or under-loaded utilization so you can plan accordingly.

Calculate Space Utilization The periodic calculation of space utilization (labeled Schedule Load Utilization within Inventory Management) involves several factors as described below.

- The maximum weight and volume specified for each bin location's capacity, aggregated into the total capacity for all bin locations within a warehouse.

- The weight and volume specified for each item.

- The existing inventory of items within bin locations—with weight and volume aggregated into a total for the first daily increment within the time horizon

- The expected receipts and issues for an item and warehouse with weight and volume aggregated into a total for each daily increment. The calculation of expected receipts/issues reflects a specified set of master plan data and a specified time horizon.

Review Space Utilization Calculations The report for space utilization (labeled the Warehouse Load Utilization report within Inventory Management) involves several options. The report dialogue provides options about the choice of weight or volume for displaying utilization and the applicable site(s) and warehouse(s). The report displays one line for each warehouse, where the line includes daily increments of space utilization. As an option, you can drill down to the detailed receipts and issues for a selected daily increment. The report can also be viewed from the warehouse manager's role-centered page.

3.6 Executive Summary

Several fundamentals of the Basic Inventory approach provide the foundation for explaining business processes in subsequent chapters. These fundamentals include key setup information such as the definition of warehouse locations and the item-related policies for warehouse management. They include basic inventory transactions such as transfers, adjustments, and cycle counts. Related topics include calculations of space utilization and cycle counting statistics.

Chapter 4

Significance of Inventory Status

The use of Inventory Status only applies to WMS-enabled items. WMS-enabled items represent a special case in the Basic Inventory approach and a prerequisite for the Advanced WMS approach. The use of Inventory Status can support additional capabilities. At its simplest, a single value can be used for Inventory Status so that the additional capabilities do not apply. However, most scenarios employ multiple user-defined values for Inventory Status for solving a broad range of warehouse management requirements.

The significance of Inventory Status is largely determined by user-defined values. One value typically indicates good inventory, such as a value of *Available* or *Good.* One or more values can be defined and designated as blocked in order to prevent usage of inventory with the assigned value. Examples of these user-defined values include *Blocked* or *Damaged.* The user-defined values can indicate needed action when assigned to existing inventory. Examples include *Needs-Inspection* or *Needs-Rework*. The user-defined values can also indicate the grade or condition of inventory that affects sales or purchase prices. Examples include *Off-Spec, Refurbished,* or *Used.* Numerous case studies provide other illustrative examples. The values for Inventory Status can be assigned to inventory during the receiving process and subsequently changed. These topics are reflected in the following sections within the chapter.

1. Two Different Meanings of the Term Inventory Status
2. Significance of Inventory Status
3. Assign a Value for Inventory Status to Orders
4. Key Characteristics of Inventory Status
5. Assign Inventory Status During the Receiving Process

6. Change Inventory Status for Existing Inventory
7. Allowable Transactions for Inventory with a Blocked Inventory Status
8. Assign Inventory Status During Purchase Order Arrival

4.1 Two Different Meanings of the Term Inventory Status

The term "inventory status" has many different meanings in different ERP systems. It has two different meanings in AX. As the primary focus of this article, the Inventory Status capabilities only apply to WMS-enabled items, where the Storage Dimension Group assigned to an item has been enabled to "use warehouse management processes." Inventory Status refers to one of the mandatory dimensions within this Storage Group Dimension. The unique aspects of Inventory Status include user-defined values and a related policy indicating whether a value represents available or blocked inventory. A value for Inventory Status must be assigned to all inventory transactions, just like the other storage dimensions for site and warehouse.

The term "inventory status" also refers to the AX viewpoint of inventory transactions, where the status indicates steps in the life cycle of orders for an item. The system-assigned values of an inventory status differ for each type of order. For example, the applicable values for a purchase order line indicate whether the item has been *Ordered*, *Received*, or *Purchased*, and the status is automatically updated by different steps in the business process. In order to differentiate the two different meanings, we will use capital letters for Inventory Status to indicate use of the Storage Group Dimension, and lower case letters for inventory status when referring to the AX viewpoint of inventory transactions.

4.2 Significance of Inventory Status

Inventory Status has a broad range of potential uses so that its significance depends on the scenario. The key aspects of its significance are determined by policies in the Storage Dimension Group assigned to items and by the user-defined values for Inventory Status. For example, a value can be designated as blocked—thereby preventing further usage of existing inventory that has been assigned the blocked status. These two factors are summarized below.

Several characteristics are particularly important for warehouse and quality management purposes, such as the ability to assign a different value during the receiving process, the different approaches of changing Inventory Status for existing inventory, and the allowable transactions for existing inventory with a value representing a blocked status. Subsequent sections provide further explanation of these key characteristics.

Significance Based on Policies in the Storage Dimension Group

Several policies within the Storage Dimension Group assigned to an item determine the significance of Inventory Status and its values. First, the values of Inventory Status are always tracked in physical inventory; blank values are not allowed for receipts and issues. Second, it is never tracked in financial inventory so that different standard costs or actual costs do not apply to different values of an Inventory Status. Three other policies indicate additional significance for values representing an "unblocked" Inventory Status. They do not apply to values representing a blocked status.

- *Sales Price based on the value of Inventory Status.* Some scenarios require different sales pricing based on the value of Inventory Status, such as different pricing for off-spec material which is illustrated in Case 14. For example, the different pricing can be defined in trade agreements about sales prices or discounts.

- *Purchase Price based on the value of Inventory Status.* Some scenarios require different purchase pricing based on the value of Inventory Status, such as different pricing for off-spec material. For example, the different pricing can be defined in trade agreements about purchase prices or discounts.

- *Coverage Planning based on the value of Inventory Status.* Some scenarios will define demands for different values of Inventory Status so that master scheduling logic will generate planned supply orders for the specified value.

For simplicity's sake, further explanation assumes none of these polices are being used unless specified otherwise.

Significance Based on the User-Defined Values for Inventory Status

You create a user-defined value and name using the Inventory Status form. One value typically indicates good inventory, such as a user-defined value of *Available* or *Good.* One or more values can be defined and designated as blocked in order to prevent usage of inventory with the assigned value, such as a value of *Blocked.* A blocked status prevents warehouse transactions (with a few exceptions) until it has been changed to an available status. As an additional factor, master scheduling logic considers the "blocked" inventory as non-nettable; it is assumed the inventory cannot be used.

You can define multiple values to differentiate the significance of a blocked Inventory Status for warehouse/quality purposes. Illustrative values include *To-Be-Scrapped* and *Return-to-Vendor*. Multiple values can also be defined to differentiate the significance of available inventory, such as the illustrative values of *Good* and *Off-Spec*. Illustrative values in the other case studies indicate the broad range of potential uses. Some pundits refer to the Inventory Status field as the "duct tape of AX."

Significance of Inventory Status in the Reservation Hierarchy The reservation hierarchy indicates whether Inventory Status should be treated as critical or simply informational. Most scenarios will employ a reservation hierarchy with Inventory Status above the Location so that it is treated as critical for reservation purposes. Others will place it below the Location so that it is treated as informational.

4.3 Assign a Value for Inventory Status to Orders

A value for Inventory Status must be entered for every type of order. This includes line items on purchase orders, transfer orders, and sales orders, as well as production orders and the related lines in a Production BOM. A value is also required on basic inventory transactions. The use of default values for Inventory Status can help streamline data entry, especially for modeling a normal business. The use of default values can also reflect different purposes of Inventory Status.

Use Default Values for Modeling the Normal Business A default value of *Available* or its equivalent should be assigned as a companywide policy and to every site and warehouse involved in normal business. In this way, every transaction will inherit an available status unless a different source of the default value applies, as illustrated by examples in subsequent points.

Use Default Values for Modeling an Item's Inspection Requirements The requirements for a purchased item can be identified by the Inventory Status capabilities, thereby providing an alternative to the use of Quality Associations for defining inspection requirements. For example, the value of *Receiving-Inspection-Required* (or its equivalent) can be assigned to an item and its supplying vendor so that the value is automatically inherited by a purchase order line and communicated to receiving clerks at the time of reporting arrival.

Use Default Values for a Warehouse or Site A different value than *Available* may apply to all transactions for a given warehouse or site. For example, a given warehouse may be dedicated for stocking "Refurbished" products so that you might assign a default value of *Refurbished* to the warehouse. A default value can also be assigned to a site.

Hierarchy of Inheriting a Default Value A default value for Inventory Status can be defined for a company, site, warehouse and/or item, and these represent increasing levels of specificity. In other words, an item-specific default value will be used (if defined), otherwise the default value will be inherited from the related warehouse or site (if defined) or the companywide default value.

4.4 Key Characteristics of Inventory Status

There are several key characteristics of Inventory Status for warehouse and quality management purposes. These include (1) the ability to assign a different value during the receiving process, (2) the different approaches of changing Inventory Status for existing inventory, and (3) the allowable transactions for existing inventory with a value representing a blocked status. The key characteristics are summarized in Figure 4.1 relative to the applicable types of transactions, and are explained further in the next three sections.

Figure 4.1 Key Characteristics of Inventory Status

Type of Transaction		Ability to Assign Status on Receipt	Ability to Change Inventory Status	Allowed Transactions for Blocked Status
Purchase Order	Purchase Order Arrival	Yes		
	Purchase Order Return			Yes
Sales Order	Sales Order Picking/Shipping			
	RMA Arrival	Yes		
Transfer Order	Transfer Order Picking/Shipping			
	Transfer Order Arrival	No		
Production Order	Production Order Picking		Yes issue item to rework order	
	Production Order Receiving	Yes but not to blocked		
Basic Inventory Transactions	Inventory Transfer (Movement)			
	Inventory Adjustment - Out			Yes
	Inventory Adjustment - In	Yes		
	Quantity Adjustment	Yes for adding new inventory		Yes for existing inventory
	Cycle Count			
Quality	Change Inventory Status			
	Quality Order for the Item		Yes	Yes

4.5 Assign Inventory Status during the Receiving Process

The ability to assign Inventory Status during the receiving process is one of the key characteristics identified in Figure 4.1. It applies to all types of orders except transfer orders.

Assign Inventory Status During Purchase Order Receiving The value of Inventory Status assigned to the purchase order line is inherited by a line item on an arrival journal, and it can be overridden. For example, the inherited value of *Available* can be changed when you identify a problem, such as changing the value to a status of *To-Be-Scrapped* or *Needs-Inspection.* The use of automatically-created quality orders may influence how you assign a value.

When using the advanced approach, you can assign a "combined disposition code" when reporting arrival via a mobile device which is mapped to a value of the Inventory Status.

Assign Inventory Status During RMA Receiving The value of Inventory Status assigned to the RMA line can be overridden when the material is received. For example, the value will be inherited by a line item on an arrival journal (much like a purchase order arrival) and it can be overridden. In addition, you must select a value for the RMA disposition code, which indicates whether the material is scrapped or placed into inventory.

When using the advanced approach, you can assign a "combined disposition code" when reporting arrival via a mobile device which is mapped to a value of the Inventory Status and an RMA disposition code.

Transfer Order Receiving and Inventory Status The value of Inventory Status assigned to the transfer order line cannot be overridden when the material is received. For example, the value will be inherited by a line item on the arrival journal, but it cannot be overridden. You can change the value after the transfer order receipt has been posted using any of the approaches for changing inventory status (Section 4.6). As an additional consideration, you can indicate a scrap quantity when posting the transfer order receipt. This often represents a "lost in transit" quantity.

Assign Inventory Status During Production Order Receiving The value of Inventory Status assigned to the production order is inherited when reporting a finished quantity, and it can be overridden to an unblocked status. It cannot be assigned a blocked status. As an additional consideration, you can indicate a trashed quantity when reporting the finished quantity.

Assign Inventory Status on Inventory Adjustments for an Addition The value of Inventory Status can be assigned when reporting an Inventory Adjustment for an addition to inventory. An initial value will be inherited based on default values for the warehouse or site (if defined). The value can also be assigned for additions to inventory via quantity adjustments or cycle counts.

4.6 Change Inventory Status for Existing Inventory

The ability to change the Inventory Status for existing inventory is one of the key characteristics identified in Figure 4.1. As shown in the figure, it can be changed by standard transactions or quality orders; it can also be changed via a rework order. It cannot be changed via a transfer journal.

Change Inventory Status via Standard Transactions The Inventory Status of existing inventory can be changed from one value to another using two forms. The forms are titled Warehouse Inventory Status Change and Change Inventory Status, and their functionality is not intuitively obvious based on the title. One approach changes status for selected existing inventory with a specified status, and the other approach changes status for all existing inventory at a selected location.

- *Change Inventory Status for Selected Existing Inventory.* Using the Warehouse Inventory Status Change form, you first identify the relevant site and warehouse. The form displays all values of Inventory Status. By selecting one of the displayed values and identifying a desired value, you can then view the details about all existing inventory with the selected status. Each detail line identifies the item, location, and quantity (and license plate if applicable). You select one or more of the detail lines in order to change their value to the desired value.

- *Change Inventory Status for all Existing Inventory at a Location.* Using the Change Inventory Status form, you identify the desired value and define the query criteria for the relevant location. All of the existing inventory at the location will be assigned the desired status. Other query criteria may also be applicable.

Change Inventory Status via Rework Orders The value of Inventory Status can be changed by a rework order. For example, an item's inventory may be assigned an unblocked status of *Needs-Rework*, and you can create a rework order in order to change the status to *Available*. More specifically, you identify the item and the *Available* status when creating the rework order and define the same item (with a status of *Needs-Rework*) as a component in the Production BOM. You issue the component's inventory and then receive the finished quantity for the rework order. The rework order approach only works for inventory with an unblocked status; inventory with a blocked status cannot be issued to a rework order.

Change Inventory Status via Quality Orders A quality order can be used to change status of existing inventory based on the test results. The quality order can be manually or automatically generated, and the material being tested can have a blocked or unblocked status. As part of the quality order information, you specify the associated value for "fail" and another value for "pass" so that validation of the test results will automatically change the status. A subsequent chapter about quality management provides further explanation of quality orders (Section 26.3).

Case 13: Use a Quality Order to Assign Inventory Status

The quality management team at a manufacturer wanted to use quality orders as part of the receiving inspection process for manufactured items. They defined multiple values of an Inventory Status to identify prescriptive actions upon validation failure. Example values included a blocked status of *To-Be-Scrapped* and an unblocked status for *Needs-Rework.* A quality control clerk identified the prescriptive action for each quality order so that the Inventory Status was automatically updated based on the validation outcomes of pass or failed.

4.7 Allowable Transactions for Inventory with a Blocked Inventory Status

A blocked status for existing inventory prevents warehouse transactions (with a few exceptions) until it has been changed to an available status. The allowable transactions are one of the key characteristics identified in Figure 4.1. As shown in the figure, they include purchase order returns, inventory adjustments out, inventory transfers, and quality orders.

- *Purchase Order Returns.* A purchase order return can be reported for inventory with a blocked status. In addition, when claiming scrap on a purchase order return, the applicable inventory needs to be reported as scrapped via an inventory adjustment.

- *Inventory Adjustments Out.* Scrap can be reported for inventory with a blocked status using inventory adjustment transactions. A relevant ledger account can also be specified. Other subtractions can be reported via quantity adjustments or cycle counts.

- *Inventory Transfers.* Inventory with a blocked status can be reported as moved by using the Inventory Transfer journal. It cannot be moved using transfer orders. It can also be moved using a mobile device transaction when using the advanced approach.

- *Quality Orders.* Inventory with a blocked status can be processed by a quality order.

4.8 Assign Inventory Status During the Purchase Order Arrival process

The significance of user-defined values for Inventory Status is more easily explained in the context of a common scenario. One scenario involves the assignment of an Inventory Status when reporting purchase order arrival, as described in Case 14.

Case 14: Receiving Clerk Assigns Inventory Status During Purchase Order Arrival

The warehouse manager and quality manager at a manufacturing company were considering options for reporting quality problems at the time of purchase order arrival. One approach involved the user-defined values for Inventory Status with possible values of *Good*, *To-Be-Scrapped*, *Return-to-Vendor*, *Needs-Rework*, and *Needs-Inspection*. The default value for Inventory Status was typically identified as *Good* on purchase order lines.

If the receiving clerks noticed a quality problem when reporting purchase order arrival, they would override the Inventory Status to a value of *Needs-Inspection* on the arrival journal. The two managers prepared a diagram of the proposed business process shown in Figure 4.2. They also prepared a similar diagram for the Advanced WMS approach for comparison purposes (Case 58).

After the receiving clerk identifies received material with a blocked status of *Needs-Inspection*, it is listed on the Blocked inventory form to communicate needed follow up by quality management. The quality control clerk can subsequently make a determination by changing the value of Inventory Status to a value of *Good*, *To-Be-Scrapped*, *Return-to-Vendor*, or *Needs-Rework*. As an additional option, the quality control clerk can manually create and process a quality order. Other roles were typically responsible for the additional steps of processing a purchase order return or a rework order.

Figure 4.2 Assign Inventory Status During Purchase Order Arrival

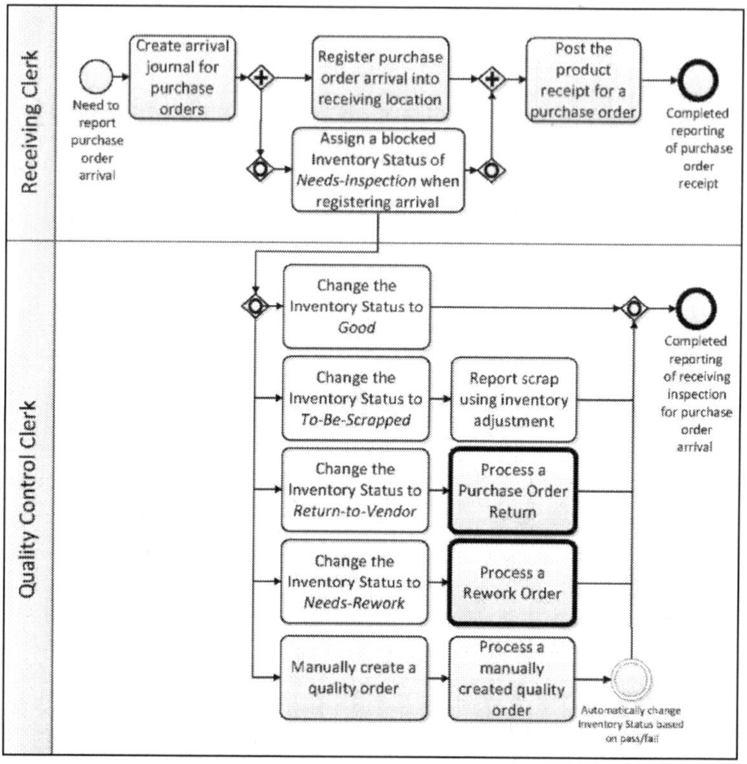

As an alternative, the receiving clerks could be responsible for assigning the other values of the Inventory Status. However, the quality manager was reluctant to have receiving clerks report anything more than simply assigning a value of *Needs-Inspection*; they preferred that a quality control clerk make any further determination.

Many of the steps in Figure 4.2 have been explained within this chapter. Subsequent chapters describe the other steps, including the use of arrival journals (Section 5.5), purchase order returns (Section 5.9), and quality orders (Section 26.3).

4.9 Additional Case Studies

Case 15: Identify Off-Spec or Blemished Products Using Inventory Status A manufacturing/distribution company of sporting goods occasionally had off-spec products that could be sold at a reduced price. They defined two values of Inventory Status to identify products as "Good" and "Off-Spec," and assigned the "Off-Spec" value to finished goods when applicable. They also defined lower sales prices in their sales price trade agreements for items with an Inventory Status of "Off-Spec." On the occasion off-spec products were also purchased for their distribution warehouse, they similarly used purchase price agreements.

Case 16: Use a Single Value for the Inventory Status A distribution company was implementing AX in a short timeframe, and did not want any additional complexities that would delay the cutover. In terms of using different values of an Inventory Status, they were not quite ready to think through the potential impacts on all business processes. They defined a single value of *Available,* defining it as the default for all possible transactions. They planned to revisit the use of Inventory Status after the initial cutover to AX.

Case 17: Indicate the Need for Inspection Using the Item's Default Value for Inventory Status The quality manager defined a value of *Receiving-Inspection-Required* for Inventory Status, and assigned it as the default value for selected items (and supplying vendor) so that the value is automatically inherited by a purchase order line and communicated to receiving clerks at the time of reporting arrival. This approach provided an alternative to using quality orders to communicate the need for inspection at the time of purchase order arrival.

4.10 Executive Summary

The use of Inventory Status only applies to WMS-enabled items. WMS-enabled items represent a special case in the Basic Inventory approach, and a prerequisite for the Advanced WMS approach. Inventory Status has a broad range of potential uses. Its significance depends on the scenario. Key aspects of its significance are determined by policies in the Storage Dimension Group assigned to items, but its significance is largely determined by user-defined values. For example, a value can be designated as blocked, thereby preventing further usage of existing inventory that has been assigned the blocked status.

Case studies provided multiple examples of different values for Inventory Status. These included using a quality order to assign Inventory Status (Case 13), assigning Inventory Status at the time of purchase order arrival (Case 14), identifying off-spec or blemished products using Inventory Status (Case 15), using a single value for the Inventory Status (Case 16), and indicating the need for inspection using the item's default value for Inventory Status (Case 17)

Chapter 5

Purchase Order Receiving

The Basic Inventory approach supports several variations for purchase order receiving. For explanatory purposes, it is easiest to start with a simple yet typical business process, and explain the related life cycles, reversing transactions, and key constructs. The basic process provides a baseline for explaining variations, such as different approaches to receiving inspection and load planning for purchases. These topics are reflected in the following sections within the chapter:

1. Basic Process for Purchase Order Receiving
2. Additional Steps in the Basic Process
3. Life Cycles Related to the Basic Process
4. Reversing Transactions in the Basic Process
5. Key Constructs for Purchase Order Receiving
6. Major Variations for Purchase Order Receiving
7. Minor Variations
8. Receiving Inspection for Purchase Order Arrivals
9. Return to Vendor
10. Additional Case Studies

Effective procurement practices represent a critical consideration for purchase order receiving. In order to be effective, the purchase orders should reflect up-to-date S&OP game plans and up-to-date delivery dates and quantities. Additional factors include a manageable level of expediting. These considerations will make life easier for warehouse management.

5.1 Basic Process for Purchase Order Receiving

The business process for purchase order receiving can have many variations. The starting point of a simple yet typical process provides a baseline for explaining the variations. The basic process shown in Figure 5.1 consists of several steps performed by a receiving clerk and warehouse worker. The process starts with the need to report purchase order arrival, and ends with completed reporting. This section provides an overview of the basic process and describes each step in more detail.

5.1 Basic Process for Purchase Order Receiving

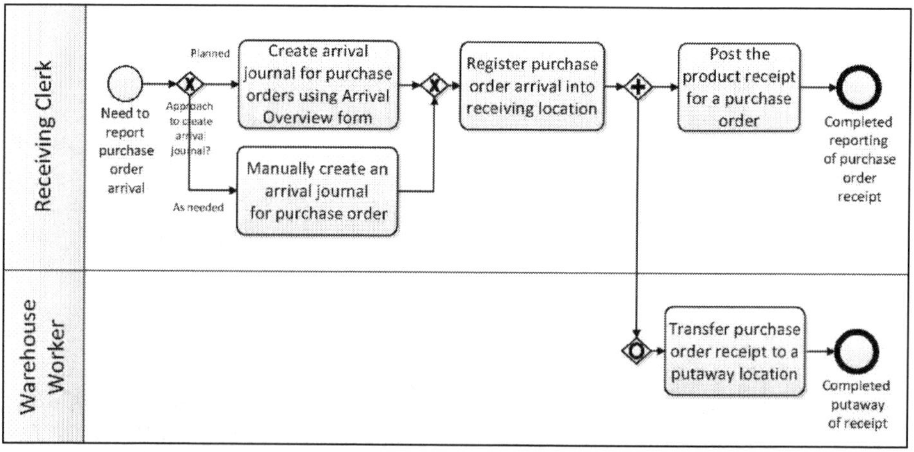

Overview The receiving clerk typically uses the Arrival Overview form to review a subset of open purchase order line items reflecting user specified criteria, such as the ship-to warehouse, delivery date and delivery mode. The receiving clerk can select purchase order lines, and then create an arrival journal containing the selected lines. Alternatively, the receiving clerk can manually create an Arrival Journal—typically to handle an unplanned receipt. The receiving clerk registers the actual receipts against each journal line item and then posts the journal to update inventory balances. The receiving clerk also identifies the vendor's packing list number when posting the product receipt for the purchase order. For received material with putaway requirements, the warehouse worker uses the Transfer Journal form to report transfers from the receiving location to the putaway location.

Create Arrival Journal for Purchase Orders using the Arrival Overview form Using the Arrival Overview form, the receiving clerk anticipates arrivals by viewing a subset of open purchase order line items reflecting user specified criteria, such as a ship-to location, delivery date, and delivery mode. The receiving clerk can select purchase order lines and then create an arrival journal containing the selected lines. When selecting purchase order lines, the receiving clerk can optionally analyze the estimated handling time and total weight/volume/pieces.

Manually Create an Arrival Journal for Purchase Orders Using the Arrival Journal form, the receiving clerk can manually create an arrival journal—typically to handle an unplanned receipt.

Register Purchase Order Arrival into Receiving Location The receiving clerk typically prints the line items within an arrival journal as a turnaround document, since it identifies the expected receipts. Using the Arrival Journal form, the receiving clerk enters the vendor's packing list number in the header information, and enters actual receipts for each journal line item (when it differs from expected receipts). The receiving clerk posts the arrival journal after completing the information, which updates inventory balances but not the financial impact.

Post the Product Receipt for a Purchase Order The receiving clerk posts the product receipt for a purchase order, which updates the financial impact of received material. The receiving clerk typically posts the product receipt as a related step on the Arrival Journal form (after posting the arrival journal). In this way, the product receipt reflects the registered information about item arrivals and the previous entry of the vendor's packing list number.

Transfer a Purchase Order Receipt to a Putaway Location When needed, the warehouse worker uses the Transfer Journal form to report a separate putaway transaction after recording purchase order arrival or product receipt into a receiving location. The warehouse worker typically prints the line items within the transfer journal as a turnaround document.

Enforcing the Major Steps in the Basic Process The major steps of registering arrival and posting the product receipt can be enforced by two policies within the Item Model Group assigned to an item. These policies are labeled as the Registration Requirements checkbox and the Receiving Requirements checkbox.

5.2 Additional Steps in the Basic Process

The basic process often includes several additional steps or slight variations. These are not shown in Figure 5.1 so that the diagram does not become too complex. The following steps may be needed.

Alternatives for Posting the Product Receipt The receiving clerk typically posts the product receipt as a related step on the Arrival Journal form (after posting the arrival journal). The Posting Product Receipt form can also be accessed from the Purchase Order form (so that it inherits information from the selected order) or accessed directly (where selection criteria can be used to populate the information). All of these approaches can reflect a quantity basis of *registered* so that the registered information about item arrivals and the previous entry of the vendor's packing list number will be used in posting the product receipt.

Receive Short When No Further Receipts are Expected When posting a product receipt for a purchase order, you can optionally indicate that a purchase order line has been received short (relative to the ordered quantity) and that no further receipts are expected. The status of the purchase order line will be updated to *Received.* Use the *Close for Receipt* checkbox for the relevant line when posting the product receipt.

Requirement for a Complete Delivery A purchase order can be flagged for complete delivery, which means the entire order quantity must be identified when posting the product receipt. It does not impact the reporting of partial quantities on the arrival journal.

Delay Posting of the Arrival Journal in Order to Indicate Putaway Locations In some scenarios, the receiving clerk enters actual quantities on the arrival journal line items, and then warehouse workers enter the actual putaway locations and post the arrival journal.

Perform Posting of Product Receipt by an Accounts Payable Clerk In some scenarios, the accounts payable clerk performs posting of product receipts. One rationale is that posting should be tightly controlled because it updates the financial information about receipts. A second rationale is that the quality order results can be considered in the quantity being posted, as illustrated in a subsequent case study (Case 18). The clerk can still start from the Arrival Journal form in order to perform posting of the product receipt.

Identify Potential Problems in Delivery Dates The delivery date for a purchase order line provides the basis for expected receiving in the warehouse. In particular, the confirmed delivery date for a purchase line (or a line within a delivery schedule) typically indicates the most realistic, up-to-date information from the vendor. Several standard inquiries identify potential problems about deliveries. You can identify purchase order lines without confirmed delivery dates or with past due delivery dates. You can also identify purchase-related backorders. These problems typically require action by the purchasing agent and coordination with the vendor, but they are also relevant for expected receiving activities in the warehouse.

Identify Purchase-Related Backorders A purchase-related backorder within AX simply refers to any purchase line with a delivery date prior to a specified date (aka the backorder date).[1] This simple definition includes purchase lines with a partially delivered quantity, where the line has not been closed short when posting the product receipt. A partially delivered quantity is the normal interpretation of a purchase backorder. Standardized inquiries can be used to identify all purchase-related backorders or just those related to a vendor. The purchasing agent typically reviews purchase-related backorders and takes action for a selected backorder. The actions include expediting delivery from the vendor, updating the confirmed delivery date, and/or reducing the quantity for the purchase line.

5.3 Life Cycles Related to the Basic Process

The basic process involves several related constructs where the status for each construct reflects various steps in the process. Figure 5.2 summarizes this information, and identifies those steps representing the minimum number of touch points for updating status. Shading highlights the key constructs of an arrival journal and a transfer journal.

5.4 Reversing Transactions in the Basic Process

The ability to reverse transactions requires an understanding of the current point within the business process and the associated status of key constructs. Borrowing from the previous figure, Figure 5.3 illustrates the steps within the basic process (shown in grey text) and the various points at which you can perform reversing transactions (shown in black text). As identified by step numbers in the figure, you can reverse transactions (3X) after posting the product receipt but prior to entering the vendor's invoice.

[1] This simple definition is critical for understanding "backordered lines" with a future delivery date when compared to a specified backorder date in the future.

Figure 5.2 Life Cycles Related to the Basic Process for Purchase Order Receiving

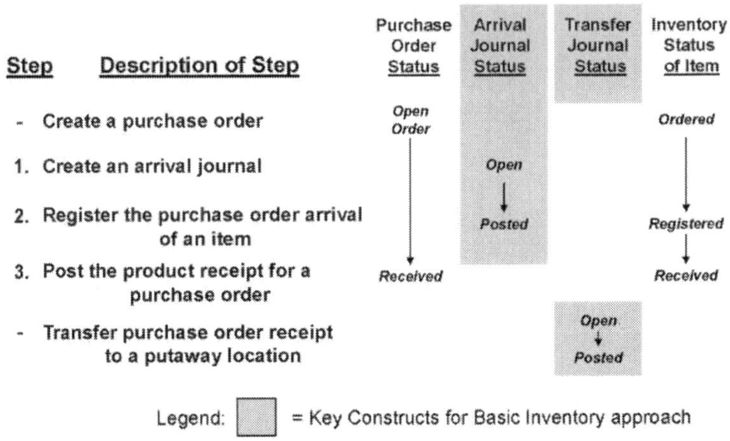

Figure 5.3 Reversing Transactions in the Basic Process for Purchase Order Receiving

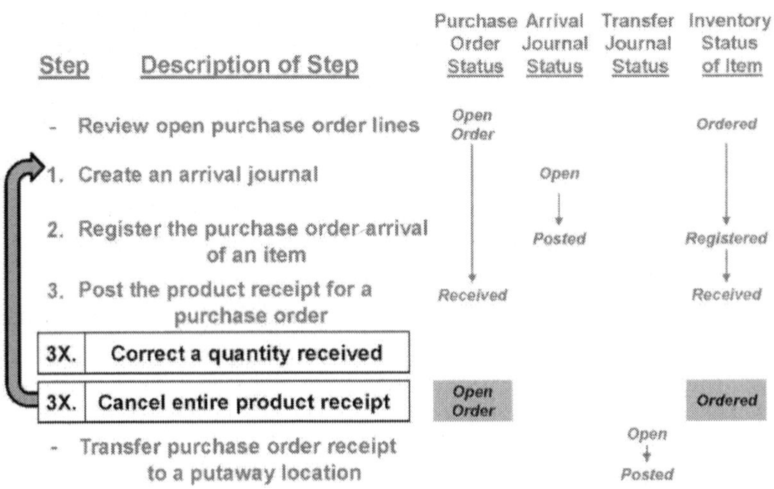

Step 3X: Correct a Quantity Received You can correct a quantity received by starting from the Product Receipt Journal form and selecting the Correct function to access the Product Receipt Correction form. You enter a different received quantity for one or more lines, and the quantity difference (with the previously entered quantity) will be reversed. You can optionally select a reason code for the correction, where codes must be defined on the Vendor Reasons form.

An additional version of a product receipt journal will be automatically created after making a correction. As part of viewing the correction history for a product receipt journal, you can view a comparison of two selected versions in order to identify the new and old values.

Step 3X: Cancel Entire Product Receipt to Reverse the Inventory Transactions You can reverse all transactions related to a product receipt (aka the vendor's packing list number) by starting from the Product Receipt Journal form and selecting the Cancel function. This will remove the items from inventory and reverse the financial impact. Figure 5.3 illustrates the impact on status of cancelling a product receipt, and the arrow indicates the resulting point in the business process. For example, you can start over with registering arrival.

5.5 Key Constructs for Purchase Order Receiving

The basic process for purchase order receiving employs an arrival journal to register receipts for updating inventory balances, and posting of the product receipt for updating the related financial transactions. The posting automatically creates a product receipt journal for viewing the financial impacts. The basic process may also employ transfer journals for putaway purposes. This section summarizes the significance of each of these constructs.

Significance of the Arrival Journal for Purchase Order Receipts An arrival journal provides the basis for identifying expected receipts and also for reporting actual receipt quantities and locations as well as batch and serial numbers if applicable. This is termed "registering the information" (or registration for short) in AX terminology.

Each arrival journal has a system-assigned identifier, and consists of header information and line items. Each line identifies the related purchase order, item and quantity to be received. You enter details about the actual receipt for each line and then post the arrival journal to update inventory balances. However, an additional step is required to update the financial information about received material.

An arrival journal and its line items typically represent the contents of a vendor's packing list, and this packing list number can be identified in the header information for an arrival journal. In this way, after posting the Arrival Journal to update inventory balances, you can easily perform the additional step to post the product receipt (and identify its related packing list number) to update the purchase order.

Significance of Posting the Product Receipt The posting of a product receipt represents the completion of the purchase order receiving process and serves several purposes. As a primary purpose, it updates the financial information about received material and automatically generates the related journal (called the Product Receipt Journal). The financial impact includes purchase price variances for standard cost items. It also updates the purchase order—such as updating the status to *received*—and provides the basis for three-way matching when entering a vendor's invoice.

As part of posting the product receipt, you identify the vendor's packing list number (aka the product receipt number); a companywide policy determines how to handle duplicate numbers.[2] You can also indicate when a purchase order line with a short receipt should be closed, indicating that no further receipts are expected. The quantity basis for posting the product receipt typically reflects the previously registered information about arrivals.

You can access the Posting Product Receipt form for a selected arrival journal or purchase order. It can also be accessed directly where you employ selection criteria for identifying one or more purchase orders.

Significance of the Product Receipt Journal A Product Receipt Journal is automatically created by posting a product receipt. Its identifier reflects the user-assigned product receipt number (aka vendor's packing list number), and consists of a header and line item information. From the header, you can view the related vouchers, distributions, and subledger journal entries. You can also perform reversing transactions for receipts (such as a correction or cancellation). For a selected journal, you can view its line items about the related item, quantity, and purchase order. You can access the Product Receipt Journal form directly or from a selected purchase order.

[2] The companywide policy (defined in the Procurement and Sourcing Parameters form) determines whether entry of a duplicate number results in a warning or rejection in order to avoid duplication of reported receipts. Alternatively, you can choose to accept entries of a duplicate number without any warning to the user.

Significance of a Transfer Journal for Purchase Order Putaway A purchase order can be received into a bin location that represents a receiving area, which typically requires an additional step to put away the inventory. However, unlike the Advanced WMS approach, the Basic Inventory approach does not generate a work order to support a separate putaway transaction. A transfer journal can be used to support a separate putaway transaction.

An alternative approach to putaway transactions is supported when using a quarantine order as part of receiving inspection so that it generates a separate putaway transaction for usable material. A subsequent chapter about quality management provides further explanation of quarantine orders (Section 26.6).

Key Forms for Purchase Order Receiving Several key forms correspond to the key constructs, and a quick summary of these key forms is provided below.

- *Arrival Journal.* Use this form to identify the expected receipts for a purchase order and to report actual receipts for updating inventory balances. You can register the actual quantity and (when applicable) the location, batch number, and/or serial numbers for the received material.

- *Posting Product Receipt.* Use this form to complete the receiving process for a purchase order and update the financial information about received material. Actual posting will automatically create a Product Receipt Journal.

  Prior to posting, you must identify the vendor's packing list number (aka product receipt number) which acts as the identifier for the Product Receipt Journal.

- *Product Receipt Journal.* Use this form to review the actual receipts related to a vendor's packing list number (aka the product receipt number), and view the vouchers and subledger entries for a selected journal. You can optionally correct or cancel a product receipt.

- *Arrival Overview.* Use this form to anticipate receiving activities and generate an arrival journal for selected purchase order lines.

5.6 Major Variations for Purchase Order Receiving

The basic process for production order picking provides the foundation for explaining major variations. The major variations include a simple inventory transaction, the use of receiving inspection and purchase order returns, and the receipts for serialized or batch-controlled items.

Simple Inventory Transaction for Reporting Purchase Order Receipts The receiving clerk can bypass the use of an arrival journal by using a simple inventory transaction, where you register the item when posting the product receipt for a purchase order. You can also identify registration information for a line item on a purchase order prior to posting the product receipt.

Receive Batch-Controlled Items A batch-controlled item involves the assignment of batch numbers when reporting purchase order arrival. It may also involve reporting of vendor batch information and/or a batch disposition code. A subsequent chapter describes the various approaches to batch number assignment, the nature of vendor batch information, and batch disposition codes (Chapter 25).

Receive Serialized Items A serialized item involves the assignment of serial numbers when reporting purchase order arrival. A subsequent chapter describes the various approaches to serial number assignment (Chapter 25).

Receiving Inspection for Purchase Order Arrivals There are many variations of receiving inspection for purchased material. For example, the receiving inspection may be performed by receiving clerks at the time of arrival into a receiving location, or by a quality control clerk reporting against an automatically-created quality order. In addition, the test results for a quality order may be reported for a small sample while the material remains in a receiving location, or the received material may be placed in a separate QC area until test results have been reported. A subsequent section provides further explanation about the variations of receiving inspection (Section 5.8).

Returns to Vendor Returning material to a vendor typically involves a different type of purchase order (termed a returned order) so that you can identify the vendor's RMA number (Return Material Authorization). It can also be handled via a purchase order line item with a negative quantity. A subsequent section provides further explanation about a typical process for purchase order returns (Section 5.9).

5.7 Minor Variations

Several minor variations apply to the basic process for purchase order receiving and its major variations. These include the use of delivery tolerances, safety margins, notes, and the Receipts List. Other minor variations were identified as part of the additional steps for the basic process, such as receiving short, requirements for a complete delivery, and posting product receipts by accounts payable.

- Receiving a Special Order
- Impact of a Vendor Hold and Other types of Stop Flags
- Impact of Delivery Tolerances on Purchase Order Receiving
- Modeling the Required Time for Purchase Order Receiving
- Effective Use of Notes for Purchase Order Receiving
- Using the Receipts List During Purchase Order Receiving

Receiving a Special Order The receipt of a special order (linked to a sales order) typically involves placement in a designated location for cross docking, so that it can be picked and shipped without putaway to a stocking location. You can identify this location on the sales line so that it is inherited by the related purchase line and displayed on the arrival journal.

An alternative approach to identifying the need for cross docking only applies to WMS-enabled items, where you can employ an Inventory Status. With this alternative, you can define one status as *Cross-Dock*, assign this status to the sales line, and then the status will be inherited by the related purchase line and displayed on the arrival journal.

The assignment of a *Cross-Dock* inventory status works best when using the Advanced WMS approach as it has difficulties with the assignment of a specified location on the sales line. You receive a warning infolog after entering the location, and the line item cannot be received via a mobile device transaction, and must be received via the client using the Basic Inventory approach.

Impact of a Vendor Hold and Other Types of Stop Flags The assignment of a vendor hold for "all" transactions will prevent posting of product receipts and result in a corresponding infolog. However, it does not prevent registration of purchase order arrivals from the vendor. Other types of stop flags include the following.

- *Impact of Stopped Transactions for an Item.* The purchase order transactions for an item can be stopped, either as a companywide or site-specific policy. The stopped flag prevents further transactions for an item's existing purchase orders (including registration of arrivals and posting of product receipts) and results in a corresponding infolog. A similar stopped flag can be specified for an item's inventory transactions, which also prevents further transactions.

- *Impact of a Stopped Flag on a Purchase Order Line.* The assignment of a stopped flag for a purchase order line prevents further transactions (including registration of arrivals and posting of product receipts) until it has been removed and results in a corresponding infolog.

Impact of Delivery Tolerances on Purchase Order Receiving When delivery tolerances are acceptable, they determine how much the quantities being received can differ from the ordered quantity. Over- and under-delivery tolerances (related to purchase orders) are expressed as a percentage; the values assigned to an item act as defaults for a purchase order line item. Delivery tolerances of zero percent for a purchase order line mean that the received quantity must equal the ordered quantity. A companywide policy (embedded in the Procurement and Sourcing parameters) determines whether over- and under-deliveries will be acceptable for purchase orders. The delivery tolerances are enforced when posting the packing slip for a purchase order, and the over-delivery tolerance is also enforced when reporting arrivals.

Modeling the Required Time for Receiving/Inspection Activities Some scenarios have a significant time requirement for receiving and inspection activities related to an item's receipt, such as one (1) or more days. A significant time requirement should be included in the supply chain model so that purchase order delivery dates will correctly reflect the required time. The required time can be identified as the receipt safety margin, where you define the number of days as part of the Coverage Group assigned to the item. It is normally assigned as part of the Item Coverage information for the item.

Effective Use of Notes for Purchase Order Receiving Purposes Notes can be entered for a purchase order header and lines, and included in the standard format for printed purchase orders. These notes can be inherited from the vendor and item respectively. However, the notes specific to receiving instructions are not currently included in standard formats; use of notes will require customized formats.

Using the Receipts List During Purchase Order Receiving A printed version of a Receipts List provides reference information for identifying the expected receipts for line items on a purchase order. For example, the expected receipt information includes the item and quantity for each line item. It represents reference information (rather than a turnaround document) because you cannot record actual receipts against the receipts list.

When posting a receipts list for a purchase order, you can optionally specify additional selection criteria (such as the ship-to warehouse and expected delivery date) so that only the applicable lines will be included. Posting the receipts list will automatically generate a Receipts List Journal, which can be subsequently viewed or used for reprinting the document. You can access the Posting Receipts List form for a selected purchase order. It can also be accessed directly or performed via batch processing, where you employ selection criteria for identifying multiple purchase order lines.

5.8 Receiving Inspection for Purchase Order Arrivals

There are many variations of receiving inspection for purchased material. For example, the receiving inspection may be performed by receiving clerks at the time of arrival into a receiving location, or by a quality control clerk using an automatically-created quality order. The test results for a quality order may be reported for a small sample while the material remains in a receiving location, or the received material may be placed in a separate QC area until test results have been reported. Validation results of pass or fail can automatically update the Inventory Status of the received inventory or the batch disposition code of batch-controlled items.

As an explanatory approach, the different inspection approaches are more easily explained via case studies. A subsequent chapter on quality management summarizes many of the different approaches and the related case studies (Section 26.2). A common scenario involves the assignment of an Inventory Status to received material based on the test results for a quality order, as described in the following Case 18. Additional case studies illustrate some other approaches.

Case 18: Assign Inventory Status Based on Test Results for a Quality Order

The warehouse manager and quality manager at a manufacturing company were considering options for identifying needed action about received material based on the test results for a quality order. One approach involved the user-defined values for Inventory Status with possible values of *Good*, *To-Be-Scrapped, Return-to-Vendor and Needs-Rework*. The default value for inventory status was always identified as *Good* on purchase order lines. This approach differs slightly from another option considered by the managers where Inventory Status is assigned by receiving clerks during purchase order arrival, as described in Case 14.

The proposed approach employs automatically-created quality orders for purchase order arrivals, where the quality control clerk identifies the applicable value when tests result in a failed validation. In addition, the approach identifies an accounts payable clerk as responsible for posting of product receipts so that the quality order results can be considered. The two managers prepared a diagram (Figure 5.4) of the proposed business process.

The receiving inspection process starts with registration of a purchase order arrival into a receiving location which automatically generates a quality order, and it has multiple end points reflecting the test results of the quality order. The inventory remains in the receiving location until completion of the quality order. The process consists of several steps performed by different roles, and three of these steps merit further explanation.

Figure 5.4 Receiving Inspection Using a Quality Order and Inventory Status

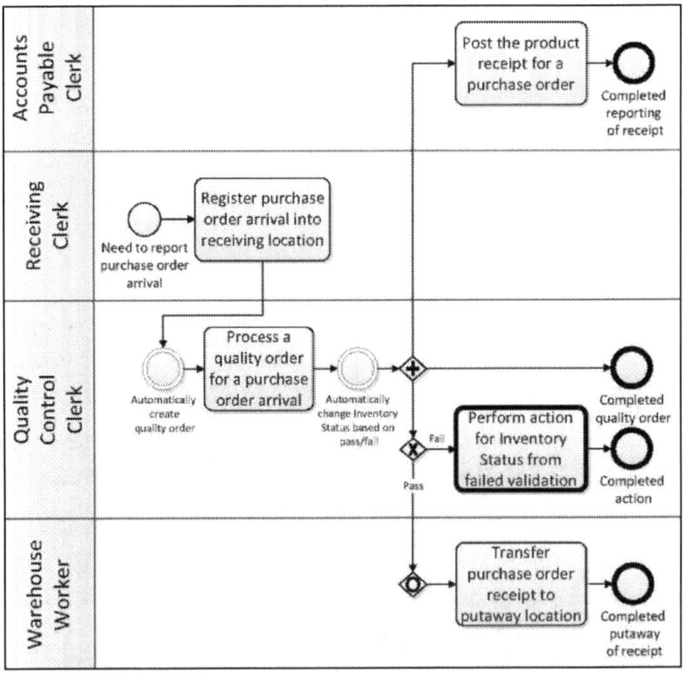

- *Process a Quality Order for a Purchase Order Arrival.* The activities of quality control clerks are coordinated based on a review of open quality orders, using either the Quality Orders form or the Inventory Blocking form. When reporting test results for a given quality order, the quality control clerk indicates the applicable Inventory Status for validation failure, such as *Scrap, Return-to-Vendor,* or *Needs-Rework.* Validation automatically updates the Inventory Status of the received material.

If applicable, the quality control clerk creates a nonconformance related to problems with the item, purchase order or vendor, and/or creates a case about the problem.

- *Perform Action for Inventory Status from Failed Validation.* The quality control clerk reports an inventory adjustment for material assigned an Inventory Status of *Scrap.* The production planner creates a rework order for material with a *Needs-Rework* status. The accounts payable clerk creates a purchase order return for material with a *Return-to-Vendor* status. For material with a *Good* status, the warehouse worker reports a transfer from the receiving location to a stocking location.

- *Post the Product Receipt for a Purchase Order.* The accounts payable clerk posts the product receipt after completion of the quality order. In this way, the posting can be blocked until completion, and a validation failure will be communicated (via an infolog message) when posting the product receipt.

Many of the steps related to Case 18 and Figure 5.2 are explained in other chapters, including the use of Inventory Status (Chapter 4), purchase order returns (Section 5.9), and quality orders (Section 26.3).

Case 19: Receiving Inspection and Batch Disposition Codes The quality manager defined several batch disposition codes with policies about restricted usage and expected scrap, and the relevant code was assigned to inventory by a quality control clerk. For example, the code *Scrap* indicated non-nettable inventory with all of the restricted usage policies, whereas the code *Good* did not have any restricted usage policies. The code was initially assigned to receipts as the result of a quality order, where the quality control clerk identified the batch disposition code that should be assigned for validation failure and also for pass. The batch disposition code for existing inventory was also updated when needed.

Case 20: Report Quality Order Results After Putaway The quality manager at a food products manufacturer employed quality orders to record the vendor-supplied certificate of analysis (COA) information about received material. For example, the test results for the salt percentage and moisture percentage were simply recorded based on the COA information for a given batch, and did not involve additional testing activities. Quality orders were automatically generated by purchase order arrivals into a receiving location, and the material was immediately put away into a stocking location. The quality control clerk typically reported the quality order results soon after arrival, and did not need to review the material in its stocking location.

Case 21: Receiving Inspection with Delayed Testing Results Some of the purchased material for a manufacturing company required testing by an outside agency that involved several days turnaround. In a typical case, a small sample of the batch-controlled item was sent to the outside agency to obtain the testing results, and the material was placed in its putaway location but blocked until the test results could be reported. The test and sample size were identified by the quality order for the received material, and an expected date was assigned that reflected completion of the outside testing results. Blocking of the entire received quantity was also enforced by the quality order. When the testing results were received, the quality control clerk reported them and then validated the quality order. This removed the blocking associated with the quality order, so that material with a failed validation was typically assigned an Inventory Status with blocking or a batch disposition code with restricted usage policies.

A failed validation sometimes involved additional testing, so that the quality order was reopened until the test results could be reported, thereby providing further blocking of the material. In other cases, the material with a failed validation was scrapped or reworked, or returned to the vendor.

In order to model the required time for reporting delayed test results, the purchased items were assigned a Receiving Safety Margin (as part of the Coverage Group assigned to the item) so that receipts were scheduled for arrival prior to their required date.

Case 22: Receiving Inspection with a Separate QC Area For certain purchased items at a manufacturing company, the entire quantity of each purchase order arrival was placed in a separate QC location so that a quality control clerk could report the testing results for the quality order. After validation, a warehouse worker would report transfers from the QC location to a stocking location. This reflects a different approach than simply reporting test results for a small sample, where the received material stays in a receiving location until validation of the test results.

5.9 Returns to Vendor

Returning material to a vendor typically involves a different type of purchase order (termed a returned order), so that you can identify the vendor's RMA number (Return Material Authorization). It can also be handled via a purchase order line item with a negative quantity. When using returned orders, the typical process consists of several steps performed by different roles, as illustrated in Figure 5.5 and summarized below. The process starts with a request for a return to vendor, and ends with a completed purchase order return.

Figure 5.5 Typical Process for a Purchase Order Return

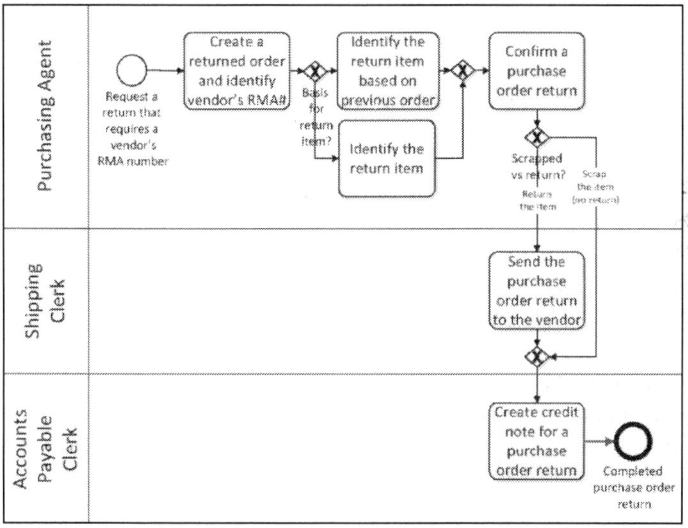

Overview The purchasing agent creates a returned order for a specified vendor and identifies the vendor's RMA number. The purchasing agent also creates a line item for each returned item, where the line item identifies an item, a negative quantity, purchase price, ship-from location, and the requested ship date. The line item information can also be created by selecting lines from a previously invoiced purchase order, which helps identify the original purchase price. The purchasing agent confirms a purchase order when information has been completely entered. In some scenarios, these steps are performed by an accounts payable clerk.

The shipping clerk typically reports the item(s) being sent back for a returned order. The accounts payable clerk creates the vendor's credit note based on the quantity of each item returned, or based on the returned order quantity (when there is no return).

Create a Purchase Order Return and Identify the Vendor's RMA Number The purchasing agent manually creates a returned order for a specified vendor, and identifies the vendor's RMA number. If applicable, the purchasing agent identifies the related blanket purchase order with the vendor. The purchasing agent also creates a line item for each returned item, where the line item identifies an item, a negative quantity, a purchase price, ship-from location, and the requested ship date.

Identify the Return Item Based on Previously Invoiced Purchase Order The purchasing agent creates a line item on a returned order by finding a previously invoiced purchase order for the pay-to vendor and selecting the line item(s) and quantity being returned. The search can be based on the item number or purchase order number. Each selected line item creates a line item on the returned order, along with the original purchase price (which acts as the credit amount).

Identify the Return Item for a Return to Vendor The purchasing agent creates a line item on the returned order, which specifies the item number, a negative quantity, and a purchase price representing the credit amount. The credit amount defaults to the item's current purchase price with the vendor, and it may be adjusted to reflect partial credit.

Confirm a Purchase Order Return The purchasing agent confirms a purchase order return when information has been completely entered. The confirmation enables subsequent steps in purchase order processing such as sending the return. The purchase order must be confirmed again after updating information. Each confirmation creates a history record so that the purchasing agent can track historical versions.

Send the Purchase Order Return to the Vendor The shipping clerk reports the item(s) being sent back for a purchase order return, including the batch number for a batch-controlled item. The shipping clerk uses the Posting Product Receipt form to select a line representing a return, and then identifies the "pick" information about the inventory being returned. The posting can print the packing slip to accompany the items being sent, and it automatically creates a Product Receipt Journal that identifies the financial impact.

The significance of the Product Receipt Journal was previously explained as one of the key constructs for purchase order receiving (Section 5.5), and it can be used to reverse transactions (Section 5.4).

Create the Vendor Credit Note for a Purchase Order Return The accounts payable clerk creates the vendor's credit note based on the quantity of each item returned, or based on the returned order quantity (when there is no return).

5.10 Additional Case Studies

Case 23: Correcting Errors about Reported Receipts The receiving clerks at a manufacturing/distribution company would sometimes make a mistake in the reported quantity received. In order to correct the mistake, the supervisor would access the Product Receipt Journal form and select the "Correct" function to access the Product Receipt Correction form. The supervisor would enter the correct quantity for the relevant line and select a reason code for the correction. In this way, the inventory balances and financial information would reflect the correction.

Case 24: Cross Docking for Special Orders A large number of sales orders for a distribution company represented a special order where the purchased item would be received and then immediately shipped to the customer. Two different approaches were being considered to communicate the need for cross-docking. The sales order line item could be assigned a specific location of "Cross-Dock," or an Inventory Status of "Cross-Dock," so that the values were inherited by the related purchase line and displayed on the arrival journal. Both approaches work for the basic approach to warehouse management. The second approach, using an Inventory Status, also works for the advanced approach.

Case 25: Indicate Need for a Quarantine Order When Reporting a Purchase Order Arrival The receiving clerks at a manufacturing/distribution company could identify the need for a quarantine order when reporting purchase order arrival via the arrival journal. This resulted in an automatically-generated quarantine order in order to communicate the need for further inspection. The receiving clerks also placed the inventory in a bin location within the quarantine warehouse.

Case 26: Modeling the Required Time for Purchase Order Receiving/Inspection A food products manufacturer required test results from an outside service for certain raw materials, which often took five (5) days before the results could be reported for the associated quality order. The five (5) days were included in the receipt safety margin for each item so the material would be scheduled for delivery before the required date. The five (5) days were also reflected in the expected completion date of the quality order so that master scheduling logic recognized the scheduled availability.

Case 27: Vendor Performance Metrics Based on Quality Order Tests A manufacturer wanted to track several user-defined vendor performance metrics based on quality order test results. Examples of a user-defined performance metric include COA included (with enumerated outcomes of yes/no for the Certificate of Analysis) and order complete (with enumerated outcomes of exact quantity, under delivery within tolerance %, and under delivery outside tolerance %). Using standard AX capabilities for quality orders, each performance metric can be defined as a test, and the test results can be captured on the automatically-generated quality order. A customized Vendor Performance report reflects the performance metrics from quality order tests.

5.11 Executive Summary

The Basic Inventory approach supports several variations for purchase order receiving. This chapter started with a simple yet typical business process, and explained the related life cycles, reversing transactions, and key constructs. This basic process provided a baseline for explaining variations, such as different approaches to receiving inspection and load planning for purchases.

Case studies illustrated some of the variations for purchase order receiving, especially those related to quality. These included assigning Inventory Status based on test results for a quality order (Case 18), receiving inspection and batch disposition codes (Case 19), reporting quality order results after putaway (Case 20), receiving inspection with delayed testing results (Case 21), receiving inspection with a separate QC area (Case 22), indicating the need for a quarantine order when reporting a purchase order arrival (Case 25), and vendor performance metrics based on quality order tests (Case 27). Other cases covered correcting errors about reported receipts (Case 23), cross-docking for special orders (Case 24), and modeling the required time for purchase order receiving/inspection (Case 26).

Chapter 6

Sales Order Picking/Shipping

The Basic Inventory approach employs an order-based picking list and a related shipment to report sales order fulfillment. For explanatory purposes, it is easiest to start with a simple yet typical business process, and explain the related life cycles, reversing transactions, and key constructs. The basic process provides a baseline for explaining variations, such as the variations of generating picking lists and the use of wave picking. These topics are reflected in the following sections within the chapter:

1. Basic Process for Sales Order Picking/Shipping
2. Additional Steps in the Basic Process
3. Life Cycles Related to the Basic Process
4. Reversing Transactions in the Basic Process
5. Key Constructs for Sales Order Picking/Shipping
6. Major Variations of Sales Order Picking/Shipping
7. Minor Variations
8. Selection Criteria for Generating Picking Lists
9. Generate Picking Lists using the Picking Workbench form
10. Extended Explanation of Related Life Cycles for Picking/Shipping
11. Additional Case Studies

Realistic delivery promises on sales orders represent a critical consideration for sales order picking/shipping. Delivery promises should reflect S&OP game plans and the delivery dates should reflect up-to-date information. Other factors may apply such as a manageable level of expediting. These considerations will make life easier for warehouse management.

6.1 Basic Process for Sales Order Picking/Shipping

The business process for sales order picking/shipping can have many variations. A simple yet typical process provides a baseline for explaining the variations. The basic process shown in Figure 6.1 consists of several steps performed by a shipping clerk and warehouse worker. The process starts with the need for sales order picking/shipping and ends with completed shipments. This section provides an overview of the basic process and describes each step in more detail.

Figure 6.1 Basic Process for Sales Order Picking/Shipping

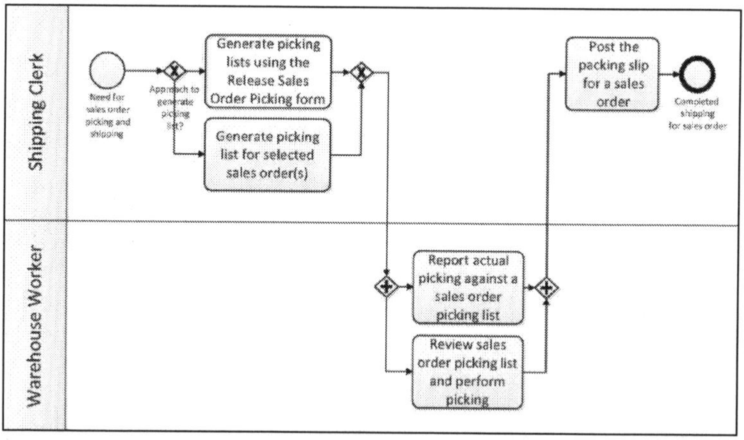

Overview The shipping clerk typically uses the Release Sales Order Picking form to review and select open sales order lines that require picking/shipping, and then generate the picking lists for selected orders. The generation of a picking list will reserve the item's inventory for the sales line (if not already reserved). The warehouse worker reports actual picking against a sales order picking list, and the shipping clerk reports actual shipment by posting the sales order packing slip for picked items.

Generate Picking Lists Using the Release Sales Order Picking Form The shipping clerk uses the Release Sales Order Picking form to view a subset of open sales order lines based on selection criteria such as the ship-from warehouse, ship date, mode of delivery and/or customer. The displayed information indicates whether a sales line already has reserved inventory stemming from order entry. When viewing the open sales lines, the shipping clerk can analyze which orders can be picked using available inventory, and then simulate allocation of the inventory to selected sales lines. The selected sales lines can then be released for picking. This step displays the Posting Picking List form for the selected lines, so that actual posting will generate the picking lists.

Generate Picking List for Selected Sales Order(s) The shipping clerk uses the Posting Picking List form to generate and print the picking list for selected sales order(s), where the query criteria can identify the selected orders. Typical selection criteria include the ship-from warehouse, ship date, mode of delivery and/or customer, and a set of criteria can be predefined with a user-definable name. Alternatively, the customer service rep can generate the picking list as part of order entry for a sales order, where accessing the Posting Picking List form will inherit selection criteria from the sales order.

Review Sales Order Picking List and Perform Picking The warehouse worker can review a printed picking list and perform the picking. The printed picking list identifies the reserved inventory.

Report Actual Picking Against a Sales Order Picking List The warehouse worker uses the Picking List Registration form for reporting actual picking against a picking list and to reduce on hand inventory. In many cases, the shipping clerk simply confirms that the reserved inventory was actually picked. If needed, the shipping clerk can identify the alternative quantity or location that was picked.

Post the Packing Slip for a Sales Order The shipping clerk posts and prints a sales order packing slip (which reflects the picked items) to indicate actual shipment and update the financial information.

Enforcing the Major Steps in the Basic Process The major steps of picking and shipping a sales order can be enforced by two policies within the item model group assigned to an item. These policies are labeled Picking Requirements and Deduction Requirements.

6.2 Additional Steps in the Basic Process

The basic process often involves additional steps or slight variations not shown in Figure 6.1 so that the diagram does not become too complex. Examples include the following steps.

Generate/Update the Bill of Lading for a Sales Order Shipment Posting the packing slip can also result in automatic generation of a bill of lading, which has a system-assigned identifier. Some information pertaining to the bill of lading is automatically updated, such as the customer, sales order number, delivery address, and the shipped items and quantities. Other information must be manually maintained, including each package type (such as carton), quantity, and weight. Use the Bill of Lading form for data maintenance and document printing. A bill of lading can be manually created to support other types of shipments (such as office furniture) or to support a master bill of lading (such as shipments to a freight forwarder). After creating a bill of lading identifier, for example, you explicitly designate it as a master bill of lading and also assign the identifier to the individual bills of lading associated with it.

Identify and Close a Sales Order Line that is Shipped Short You can indicate that a sales line with a shipped short quantity should be closed when posting the packing slip for the sales order.

Identify Sales Orders with Partial Picking One indicator of needed actions for warehouse management consists of sales orders with partially completed picking. You can identify these needed actions using a standard form (labeled All Partially Picked Orders, within Accounts Receivable). The form identifies any sales order with one or more line items that have a partially picked quantity. It does not include sales orders with a delivered status where a sales line was shipped short and closed.

Identify Sales Order Lines Picked but not yet Shipped One indicator of needed actions for warehouse management consists of sales order line items which have been picked but not yet shipped as of today's date. You can identify these needed actions using a standard report (labeled Inventory Picked not Delivered, within Inventory Management).

Identify Sales Order Lines with Past Due Ship Dates One indicator of needed actions for warehouse management consists of sales order line items with past-due ship dates You can identify these needed actions using a standard form (labeled Delayed Shipments, within Sales and Marketing), which lists the sales lines with a promised ship date that is past due relative to a specified backorder date.

Identify Sales-Related Backorders A sales-related backorder within AX simply refers to any sales line with a ship date prior to a specified date (aka the backorder date).[1] This simple definition also applies to a sales line with an unshipped or partially shipped quantity, where the line has not been closed short when reporting actual shipment. This represents the more common interpretation of a sales-related backorder. Some scenarios need to identify the quantity for an

[1] This simple definition is critical for understanding "backordered lines" with a future ship date when compared to a specified backorder date in the future.

unshipped or partially shipped line as "backordered" on sales order documents.[2] A standard inquiry provides information about sales-related backorders (labeled Backorder Lines, within Sales and Marketing).

The customer service rep typically reviews sales-related backorders and takes action for a selected backorder, but the information is also critical for the warehouse manager. The actions include updating the promise date or reducing the quantity for the sales order line, or a request to expedite a supply order.

Impact of an Order Hold on Sales Order Picking/Shipping The assignment of a Hold Code to a sales order will prevent any picking/shipping transactions until the Hold Code has been cleared. It results in a corresponding infolog when attempting to enter transactions.

Review Performance Metrics for On-Time Delivery and Full Quantity Two performance metrics include on-time delivery and full quantity delivery, typically measured over a specified time interval. Each performance metric reflects several underlying assumptions, as described below.

- *On Time Delivery*. On-time delivery for a sales line reflects a comparison between the actual and promised ship date. The basis of the promised date can be the requested or confirmed date for the sales line; either option should reflect consistent assignment of the promised date. In addition, achievement of on-time delivery typically reflects an exact match between dates or early delivery so that only late shipments indicate a performance problem.

- *Full-Quantity Delivery*. Full-quantity delivery for a sales line reflects a comparison between the ordered quantity and the actual shipped quantity. The achievement of full delivery typically requires an exact match between quantities so that quantity differences indicate a performance problem. Some would argue that delivery tolerances for over- and under-shipment quantities on a sales line (expressed as a percentage) should be considered in the performance metric.

You can identify these two performance metrics and their underlying assumptions using a standard report (labeled Top Sales Order Lines Not Shipped in Full or Not Shipped on Time, within Inventory Management), where the report dialogue also specifies the applicable time interval and warehouses(s). The standard report does not account for delivery tolerances.

---

[2] The treatment of unshipped and partially shipped line items is defined by the Backorder Tracking policy for printing packing slips and invoices (within the Forms Setup form in Accounts Receivable).

A standard inquiry provides a similar performance metric for on-time delivery (labeled Deviations Between Actual and Expected Shipments, within Sales and Marketing). The displayed information identifies sales lines with late shipments, and reflects a selected basis for the promised ship date and time interval (expressed as a number of look-back days).

6.3 Life Cycles Related to the Basic Process

The basic process involves several related constructs, where the status for each construct reflects various steps in the process. Figure 6.2 summarizes this information for the basic process, and only displays those steps representing the minimum number of touch points for updating status. Grey shading highlights the key constructs of a picking list, output order and shipment.

Figure 6.2 Life Cycles Related to the Basic Process for Sales Order Picking/Shipping

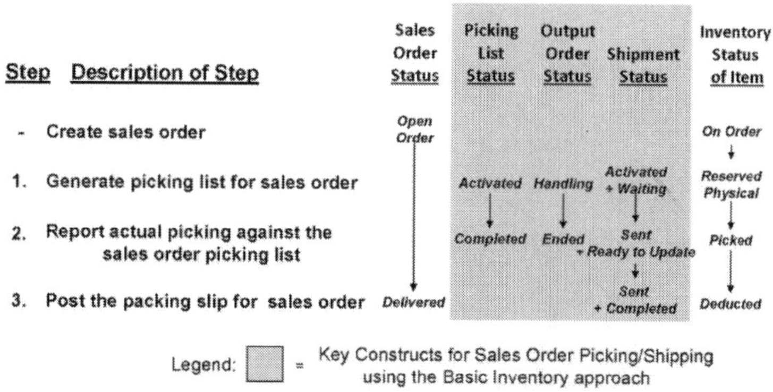

As shown in the figure, the first step will create a picking list (with line items reflecting output orders) and a corresponding shipment. It should be noted that the status for a shipment is identified by the combination of two fields termed the Shipment Status and the Physical Update Status. For example, the combination of *Activated* + *Waiting* indicates the shipment has been created. The right side of the figure shows the inventory status for an item on a sales order line. For example, various steps in the process will change this status from *on order* to *reserved physical*, *picked,* and *deducted.*

Information about related life cycles provides the foundation for explaining the reversing transactions which is covered in the next section. An extended explanation of each status is deferred until the end of the chapter (Section 6.10).

6.4 Reversing Transactions in the Basic Process

The ability to reverse transactions requires an understanding of the current point within the business process and the associated status of key constructs. Borrowing from the previous figure, Figure 6.3 illustrates the steps within the basic process (shown in grey text), and the various points at which you can perform reversing transactions (shown in black text). The figure also illustrates the impact of a reversing transaction on status, and the arrows indicate the resulting point in the business process. As identified by step numbers in the figure, you can reverse transactions (1X) after initially generating a picking list (2X) after reporting actual picking and (4X) after reporting actual shipment.

Figure 6.3 Reversing Transactions in the Basic Process for Sales Order Picking/Shipping

Step 1X: Reverse Transaction after Generating Picking List You can delete an output order (on the Output Order form) prior to actual picking, which automatically deletes the corresponding line on a picking list. Alternatively, you can cancel a picking list line or the entire picking list, which also deletes the corresponding output order(s). A deleted output order no longer has a status, as shown by a value of "N/A" within the figure.

Step 2X: Reverse Transaction after Actual Picking You can unpick a transaction prior to actual shipment by using the Unpick function on the Picking List Registration form.

Step 3X: Correct the Shipped Quantity or Cancel the Packing Slip Information can be corrected or cancelled after posting the sales order packing slip but before you generate the invoice. You perform the correction or cancellation from the Packing Slip Journal form, as described below.

- *Correct the quantity for a packing slip.* When you select the Correct function, you access the Correct Packing Slip form in order to enter a different shipped quantity. The quantity difference (with the previously entered quantity) will be reversed.

- *Cancel a packing slip.* When you select the Cancel function, you will cancel the sales order packing slip.

6.5 Key Constructs for Sales Order Picking/Shipping

The Basic Inventory approach for sales order picking/shipping involves several key constructs in addition to the sales order. These constructs include output orders, picking lists, and shipment. An output order represents a request for picking a sales order line item, and provides the basis for line items on a picking list. A picking list indicates what needs to be picked, and the printed picking list serves as a turnaround document for warehouse workers. You report actual picking against the picking list.

Significance of an Output Order for Sales Order Picking An output order (also termed an Inventory Order) represents a request for picking a sales order line item. Each output order has a system-assigned number and identifies the source information such as the sales order, item, quantity, ship-from warehouse, and ship date. When generating a picking list for a sales order, the system automatically creates an output order for each applicable line item and assigns it to the picking list. You can subsequently view the output orders that have been assigned to a picking list. Actual picking will automatically update the output order status from the initial value of *handling* to *ended,* and you can view the inventory transactions associated with the output order.

An output order can be deleted from a picking list prior to actual picking. Deletion of all output orders assigned to a picking list will also delete the picking list itself. Generating another picking list for the sales order will automatically create the output orders.

After generating a sales order picking list, and making changes to the sales order such as a quantity increase or an additional line, you can generate an additional picking list that will also automatically create output orders for the related changes.

Significance of the Picking List for a Sales Order A picking list indicates what needs to be picked, and the printed picking list serves as a turnaround document for warehouse workers. You report actual picking against the picking list. A sales order will have a single picking list in a simple scenario, such as a sales order with a single ship-from warehouse, one delivery mode, and a single ship date.

Each sales order picking list has a system-assigned identifier (also termed the picking route number), and one or more line items reflect the assignment of output orders to the picking list. A customer service rep can generate the picking list(s) from the Sales Order form in the context of order entry. Alternatively, the warehouse personnel can use other approaches to subsequently generate the picking lists based on selection criteria. In either case, the generation of a picking list reserves inventory for each sales order line (if not already reserved), and the printed picking list identifies the reserved material. Several options can be used to print or e-mail the picking list. After generating a picking list, it can be viewed on the Picking List Journal form and optionally reprinted.

Separate picking lists will be generated for a sales order when the sales lines identify more than one ship-from site or mode of delivery.[3] Separate picking lists may also reflect the selection criteria within the approach for generating picking lists, such as selection criteria about different ship dates or expedite codes on sales lines.

Significance of a Shipment for a Sales Order Each sales order picking list has a related shipment which the system automatically creates when you generate a picking lists. Each shipment has a system-assigned identifier. A shipment has no particular significance for the Basic Inventory approach. As a confusing factor, the Advanced WMS approach employs a different construct with the same name.

Significance of the Packing Slip for a Sales Order You post a sales order packing slip to indicate actual shipment of the picked items and to update the financial information. You can also print the packing slip.

Posting a sales order packing slip creates a packing slip journal, which can be viewed on the Packing Slip Journal form. Each journal has a system-assigned number. When viewing a selected packing slip journal, you can print the related packing slip, review additional information (such as related voucher

[3] A companywide policy (within the Accounts Receivable Parameters) determines whether separate picking lists will be generated for different delivery modes on sales lines within a sales order.

transactions), and send an electronic version of the Advanced Ship Notice (ASN) to the customer. You can also correct a transaction quantity or cancel the related shipment transactions, but only before the related invoice has been posted.

Key Forms for Sales Order Picking/Shipping Several key forms correspond to the key constructs, and a quick summary of these key forms is provided below.

- *Posting Picking List.* Use this form to generate and print picking lists for selected sales order line items. Actual posting will automatically create a Picking List Journal.

- *Picking List Journal.* Use this form to review sales order picking lists as well as access the Picking List Registration form for a selected picking list.

- *Picking List Registration.* Use this form to report actual picking against a sales order picking list.

- *Posting Packing Slip.* Use this form to post the packing slip for selected sales orders. Actual posting will automatically create a Packing Slip Journal.

- *Packing Slip Journal.* Use this form to review sales order packing lists and related information about vouchers and subledger entries. You can also make corrections to a selected packing slip or cancel it.

- *Release Sales Order Picking.* Use this form to review a subset of sales order line items based on selection criteria. When you release selected lines for picking, you automatically access the Posting Picking List form to generate and print the picking lists.

6.6 Major Variations of Sales Order Picking/Shipping

The basic process for sales order picking/shipping provides the baseline for explaining variations. These variations include a simple inventory transaction—the picking of serialized or batch-controlled items, the selection criteria for generating picking lists, and use of the Picking Workbench for wave picking purposes. One of the variations in the basic process—for using the Release Sales Order Picking form—is repeated here for completeness sake.

Simple Inventory Transaction for Sales Order Picking/Shipping The shipping clerk can bypass the use of picking lists and shipments by using a simple inventory transaction, where you report actual picking when posting the packing slip for a sales order. This simple inventory transaction applies to both the Basic Inventory Approach and the Advanced WMS approach.

Picking Batch-Controlled Items The sales order picking list can identify the reserved material for the specific batch(es) to be picked. With shelf-life items and FEFO reservation logic, for example, the reserved material reflects the inventory's expiration date and the customer requirements for remaining shelf life. Alternatively, the reserved material can reflect a batch reservation during sales order entry based on the customer's requirements for batch attributes. A subsequent chapter provides more detailed explanations about these considerations for batch-controlled items (Section 25.3).

Picking Serialized Items The serial number(s) can be identified when reporting actual picking against the sales order picking list. A subsequent chapter provides more detailed explanations about serialized items (Section 25.1).

Shipping Serialized Items with Deferred Assignment of Serial Numbers With the deferred approach, you register the item's serial number(s) when posting the sales order packing slip by accessing the Serial Numbers form for the line item. The serial numbers are not identified when reporting actual picking against the sales order picking list. A subsequent chapter provides more detailed explanations about deferred assignment serialized items (Section 25.2).

Selection Criteria for Generating Sales Order Picking Lists Different selection criteria can be used to generate sales order picking lists, such as the ship-from warehouse, ship date, customer and/or mode of delivery. Additional criteria include expedite policies that have been assigned to the sales order header and line items, and the customer classification code assigned to customers. A subsequent section provides further explanation of the variations in selection criteria (Section 6.8).

Generate Picking Lists Using the Release Sales Order Picking Form The shipping clerk uses the Release Sales Order Picking form to view a subset of open sales order lines based on selection criteria, and release selected lines in order to generate picking lists. As one advantage, this form displays related information about the ability to deliver the order and the need for allocation. You can temporarily reserve the inventory for selected lines. It also displays information about other requirements for the item stemming from production or transfers. As a result, it makes it easier to selectively identify which sales lines should be released for picking. As a related advantage, the form supports a stepwise allocation of available inventory based on selection criteria (including the Customer Classification Code about customer priority), thereby avoiding the complexities of automatic allocation approaches.

In terms of shortcomings, the form does not display a sales line when no inventory exists for the item, but this can be corrected via customization. A related shortcoming concerns the lack of visibility about scheduled receipts, which would be helpful when production orders (or other supply orders) will be imminently received.

Generate Picking Lists Using the Picking Workbench Approach The Picking Workbench provides an alternative approach to the generation of sales order picking lists that reflects the wave picking concept. That is, the picking lists can be grouped together under a separate identifier (termed a picking batch) and assigned to a warehouse worker. In addition, it can suggest the appropriate box size(s) and number of boxes for packing the items when generating the picking lists. A subsequent section provides further explanation of the Picking Workbench approach (Section 6.9).

6.7 Minor Variations

Several minor variations apply to the basic process of sales order shipping/shipping and its major variations. These variations are listed below and explained in the following subsections. Other minor variations were identified as part of the additional steps for the basic process, such as identifying needed actions for warehouse management and performance metrics.

- Quality Orders for Sales Order Picking/Shipping
- Impact of a Customer Pickup on Picking/Shipping
- Impact of a Sales Order Hold and Other Types of Holds
- Significance of Ship Complete Policies for a Sales Order
- Impact of Delivery Tolerances on Picking/Shipping
- Significance of Expedite Policies for Picking/Shipping
- Modeling the Required Time for Picking/Shipping Activities
- Relevance of Order Entry Deadlines for Picking/Shipping Activities
- Effective Use of Notes for Picking/Shipping Purposes

Quality Orders for Sales Order Picking/Shipping A quality order can be automatically generated when you generate a picking list or post the packing slip for a sales order, as defined by Quality Associations related to sales orders for an item. For example, tests may be required before an item can be actually picked (or shipped), and the associated blocking rules can prevent further transactions (such as actual picking or shipping) until the quality order has been validated. In addition, an infolog warning is displayed on subsequent transactions when validation fails. A subsequent chapter about quality management provides further explanation of quality orders (Section 26.3).

Impact of a Customer Pickup on Picking/Shipping The Sales Pickup form displays sales orders having one or more line items with a delivery mode for customer pickup, and provides a short-cut approach for reporting shipment and invoicing transactions. However, you can also perform the normal picking and shipping steps for a customer pickup.

Impact of a Sales Order Hold and Other Types of Holds The assignment of a Hold Code to a sales order will prevent any picking/shipping transactions until the Hold Code has been cleared. Other types of holds include customer holds and stopped flags.

- *Impact of a Customer Hold.* The assignment of the hold policy of "all" to a customer will prevent any picking/shipping transactions for the customer.

- *Impact of Stopped Transactions for an Item.* The sales order transactions for an item can be stopped, either as a companywide or site-specific policy within the item's default order policies. The stopped flag prevents further transactions for an item's existing sales orders, including picking/shipping transactions. A similar stopped flag can be specified for an item's inventory transactions, which also prevents further transactions.

Significance of Ship Complete Policies for a Sales Order A sales order line can be flagged as "ship complete," so that you will receive an error unless you ship the entire quantity when posting the sales order packing slip. An additional "ship complete" flag for the entire sales order has a slightly different significance as it prevents the generation of a sales order picking list until all lines have sufficient inventory to be reserved for the ordered quantity. Hence, using both policies will help ensure that all lines will be picked, and that order quantities for individual lines will be shipped complete.

As an alternative approach, the concept of "ship complete" can be enforced using the delivery tolerance functionality, since delivery tolerances of zero percent for a sales line mean that the shipped quantity must equal the ordered quantity. It is also possible to enforce a companywide policy so that any over- and under-delivery quantities are not acceptable. The next point provides further explanation of delivery tolerances.

Impact of Delivery Tolerances on Picking/Shipping When delivery tolerances are acceptable, they determine how much the quantities being picked and shipped for a sales line can differ from the ordered quantity. Over- and under-delivery tolerances (related to sales orders) are expressed as a percentage; the values assigned to an item act as defaults for a sales order line item. Delivery tolerances of zero percent for a sales line mean that the shipped quantity must equal the ordered quantity. A companywide policy (embedded in the A/R parameters) determines whether over- and under-deliveries will be acceptable for sales orders.

An over-delivery tolerance applies to both the picked quantity and the shipped quantity for a sales line. For example, the system displays an error message infolog and prevents over-picking (beyond the over-delivery tolerance) when reporting the quantity picked, as well as over-shipping (beyond the delivery tolerance) when posting the sales order packing slip.

An under-delivery tolerance only applies to the shipped quantity for a sales line. For example, you cannot post the packing slip for an under-shipped quantity (beyond the under-delivery tolerance) in conjunction with the "close short" flag—the system displays an error message infolog.

Significance of Expedite Policies on Picking/Shipping Expedite policies can be assigned to a sales order header and line items, and they provide selection criteria for generating sales order picking lists. They do not directly impact picking/shipping activities, and they are sometimes included in printed picking lists as reference information. A subsequent section provides further explanation of expedite codes in the context of generating picking lists (Section 6.8).

Modeling the Required Time for Picking/Shipping Activities Some scenarios have a significant time requirement for picking/shipping activities related to a sales order (such as 1 or 2 days), while many others have a much shorter preparation time. A significant time requirement should be included in the supply chain model so that (1) promised ship dates will reflect the required time and (2) picking will be scheduled prior to the ship date.

- *Identify the Required Time for Picking/Shipping as a Safety Margin for a Salable Item.* The required time can be identified as the issue safety margin for a salable item, where you define the number of days as part of the

Coverage Group assigned to the item. For example, when demands exist for an item with one day prep time, master scheduling logic will generate planned orders to arrive one day before the demand date. As another consideration, when using the Release Sales Order Picking form to anticipate picking activities, you should release orders for picking one day prior to the ship date.

- *Include Required Time for Picking/Shipping in Delivery Promises* The required time (expressed as the issue safety margin described above) can be included in delivery promises based on ATP logic, where you assign a delivery date control policy of "ATP plus issue margin" to the saleable item as part of its default order policies. For example, when entering a sales line for a stocked item with one day prep time, the earliest possible promised date will be one day later.

  Some scenarios do not use ATP logic as the basis for delivery promises, such as using CTP logic for make-to-order items. In many of these scenarios, the required time can be modeled by the sales lead time assigned to an item as part of its default order policies.

Relevance of Order Entry Deadlines for Picking/Shipping Activities Some scenarios involve same day shipments for sales orders that have been entered by a specified deadline. This order entry deadline frequently represents a prerequisite for meeting the departure time of a shipping vehicle so that adequate time is available for picking/shipping activities. An order entry deadline also means that an order entered after the specified time will be treated as if it were entered the next day, thereby affecting the assignment of a promised ship date. You define a set of deadlines for each day within a week (termed an order entry deadline group), and then assign the deadline group to each customer and site.

Effective Use of Notes for Picking/Shipping Purposes The printed version of a picking list and packing list can optionally include notes about the sales order header and/or line items that can guide picking/shipping activities. It is often helpful to create a user-defined note type that is only applicable to picking/shipping instructions so that notes can be entered (and printed) for just the applicable note type.

6.8 Selection Criteria for Generating Sales Order Picking Lists

Several approaches can be used to generate picking lists based on selection criteria. Example selection criteria are summarized in Figure 6.5 and described below. The figure indicates the applicable constructs for each selection criteria, such as the sales order line or header. It also highlights several selection criteria (via light grey shading) which provide the basis for prioritizing picking/shipping activities, such as the ship date and expedite code for a sales line.

Figure 6.4 Example Selection Criteria for Generating Sales Order Picking Lists

	Field Name	Applicable Construct		
		SO Line	SO Header	Customer
	Ship from site/warehouse	Yes	Yes	N/A
Basis for Prioritizing Picking and Shipping	Ship date	Yes	Yes	N/A
Basis for Prioritizing Picking and Shipping	Mode of delivery	Yes	Yes	N/A
Basis for Prioritizing Picking and Shipping	Expedite code	Yes	Yes	N/A
Basis for Prioritizing Picking and Shipping	Expedited shipment flag	N/A	Yes	N/A
Basis for Prioritizing Picking and Shipping	Sales order priority for fulfillment	N/A	Yes	N/A
Basis for Prioritizing Picking and Shipping	Customer classification group	N/A	N/A	Yes
	Customer	N/A	Yes	N/A
	Ship-to address information	Yes	Yes	N/A
	Shipping carrier/service	Yes	Yes	N/A

- *Ship-From Site and Warehouse*. The ship-from site and warehouse provide an organizing focus for picking/shipping activities.

- *Ship Date*. The ship date provides the primary basis for scheduling and prioritizing the picking/shipping activities, and is frequently used in conjunction with other prioritization criteria. The confirmed ship date is typically used, although the requested ship date may be used in some cases.

- *Mode of Delivery*. The mode of delivery provides another organizing focus for picking/shipping activities, especially when preparing shipments for a scheduled pickup time. A sales order may have multiple picking lists that reflect different delivery modes on sales lines. A delivery mode may reflect faster or expedited delivery, and can be associated with an Expedite code.

- *Expedite Code.* A user-defined Expedite code can be assigned to a sales order header and/or line item to indicate the need for expediting. In addition, you can associate an Expedite code with a mode of delivery so that selecting the expedited mode of delivery also updates the Expedite code on a sales order.

- *Expedited Shipment Flag.* The expedite shipment flag can only be assigned to a sales order header, and it provides an additional basis for expediting. As the primary purpose, it works in conjunction with the shipping carrier assigned to a sales order in order to include the carrier's shipping charges (for expedited shipment) when they are normally considered as free for orders exceeding a specified total amount.

- *Sales Order Priority for Fulfillment.* A predefined priority can only be assigned to a sales order header, and it provides an additional basis for expediting. The ten predefined values reflect different priorities, ranging from High (1) to Low(10).

- *Customer Classification Group.* A user-defined customer classification group can be assigned to a customer, and provides one approach to prioritize the generation of picking lists when using the Release Sales Order Picking form.

- *Customer.* A selected customer provides another organizing focus for picking/shipping activities, such as generating picking lists for shipping sales orders to a customer.

- *Ship-To Address Information.* Various elements of the address can be used as an organizing focus of picking/shipping activities, such as generating picking lists for shipping sales orders to the same address.

- *Shipping Carrier and Carrier Service.* The shipping carrier and carrier service can be used as an organizing focus of picking/shipping activities, especially when preparing shipments for a scheduled pickup time by the carrier.

6.9 Generate Picking Lists Using the Picking Workbench form

The Picking Workbench provides an alternative approach to the generation of sales order picking lists that reflects the wave picking concept. That is, the picking lists can be grouped together under a separate identifier (termed a picking batch) and assigned to a warehouse worker. It optionally provides boxing logic to suggest the appropriate box size(s) and number of boxes for packing the items.

This alternative approach involves several additional constructs for coordinating picking lists with a wave-picking concept. Two key constructs are labeled a picking session and a picking batch. A picking batch consists of one or more picking lists; a picking session consists of one or more picking batches. A packing batch represents a manageable amount of work that can be assigned to a worker. The steps for using the Picking Workbench are summarized in Figure 6.5 and described below.

Figure 6.5 Typical Process for Using the Picking Workbench Approach

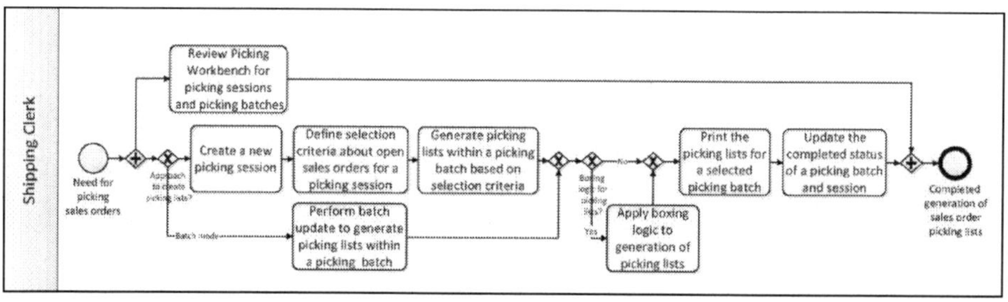

Review Picking Workbench for Picking Sessions and Picking Batches The shipping clerk uses the Picking Workbench form to review existing sessions and create new sessions for sales order picking. The form itself consists of several sections identifying (1) the picking sessions, (2) the batches within a selected picking session, (3) the picking lists within a selected picking batch, and (4) the line items within a selected picking list. An additional section identifies (5) the selection criteria about open sales order line items for generating picking lists within picking batches. All of the steps described here can be performed from the Picking Workbench form as well as reporting actual picking against a picking list.

Create a New Picking Session The shipping clerk creates a new picking session as the first step in generating sales order picking lists.

Define Selection Criteria About Open Sales Orders for a Picking Session For a new picking session, the shipping clerk defines the selection criteria for open sales order lines. Example criteria include the ship-from warehouse, ship date and/or mode of delivery. A set of criteria can be predefined as a Workbench Profile with a user-definable identifier and description.

Generate Picking Lists (Within a Picking Batch) Based on Selection Criteria The shipping clerk generates the picking lists (within a picking batch) for a selected picking session, which defines the selection criteria for open sales order line items.

In order to segment the amount of picking effort, a warehouse-specific policy can optionally define the maximum number of picking lists within a picking batch and the number of lines per picking list.

Apply Boxing Logic to the Generation of Picking Lists With boxing logic, the generation of picking lists can identify the suggested box size for the item's quantity on a printed picking list. In addition to the item's quantity, the suggested box size reflects the physical dimensions of the item and the user-defined box names. Multiple picking lists will be generated when the item's quantity and physical dimensions require more than one box so that each printed picking list identifies the appropriate box size. The printed picking list can also identify a "standalone item" that already has an individual box per item.

Use of boxing logic requires several aspects of setup information. First, it requires a companywide policy to support boxing logic (embedded in the Inventory Management Parameters form). Second, the relevant salable items must be designated for using boxing logic, and have their physical dimensions specified per inventory unit. Boxing logic only applies to designated items. These physical dimensions include depth, width, height, weight, and volume. An item can also be designated as a "standalone item" when it already has an individual box per item. Third, the applicable box names must be defined along with their physical dimensions. Examples of a user-defined box name include *LargeBox* and *SmallBox*. Based on this setup information, the suggested box name is only displayed on the printed picking list, and multiple picking lists may be generated to identify the suggested box name on each picking list.

Print the Picking Lists for a Selected Picking Batch The shipping clerk prints the picking lists for a selected picking batch, which automatically updates the status of the picking batch from *created* to *printed*.

Update the Completed Status of a Picking Batch and Session The shipping clerk indicates completion of the picking lists within a selected picking batch, which automatically updates the status of the picking batch from *printed* to *completed*. In a similar fashion, the shipping clerk also indicates completion of the picking lists within a selected picking session. Actual picking can be reported before or after you indicate completion of the picking lists.

Perform Batch Update to Generate Picking Lists for the Picking Workbench The shipping clerk can setup a batch job for the Picking Workbench (which involves a dialogue for defining the selection criteria about open sales order lines), and then perform or schedule the batch update. The batch update will automatically create a picking session and picking batch(es) and generate the picking lists.

Life Cycles Related to Picking Workbench Approach The process of generating picking lists from the Picking Workbench involves two additional constructs (for the Picking Session and Picking Batch) as part of supporting a wave-picking concept. The life cycle and status of these constructs are summarized in Figure 6.6 in terms of the major steps in the process.

Figure 6.6 Life Cycles Related to Picking Workbench

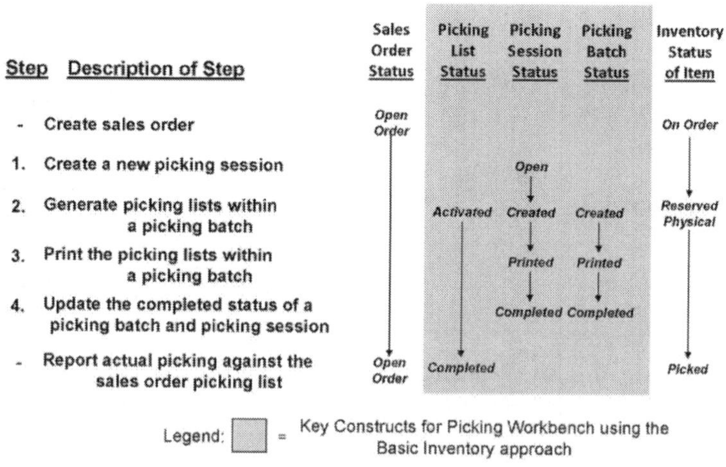

The status for a picking session and a picking batch are normally updated automatically by steps in the business process, but you can manually assign the completed status.

6.10 Extended Explanation of Related Life Cycles for Picking/Shipping

The basic process for sales order picking/shipping involves several related constructs of picking lists, output orders and shipments, with a status automatically updated by steps in the process. The life cycles were previously illustrated for the basic process (Figure 6.2). The same constructs and life cycles are also employed in transfer order picking/shipping (Figure 7.2). This section provides an extended explanation of the status for each construct, and it applies to both sales orders and transfer orders.

Status of a Picking List A status applies to a picking list and each line item. The status for a picking list indicates the following steps in its life cycle:

- *Activated.* The status indicates the picking list has been created. The picking list can be cancelled.
- *Started.* The status indicates that one line item has been picked when the picking list contains multiple lines. Alternatively, the status reflects a manual update to indicate that picking has started.
- *Completed.* The status indicates all line items have been picked for the picking list.
- *Cancelled.* The status indicates the picking list has been cancelled, or that all line items have been cancelled.

Status of a Line Item on a Picking List The status for a line item on a sales order picking list indicates the following steps in its life cycle.

- *Activated.* The status indicates the line item has been created. The line item can be deleted or cancelled if needed for reversing transactions.
- *Picked.* The status indicates the line item has been picked. The line item can be unpicked if needed for reversing transactions.
- *Completed.* The status indicates the line item has been picked for the picking list.
- *Cancelled.* The status indicates the line item has been cancelled.

Status of an Output Order The status for an output order indicates the following steps in its life cycle.

- *Handling.* The status indicates the output order has been created for a line item on an order, and assigned to a picking list line item. It also applies to an output order for a picking list line item that has been partially picked.
- *Ended.* The status indicates the related picking list line item has been completely picked. It can also indicate the related picking list line item has been cancelled.

Status of a Shipment The status for a shipment is identified by the combination of two fields—termed the Shipment Status and the Physical Update Status—which indicate the following steps in its life cycle. For example, the combination of *Activated* + *Waiting* indicates the shipment has been created.

- *Activated + Waiting.* The status indicates the shipment has been created, along with its associated picking list.
- *Sent + Ready for Update.* The status indicates the associated picking list has been completely picked.
- *Sent + Completed.* The status indicates the associated order has been shipped.
- *Cancelled.* The status indicates the associated picking list has been cancelled.

6.11 Additional Case Studies

Case 28: Sales Order Shipments from a Remote Warehouse Several remote warehouses for a distribution operation did not have on-line access for reporting AX transactions. In order to communicate the need for sales order shipments from the remote warehouses, the DRP coordinator generated the sales order picking lists and e-mailed a copy to the relevant contact person. The contact person sent a return e-mail after completing the requested shipments, and the DRP coordinator simply posted each completed picking list and the related sales order packing slip.

Case 29: Expedite Policies for Sales Order Picking The customer service reps at a manufacturing/distribution company used several different approaches to indicate the need for expediting when the rep was entering a sales order or its line items. As the starting point, the assignment of shipment and delivery dates reflected available to promise logic so that unrealistic dates could not be assigned. The customer service reps could then assign an expedited mode of delivery which also resulted in the automatic assignment of a expedite code. The shipping clerks would use this expedite code (and mode of delivery) to help prioritize the generation of sales order picking lists and ultimately provide expedited service.

Case 30: Correcting Errors about a Reported Shipment The warehouse workers and shipping clerks at a manufacturing/distribution company would sometimes make a mistake in the reported quantity shipped. In order to correct the mistake, the supervisor would access the Packing Slip Journal form and select the "Correct" function to access the Correct Packing Slip form. In this way, the inventory balances and financial information would reflect the correction.

Case 31: Performance Metrics for On-Time Delivery and Full Quantity The performance metrics for each ship-from warehouse (in a multisite distribution operation) included on-time delivery and full quantity; the weekly results were closely monitored. The standardized inquiries on these performance metrics were sufficient for most purposes, but several customizations were being considered. One customization involved the additional consideration of delivery tolerances for the full quantity metric. Another customization involved the addition of a similar tolerance (expressed in days) for the on-time metric. A third customization involved the assignment of reason codes to understand what was causing under-performance against the metrics.

6.12 Executive Summary

The Basic Inventory approach employs an order-based picking list and a related shipment to report sales order fulfillment. This chapter started with a simple yet typical business process, explaining the related life cycles, reversing transactions, and key constructs. The basic process provided a baseline for explaining variations, such as the variations of generating picking lists and the use of wave picking.

Several case studies illustrated variations for sales order picking/shipping. These included sales order shipments from a remote warehouse (Case 28), expedite policies for sales order picking (Case 29), correcting errors about a reported shipment (Case 30), and performance metrics for on-time delivery and full quantity (Case 31).

Chapter 7

Transfer Order Picking/Shipping

The Basic Inventory approach employs an order-based picking list and a related shipment to report transfer order fulfillment. As an explanatory approach, it is easiest to start with a simple yet typical business process, and explain the related life cycles, transactions, and key constructs. The basic process provides a baseline for explaining variations, such as different ways to generate picking lists and the use of wave picking. These topics are reflected in the following sections within the chapter:

1. Basic Process for Transfer Order Picking/Shipping
2. Additional Steps in the Basic Process
3. Life Cycles Related to the Basic Process
4. Reversing Transactions in the Basic Process
5. Key Constructs for Transfer Order Picking/Shipping
6. Major Variations of Transfer Order Picking/Shipping
7. Minor Variations

Effective distribution planning represents a critical consideration for transfer order picking/shipping and receiving. In order to be effective, the requirements for transfer orders should reflect S&OP game plans, a reasonable model of the supply chain, and other factors such as a manageable level of expediting. These considerations will make life easier for warehouse management.

The AX functionality for picking/shipping a transfer order shares a high degree of similarity with the functionality for sales orders, but there are several differences. These differences include the approach for reporting actual shipment and the ability to reverse shipment transactions. In addition, the use of order holds, expedite codes, and quality orders do not apply to transfer orders. Hence, this chapter provides a completely separate explanation about transfer orders, even though a few topics must be repeated for completeness sake.

7.1 Basic Process for Transfer Order Picking/Shipping

The business process for transfer order picking/shipping can have many variations. A simple yet typical process provides a baseline for explaining the variations. The basic process shown in Figure 7.1 consists of several steps typically performed by a shipping clerk and a warehouse worker. The process starts with the need for transfer order picking/shipping and ends with completed shipments. This section provides an overview of the basic process and describes each step in more detail.

Figure 7.1 Basic Process for Transfer Order Picking/Shipping

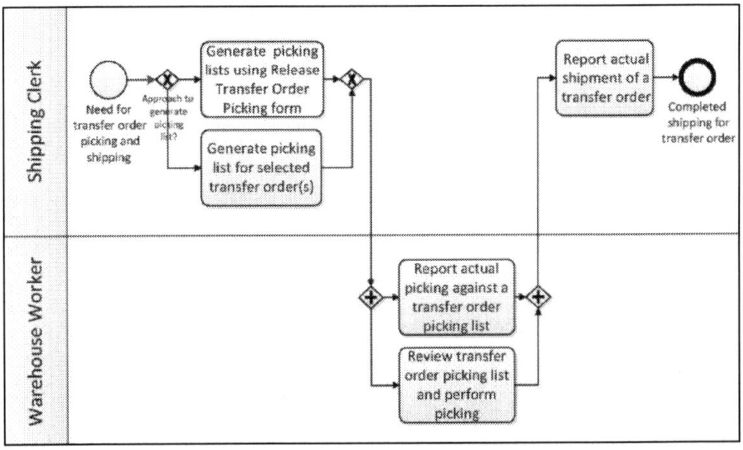

Overview The shipping clerk typically uses the Release Transfer Order Picking form to review and select open transfer order lines that require picking/shipping, and then generate the picking lists for selected orders. The generation of a picking list will reserve the item's inventory (if not already reserved). The warehouse worker reports actual picking against a transfer order picking list, and the shipping clerk reports actual shipment of the transfer order.

Generate Picking Lists Using the Release Transfer Order Picking Form The shipping clerk uses the Release Transfer Order Picking form to view a subset of open transfer order lines based on selection criteria. The displayed information indicates whether a transfer line already has reserved inventory. The shipping clerk can analyze which lines can be picked using available inventory, and then simulate allocation of the inventory to selected transfer lines. The selected transfer lines can then be released for picking, which displays the Posting Picking List form for the selected lines so that actual posting will generate the picking lists. Generation of a picking list will reserve the item's inventory for each transfer line (if not already reserved).

Generate Picking List for Selected Transfer Order(s) The shipping clerk generates and prints the picking list for selected transfer orders by using the Posting Picking List form. It can be accessed from the Transfer Order form for a selected order, although it is commonly accessed directly in order to generate picking lists for multiple orders based on selection criteria. Typical selection criteria include the ship-from warehouse, ship date, and mode of delivery. Different sets of selection criteria are commonly predefined with a user-definable name in order to model typical variations in the business process. Generation of a picking list will reserve the item's inventory for each transfer line (if not already reserved).

Review Transfer Order Picking List and Perform Picking The warehouse worker can review a printed picking list and perform the picking. The printed picking list identifies the reserved inventory.

Report Actual Picking Against a Transfer Order Picking List The warehouse worker reports actual picking against a picking list using the Picking List Registration form. It can be accessed from the Transfer Order form for a selected order, although it is commonly accessed directly in order to report actual picking for one or more transfer orders based on selection criteria. Typical selection criteria include the transfer order number, ship-from warehouse, ship date, and/or mode of delivery. In many cases, the shipping clerk simply confirms that the reserved inventory was actually picked. If needed, the shipping clerk can identify the alternative quantity or location that was picked, or close a line item when reporting less than the ordered quantity.

Report Actual Shipment of a Transfer Order The shipping clerk reports actual shipment of a transfer order using the Shipment [for Transfer Orders] form. It can be accessed from the Transfer Order form for a selected order, although it is commonly accessed directly in order to report actual picking for one or more transfer orders based on selection criteria. Typical selection criteria include the transfer order number, ship-from warehouse, ship date, and/or mode of delivery. The shipping clerk typically employs the actual picking information as the basis for actual shipment, and can optionally specify a tracking ID for the shipment.

Enforcing the Major Steps in the Typical Business Process The major step of picking a transfer order can be enforced by the Picking Requirement policy within the Item Model Group assigned to an item.

7.2 Additional Steps in the Basic Process

The basic process typically includes several additional steps not shown in Figure 7.1 so that the diagram does not become too complex. Examples include the following steps.

Ship Short When No Further Shipments are Expected When using the Shipment form to report actual shipment of a transfer order line, you can optionally indicate that a line has been shipped short (relative to the order quantity) and that no further shipments are expected. Use the *Close* checkbox for the relevant line, and this will also update its status to *Shipped.*

Assign a Tracking ID to a Transfer Order Shipment You can optionally assign a Tracking ID when reporting actual shipment using the Shipment form. The Tracking ID only provides reference information.

Identify Transfer Order Lines Picked but not yet Shipped One indicator of needed actions for warehouse management consists of transfer order line items which have been picked but not yet shipped as of today's date. You can identify these needed actions using a standard report labeled Inventory Picked not Delivered.

Print Shipment Documents for Transfer Orders You can print a Transfer Order Shipment from the Transfer Order form, or by using the Transfer Order Shipment report and its associated dialogue about selection criteria. The document identifies the transfer order number and related information, such as the ship-to address, mode of delivery, posting date, and tracking number (if specified), as well as information about its line items.

Review In Transit Inventory for an Item You can view an item's in-transit inventory on various on-hand inquiries, or view the on-hand inquiries for the in-transit warehouse and its location.

Review Transfer Order History The Transfer Order History form displays all transfer orders with separate lines for the related shipment and receipt transactions, and the related line items for a selected transaction. It displays the posting date and voucher for each transaction line, and the tracking ID (if specified) for a shipment transaction.

Review the Transfer Overview Report This report provides a one line summary of each transfer order, including its status, the ship-from and ship-to warehouses, and the ship and receipt dates. It also identifies the item and quantity for each line item on a transfer order. You can specify selection criteria as part of the associated report dialogue—such as the relevant ship-from warehouse, ship date and order status—in order to view the desired subset of transfer orders.

7.3 Life Cycles Related to the Basic Process

The basic process for transfer order picking/shipping involves several related constructs, where the status for each construct reflects various steps in the process. Figure 7.2 summarizes this information for the basic process, and only displays those steps representing the minimum number of touch points for updating status. Grey shading highlights the key constructs of a picking list, output order, and shipment.

Figure 7.2 Life Cycles Related to the Basic Process for Transfer Order Picking/Shipping

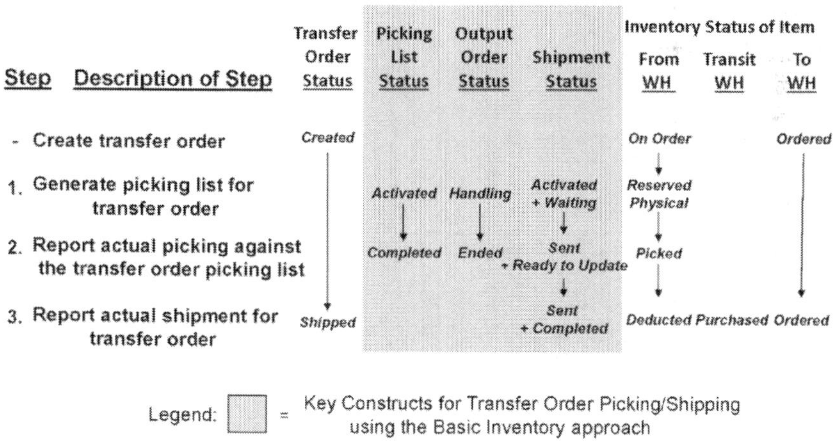

As shown in the figure, the first step will create a picking list (with line items reflecting output orders) and a corresponding shipment. It should be noted that the status for a shipment is identified by the combination of two fields termed the Shipment Status and the Physical Update Status. For example, the combination of *Activated + Waiting* indicates the shipment has been created. The right side of the figure shows the inventory status for an item on a transfer order line. At the ship-from warehouse, for example, various steps in the process will change this status from *on order* to *reserved physical*, *picked* and *deducted*.

Information about the related life cycles provides the foundation for explaining the reversing transactions and is covered in the next section. An extended explanation of each status was provided in the previous chapter (Section 6.10).

7.4 Reversing Transactions in the Basic Process

The ability to reverse transactions requires an understanding of the current point within the business process and the associated status of key constructs. Borrowing from the previous figure, Figure 7.3 illustrates the steps within the basic process (shown in grey text), and the various points at which you can perform reversing transactions (shown in black text). The figure also illustrates the impact of a reversing transaction on status, and the arrows indicate the resulting point in the business process. As identified by step numbers in the figure, you can reverse transactions (1X) after initially generating a picking list and (2X) after reporting actual picking.

Figure 7.3 Reversing Transactions in the Basic Process for Transfer Order Picking/Shipping

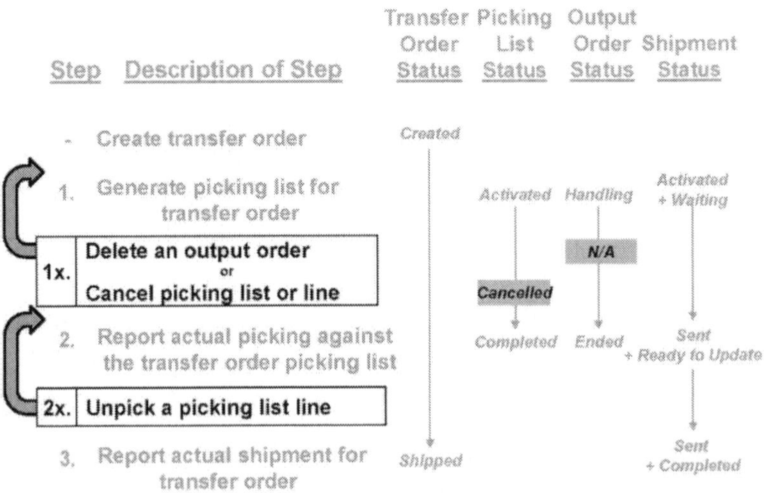

Step 1X: Reverse Transaction After Generating Picking List You can delete an output order (on the Output Order form) prior to actual picking, which automatically deletes the corresponding line on a picking list. Alternatively, you can cancel a picking list line or the entire picking list, which also deletes the corresponding output order(s). A deleted output order no longer has a status, as shown by a value of "N/A" within the figure.

Step 2X: Reverse Transaction After Actual Picking You can unpick a transaction prior to actual shipment by using the Unpick function on the Picking List Registration form. Unpicking all line items will reset the picking list status to *Activated.*

Reversing Transactions After Actual Shipment of a Transfer Order Information cannot be corrected or cancelled after reporting actual shipment of a transfer order, and the shipment must be completely received at the ship-to warehouse. Transfer journals provide one approach for making corrections. In order to correct an over-reported quantity, for example, the shipped material must be reported as received; a transfer journal can be used to move it back.

7.5 Key Constructs for Transfer Order Picking/Shipping

The Basic Inventory approach for transfer order picking/shipping involves several key constructs in addition to the transfer order. These constructs include output orders, picking lists and shipments, which are the same constructs for sales order picking/shipping. The previous chapter provided a detailed explanation of these constructs for sales orders (Section 6.5).

One key difference between transfer orders and sales orders involves the reporting of actual shipments. You use the Posting Packing Slip form for sales orders, whereas you use the Shipment form for transfer orders. Another key difference involves the selection criteria for generating transfer order picking lists. These differences and other minor ones merit a separate explanation of the key constructs for transfer orders.

In summary, an output order represents a request for picking a transfer order line item, and provides the basis for line items on a picking list. A picking list indicates what needs to be picked, and the printed picking list serves as a turnaround document for warehouse workers. You report actual picking against the picking list. Reporting actual shipment of a transfer order updates the inventory and the financial information.

Significance of an Output Order for Transfer Order Picking An output order (also termed an Inventory Order) represents a request for picking a transfer order line item. Each output order has a system-assigned number which identifies the source information such as the transfer order, item, quantity, ship-from warehouse and ship date. When generating a picking list for a transfer order, the system automatically creates an output order for each applicable line item and assigns it to the picking list. You can subsequently view the output orders that have been assigned to a picking list. Actual picking will automatically update the output order status from the initial value of *handling* to *ended,* and you can view the inventory transactions associated with the output order.

An output order can be deleted from a picking list prior to actual picking. Deletion of all output orders assigned to a picking list will also delete the picking list itself. Generating another picking list for the transfer order will automatically create the output orders.

After generating a transfer order picking list and making changes to the transfer order, such as a quantity increase or an additional line, you can generate an additional picking list that will also automatically create output orders for the related changes.

Significance of the Picking List for a Transfer Order A picking list indicates what needs to be picked, and the printed picking list serves as a turnaround document for warehouse workers. You report actual picking against the picking list. A transfer order will typically have a single picking list in a simple scenario, such as a transfer order with a single ship date that represents a single shipment. Different picking lists may be required when the transfer order lines have different ship dates.

Each transfer order picking list has a system-assigned identifier (also termed the picking route number), and one or more line items reflect the assignment of output orders to the picking list. The generation of a picking list reserves inventory for each transfer order line (if not already reserved), and the printed picking list identifies the reserved material. After generating a picking list, it can be viewed on the Picking List Journal form and optionally reprinted.

Several approaches can be used to generate a picking list for transfer orders. For example, a picking list can be generated for a single order by starting from the Transfer Order form, or you can start from the Posting Picking List form to generate picking lists for multiple orders based on selection criteria. The selection criteria about transfer orders differ considerably from the selection criteria about sales orders. The next section provides further explanation of these selection criteria about transfer orders (Section 7.6).

Significance of a Shipment for a Transfer Order Each transfer order picking list has a related shipment which the system automatically creates when you generate a picking list. A shipment has no particular significance for the Basic Inventory approach. The actual shipment of a transfer order is reported on a form labeled Shipment [for a Transfer Order].[1]

Key Forms for Transfer Order Picking/Shipping Several key forms correspond to the key constructs. A quick summary of these key forms is provided below.

- *Posting Picking List.* Use this form to generate and print picking lists for selected transfer order line items. Actual posting will automatically create a Picking List Journal.

- *Picking List Journal.* Use this form to review transfer order picking lists and to access the Picking List Registration form for a selected picking list.

- *Picking List Registration.* Use this form to report actual picking against a transfer order picking list.

- *Shipment [for a Transfer Order].* Use this form to report actual shipment for a transfer order and, optionally, close a line item when the order quantity cannot be completely shipped.

- *Release Transfer Order Picking.* Use this form to review a subset of transfer order line items based on selection criteria. When you release selected lines for picking, you automatically access the Posting Picking List form to generate and print the picking lists.

7.6 Major Variations for Transfer Order Picking/Shipping

The basic process for transfer order picking/shipping provides the foundation for explaining variations. The major variations include a simple inventory transaction, the selection criteria for generating picking lists, and two different approaches for generating picking lists. Another major variation involves a single-step shipment with automatic receipt.

[1] A shipment is not created when using the Shipment [for a Transfer Order] form as part of a simple inventory transaction, nor does it involve picking lists and output orders.

Simple Inventory Transaction for Transfer Order Picking/Shipping The shipping clerk can bypass the use of picking lists and shipments by using a simple inventory transaction where you simply report actual shipment of the transfer order.

Picking Batch-Controlled Items The transfer order picking list can identify reserved material for the specific batch(es) to be picked. With shelf-life items and FEFO reservation logic, for example, the reserved material reflects the inventory's expiration date. Alternatively, the reserved material can reflect a batch reservation based on the requirements for batch attributes. A subsequent chapter provides further explanation about batch-controlled items (Section 25.3).

Picking Serialized Items The serial number(s) can be identified when reporting actual picking against the transfer order picking list. A subsequent chapter provides further explanation about serialized items (Section 25.1).

Selection Criteria for Generating a Transfer Order Picking List Several approaches can be used to generate picking lists based on selection criteria. Example selection criteria are summarized in Figure 7.4. The figure indicates the applicable constructs for each selection criteria, such as the transfer order line or header. It also highlights several selection criteria (via shading) which provide the basis for prioritizing picking/shipping activities, such as the ship date and the mode of delivery.

Generate Picking Lists Using the Release Transfer Order Picking Form The shipping clerk uses the Release Transfer Order Picking form to view a subset of open transfer order lines based on selection criteria, and releases selected lines in order to generate picking lists. As one advantage, this form displays related information about the ability to deliver the order and the need for allocation. You can temporarily reserve the inventory for selected lines. It also displays information about other requirements for the item stemming from production or sales. As a result, it makes it easier to selectively identify which transfer lines should be released for picking.

In terms of shortcomings, the form does not display a transfer line when no inventory exists for the item, but this can be corrected via customization. A related shortcoming concerns the lack of visibility about scheduled receipts, which would be helpful when production orders (or other supply orders) will be received shortly.

Figure 7.4 Example Selection Criteria for Generating Transfer Order Picking Lists

Basis for Prioritizing Picking/Shipping (Mode of Delivery, Ship Date)

<table>
<tr><th rowspan="2">Field Name for a Transfer Order</th><th colspan="2">Applicable Construct</th></tr>
<tr><th>Order Header</th><th>Order Line</th></tr>
<tr><td>Ship-from Warehouse</td><td rowspan="6">Yes</td><td rowspan="2">N/A</td></tr>
<tr><td>Mode of Delivery</td></tr>
<tr><td>Ship Date</td><td>Yes</td></tr>
<tr><td>Transfer Order Number</td><td rowspan="2">N/A</td></tr>
<tr><td>Ship-to Warehouse</td></tr>
<tr><td>Receive Date</td><td>Yes</td></tr>
</table>

Generate Picking Lists Using the Picking Workbench Approach The Picking Workbench provides an alternative approach to the generation of transfer order picking lists that reflects the wave picking concept. That is, the picking lists can be grouped together under a separate identifier (termed a picking batch) and assigned to a warehouse worker. In addition, it can suggest the appropriate box size(s) and number of boxes for packing the items when generating the picking lists. The previous chapter provided further explanation of the Picking Workbench approach (Section 6.9).

Single Step for Transfer Order Shipment with Automatic Receipt When reporting actual shipment for a sales order, you can indicate (via the Auto Receive checkbox) that the material should be automatically reported as received at the ship-to warehouse.

7.7 Minor Variations of Transfer Order Picking/Shipping

Several minor variations apply to the basic process of transfer order picking/shipping, such as the use of delivery tolerances and safety margins. Other minor variations were identified as part of the additional steps for the basic process, such as the needed actions for warehouse management.

Impact of Delivery Tolerances on Transfer Order Picking/Shipping When delivery tolerances are acceptable, they determine how much the quantities being picked and shipped for a transfer line can differ from the ordered quantity. Over- and under-delivery tolerances (related to transfer orders) are expressed as a percentage; the values assigned to an item act as defaults for a transfer order line item. Delivery tolerances of zero percent for a transfer line mean that the shipped quantity must equal the ordered quantity. A companywide policy (embedded in the Inventory Management parameters) determines whether over- and under-deliveries will be acceptable for transfer orders.

An over-delivery tolerance applies to both the picked quantity and the shipped quantity for a transfer line. For example, the system displays an error message infolog and prevents over-picking (beyond the over-delivery tolerance) when reporting the quantity picked, as well as over-shipping (beyond the delivery tolerance) when reporting a shipped quantity.

An under-delivery tolerance only applies to the shipped quantity for a transfer line. For example, you cannot report a shipment for an under-shipped quantity (beyond the under-delivery tolerance) in conjunction with the "close short" flag or the system will display an error message infolog.

Modeling the Required Time for Picking/Shipping Activities Some scenarios have a significant time requirement for picking/shipping activities related to a transfer order (such as 1 or 2 days), while many others have a much shorter preparation time of minutes. A significant time requirement should be included in the supply chain model so that (1) promised ship dates will reflect the required time and (2) picking will be scheduled prior to the ship date.

- *Identify the Required Time for Picking/Shipping as a Safety Margin* The required time can be identified as the issue safety margin, where you define the number of days as part of the Coverage Group assigned to the item. It is normally assigned as part of the Item Coverage information for the item and ship-to warehouse, where you identify the source warehouse for planned transfer orders and also override the normal Coverage Group assigned to the item.

  For example, when demands exist for an item with one day prep time, master scheduling logic will generate planned orders to arrive one day before the demand date. As another consideration, when using the Release Transfer Order Picking form to anticipate picking activities, you should release orders for picking one day prior to the ship date.

- *Include Required Time for Picking/Shipping in Delivery Promises* The required time (expressed as the issue safety margin, described above) can be included in delivery promises based on ATP logic, where you assign a delivery date control policy of "ATP plus issue margin" to the item as part of its default order policies for inventory. For example, when manually entering a transfer order line for an item with one day prep time, the earliest possible ship date will be one day later.

  Some scenarios do not use ATP logic as the basis for delivery promises. In many of these scenarios, the required time can be modeled by the sales lead time assigned to an item as part of its default order policies for inventory.

7.8 Executive Summary

The Basic Inventory approach employs an order-based picking list and a related shipment to report transfer order fulfillment. This chapter focused on transfer order picking/shipping, and the next chapter covers transfer order receiving. This chapter started with a simple yet typical business process and explained the related life cycles, transactions, and key constructs. The basic process provided a baseline for explaining variations, such as different ways to generate picking lists and the use of wave picking.

Chapter 8

Transfer Order Receiving

The order-based approach to transfer order picking/shipping also extends to receiving. As an explanatory approach, it is easiest to start with a simple yet typical business process and explain the related life cycles, reversing transactions, and key constructs. This basic process provides a baseline for explaining variations. These topics are reflected in the following sections within the chapter:

1. Basic Process for Transfer Order Receiving
2. Additional Steps in the Basic Process
3. Life Cycles Related to the Basic Process
4. Reversing Transactions in the Basic Process
5. Key Constructs for Transfer Order Receiving
6. Variations of Transfer Order Receiving
7. Additional Case Studies

Effective distribution planning represents a critical consideration for transfer order receiving. In order to be effective, the transfer orders should reflect S&OP game plans, a reasonable model of the supply chain, and other factors such as a manageable level of expediting. These considerations will make life easier for warehouse management.

8.1 Basic Process for Transfer Order Receiving

The basic process for transfer order receiving consists of several steps typically performed by a shipping clerk and a warehouse worker and is illustrated in Figure 8.1. The process starts with the need for reporting arrival and ends with completed receipts. This section provides an overview of the basic process and describes each step in more detail.

Figure 8.1 Basic Process for Transfer Order Receiving

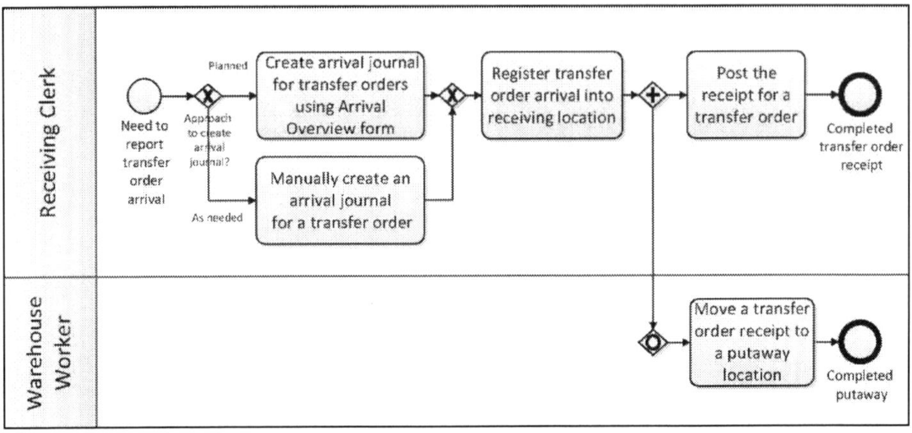

Overview The receiving clerk typically uses the Arrival Overview form to review a subset of shipped transfer orders reflecting user-specified criteria such as the ship-to warehouse, delivery date, and delivery mode. The receiving clerk can select transfer order lines and then create an arrival journal containing the selected lines. Alternatively, the receiving clerk can manually create an Arrival Journal (typically to handle an unplanned receipt). In either case, the receiving clerk registers the actual receipts against each journal line item and posts the journal to update inventory balances. As a final step, the receiving clerk posts the receipt for a transfer order.

For received material with putaway requirements, the warehouse worker uses the Transfer Journal form to report transfers from the receiving location to the putaway location.

Create Arrival Journal for Transfer Orders using the Arrival Overview Form The receiving clerk uses the Arrival Overview form to anticipate arrivals by viewing a subset of shipped transfer order line items reflecting user-specified criteria such as a ship-to location, delivery date, delivery mode, and/or transfer order number. The receiving clerk can select transfer order lines and then create an arrival journal containing the selected lines. When selecting transfer order lines, the receiving clerk can optionally analyze the estimated handling time and total weight/volume/pieces.

Manually Create an Arrival Journal for a Transfer Order The receiving clerk uses the Arrival Journal form to manually create an arrival journal and its line items (typically to handle an unplanned receipt of a transfer order).

Register Transfer Order Arrival into Receiving Location The receiving clerk uses the Arrival Journal form to register the actual quantities for each journal line item and posts the arrival journal to update on-hand inventory balances. As a last step, after posting the arrival journal, the receiving clerk typically uses the Arrival Journal form to post the transfer order receipt(s) for updating financial information about the received inventory.

Post the Receipt for a Transfer Order The receiving clerk typically posts the transfer order receipt as a related step on the Arrival Journal form (after posting the arrival journal) by accessing the Receive form It is also termed the Receive a Transfer Order form. On the Receive form, you can select the update basis for the receipt quantity—such as the registered information—and post the receipt. The Receive form can also be accessed from the Transfer Order form (so that it inherits information from the selected order) or accessed directly (where selection criteria can be used to populate the information).

Move a Transfer Order Receipt to a Putaway Location The warehouse worker uses the Transfer Journal to report a separate putaway transaction after recording transfer order arrival or receipt, typically when the received material has been placed in a bin location representing a receiving location.

Enforce Major Steps in the Basic Process The major step of recording registration (via the arrival journal) can be enforced by the Registration Requirements policy embedded within the Item Model Group assigned to an item.

8.2 Additional Steps in the Basic Process

The basic process sometimes includes several additional steps not shown in Figure 8.1 so that the diagram does not become too complex. These steps include scrap reporting and delayed posting of the arrival journal. Other related steps about Transfer Order History and in-transit inventory were described in the previous chapter (Section 7.2).

Report a "Lost in Transit" Quantity or a "Scrap" Quantity When Reporting a Transfer Order Receipt The receiving clerk can optionally identify that a scrap quantity applies to the received quantity. The scrap quantity may reflect material that has been lost in transit or scrapped material at the time of receipt. For example, a scrap quantity of 5 for the received quantity of 100 would result in an on-hand inventory of 95. The scrap quantity will automatically create two transactions to add and subtract the inventory.

Delay Posting of Arrival Journal in Order to Indicate Putaway Locations In some scenarios, the receiving clerk enters actual quantities on the arrival journal line items, and then warehouse workers enter the actual putaway locations and post the arrival journal.

8.3 *Life Cycles related to the Basic Process*

The basic process for transfer order receiving involves several related constructs, where the status for each construct reflects various steps in the process. Figure 8.2 summarizes this information for the basic process, and only displays those steps representing the minimum number of touch points for updating status. Grey shading highlights the key construct of an arrival journal.

Figure 8.2 Life Cycles Related to Basic Process for Transfer Order Receiving

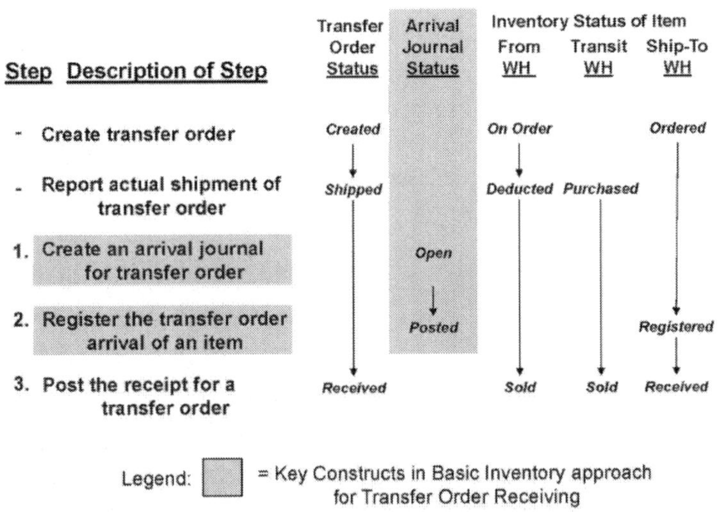

As shown in the figure, the steps will create an arrival journal (with line items reflecting transfer order lines), register the arrival (which updates inventory), and post the receipt for transfer orders (which updates financial information). The right side of the figure shows the inventory status for an item on a transfer order line. At the ship-to warehouse, for example, various steps will change this status from *ordered* to *registered* and *received.*

8.4 Reversing Transactions in the Basic Process

An arrival journal can be created and then deleted prior to posting. However, you still need to report arrival; otherwise, information cannot be corrected or cancelled after reporting actual shipment of a transfer order. In addition, the entire shipped quantity must ultimately be reported as received; it cannot remain in transit. When material has been lost in transit or gets scrapped upon receipt, you can identify the scrap quantity when posting the transfer order receipt.

Transfer journals provide one approach for making corrections. In order to correct an over-reported shipped quantity, for example, the shipped material must be reported as received and then a transfer journal can be used to move it back.

8.5 Key Constructs in the Basic Process

The basic process for transfer order receiving employs the key construct of an arrival journal and the related forms of an Arrival Journal and an Arrival Overview. A quick summary of these forms is provided below. The same constructs were also used and described for purchase orders (Section 5.5)

- *Arrival Overview.* Use this form to anticipate receiving activities and generate an arrival journal for selected transfer order lines.

- *Arrival Journal.* Use this form to identify the expected receipts for a transfer order and to report actual receipts. You can register the actual quantity and (when applicable) the location, batch number, and/or serial numbers for the received material. Posting the arrival journal will update on-hand inventory, but does not update financial information.

- *Receive [a Transfer Order]* Use the Receive form as the final step of transfer order receiving, which provides a financial update of the received inventory. It can be accessed in different ways. It can also update the line status and order status to *Received* when material has been completely received.

8.6 Variations of Transfer Order Receiving

The major variations include a simple inventory transaction and a single-step shipment; minor variations include modeling the time required for receiving activities. The use of automatically-generated quality orders does not apply to transfer order receiving.

Simple Inventory Transaction for Transfer Order Receiving The receiving clerk can bypass the use of arrival journals by simply posting the transfer order receipt and using an update basis of the shipped quantity rather than the registered quantity.

Single Step for Transfer Order Shipment with Automatic Receipt When reporting actual shipment for a sales order, you can indicate (via the Auto Receive checkbox) that the material should be automatically reported as received at the ship-to warehouse.

Receiving Batch-Controlled Items There is no specialized reporting of batch numbers since they are already identified for the shipped items.

Receiving Serialized Items There is no specialized reporting of serial numbers since they are already identified for the shipped items.

Modeling the Required Time for Transfer Order Receiving Activities Some scenarios have a significant time requirement for receiving activities related to a transfer order (such as 1 or 2 days), while many others have a much shorter preparation time of minutes. A significant time requirement should be included in the supply chain model so that receiving will be scheduled prior to the ship date.

The required time can be identified as the receipt safety margin, where you define the number of days as part of the Coverage Group assigned to the item. It is normally assigned as part of the Item Coverage information for the item and ship-to warehouse, where you identify the source warehouse for planned transfer orders and also override the normal Coverage Group assigned to the item.

8.7 Additional Case Studies

Case 32: Reporting "Lost in Transit" for a Transfer Order A transfer order shipment was sometimes "lost in transit," such as an individual line item or a partial quantity of a line item. In these cases, the receiving clerk at the ship-to warehouse identified this as a separate scrap quantity when reporting the total received quantity.

Case 33: Transfer Orders to/from a Subcontractor Warehouse As part of supporting their co-packers, a food products manufacturer sometimes used transfer orders to send the supplied material to the subcontractor warehouse and also receive the finished quantities. The actual receipt of a transfer order at the co-packer was entered into AX (by a coordinator role) as a simple inventory transaction. A simple inventory transaction was also entered for actual shipment of a transfer order from the co-packer.

Case 34: Updating the Transfer Order Receipt Date for Overseas Deliveries A manufacturer/distributor purchased many of its end items from suppliers in Asia. They took ownership when the items were still at the supplier, and then used transfer orders to coordinate deliveries to their U.S. warehouses. Each transfer order represented a container, and the line items represented the container contents. The transfer order receipt date was continually updated to reflect the expected date.

8.8 Executive Summary

The order-based approach to transfer order picking/shipping also extends to receiving. This chapter started a simple yet typical business process for transfer order receiving as well as explained the related life cycles, reversing transactions, and key constructs. This basic process provided a baseline for explaining variations.

Several case studies illustrated the variations. These included reporting "Lost in Transit" for a transfer order (Case 32), transfer orders to/from a subcontractor warehouse (Case 33), and updating the transfer order receipt date for overseas deliveries (Case 34).

Chapter 9

Production Order Picking

The Basic Inventory approach supports several variations in picking and receiving material for production orders. This chapter covers topics related to picking, and the next chapter covers topics related to receiving. The explanation focuses on production orders (for BOM items) but also covers batch orders (for formula items) as one of the major variations of the business process.

A simple production scenario provides the context for explaining the basic processes for picking and receiving, especially the differing viewpoints of engineering, production reporting, and warehouse management. Given this context, it is easiest to start with a simple yet typical business process that represents order-based picking for production orders and then explain the related life cycles, reversing transactions, and key constructs. The basic process provides a baseline for explaining variations, some of which involve an extended explanation. These topics are reflected in the following sections within the chapter:

1. Production Scenario #1 for Internal Manufacturing
2. Basic Process for Production Order Picking
3. Additional Steps in the Basic Process
4. Life Cycles Related to the Basic Process
5. Reversing Transactions in the Basic Process
6. Key Constructs for Production Order Picking
7. Major Variations of Production Order Picking
8. Significance of the Picking List Journal for Production Orders
9. Define the Warehouse Source of Components in BOM/Route Information
10. Additional Case Studies

Effective production scheduling represents a critical consideration for production order picking and receiving. A production schedule should reflect up-to-date S&OP game plans, capacity and material constraints, near term stability, and other factors such as production sequencing and a manageable level of expediting. One factor involves the time span associated with a production order quantity where large time spans (such as orders representing a month's worth of production) oftentimes do not provide sufficient granularity for coordinating warehouse activities or providing the visibility of expected receipts. These considerations will make life easier for warehouse management.

9.1 Production Scenario #1 for Internal Manufacturing

A simple production scenario provides a baseline for explaining the basic business processes related to production order picking and receiving. The simple scenario represents one of many variations in production, and there are several viewpoints of this scenario. From an engineering viewpoint, the scenario consists of a single-level bill of material (BOM) to produce an end-item from raw material components and a single operation within the routing. The warehouse is responsible for reporting picked material from raw material locations, and production is responsible for producing the end-item and reporting any adjustments to actual material usage. Work in process will be updated by the picked material and adjustments, and by reporting finished quantities. A finished quantity can be reported by production or warehouse workers. Figure 9.1 summarizes these engineering, production reporting, and warehouse management viewpoints. Arrows identify the various transactions.

The figure identifies the single-level bill of material and routing for the simple scenario where End-Item #1 is produced from Raw Material A (and other components) by a routing operation at Work Center #1 (aka a resource). A resource group identifies several similar work centers; the resource group has a common production input location (located at the start of production) and a common output location (located at the end of production). These are commonly termed floorstock or lineside locations and reflect the lean principle of stocking at the point of use.

Figure 9.1 Production Scenario #1 for Internal Manufacturing

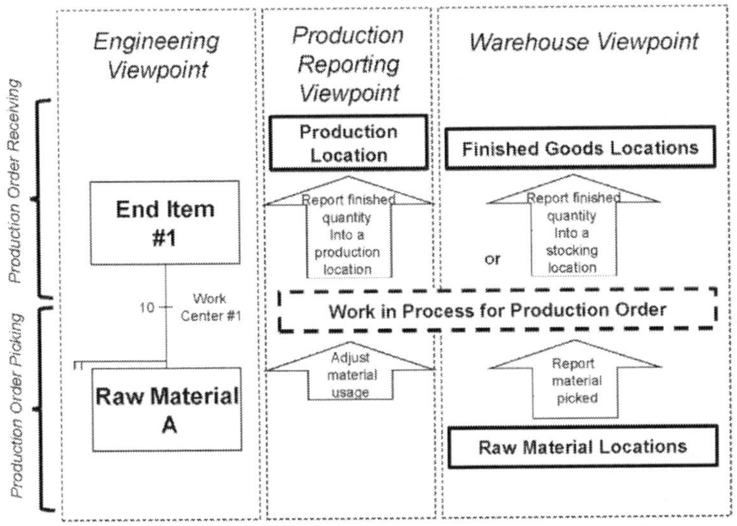

The arrows indicate key transactions for production and warehouse reporting. The figure indicates the different alternatives for reporting the finished quantity into a stocking location or a production location. The figure also identifies the relevant warehouse locations for raw material and finished goods as well as the work in process for the production order. The left side of the figure indicates the segmentation of book chapters about production order picking and receiving.

9.2 Basic Process for Production Order Picking

The basic process reflects the previously-described baseline of a simple production scenario and the related transactions. It also reflects order-based picking and normal material rather than serialized or batch-controlled material. Subsequent sections describe these variations to the basic process.

The basic process shown in Figure 9.2 consists of several steps typically performed by a machine operator and warehouse worker; however, there are many variations about the role responsibilities and steps. The figure also identifies the automatic step for generating the picking list journal. The process starts with the need to issue goods to production and ends with completed issues. This section provides an overview of the basic process and describes each step in more detail.

Figure 9.2 Basic Process for Production Order Picking

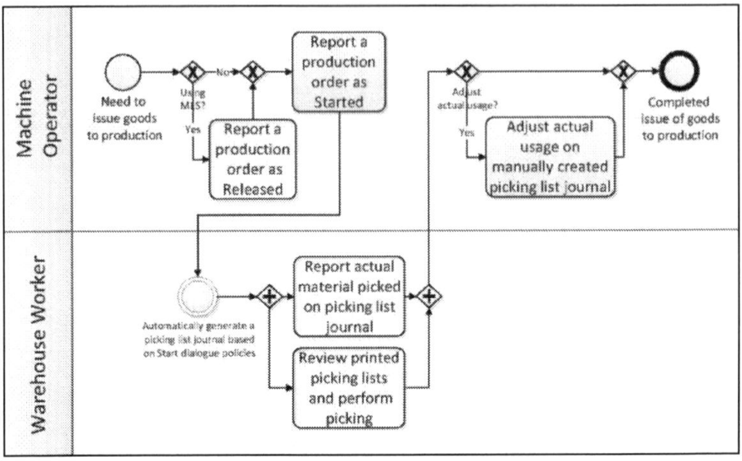

Overview The machine operator reports a production order as Started which acts as the trigger for creating a picking list journal (based on the Start dialogue policies). The operator may release the production order beforehand when using the Manufacturing Execution System (MES) functionality which generates route cards (that reflect routing information) so that a production supervisor can manually edit the production schedules.

The warehouse worker reviews the printed version of the picking list journal and reports actual material picked. The picked material is charged to work in process for the production order and deducted from inventory. It is typically delivered physically to production but not to a specific location.

In some cases, the machine operator may need to revise actual usage relative to the picked material. The machine operator manually creates a picking list journal containing the adjustments and then posts it.

Report a Production Order as Released The machine operator optionally reports a production order as Released, which can generate production paperwork (such as route cards) and also support MES functionality about detailed scheduling prior to reporting the order as Started.

Report a Production Order as Started The machine operator reports a production order as Started, which automatically generates a picking list journal based on the Start dialogue policies. As part of the Start dialogue, for example, the machine operator will start the entire order quantity and generate the picking list journal for components with a flushing principle of *Start*.

Report Actual Material Picked on the Picking List Journal The warehouse worker reports actual material picked by entering the data on the picking list journal and then physically delivering the components to production.

Review Printed Picking Lists The warehouse worker reviews the printed version of the picking list journal as a guide for performing activities. The printed document indicates the reserved quantity and location for each component, and provides bar-coded information to simplify data collection.

Adjust Actual Usage on a Manually-Created Picking List Journal In some cases, the machine operator may need to adjust actual usage relative to the picked material. The machine operator manually creates a picking list journal to identify the adjustments and then posts it.

Enforce the Sequence of Major Steps in the Basic Process Some scenarios need to limit the ability to change production order status, such as preventing a jump to a Started status so that orders must be reported as scheduled before they can be started. These companywide policies (defined on the Production Control Parameters form) consist of a matrix about the allowed changes from one status to another.

9.3 Additional Steps in the Basic Process

The basic process often includes several additional steps which are not shown in Figure 9.2 so that the diagram does not become too complex. Examples include identifying material shortages, reporting scrap, and completion of picking activities as well as assigning a stop flag to a production order.

Indicate Completion of Picking Activity The remaining component requirements are ignored when (1) a specific component has been flagged as completely picked, (2) when a picking list journal has been flagged as complete, (3) when an operation linked to the material has been flagged as complete, or (4) when the production order status has been updated to reported as finished.

Identify the Material Shortages for Production Order A material shortage represents the remaining requirements for a component in the Production BOM for a started production order. The system ignores a component's remaining required quantity when you indicate completion of picking activities, as described in the previous point. You can view these shortages on the Material Stock-Out List inquiry.

Indicate Component Scrap When Reporting Actual Material Usage You can report component scrap for a line item on the picking list journal, where you identify a separate scrap quantity and an optional reason code.

Report Actual Usage of Additional Components You can report usage of an additional component by adding it as a line item on the picking list journal.

Move Unused Raw Material Back to Stocking Location In some scenarios, actual material usage is less than the picked quantity for a component; the unused inventory needs to be returned to a stocking location. It is first necessary to reverse the picked quantity (out of work in process) via a manually-created picking list journal. You can indicate the stocking location on the journal line before posting the journal.

Assign (and Remove) a Stop flag for a Production Order Prior to Started Status The Stop flag primarily serves warehouse management purposes and prevents changes in order status prior to starting a production order. For example, assigning the Stop flag to a scheduled order prevents a change in order status to Started, which prevents creation of a picking list journal and reporting of actual picked material. The Stop flag also prevents resetting order status. You assign and remove the Stop flag as an explicit step on the Production Orders form. A Stop checkbox is also displayed as part of the warehouse management information for the order. The Stop flag has no impact when assigned after a production order has been started.

9.4 Life Cycles Related to the Basic Process

The basic process involves several related constructs where the status for each construct reflects various steps in the process. Figure 9.3 summarizes this information for the basic process. The steps represent the minimum number of touch points for updating status. Shading highlights the key constructs related to the Basic Inventory approach. These constructs include the production order and its picking list journal.

Reporting a production order as Started provides the starting point of the process, since this will automatically generate the picking list journal based on the Start dialogue policies. In many scenarios, starting the order also reserves component inventory (based on the reservation policy for the order). The component's inventory status changes to *deducted* after reporting actual material picked and posting the picking list journal. The inventory status of a component and the parent item are shown on the right side of the figure. Their status will also be updated by reporting a finished quantity and by ending an order.

Figure 9.3 Life Cycles Related to the Basic Process for Production Order Picking

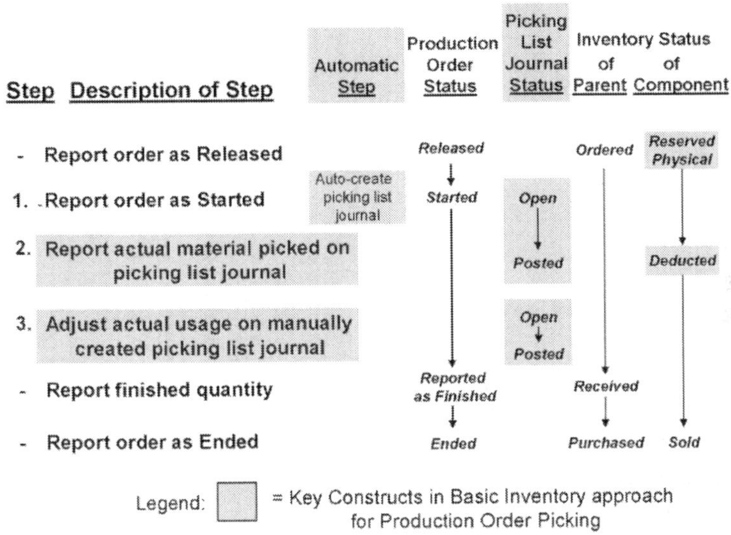

9.5 *Reversing Transactions in the Basic Process*

The ability to reverse transactions requires an understanding of the current point within the business process and the associated status of key constructs. Borrowing from the previous figure, Figure 9.4 illustrates the steps within the basic process (shown in grey text) and the various points at which you can perform reversing transactions (shown in black text). The figure also illustrates the impact of a reversing transaction on status, and the arrow indicates the resulting point in the business process. As identified by step numbers in the figure, you can reverse transactions (3X) after reporting actual material usage on the picking list journal and (AnyX) at any time prior to ending the production order.

Step 3X: Create a Picking List Journal with Reversing Entries You can reverse one or more transactions from a previously posted picking list. As the starting point, you manually generate a picking list journal with lines created from a previously-posted picking list. The lines (with a negative quantity) can be adjusted prior to posting the picking list. For example, some of the transactions can be deleted (because they do not need to be reversed) or the negative quantity can be reduced to indicate a partial reversal.

Figure 9.4 Reversing Transactions in the Basic Process for Production Order Picking

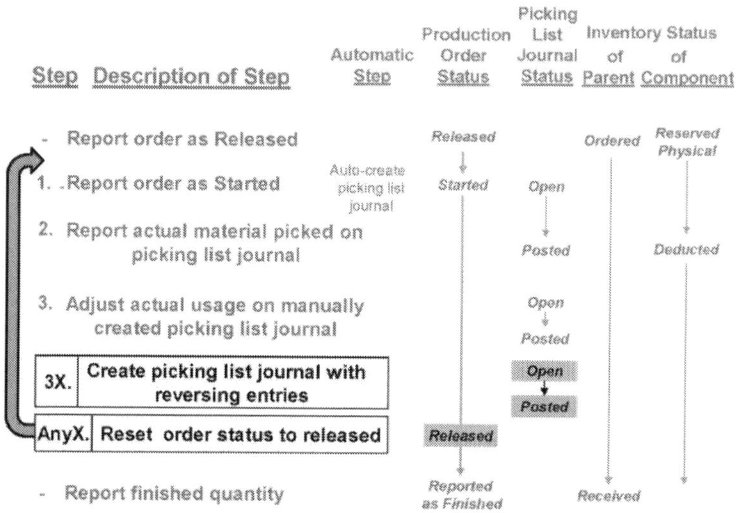

Step AnyX: Reset Order Status for a Production Order A production order can be reset to a previous status at any time prior to the *Ended* status. You indicate the desired order status on the reset order dialogue. For example, as shown in the figure, order status may be changed to *Released* from *Started* so that all transactions about actual production activities will be reversed.

9.6 Key Constructs in the Basic Process

The key constructs include production orders and picking list journals, and also the reservations for components.

Production Orders and Picking List Journals The production order and its related picking list journal(s) represent critical tools for coordination and reporting of production and warehouse activities. Their significance can differ widely depending on the scenario. In the simple scenario, for example, the production order represents a single production run and the picking list journal contains all components and reflects the entire order quantity. An extended explanation of these constructs is provided in a subsequent section (Section 9.8).

Reservations for Production Order Components The reservation policy assigned to a production order determines when components will be reserved relative to order status. The reservation policy for an order is initially inherited as a companywide or site-specific policy and it can be overridden. In most scenarios, you select a reservation policy so that components will be automatically reserved at the time of releasing or starting the production order. Some scenarios employ a reservation policy of Manual. You can view and update reservations for components in the Production BOM or the Picking List Journal by accessing the Reservations form.

A related reservation policy only applies to the Advanced WMS approach, and it determines whether components must be fully reserved or partially reserved when releasing a production order to the warehouse.

9.7 Major Variations of Production Order Picking

The basic process for production order picking provides the baseline for explaining major variations. Some variations entail a brief explanation. Other variations entail more extensive explanations, so they will be summarized here and explained further in subsequent sections. The major variations are listed below.

- Variations in the Significance of a Picking List Journal
- Variations in Defining the Warehouse Source of Components
- Report Production Order Picking via Auto-Deduction
- Report Batch Order Picking
- Report Production Order Picking for a Rework Order
- Picking Batch-Controlled Items
- Picking Serialized Items

Variations in the Significance of a Picking List Journal The picking list journal provides a critical tool for coordination and reporting of production activities and can be used in different ways. For example, it may be used by a warehouse worker for reporting actual picked quantities, or by a production worker for reporting or reversing actual material usage. Some variations stem from the significance of a single production order and the approach for generating and posting a picking list journal, as described in a subsequent section (Section 9.8). Other variations stem from the approach for defining the warehouse source of components (Section 9.9).

Variations in Defining the Warehouse Source of Components A component's warehouse source indicates where to pick the item for a production order, and it impacts master scheduling logic about material requirements for the item and warehouse. You define a component's warehouse source as part of the BOM and routing information, and this information will be inherited by the Production BOM and, ultimately, by the picking list journal.

There are three basic options for identifying the warehouse source of components in the BOM and routing information. A fourth option applies when components must be delivered to a production input location for a scheduled resource (or resource group) so that you report actual material usage (rather than picked material) on the picking list journal. A subsequent section provides further explanation about the variations in the warehouse source of components (Section 9.9).

Report Production Order Picking via Auto-Deduction Reporting a production order as *Started* can trigger automatic deduction of components based on policies in the Start dialogue. For example, as a result of starting an order, the picking list journal can be generated and posted immediately for components with a flushing principle of *Start.*

Reporting the finished quantity for a production order can also trigger automatic deduction based on policies in the Report as Finished dialogue. For example, as a result of reporting a finished quantity, the picking list journal can be generated and posted immediately for components with a flushing principle of *Finish.*

Report Batch Order Picking The same warehouse management considerations of production order picking also apply to batch orders. For example, the picking list journal applies to both types of orders.

Batch orders can have several unique variations that do not apply to production orders. For example, the picking and receiving transactions for a bulk/pack scenario involve coordination between the batch orders for the bulk item and packed items. Additional coordination is also required when using potency-based formulas, since the potency of a component can determine its required batch number and quantity. One other variation of batch orders involves catch weight items. The catch weight unit of measure (i.e., pieces rather than weight) applies to component picking and to reporting finished quantities

Report Production Order Picking for a Rework Order Rework may be necessary for the finished quantity of a production order that has not been reported as scrapped. A rework order can be created, and the same approaches can be employed for generating a picking list and reporting actual material usage.

Picking Batch-Controlled Items The picking list journal can identify the reserved material for picking a specific batch. With shelf-life items and FEFO reservation logic, for example, the reserved material reflects the inventory's expiration date. Alternatively, the reserved material can reflect a batch reservation based on attributes of an inventory batch. A subsequent chapter provides more detailed explanations about batch-controlled items (Sections 25.3).

Picking Serialized Items The serial number(s) can be identified when reporting actual picking against the picking list journal. A subsequent chapter provides further explanation about serialized items (Section 25.1).

9.8 Significance of the Picking List Journal for Production Orders

The picking list journal provides a critical tool for coordination and reporting of production activities, and it can be used in different ways. For example, it may be used by a warehouse worker for reporting actual picked quantities, or by a production worker for reporting actual material usage. This section provides a quick introduction of several factors impacting the use of picking list journals. These factors include the significance of a single production order and its order status, the significance of the flushing principle, and the variations for generating and posting a picking list journal.

Significance of a Single Production Order The significance of a single production order can vary in different scenarios, especially those involving manufactured items with batch tracking. It may represent a single production run (aka physical batch) in some scenarios, or the order quantity may represent multiple production runs within a day or week in other scenarios. Depending on the significance of a single order, it impacts the reporting of the started quantity for an order, the automatic generation of picking list journals for the started quantity, the reporting of finished quantities for the order, and the assignment of batch numbers to finished quantities.

The time span represented by the order quantity for a single production order is also important for warehouse management purposes. A worst case example might be a production order representing a monthly production quantity, which provides no granularity for expected component requirements and finished good receipts throughout the month.

A production order can be created in different ways, such as firming a planned order or manually creating the order. A key aspect involves the bill of material at the time you create the production order (termed a Production BOM or an order-dependent BOM), which is typically inherited from the item's active bill of material, but the component information can be overridden on the Production BOM.

The Production BOM provides the basis for line items in a picking list journal. Multiple aspects of this BOM information impact the generation and use of the picking list journal. For example, one aspect involves the approach to defining a component's required quantity. Another aspect involves the BOM line type (such as phantom) for a manufactured component, and the resulting impact on required components. Other aspects involve the impact of planned scrap factors on component quantities, and the operation number assigned to components. A comprehensive explanation of these aspects falls outside the book's scope.[1]

Significance of Production Order Status The life cycle of a production order consists of several steps represented by an order status. The order status represents a linear progression that affects order behavior, such as the ability to report actual production activities. When you skip reporting of steps in the linear progression, the system will automatically perform (or prompt you to perform) the intervening update tasks. Steps can also be reversed by resetting order status. Each step involves a user-initiated update task (and an associated dialogue) and results in a change to order status. For example, changing order status to *Started* involves a start task and an associated start dialogue; default values can be defined for many of the dialogue fields. A comprehensive explanation of production orders and order status falls outside the book's scope.[2]

The current status of a production order impacts system behavior and the ability to perform various tasks, such as the ability to report actual material usage and finished quantities. Figure 9.5 summarizes the significance of production order status for warehouse management purposes.

[1] Extended explanations about defining BOM and routing information are provided in the 2016 Edition of the two companion books titled Supply Chain Management and Process Manufacturing.

[2] Extended explanations about using production orders and batch orders are provided in the 2016 Edition of the two companion books titled Supply Chain Management and Process Manufacturing.

Figure 9.5 Significance of Production Order Status for Warehouse Management Purposes

Significance of Current Order Status	Current Order Status: Created	Estimated	Scheduled	Released	Started	Reported as Finished	Ended
Recognize Component Requirements	No	Yes				No	
Timing Option for Automatic Reservations	No	Yes				No	
Split a Production Order	Yes					No	
Create Work Order for raw material picking	No			Yes	No		
Generate Picking List Journal	No				Yes		No
Report Actual Picking or Material Usage	No				Yes		No
Report Finished Quantity	No				Yes		No
Reset Production Order Status	N/A	Yes					No

Legend: [shaded box] = Additional capability for Advanced WMS approach

Significance of the Flushing Principle for Populating Picking Lists The flushing principle assigned to a component item provides the basis for populating a picking list journal. For example, a flushing principle of *Start* provides the basis for populating a picking list when you report an order as Started. A flushing principle of *Finish* provides the basis for populating a picking list when reporting finished quantities for an order. A flushing principle of *Manual* may apply to items that should not be included when generating a picking list.

In order to effectively use the flushing principle, it must be considered in the Start dialogue when reporting an order as Started, and in the Report as Finished dialogue when reporting a finished quantity. As part of the Start dialogue, you can optionally populate the picking list with all components (regardless of flushing policy) or immediately post the picking list (which provides auto-deduction of components).

Variations in Generating and Posting a Picking List Journal Material usage can only be reported through a picking list journal. There are multiple variations for generating a picking list, where the variations reflect differences in modeling the business process. In the basic process, for example, starting a production order generated a single picking list journal for all components and a manually-created picking list was used for reporting adjustments and corrections. The following examples illustrate some of the variations.

- *Generate a Single Picking List Based on Starting the Entire Order Quantity.* This represents the simplest scenario, where the picking list would be populated by all components with a flushing principle of Start.

- *Generate Multiple Picking Lists Based on Different Start Quantities.* A typical scenario involves a production order quantity that represents multiple physical batches. You report a started quantity for each physical batch so that the picking list journal identifies component quantities for just one batch. Another scenario involves a production order quantity that represents a week's worth of production, but picking occurs in daily increments. You report a started quantity for each daily increment.

- *Generate Multiple Picking Lists Based on Different Operation Numbers.* A typical scenario involves a production order with multiple operations and differing component requirements at each operation. For example, you can report the entire order quantity as started but segment the picking lists by operation. Another scenario also involves an extended time between operations so that you only report the started quantity for a specified operation.

- *Generate and Immediately Post a Picking List Based on the Started Quantity.* This approach is commonly termed forward flushing because the picking list is generated and then automatically posted. The approach reflects a policy in the Start dialogue.

- *Generate and Immediately Post a Picking List Based on the Finished Quantity.* A typical scenario would populate the picking list with components assigned a flushing principle of Finish. This approach is commonly termed back flushing because the picking list is automatically posted. The approach reflects the policies in the Report As Finished dialogue.

- *Manually Generate a Picking List.* This approach starts from the Picking List Journal where you specify the basis for automatically populating a picking list via a Create Lines dialogue. For example, you can automatically create lines based on a specified quantity or the order's started quantity. You post the picking list after reporting actual material usage. The approach ignores the flushing principle assigned to component items.

- *Reverse the Entries for a Previously-Posted Picking List.* When manually generating a picking list (described above), the basis for automatically populating the picking list can reflect reversing entries for a previously-posted picking list. The resulting line items have a negative quantity, and line items can be deleted and modified. This approach is typically employed to record adjustments or corrections.

- *Issue Unexpected Components to an Order.* This approach starts from the Picking List Journal where you manually add a line item for issuing the component. A manually-created line item represents an unexpected component which will be added to the Production BOM with a required quantity of zero. It will also result in a material substitution variance for a standard cost item. It does not represent an additional quantity for an existing component.

9.9 Define the Warehouse Source of Components in BOM/Routing Information

A component's warehouse source indicates where to pick the item for a production order, and impacts master scheduling logic about material requirements for the item and warehouse. You define a component's warehouse source as part of the BOM and routing information, and this information will be inherited by the Production BOM and then by the picking list journal.

For many scenarios, the warehouse workers use the picking list journal as the basis for reporting actual material picked, and it identifies the reserved material at stocking locations. It is typically posted immediately upon completion of picking activities, but posting may be delayed. After posting, the picked inventory is not visible for on-hand inquiries because it has been charged to work in process for the production order. There are three basic options for supporting this purpose of the picking list journal, as summarized in Figure 9.6 and explained below. Each option involves considerations about BOM and routing information, and the requirements for additional information vary by option.

The fourth option displayed in Figure 9.6 represents a different purpose for the picking list journal. It assumes components will be delivered to a production input location which will be identified on the picking list journal for reporting actual material usage (rather than material picked). This option also applies to the Basic Inventory approach. However, it represents the only option for supporting the Advanced WMS approach to raw material picking work and wave picking, as described in a subsequent chapter (Chapter 19).

Figure 9.6 Variations in Warehouse Source of Components

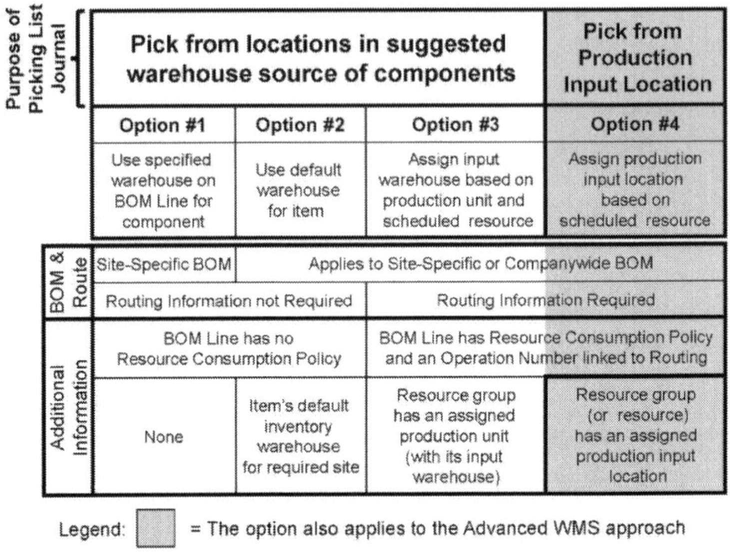

Option #1: Use the specified warehouse on the BOM line for the component The first option only applies to a site-specific BOM version, and the specified warehouse must belong to the site. After creating a production order for the manufactured item, the component in the Production BOM inherits the component's specified warehouse.

Option #2: Use the default warehouse for the item The second option does not specify a component warehouse on the BOM line, and requires additional information about the item's default inventory warehouse for each site (as defined in the item's site-specific order settings). After creating a production order, the component in the Production BOM inherits the component's default inventory warehouse for the required site.

A shown in the figure, the first two options do not require routing information, and they represent the most straightforward approach. In addition, they do not employ the "resource consumption" policy on a BOM line, even when routing information has been defined.

Option #3: Automatically assign an input warehouse based on the scheduled resource and its related production unit The third option requires routing information and operation numbers linking BOM lines to specific operations.[3] It employs the "resource consumption" policy for each BOM line, which defers assignment of a warehouse source until a resource (or resource group) has been scheduled for each routing operation. A resource group has an assigned production unit which might be assigned to multiple resource groups with a common warehouse source of components. This is termed the input warehouse for a production unit. After scheduling a production order, the component in the Production BOM inherits the input warehouse associated with the resource group performing the operation.

Option #4: Automatically assign a production input location based on the scheduled resource The fourth option represents a different purpose for the picking list journal, as mentioned earlier. It assumes components will be delivered to a production input location which will be identified on the picking list journal for reporting actual material usage (rather than material picked). Delivering components to a production input location typically involves transfer journals (or withdrawal kanbans) in the Basic Inventory approach. It involves Raw Material Picking work in the Advanced WMS approach, where the component must be a WMS-enabled item and production occurs at a WMS-enabled warehouse.

The fourth option requires routing information and operation numbers linking BOM lines to specific operations, and it also employs the "resource consumption" policy for each BOM line, just like the third option.

You define a location representing each production input location within a warehouse, so that it can be assigned to a resource group or for individual resources within the group. After scheduling a production order, the component in the Production BOM inherits the production input location associated with the resource group (or resource) performing the operation.

It is feasible to assign both a production input location and a production unit to a resource group, but the former will be used by scheduling logic for assigning the location to components in the Production BOM.

[3] The system assumes that a BOM line not linked to an operation number is required for the first operation.

9.10 Additional Case Studies

Case 35: Warehouse Source of Components in a Multisite Operation A manufacturer produced items at different sites and employed site-specific BOM versions to define the components. The warehouse source for each component's inventory could be specified as part of the BOM line information. The company felt this approach was the most straightforward to understand and the simplest to maintain. After creating a production order for the manufactured item, the component in the Production BOM inherited the component's specified warehouse.

Case 36: Preferred Equipment and the Warehouse Source of Components A manufacturing company used routing information to indicate the preferred equipment for producing an item. For example, the resource requirements for a routing operation can identify a dedicated machine (specified as the required resource for the operation), or as any machine within an interchangeable group of machines (specified as the required resource group for the operation). Other routing operations indicated a preferred machine based on the required capability or a minimum capability, or the production quantity (specified as a different route version with a quantity breakpoint). The scheduling logic would suggest the preferred machine, and the assigned resource determined which warehouse location should supply the components.

Case 37: Substitution Logic for an Ingredient The production planner at a food products manufacturing firm worked with the product engineers to define substitute ingredients in the formulas for different products. The substitute ingredients were automatically considered in the planned batch orders generated by master scheduling logic and also in planned orders that were manually entered. With this logic, a substitute ingredient was considered when there was insufficient inventory of the original ingredient. In some cases, the formula lines for a planned order identified some of the original ingredient and some of the substitute ingredient. This information was identified in the picking list journal for the batch order.

Case 38: Correcting Errors About the Picked Components The warehouse workers at a manufacturing company sometimes made a mistake in reporting the quantity picked for a production order or they needed to completely reverse an entire picking list. In these cases, they manually generated a picking list journal with lines created from the previously posted picking list. The lines (with a negative quantity) were adjusted prior to posting the picking list. For example, some of the lines were deleted (because they did not need to be reversed) or the negative quantity was reduced to indicate a partial reversal or correction.

9.11 Executive Summary

The Basic Inventory approach supports several variations in picking and receiving material for production orders. As a starting point, a simple production scenario for internal manufacturing provided the context for explaining the basic processes for picking and receiving. Given this context, the chapter described a simple yet typical business process that represents order-based picking for production orders as well as explained the related life cycles, reversing transactions, and key constructs. The basic process provided a baseline for explaining variations, such as the variations in the significance of a picking list, the warehouse source of components, and the use of auto-deduction.

Several case studies illustrated the variations. These included the warehouse source of components in a multisite operation (Case 35), preferred equipment and the warehouse source of components (Case 36), substitution logic for an ingredient (Case 37), and correcting errors about the picked components (Case 38). A related case study involves customer supplied material (Case 76).

Chapter 10

Production Order Receiving

The Basic Inventory approach supports several variations of issuing and receiving goods for production orders. This chapter covers topics related to receiving and the previous chapter covered topics related to picking. The explanation focuses on production orders (for BOM items) but also covers batch orders (for formula items) as one of the major variations of the business process.

A simple production scenario—described in the previous chapter—provides the context for explaining a basic process for receiving. Given this context, it is easiest to start with a simple yet typical process and then explain the related life cycles, reversing transactions and key constructs. The basic process provides a baseline for explaining several variations. These topics are reflected in the following sections within the chapter:

1. Basic Process for Production Order Receiving
2. Additional Steps in the Basic Process
3. Life Cycles Related to the Basic Process
4. Reversing Transactions in the Basic Process
5. Major Variations of Production Order Receiving
6. Alternatives for Reporting Production Order Receipts
7. Production Inspection of Finished Quantities
8. Report Production using a BOM Journal

Effective production scheduling represents a critical consideration for production order picking and receiving. In order to be effective, the production orders should reflect up-to-date S&OP game plans for required material, material and capacity constraints, a reasonable model of the supply chain, and other factors such as a manageable level of expediting. These considerations will make life easier for warehouse management.

The AX terminology about reporting a finished quantity can become confusing because the AX term "Report as Finished" has multiple contexts. The primary context involves the production order status of *Report as Finished*, which means all production activities have been reported. You can report a finished quantity using several different approaches, including the Report as Finished form and the Report as Finished Journal, where indicating the "report as finished flag" can also update order status. In addition, you can use the route card journal for reporting a good quantity at the last operation, and indicating the "production report as finished flag" will update the finished quantity. This explanation will primarily use the terms "production order receipts" and "reporting a finished quantity," and explain the context when applicable.

10.1 Basic Process for Production Order Receiving

A simple production scenario described in the previous chapter provides a context for explaining a basic business for production order receiving. The basic process shown in Figure 10.1 consists of several steps typically performed by a machine operator and warehouse worker, but there are many variations about the role responsibilities and reporting approaches. The process starts with the need to receive a finished quantity and ends with a completed receipt. This section provides an overview of the basic process and describes each step in more detail.

Figure 10.1 Basic Process for Production Order Receiving

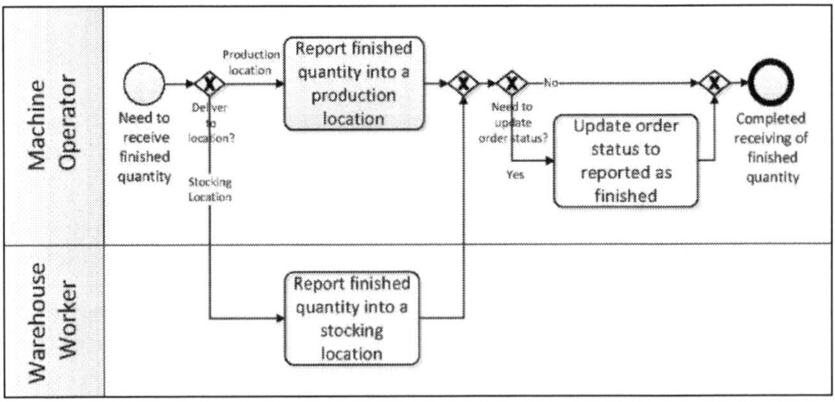

Overview The finished quantity of a production order can be reported by different roles using different approaches and delivered to different locations. As illustrated in the figure, a finished quantity may be reported into a production location by the machine operator, or it may be reported into a stocking location by a warehouse worker. The finished quantity may be reported multiple times for a given order, or reported once when it represents the entire order quantity. The machine operator updates the order status to *reported as finished* after all production output has been reported.

Report the Finished Quantity into a Production Location The machine operator can report the finished quantity into a production location. The finished quantity can be reported for the entire order quantity, or it may be reported for multiple receipts. Reporting a finished quantity that represents the last of the production output can be flagged, so that the order status will be updated to *reported as finished.*

Report the Finished Quantity into a Stocking Location The warehouse worker can report the finished quantity into a stocking location. The finished quantity can be reported for the entire order quantity, or it may be reported for multiple receipts. Reporting a finished quantity that represents the last of the production output can be flagged, so that the order status will be updated to *reported as finished.*

Update Order Status to Reported as Finished When reporting finished quantities, the last of the production output can be flagged so that the order status will be updated to *Reported as Finished.* If needed, you can report a zero quantity in order to update the order status. An order status of *Reported as Finished* means that any remaining requirements for material or capacity will be ignored, and any difference between the ordered quantity and received quantity will also be ignored.

10.2 Additional Steps in the Basic Process

The basic process often includes several additional steps which are not shown in Figure 10.1 so that the diagram does not become too complex. The following additional steps may be needed.

Report a Trashed Quantity for a Production Order Some scenarios will identify scrap when reporting a finished quantity rather than receiving the inventory for subsequent reporting of scrap. This scrapped quantity is also termed the error quantity or trashed quantity. The trashed quantity represents an incremental output in addition to good quantity. The trashed quantity is not tracked in inventory and does not result in an inventory transaction. The value of the trashed quantity can be charged to a specific G/L account but only for actual cost items, and it is identified as a substitution variance for standard cost items.

Move Unused Raw Material Back to Stocking Location In some scenarios, actual material usage is less than the picked quantity for a component, and the unused inventory needs to be returned to a stocking location. It is first necessary to reverse the picked quantity (out of work in process) via a manually-created picking list journal. You can indicate the stocking location on the journal line before posting the journal.

10.3 Life Cycles related to the Basic Process

The basic process involves several related constructs, where the status for each construct reflects various steps in the process. Figure 10.2 summarizes this information for the basic process, and only displays those steps representing the minimum number of touch points for updating status. The major constructs include the production order and an inventory journal for each finished quantity (termed the Report as Finished Journal).

Figure 10.2 Life Cycles Related to the Basic Process for Production Order Receiving

Step	Description of Step	Automatic Step	Production Order Status	Report as Finished (RAF) Journal Status	Inventory Status of Parent	Inventory Status of Component
-	Report order as Started and report actual material usage		*Started*		*Ordered*	*Deducted*
1.	Report a finished quantity for production order	Auto-create & post RAF journal		*Posted*	*Received*	
2.	Update production order status to reported as finished		*Reported as Finished*			
-	Report order as Ended		*Ended*		*Purchased*	*Sold*

Reporting a finished quantity provides the starting point of the process, and it automatically creates and posts an inventory journal for the finished quantity. There are several alternatives for reporting a finished quantity, as described in a subsequent section (Section 10.6). A separate step for updating order status only applies when it has not already been updated by reporting the last of the finished quantities. The right side of the figure illustrates the inventory status associated with the parent item and a component for the production order.

10.4 Reversing Transactions in the Basic Process

The ability to reverse transactions requires an understanding of the current point within the business process, and the associated status of key constructs. Borrowing from the previous figure, Figure 10.3 illustrates the steps within the basic process (shown in grey text) and the various points at which you can perform reversing transactions (shown in black text). As identified by step numbers in the figure, you can reverse transactions (1X) after reporting a finished quantity and (2) after updating order status to *reported as finished.*

Figure 10.3 Reversing Transactions in the Basic Process for Production Order Receiving

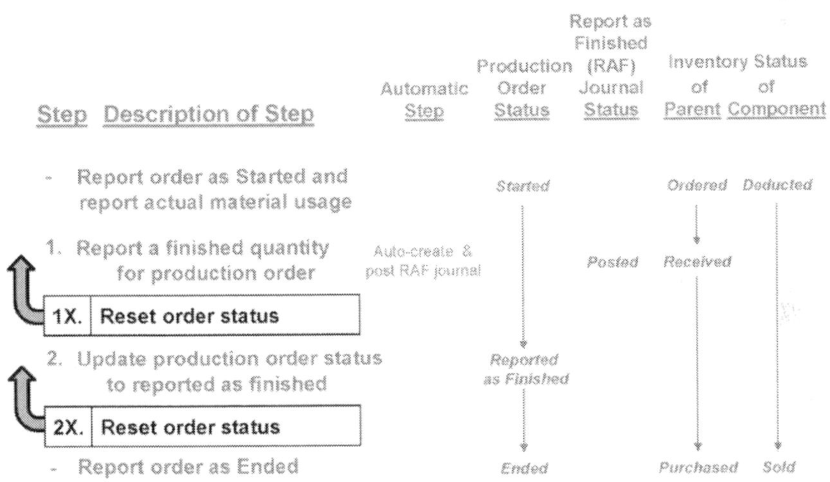

Step 1X: Reset Order Status for a Production Order You can reset the order status from Started to Released (or earlier) in order to back out all transactions for finished quantities and picking transactions.

Step 2X: Reset Order Status for a Production Order Resetting the order status from Started to Released (or earlier) will back out all transactions for finished quantities and picking transactions. Resetting to a Started status has no impact.

10.5 Major Variations of Production Order Receiving

The basic process for production order receiving provides the baseline for explaining major variations. Some variations entail a brief explanation. Other variations entail more extensive explanations, so they will be summarized here and explained further in subsequent sections. The major variations are listed below and covered in separate subsections.

- Alternatives for Reporting the Finished Quantity
- Production Inspection of Finished Quantities
- Receive Batch-Controlled Items
- Receive Serialized Items
- Report Batch Order Receiving
- Report Batch Order Receiving of Co/By-Products
- Production Order Arrivals Using an Arrival Journal
- Report Production Using the BOM Journal

Alternatives for Reporting the Finished Quantity The finished quantity of a production order can be reported in different ways. Each approach enables you to indicate the last of the finished quantities so that order status will be updated to *Reported as Finished.* However, the attempts to update order status will be prevented when there are missing transactions or errors. An infolog warning identifies these conditions so that you can finish or correct the transactions. Alternatively, you can choose to accept any errors in order to update order status. A subsequent section provides further explanation about these alternatives (Section 10.6).

Production Inspection of Finished Quantities There are many variations of production inspection for the finished quantity of a production order. For example, the inspection may be performed by machine operators at the time of reporting production output, or by a quality control clerk reporting against an automatically-created quality order. In addition, the test results for a quality order may be reported for a small sample while the material remains in a production location, or the finished quantity may be placed in a separate QC area until test results have been reported. A subsequent section provides further explanation about the variations of receiving inspection (Section 10.7).

Receive Batch-Controlled Items A batch-controlled item involves the assignment of batch numbers when reporting a finished quantity. It may also involve reporting of a batch disposition code. A subsequent chapter describes the various approaches to batch number assignment (Section 25.3) and batch disposition codes (Section 25.8).

Receive Serialized Items A serialized item involves the assignment of serial numbers when reporting purchase order arrival. A subsequent chapter describes the various approaches to serial number assignment (Section 25.1).

Report Batch Order Receiving The same approaches for reporting finished quantities of a production order also apply to a batch order. Hence, it does not represent a major variation but is included for completeness sake.

Report Batch Order Receiving of Co/By-Products The same approaches for reporting finished quantities also apply to the co-products and/or by-products of a batch order. You can optionally add an unexpected co/by-product when reporting finished quantities but only when permitted by a policy on the batch order (labeled the Co/By Product Variations checkbox).

Report Production Order Arrival using an Arrival Journal The use of an arrival journal and the Arrival Overview form were previously described for purchase order arrivals (Section 5.5), and the same constructs and similar steps can be used for reporting production order arrivals. In summary, you use the Arrival Overview form to identify and select production orders to be received, and then create an arrival journal containing the selected orders.[1] You can register actual receipts against each journal line and then post the journal to update inventory balances with a *registered* status.

The similarity of approaches can be an advantage when the same workers report receiving for purchase orders and production orders. In addition, the arrival journal can be used to assign of an inventory status, typically to support quality purposes.

There are some shortcomings in this alternative approach. It still requires an additional report-as-finished step to update inventory balances to received and generate the Report as Finished Journal (with the financial impacts). You cannot identify a trashed quantity. You may want to customize the current format of the Arrival Overview form, since it currently displays all production orders regardless of order status and it does not display the scheduled completion dates.

---

[1] A production input journal rather than an arrival journal is typically used for production order receiving. They both provide the same functionality for production orders, so it is simpler to retain the arrival journal terminology in explanations.

Report Production Using the BOM Journal The Bills of Material Journal (termed BOM Journal for short) provides an alternative approach for reporting production of a manufactured item and consumption of its component inventory. The approach is described in a subsequent section (Section 10.8).

10.6 Alternatives for Reporting the Finished Quantity

The finished quantity of a production order can be reported in different ways. This section summarizes the three major options and also explains the conditions which prevent updating order status to *Reported as Finished.*[2]

Option #1: Using the Report as Finished Form The Report as Finished form can be accessed by starting from the Production Order form so that it inherits information from the selected order. When applicable, you indicate the finished quantity represents the last of the remaining production output (by selecting the checkbox labeled End Job) so that the order status will be updated to *Reported as Finished.* Processing this task will automatically create and post an inventory journal for the finished quantity (labeled the Report as Finished Journal).

The Report as Finished form can also be accessed directly in order to report the finished quantity for multiple orders. Information about multiple orders can be populated using selection criteria, such as the order's scheduled delivery date/time or the item's production pool.

Option #2: Using the Route Card Journal for Reporting Unit Completions at the Last Operation When routing data exists, reporting the unit completions at the last operation can automatically create and post the Report as Finished Journal.

Option #3: Using the Report as Finished Journal Each transaction for reporting a finished quantity will automatically create and post an inventory journal labeled the Report as Finished Journal. The journal consists of header information (identifying the production order) and one or more line items, where each line identifies an item and its finished quantity. The journal can be accessed by starting from the Production Order form so that it only displays information

[2] The term "report as finished" has several contexts within Dynamics AX that can lead to confusion. These contexts include the update task for a production order, a journal for reporting unit completions by operation, report-as-finished flags when reporting production activities, and the status of a production order.

about the selected order. It can also be accessed directly in order to display information about all orders. In either case, you can manually create a new journal and line item in order to report a finished quantity.

Update the Order Status to Reported as Finished All of the above-mentioned transactions can update order status to *Reported as Finished.* You indicate the finished quantity represents the last of the remaining production output by selecting the checkbox labeled End Job. When applicable, you can also report a zero quantity in order to update the order status.

It is assumed no more transactions need to be reported after updating order status, so that any remaining component requirements or expected receipts will be ignored. However, transactions can still be reported until order status has been updated to Ended.

Conditions Preventing Updates to Order Status Missing feedback or errors can prevent an order status update, and a warning infolog identifies the conditions when attempting to update order status. You can override these warnings by using the *accept errors* flag when reporting the finished quantity. Examples of missing feedback or errors include the following.

- Each component must be completely issued, or flagged as completed in the picking list journal.
- Each operation must be flagged as completed.
- The total finished quantity must be less than or equal to the started quantity.

10.7 Production Inspection of Finished Quantities

There are many variations of production inspection for manufactured items. For example, production inspection may be reported by a machine operator at the time of reporting the finished quantity of a production order, or reported afterward by a quality control clerk using an automatically-created quality order. The test results for a quality order may be reported for a small sample while the material remains at a production output location, or a finished quantity may be placed in a separate QC area until test results have been reported. Validation failure of the test results can automatically update the Inventory Status of the finished quantity, such as changing status to a value of *To-Be-Scrapped* or *Needs-Rework.*

As an explanatory approach, the different approaches for production inspection are more easily explained via case studies. A common scenario involves reporting by the machine operator, as described in Case 39. Another common scenario involves reporting by a quality control clerk using quality orders and Inventory Status, as described in Case 40. Additional case studies illustrate some other approaches to production inspection, and a subsequent chapter about quality management summarizes many of the variations and case studies about inspection approaches (Section 26.2).

Case 39: Production Inspection by Machine Operators The production manager at a manufacturing company wanted the machine operators to report inspection of finished quantities for production orders. A machine operator could immediately report a trashed quantity (aka the error quantity) when reporting a good quantity on the Reported as Finished form, thereby bypassing the need for additional steps. Alternatively, the machine operator could assign an inventory status of *To-Be-Scrapped*, *Needs-Rework* or *Needs-Inspection* to a received quantity, thereby indicating the need for an additional step. The corresponding steps involved an inventory adjustment, a rework order, or a quality order.

Case 40: Production Inspection using Quality Orders and Inventory Status

The warehouse manager and quality control (QC) manager at a manufacturing company were considering options for using automatically-generated quality orders for finished quantities of production orders. One option involved the use of Inventory Status, where the quality order would automatically change the value based on pass/fail validation. Passing the validation changed the value to *Good.* Failing the validation changed the value to *To-Be-Scrapped* or *Needs-Rework*, as defined by the quality control clerk performing the quality order. The proposed business process is illustrated in Figure 10.4 and described below.

The production inspection process starts with reporting a finished quantity into a production location which automatically generates a quality order. The process has multiple end points reflecting the test results of the quality order. The inventory remains in the production location until completion of the quality order. The process consists of several steps performed by different roles, and three of these steps merit further explanation.

Figure 10.4 Production Inspection Using a Quality Order and Inventory Status

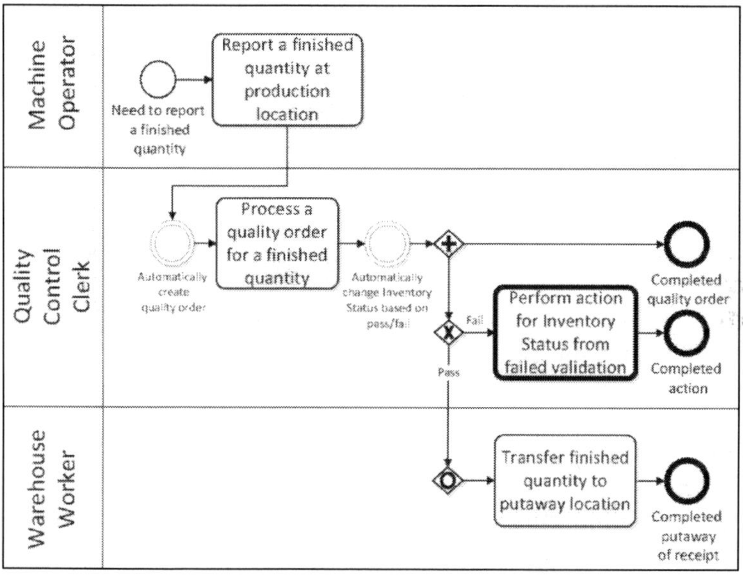

- *Process a Quality Order for a Finished Quantity.* The activities of quality control clerks are coordinated based on a review of open quality orders, using either the Quality Orders form or the Inventory Blocking form. When reporting test results for a given quality order, the quality control clerk indicates the applicable Inventory Status for validation failure, such as *To-Be-Scrapped* or *Needs- Rework.* Validation automatically updates the Inventory Status.

  If applicable, the quality control clerk creates a nonconformance related to problems with the item or production order, and/or creates a case about the problem.

- *Perform Action for Inventory Status from failed Validation.* The quality control clerk reports an inventory adjustment for material assigned an Inventory Status of *To-Be-Scrapped.* The production planner creates a rework order for material with a *Needs-Rework* status. For material with a *Good* status, the warehouse worker can report a transfer from the production location to a stocking location.

Case 41: Quality Orders during the Production Process The quality manager at a manufacturing company wanted to obtain test results during the production process for a manufactured item. The item's routing information identified multiple operations with operation numbers (such as 10, 20, 30 and 40), and the test results were needed at selected operation numbers (such as 20 and 30). These testing requirements were defined as part of a Quality Association for the item and each selected operation number, which would trigger automatic creation of a quality order after the operation was reported as finished.

10.8 Report Production using a BOM Journal

The Bills of Material Journal (termed BOM Journal for short) supports an order-less approach to reporting production of a manufactured item and consumption of its component inventory. It can be used for manufactured items with a product structure defined by the BOM approach or the Formula approach, although this explanation employs the terminology for the BOM approach.

A BOM Journal has a system-assigned identifier and consists of a header and line items, much like the previously described inventory journals for basic inventory transactions (Section 3.2). However, the BOM journal works slightly differently because one line item identifies the parent item and the other line items identify its components. The creation of journal line items is also different.

You can directly access the BOM Journal form in order to create a BOM Journal. After creating a BOM journal, you access a separate form (termed the Report as Finish form) from the journal lines in order to identify the parent item and some additional information. The additional information includes the intended location (site, warehouse and bin), quantity, BOM version, and an explosion policy. The explosion policy determines the basis for automatically creating the journal lines for components, as described below. Accepting the completed information will automatically create a BOM Journal and display the journal lines for the parent and its components.

- *Never Explode*. The underlying bills for manufactured components are never exploded, so that the components reflect the single-level bill. However, the system still explodes requirements through phantom components.

- *Always Explode*. The underlying bills for manufactured components are always exploded regardless of inventory availability, so that components only reflect purchased items.

- *Explode Only When Shortage Exists.* The explosion of underlying bills for manufactured components reflects available inventory.

As a short cut, by starting from the Released Products form for a selected manufactured item, you can access the above-mentioned Report as Finish form and specify the additional information. Accepting the completed information has the same results. It will automatically create a BOM Journal and display the journal lines for the parent and its components.

After automatic creation of the journal lines, you can override the information about the intended quantity and location for the parent item and components. The journal line for a component can also be manually added or deleted.

The BOM journal can be printed for coordinating production and acts as a turnaround document. You report the actual production of the parent item and the actual component consumption against the journal line items, and then post the BOM Journal to update inventory.

10.9 Executive Summary

The Basic Inventory approach supports several variations in picking and receiving material for production orders. This chapter focused on receiving the finished quantities for a production. It started with a simple yet typical business process and then explained the related life cycles, reversing transactions and key constructs. The basic process provided a baseline for explaining variations, such as the alternatives for reporting finished quantities and variations of production inspection.

Several case studies illustrated the variations, especially those related to quality. These included production inspection by machine operators (Case 39), production inspection using quality orders and inventory status (Case 40), and quality orders during the production process (Case 41).

Chapter 11

Subcontracted Production

Subcontracted production and internal production share many similarities in the use of basic constructs like production orders and picking list journals. However, subcontracted production involves significant differences and several variations that merit a separate explanation. One key difference stems from the AX approach to modeling subcontracted production, which requires a unique item representing the subcontracted service, and a BOM line specifying the item as a buy-to-order component. As a result, scheduling a production order for the parent item automatically creates the purchase order for the subcontracted service. The dual constructs of a production order and its related purchase order involve additional complexity. The two different orders can be received separately, or a single purchase order receipt can be employed for updating both orders.

Subcontracted production can have many variations of the supplied material and handling of the finished quantities. A basic issue concerns the visibility of inventory at the subcontractor site and the in-transit inventory.

For explanatory purposes, it is easiest to view the variations of subcontracted production in terms of a single-level BOM and a single routing operation for the manufactured item. The BOM lines identify the supplied material and an additional component representing the subcontracted service. The routing operation typically identifies the turnaround time at the subcontractor and has no costing impact. Other variations will be covered as case studies, such as a multi-step routing with one or more outside operations or subcontracted production without routing data. These considerations are reflected in the following sections within the chapter.

1. Variations of Supplied Material for Subcontracted Production
2. Variations of Finished Quantities for Subcontracted Production

3. Key Constructs for Subcontracted Production
4. Case Studies for Subcontracted Production

Several aspects of supply chain management represent critical considerations for subcontracted production. The requirements should reflect S&OP game plans, a reasonable model of the supply chain, and up-to-date information about the subcontracted production order and its supplied material. In many cases, up-to-date information is also needed for purchase order or transfer order deliveries of supplied material, as well as transfer order deliveries of finished quantities. Other factors may apply such as a manageable level of expediting.

11.1 Variations of Supplied Material for Subcontracted Production

Subcontracted production involves supplied material—either completely supplied or partially supplied—and there are several delivery options as well as options for reporting usage.[1] In the simplest case, the picked material for a subcontracted production order reflects delivery and usage. This approach provides no visibility of component inventory at the subcontractor or in transit.

Other delivery options for supplied material include receipts of purchase orders or transfer orders, with inventory visibility at the subcontractor (and in transit). In this case, the picking list for the production order provides the basis for usage, typically via backflushing (based on reporting a finished quantity) but also via reporting actual usage. For example, reporting actual usage of batch numbers may be critical. Figure 11.1 illustrates these variations of supplied material in terms of three delivery options (labeled 1 thru 3) and three options for usage reporting (labeled A thru C).

The figure includes a fourth option for usage reporting which also applies to the other three options, where you can adjust the actual usage of supplied material when needed. In a typical scenario, you manually create an additional picking list journal to identify the adjustments. A previous chapter explained the significance of a picking list journal (Section 9.8).

[1] Subcontracted production of a "turnkey" item does not require supplied material, and is typically coordinated via a purchase order rather than a subcontracted production order.

Figure 11.1 Variations of Supplied Material

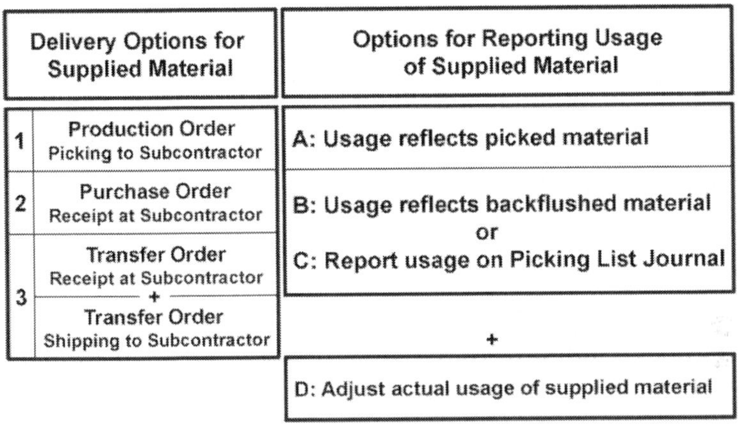

Case 42: Identify BOM Components provided by the Subcontractor
A food products manufacturer found it helpful to define formula information that included material provided by the co-packer. These are sometimes called reference ingredients. In this way, the food engineers could specify the exact recipe information with all ingredients. The theoretical usage (of reference ingredients) could be calculated for each production order, which helped reconcile a co-packer's claims about actual usage. Other benefits included a comparative cost calculation with all ingredients included, and the calculated requirements (for the reference ingredients) helped in negotiating agreements with suppliers.

11.2 Variations of Receiving a Finished Quantity for Subcontracted Production

The variations in subcontracted production are especially apparent in the options for receiving and handling a finished quantity. In addition to the previously-described alternatives for reporting a finished quantity (Section 10.6), a new option is available based on receiving the purchase order for the subcontracted service. Figure 11.2 illustrates these two basic options for receiving a finished quantity for subcontracted production. They are labeled (1) receive the purchase order for a subcontracted service and (2) receive the subcontracted production order.

Figure 11.2 Variations of Receiving a Finished Quantity

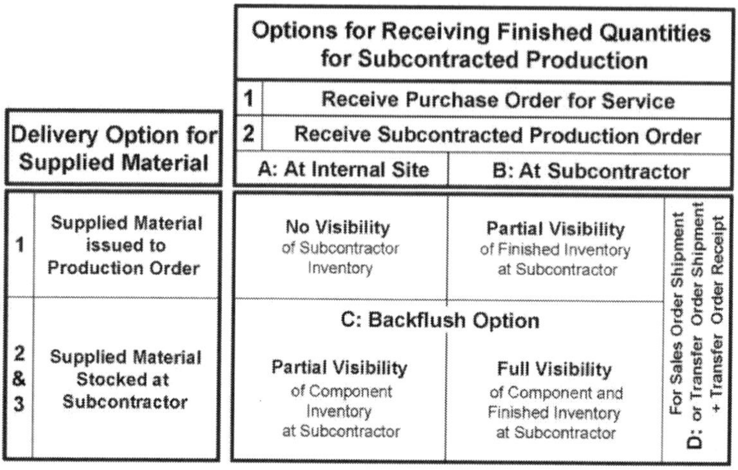

The figure also illustrates several related options for the finished quantity. It can be received at (A) an internal site or (B) at the subcontractor site, and it can (C) trigger backflushing of supplied material stocked at the subcontractor site. When received at the subcontractor site, the handling options include (D) stocking the inventory for subsequent sales order shipments or transferring the inventory to another site (such as an internal warehouse).

Visibility of Inventory at Subcontractor Site A basic issue in subcontracted production concerns the visibility of inventory at the subcontractor site and the in-transit inventory. Figure 11.2 summarizes the three major variations of inventory visibility at the subcontractor site—consisting of no visibility, partial visibility and full visibility. The use of transfer orders for supplied material and finished quantities provide additional visibility of in-transit inventory.

11.3 Key Constructs for Subcontracted Production

Subcontracted production and internal production share many similarities in the use of basic constructs like production orders and picking list journals. However, subcontracted production involves significant differences and several variations. In particular, the dual constructs of a production order and its related purchase order (for the subcontracted service) can be received separately, or a single purchase order receipt can be employed for updating both orders.

Key Constructs Related to a Production Order Previous chapters covered the significance of a production order and its picking list journal (Section 9.8), the warehouse source of components (Section 9.), the alternatives for reporting production order receipts (Section 10.6), and production inspection of a finished quantity (Section 10.7). The life cycles and reversing transactions were also explained for production order picking (Sections 9.4 and 9.5) and receiving (Sections 10.3 and 10.4).

Other Warehouse-Related Transactions for Subcontracted Production Subcontracted production sometimes involves transfer order shipments of supplied material (Chapter 7) or transfer order receipts of finished quantities (Chapter 8), purchase order receipts of supplied material delivered to the subcontractor location (Chapter 5), and/or sales order shipments from the subcontractor site (Chapter 6).

Simple Inventory Transactions A simple inventory transaction is typically employed for reporting transactions occurring at the subcontractor site. The previous point summarized these transactions.

Receive a Purchase Order for the Subcontracted Service The dual constructs of a production order and its related purchase order can be received separately, as illustrated in Case 46. Alternatively, a single receipt transaction (for the purchase order) can update both orders, as illustrated in Case 47.

The single receipt transaction triggers several automatic steps based on setup information. It will (1) automatically generate and post a route card journal for the outside operation. The journal line inherits a "good quantity" (from the receipt) and the reported-as-finished flag. This acts as a trigger to (2) automatically update the finished quantity for the related production order, which also acts as a trigger to (3) automatically backflush the component representing the subcontracted service, and possibly backflush the supplied material stocked at the subcontractor site. A complete explanation of the setup information falls outside the book's scope.[2]

11.4 Case Studies for Subcontracted Production

Case studies can be used to illustrate the variations of subcontracted production. For example, the simplest scenario involves production order picking and receiving with no visibility of inventory at the subcontractor or in transit (Case 43). Another scenario involves complete visibility of this inventory (Case 44).

---

[2] Further explanation of the setup information for subcontracted production is provided in the 2016 Edition of the two companion books titled Supply Chain Management and Process Manufacturing.

Case 43: Subcontracted Production with No Visibility

A manufacturing company produced several products at nearby subcontractors. For a given production order, a kit of supplied material was picked and sent to the subcontractor, and the finished quantity was received at the originating warehouse. The subcontractor provided a quick turnaround for each production order, thereby minimizing the need for visibility of subcontractor inventory. The typical business process is summarized in Figure 11.3 and described below.

Figure 11.3 Subcontracted Production with No Visibility

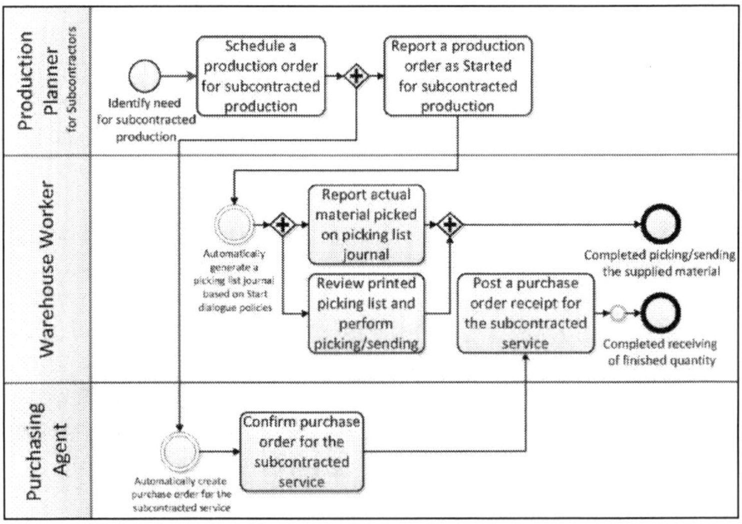

- *Overview.* Scheduling a production order automatically created a purchase order for the subcontracted service which was confirmed by the purchasing agent. The production planner reported the production order as Started to automatically generate and print a picking list journal for the supplied material. The warehouse worker picked and sent the supplied material to the subcontractor. When a finished quantity was received from the subcontractor, the warehouse worker used a simple inventory transaction to post the product receipt for the subcontracted service, which automatically updated the finished quantity for the production order.

- *Schedule a Production Order for Subcontracted Production.* After the production planner scheduled a production order (typically by firming planned orders), the corresponding purchase order for the subcontracted service was automatically created.

- *Report a Production Order as Started for Subcontracted Production.* The production planner reported a production order as Started in order to automatically generate and print the picking list for supplied material. The printed version reflected the "delivery note" format of a picking list, which identifies the delivery address of the subcontractor.

- *Report actual material picked on Picking List Journal.* The warehouse worker reported actual material picked by entering data on the picking list journal, and then physically delivered the components to shipping.

- *Review printed picking list and perform picking/sending.* The warehouse worker reviewed the printed version of the picking list journal as a guide for performing picking activities. The printed version reflected a "delivery note" format with the vendor's address. After the warehouse worker picked and delivered the components to shipping, the shipping clerk assisted in sending the kit of supplied material to the subcontractor. A copy of the picking list in "delivery note" format was included.

- *Confirm a Purchase Order for a Subcontracted Service.* The purchasing agent confirmed the automatically-generated purchase order, which enabled subsequent receiving steps.

- *Post a Purchase Order Receipt for a Subcontracted Service.* When a finished quantity was received from the subcontractor, a warehouse worker or receiving clerk used a simple inventory transaction to post the product receipt for the subcontracted service.

- *Additional Steps.* Several additional steps were often required that are not shown in Figure 11.3, as illustrated by the following additional points.

- *View Current Status of Subtracted Work.* The Subcontractor Work form displays production orders with a linked purchase order for any buy-to-order component. The buy-to-order component represents a subcontracted service in scenarios with subcontracted production. The form displays information about purchase order status, and can be used to update the production order status via the start task and report-as-finished task.

- *Update Production Order status to Reported as Finished.* If needed, the production planner updated order status by reporting a zero quantity on the Report as Finished form.

- *Adjust actual usage of Supplied Material.* Based on information provided by the subcontractor, the production planner sometimes needed to adjust actual material usage relative to the material picked and sent to the subcontractor. The production planner manually created a picking list journal to identify the adjustments and then posted it.

Case 44: Subcontracted Production with Full Visibility

A manufacturing company produced several products at subcontractors located in other states and countries. The supplied material was transferred and stocked at each subcontractor, and the finished quantities were reported prior to transferring the goods to an internal warehouse. This approach provided full visibility of inventory at the subcontractor site and in transit, and also modeled the associated transportation time. Figure 11.4 illustrates the bill of material information and the warehouse-related transactions.

Figure 11.4 Subcontracted Production with Full Visibility

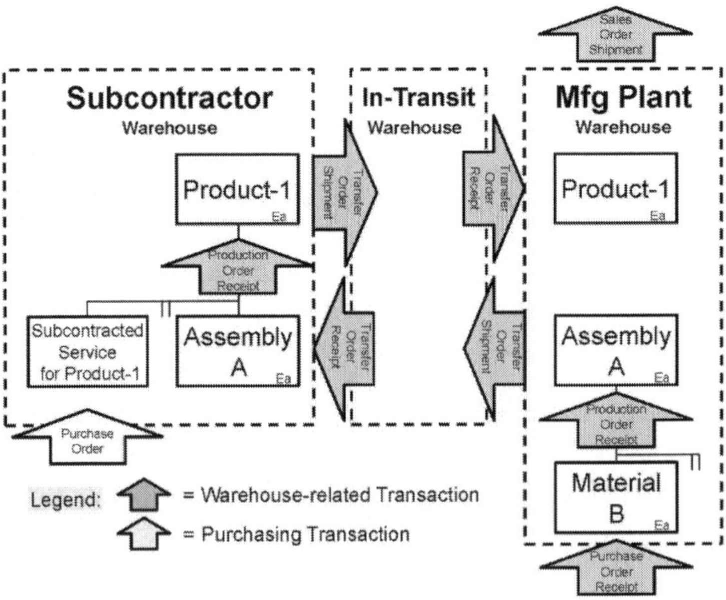

Case 45: Subcontracted Production without Routing Data A manufacturing company employed subcontractors to produce several different products, and wanted to model subcontracted production without routing data. The solution approach involved a customization so that the purchase order due date for the subcontracted service automatically aligned with the due date of the production order for the parent item. As the starting point for the customization, they identified the component requirement (for the subcontracted service) occurring at the "end" of production. Using the linkage between automatically-generated purchase order (for the subcontracted service) and the production order, the customization correctly aligned the purchase order due date.

Case 46: Separate Receipt Transactions for Reporting Subcontracted Production A manufacturing company employed subcontractors to produce several different products, which involved the dual constructs of a purchase order (for the subcontracted service) and the production order. The dual constructs required two separate receipt transactions about the purchase order (to indicate what they would pay for) and the production order (to indicate the good and trashed quantity, and to trigger backflushing of supplied components). The two quantities were frequently different.

Case 47: Single Receipt Transaction for Reporting Subcontracted Production A manufacturing company employed subcontractors to produce several different products, which involved the dual constructs of a purchase order (for the subcontracted service) and the production order. They used a single purchase order receipt transaction for the subcontracted service to also update the related production order. It resulted in a reported-as-finished quantity for the subcontracted production order, and this triggered backflushing of the supplied material.

Case 48: Multiple Subcontractors Build Same Item A manufacturing company employed multiple subcontractors to produce the same item, where the supplied components were stocked at each subcontractor. Each subcontractor's location was identified as a unique AX site, and site-specific BOM versions for a parent item defined the supplied components for each subcontractor. A subcontracted service item was defined for each parent item. Since the company was using standard costs, different site-specific standard costs were assigned to the subcontracted service item and to the supplied components. This approach also entailed the calculation of site-specific standard costs for the parent item.

Case 49: Purchase Orders Delivered to a Subcontractor Warehouse
As part of supporting their subcontractors, a manufacturer sometimes had vendors deliver the purchased items (representing the supplied material) to the subcontractor warehouse. The actual receipt of a purchase order at the subcontractor was entered into AX (by a coordinator role) as a simple inventory transaction.

Case 50: Sales Order Shipments from a Subcontractor Warehouse
A manufacturing company stocked an item's finished quantity at the subcontractor warehouse, and entered sales orders for shipment from the subcontractor warehouse. In order to communicate the need for sales order shipments from the subcontractor warehouses, the DRP coordinator generated the sales order picking lists and e-mailed a copy to the relevant contact person. The contact person sent a return e-mail after completing the requested shipments, and the DRP coordinator simply posted each completed picking list and the related sales order packing slip.

11.5 Executive Summary

Subcontracted production and internal production share many similarities. However, there are many variations of subcontracted production scenarios which involve significant differences about inventory visibility and multisite coordination, and supply chain coordination via the dual constructs of a production order and a corresponding purchase order. The chapter explained the variations associated with supplied material and finished quantities, and highlighted the key constructs.

Several case studies illustrated the variations. These included BOM components provided by the subcontractor (Case 42), subcontracted production with no visibility (Case 43) and with full visibility of inventory (Case 44), the need for routing data (Case 45), reporting subcontracted production with separate receipt transactions (Case 46) and with a single receipt transaction (Case 47), multiple subcontractors building the same item (Case 48), purchase orders delivered to a subcontractor warehouse (Case 49) and sales order shipments from a subcontractor warehouse (Case 50).

Chapter 12

Basics of Transportation

Several basic aspects of transportation apply to sales orders, transfer orders and purchase orders regardless of the warehouse management approach. Examples include the transportation times and the significance of delivery dates used in master scheduling logic, and the charges associated with freight. Several case studies can be used to illustrate these basics of transportation. These considerations are reflected in the following sections with the chapter.

1. Transportation Basics for Sales Orders
2. Transportation Basics for Transfer Orders
3. Transportation Basics for Purchase Orders
4. Carrier Interface Information for Sales Order Shipments

An additional aspect of transportation only applies to the Basic Inventory approach to sales order shipments, where standard AX can be integrated with carrier interface information. However, this approach to carrier interface information will not be included in future AX versions. It is included here for the sake of completeness.

12.1 Transportation Basics for Sales Orders

The transportation basics include sales order dates for shipment and delivery, the transportation time to a customer, the sales order promise dates, the need for expediting a sales order shipment, the sales order charges for freight/handling, and shipping documents such as a bill of lading.

Sales Order Dates for Shipment and Delivery A sales order header has a requested ship date and a requested delivery date, where the difference represents the transportation time (termed transport days) between the ship-from warehouse and the delivery address. It also has a confirmed ship date and confirmed receipt date. The assignments of these dates are affected by the delivery date control policy assigned to the sales order header, which can enforce basic rules about applicable calendars (for the ship-from warehouse, the customer, and the mode of delivery), the expected transportation time to the customer address, and order entry deadlines.

These dates within the sales order header can be inherited by the sales lines, and changes in the header dates can optionally update information for the sales lines. However, the dates for a line item are also subject to the delivery date control policy for the line item (such as ATP logic). This policy can enforce the above-mentioned rules. It is inherited from the item and can be overridden. The confirmed ship date for a sales line (if specified) will drive picking/shipping activities and master scheduling logic, otherwise the requested ship date will be used.

Transportation Time to a Customer The number of days for expected transportation time can be specified for different combinations of the ship-from warehouse, the delivery address characteristics (such as the country, state, county, or ZIP code), and the mode of delivery (such as air or truck). The mode of delivery and address can be assigned to the sales order header and inherited by the line items, or specified for each line item if needed.

A calendar can be assigned to various modes of delivery for the ship-from warehouse, where the calendar determines the working days when items can be transported. For example, a truck route may only occur on Thursdays.

The mode of delivery can be inherited from a sales agreement. For example, it can be inherited by releasing a sales order from a sales agreement or by manually creating a sales order linked to a sales agreement.

Sales Order Promise Dates for Shipment and Delivery The delivery date control policy for a sales order line can enforce several basic rules related to transportation when making delivery promises. These rules include the calendar of working days at the ship-from warehouse and at the customer receiving point, the calendar assigned to the mode of delivery, the transportation time to the customer, and the sales lead time for preparing items for shipment. These rules apply to the automatic assignment of dates when initially entering a sales order header or line, and when manually entering a date. A policy of "none" means that the basic rules will be ignored so that promise dates and transportation considerations can be unrealistic.

Need for Expediting a Sales Order Shipment The need for expediting can be identified on a sales order header and its line items, such as the expedited shipment flag and an expedite code. These can be used for generating sales order picking lists, as described in a previous chapter (Section 6.7).

Sales Order Charges for Freight/Handling The charges related to freight and handling can be manually assigned to a sales order, either as order-level charges or line item charges or both. A user-defined Charges Code identifies each type of charge and its related ledger account. The charges can be expressed as a fixed amount, an amount per piece, or a percentage of value. A fixed amount (for an order-level charge) needs to be allocated to the lines.

Some sales environments involve predefined agreements about charges, such as freight or handling charges for selected items or customers. An agreement about charges can be embedded in the sales price trade agreement information, or they can be specified separately as *auto charges*. These auto charges can be applied to an entire sales order or to individual line items, and expressed as a fixed amount, an amount per piece, or a percentage of value.

- *Order-Level Charges*. Charge agreements related to the entire sales order can be defined for a single customer, all customers or a group of customers, (identified by the *Customer Charges Group* assigned to relevant customers). Examples of an order-level charge include order preparation costs for selected customers.

- *Line Item Charges*. Charge agreements related to the sales order line item can be defined by customer and item, such as charges for a single item, all items, or a group of items (identified by the Item Charges group assigned to relevant salable items).[1] Examples of a line item charge include a setup fee for producing selected items for a customer.

Bill of Lading and Other Shipping Documents A bill of lading represents one of several shipping documents that may be needed for a sales order shipment. The capabilities for supporting these various documents—especially the options for printing standard documents—differ between the basic and advanced approaches to warehouse management. The creation and use of a bill of lading provides an illustrative example.

[1] Two policies (embedded within the A/R parameters) indicate whether the system recognizes auto charges for the entire order and for line items.

- *Bill of Lading Using the Basic Approach.* A bill of lading can be automatically created by posting a sales order packing list or invoice. Some information pertaining to the system-assigned bill of lading identifier is automatically updated, such as the customer, sales order number, delivery address, and the shipped items and quantities. The bill of lading information reflects the item number and description. Other bill of lading information must be manually maintained, including each package type (such as carton), quantity and weight. Use the bill of lading form for data maintenance and document printing. A bill of lading can be manually created to support other types of shipments (such as office furniture), or to support a master bill of lading (such as shipments to a freight forwarder). After creating a bill of lading identifier, for example, you explicitly designate it as a master bill of lading and also assign the identifier to individual bills of lading associated with it.

- *Bill of Lading Using the Advanced Approach.* A bill of lading can be automatically created for a sales order shipment or a transfer order shipment, either before or after confirming the outbound shipment. The bill of lading format reflects information about the National Motor Freight Code (NMFC) assigned to each product (rather than the item number and description).

Case 51: Identify Truck Routes for Regional Customer Deliveries A manufacturing/distribution company employed internal trucks for making regional customer deliveries, and identified the four variations of truck routes as different modes of delivery. For example, one truck route applied to northern customer locations with M-W-F deliveries and another truck route applied to the southern locations with T-R-S deliveries. The calendar assigned to each mode of delivery identified these periodic deliveries. A mode of delivery (aka truck route) was also assigned to each customer so that it would be inherited by sales orders.

Case 52: Charges for Faster-than-Normal Delivery on Sales Orders A distribution company employed several types of rules-based pricing when selling their products to retailers. The approaches included a surcharge for a small order and discounts for a large order (based on total order value), as well as discount percentages and supplementary items based on total quantity ordered for different items within a product line. A miscellaneous charge was added to items requiring faster-than-normal delivery lead time.

Case 53: Using the Basic Inventory Approach and Still Use Advanced Transportation Capabilities The capabilities within advanced transportation management were deemed critical for a company intending to use the basic approach to warehouse management. They were considering the option proposed in a blog about "using transportation management without the new warehouse management module." The proposed option employed items that were not WMS-enabled, but were still assigned the policy to "use transportation management processes." This approach would allow them to use the Load Planning Workbench to create a load for sales orders and then use the rating and routing capabilities.

Case 54: Print an MSDS Document to Accompany a Sales Order Shipment A manufacturing company produced several items that required an MSDS (Material Safety Data Sheet) document. This had several impacts. For example, when entering a sales order line for an item designated as hazardous material, an infolog warning can be displayed about sending the latest active MSDS document to the customer. This infolog warning occurs when the customer has not yet received the item's MSDS document, or when a newer version (defined by the document's effective date) needs to be sent. At the time of shipping, the shipping clerk would print the relevant MSDS documents when posting the packing list for the sales order. This transaction was prevented when a document's expiry date has been exceeded. A subsequent chapter about quality management provides further explanation of MSDS documents (Section 26.9).

12.2 Transportation Basics for Transfer Orders

The transportation basics include transfer order dates for shipment and delivery, the transportation time between warehouses, and the transfer order promise dates.

Transfer Order Dates for Shipment and Delivery The transfer order header specifies a shipment date and receipt date, along with the ship-from and ship-to site/warehouses and a mode of delivery such as air or truck. The difference between the two dates reflects the expected transportation time (expressed in days) between the two locations.
The assignments of these dates are affected by the delivery date control policy assigned to the transfer order header, which can enforce basic rules such as the working calendar for both warehouses, the calendar for the delivery mode, and the expected transportation time between a pair of warehouses.

These dates and delivery mode within the transfer order header can be inherited by the line items, and changes in the header can optionally update information for the line items. However, the dates for a line item are also subject to the delivery date control policy for the line item (such as ATP logic). This policy can enforce the above-mentioned rules. It is inherited from the item and can be overridden. The ship date for a transfer line will drive picking/shipping activities and master scheduling logic.

Transportation Time Between Warehouses You define the transportation time between a pair of warehouses using the Transport form, and the time can vary by delivery mode.

Transfer Order Promise Dates for Shipment and Delivery The delivery date control policy for a transfer line can enforce several basic rules related to transportation when making delivery promises. These rules include the calendar of working days at the ship-from warehouse and at the ship-to warehouse, the calendar assigned to the mode of delivery, the transportation time between the warehouse, and the sales lead time for preparing items for shipment. These rules apply to the automatic assignment of dates when initially entering a transfer order header or line, and when manually entering a date. A policy of "none" means that the basic rules will be ignored so that promise dates and transportation considerations can be unrealistic.

Case 55: Transportation Constraints about Transfer Orders to/from a Subcontractor An electronics manufacturer located in the United States sent supplied material via truck to its subcontractor in Mexico, and the completed subassembly was sent back via truck to its US location. The weekly truck schedules to and from Mexico were identified as two different modes of delivery, and the associated calendars identified which days the truck departed and an estimated transportation time (expressed in days). The contents of a given truck were identified as line items on a transfer order. These transportation constraints were used by master scheduling logic to suggest appropriate dates and quantities for planned transfer orders and subcontracted production orders, and coordinate the supply chain accordingly. This approach provided full visibility of inventory at the subcontractor location and in transit.

Case 56: Coordinate Transportation for Asian Subcontractors The office furniture products for a US distribution company were produced by a subcontractor in Taiwan using supplied material from vendors located in nearby countries, and the finished goods were shipped monthly from Taiwan in a container. A transfer order represented each container and the line items identified its contents. Its shipment and delivery dates reflected the 4-week transportation time to the US distribution center. The purchase orders for supplied material were delivered to the Taiwan subcontractor. Each subcontracted production order reflected the monthly shipment intervals, and finished quantities were received at the subcontractor site prior to reporting transfer order shipment. These transportation considerations were used by master scheduling logic to suggest appropriate dates and quantities for planned transfer orders as well as the related orders for subcontracted production and the purchase orders for supplied material.

12.3 Transportation Basics for Purchase Orders

The transportation basics include the significance of a confirmed delivery date, the mode of delivery for a purchase order, and purchase order charges for freight/handling.

Significance of a Confirmed Delivery Date Each purchase order line (and a line within a delivery schedule) has a delivery date and a separate "confirmed" delivery date. The confirmed delivery date is initially blank, and should be updated to reflect actual confirmation from the vendor or the carrier. If specified, the confirmed date will be used for anticipating warehouse receipts and by master scheduling logic—otherwise the delivery date will be used. For example, if the confirmed delivery date reflects a projected delay, master scheduling logic can identify (via futures messages) the impact of the projected delay in meeting a sales order shipment date.

Changing the delivery date within a purchase order header can optionally update the delivery date for every line (with a prompt or without a prompt), as defined by a companywide policy (embedded in the A/P parameters).

Mode of Delivery for a Purchase Order The mode of delivery and address can be assigned to the purchase order header and inherited by the line items, or specified for each line item if needed. A calendar can be assigned to various modes of delivery for the ship-to warehouse, where the calendar determines the working days when items can be transported.

The mode of delivery can be inherited from a purchase agreement. For example, it can be inherited by releasing a purchase order from a purchase agreement, by manually creating a purchase order linked to a purchase agreement, or by firming planned purchase orders with grouping by purchase agreement.

Purchase Order Charges for Freight/Handling The charges related to freight and handling can be manually assigned to a purchase order, either as order-level charges or line item charges or both. A user-defined Charges Code identifies each type of charge and its related ledger account. The charges can be expressed as a fixed amount, an amount per piece, or a percentage of value. A fixed amount (for an order-level charge) needs to be allocated to the lines.

Some purchase environments involve predefined agreements about charges, such as handling or freight charges for selected items or vendors. These charges can be embedded in the purchase price trade agreement information, or they can be specified separately as *auto charges*. These auto charges can be applied to an

entire purchase order or to individual line items, and expressed as a fixed amount, an amount per piece,
or a percentage of value.

- *Order-Level Charges.* Charge agreements related to the entire purchase order can be defined for a single vendor, all vendors or a group of vendors (identified by the *Vendor Charges Group* assigned to relevant vendors). Examples of an order-level charge include order preparation costs for selected vendors.

- *Line Item Charges.* Charges related to the purchase order line item can be defined by vendor and item, such as charges for a single item, all items, or a group of items (identified by the Item Charges Group assigned to relevant purchased items). Examples of a line item charge include a setup fee for purchasing selected items from a vendor.

Case 57: Freight Charges for a Purchase Order and its Invoice At a manufacturing company, the purchasing agent manually assigned the expected freight charges on a purchase order header. The charges consist of a freight charge code and an expected amount (expressed as a fixed amount) which was allocated to the purchase order lines. When entering a vendor's invoice for the purchase order, the accounts payable clerk reviewed the expected freight charges and entered the actual fright charges if different. The accounts payable clerk reviewed a comparison of actual versus expected freight charges, which highlighted discrepancies exceeding a predefined tolerance. The clerk needed to approve a vendor's invoice when a charges discrepancy exceeded the predefined tolerance.

12.4 Carrier Interface Information for Sales Order Shipments

Some scenarios using AX 2012 R3 and the Basic Inventory Approach need integration with shipping carrier software.[2] Standard AX functionality only supports this integration for sales order shipments. When you post a sales order packing slip, information about the shipment can be automatically transferred to the shipping carrier software—such as Kewill ClipperShip, UPS WorldShip, and FedEx Ship Manager—and the resulting information about freight charges and tracking numbers can be transferred back to the sales order. This helps eliminate manual entry and improve tracking visibility.

---

[2] This approach to carrier interface information is not supported in the new Dynamics AX. It is included here for the sake of completeness.

The integration with shipping carrier software requires considerable setup information, including the definition of carrier companies, the applicable charge codes, delivery modes and terms of delivery for each shipping carrier, and default shipping carrier information for each customer. A detailed explanation falls outside the book's scope.

12.5 Executive Summary

Several basic aspects of transportation apply to sales orders, transfer orders and purchase orders regardless of the warehouse management approach. Examples include the transportation times and the significance of delivery dates used in master scheduling logic, and the charges associated with freight. These transportation basics reflect key aspects of how a company models and manages its supply chain, especially in terms of the detailed game plans that everybody is working to. The additional aspects of any transportation management capabilities need to support these detailed game plans or update the details if they change—such as changing a ship date or a delivery date.

Many of the case studies identified issues that apply to basic and advanced approaches to transportation management. These case studies included truck routes for regional customer deliveries (Case 51), MSDS documents for sales order shipments (Case 54), transportation constraints about transfer orders to/from a subcontractor (Case 55), coordination of transportation for Asian subcontractors (Case 56), and freight charges for a purchase order and its invoice (Case 57).

Chapter 13

Fundamentals of the Advanced WMS Approach

Several fundamentals of the Advanced WMS approach provide the foundation for explaining business processes in subsequent chapters. These fundamentals include the key setup information, such as the definition of warehouse locations and the item-related policies for warehouse management. They include the significance of license plates and Inventory Status, as well as basic inventory transactions such as moves and adjustments. The fundamentals also include the significance of work orders, and this topic will be covered in the next chapter.

The proper starting point typically involves the key setup information, but this extended explanation is postponed until later in the chapter. These considerations are reflected in the following sections within the chapter.

1. Summary of Warehouse-Related Transactions
2. Significance of License Plates
3. Basic Inventory Transactions
4. Significance of Inventory Status (and Combined Disposition Codes)
5. Define a WMS-Enabled Warehouse and its Locations
6. Item-Related Policies for Warehouse Management

13.1 Summary of Warehouse-Related Transactions

The various types of warehouse transactions provide an organizing focus for explaining the Basic Inventory approach to warehouse management. This chapter covers the basic inventory transactions and subsequent chapters cover order-based transactions. Figure 13.1 summarizes these warehouse-related transactions, and indicates the relevant book section about each business process.

Figure 13.1 Warehouse-Related Transactions

Type of Transaction		Example Process
Basic Inventory Transactions	Inventory Transfer (Movement)	Section 13.3
	Inventory Adjustment - Out	
	Inventory Adjustment - In	
	Quantity Adjustment (Count)	
	Cycle Count	
Quality	Change Inventory Status	
Purchase Order	Purchase Order Arrival	Section 15.1
	Purchase Order Return	Section 5.10
Sales Order	Sales Order Picking/Shipping	Section 16.1
	RMA Arrival	
Transfer Order	Transfer Order Picking/Shipping	Section 17.1
	Transfer Order Arrival	Section 18.1
Production Order	Production Order Picking	Section 19.2
	Production Order Receiving	Section 20.1

Other types of inventory transactions are not considered because of book length considerations. Examples include transactions for projects and service orders, retail-specific transactions related to stores, and kanban transactions for lean manufacturing.

13.2 Significance of License Plates

A license plate can represent many different physical entities or a logical entity. The significance of a license plate is easiest to conceptualize in terms of a physical pallet, where a quantity of the same item has been placed on the pallet, and a license plate identifier has been assigned to the pallet. The license plate ID provides a convenient way to view inventory balances by pallet, and to report receipts, movement and picking. This is especially helpful for serialized or batch-controlled items, where you have placed multiple batch numbers or serial numbers on the physical pallet. The item often has a standard quantity per physical pallet, which provides the basis for a suggested number of pallets when receiving a large quantity. However, you can place a larger or smaller quantity on a pallet. In some cases, you may place multiple items on a physical pallet, where each item has a separate license plate identifier and you assign them to a parent license plate. These separate identifiers are termed nested license plates when assigned to a parent license plate.

The use of license plates only applies to warehouse locations that are license plate controlled, or LP-controlled for short. Otherwise the license plate IDs are not tracked or displayed from an end-user perspective, even though they are sometimes used for internal system purposes. Minimal use of license plate IDs represents one of the strategic options for warehouse described at the beginning of the book (Section 2.6). However, this explanation assumes that license plates and LP-controlled locations will be used, and that selected locations will not be LP-controlled.

UM Considerations Related to the License Plate for an Item An item typically has a standard quantity per physical pallet. When the typical quantity is greater than one, you must define the UM conversion between the two units of measure, such as the number of pieces per pallet. Some items involve additional UM considerations, such as pieces per box and boxes per pallet, so that multiple UM conversions must be defined for the item.

These UM considerations must also be reflected in the Unit Sequence Group assigned to the item, which defines the applicable UM codes for warehouse management purposes. For example, the UM code corresponding to a physical pallet can be designated as the default value for recording receipts and transfers via mobile devices, although you can override this suggested UM when recording the transaction. The UM code corresponding to less than a pallet quantity can be designated for "license plate grouping", which avoids a suggested pallet for every one of the units. As a key impact, the Unit Sequence Group information provides the basis for a suggested number of pallets when reporting receipts via the mobile device, including the suggested use of a single pallet when the number of pieces reflects a less-than-pallet quantity. You typically define several Unit Sequence Groups reflecting the common UM considerations related to your products, and then assign the applicable group to each item requiring mobile device transactions. A subsequent section provides further explanation of these UM considerations (Section 13.6).

Applicable Transactions for Assignment of a License Plate ID A license plate identifier is typically assigned upon receipt, such as a purchase order receipt, production order receipt or an inventory adjustment in. However, it can be assigned for other transactions, such as using a different target pallet when picking for a sales order or moving material. The label for the license plate can then be affixed to the physical pallet.

Assignment of a License Plate ID When Using Mobile Devices The identifier can be assigned manually or automatically when using mobile devices, as defined by a policy within the Mobile Device Menu Item for each applicable transaction.

- *Manual Assignment.* Some scenarios employ permanently-affixed identifiers on the physical pallets. Other scenarios employ a preprinted roll of labels (with sequential identifiers) that can be affixed to the physical pallet and scanned. In either case, when first recorded on a mobile device transaction, the identifier is automatically created within the system.

- *Automatic Assignment.* Automatic assignment reflects five different segments of information, but only three segments are controlled by user settings. The five segments are described below, and the combination of segments results in a unique identifier of a license plate.

  1. Automatic prefix of 00. This prefix represents an internal system assignment.

  2. Optional value for a GS1 number. This value (defined in the Warehouse Parameters form) represents a companywide value. It can be null, or one or more numbers (or characters).

  3. Required value for the license plate tracking type. This value (defined in the Unit Sequence Group assigned to an item) must be numeric, and consists of one or more digits. It is feasible to impute significance into the numeric number.

  4. Required number sequence code for license plates. The number sequence code for license plates (defined in the Warehouse Parameters form) should simply provide a numeric counter, with sufficient digits to handle the expected number of license plates.

  5. Automatic suffix of a single check digit. This check digit represents an internal system assignment.

  An example identifier of 00981231 reflects the automatic assignment of values for each of the five segments, consisting of 00, 9, 8, 123 and 1.

The License Plate form displays the license plate IDs created by manual or automatic assignment during mobile device transactions. It also supports manual creation of a license plate ID.

Definition of a Parent License Plate and its Nested License Plates In some cases, multiple items may be placed on a physical pallet, where each item has a separate license plate identifier and you assign them to a parent license plate. These separate identifiers are termed nested license plates when assigned to a parent license plate. The information about nested license plates can be manually defined or automatically created, as described below.

- *Manual Definition of Nested License Plates.* A mobile device must be used to define a parent license plate and assign one or more nested license plates. You can create one or more levels of nested license plates. In addition, a mobile device must be used to break down a parent license plate. These transactions cannot be performed via screen. Hence, you must define two Mobile Device Menu Items (one to build and one to breakdown the parent license plate) that reflect a mode of an indirect and the relevant activity code. An additional menu item can provide an inquiry about the contents of a license plate.

- *Automatic Definition of Nested License Plates via ASN information.* The ASN information provided by a vendor can automatically create license plate identifiers and the definition of nested license plate information. The resulting information can then be used for reporting purchase order receipts against the license plates.

Inquiries about License Plates The License Plate form displays the automatic- and manually-assigned identifiers, and supports manual creation of an identifier. It also displays the associated parent license plate when applicable. You can also define a mobile device menu item that provides an inquiry about the contents of a license plate.

13.3 Basic Inventory Transactions

The basic inventory transactions include transfers, adjustments and cycle counts. These basic transactions and some related inquiries/analyses are summarized in Figure 13.2, which provides an organizing focus for further explanation. The grey shading indicates mobile device transactions.

Figure 13.2 Summary of Basic Inventory Transactions

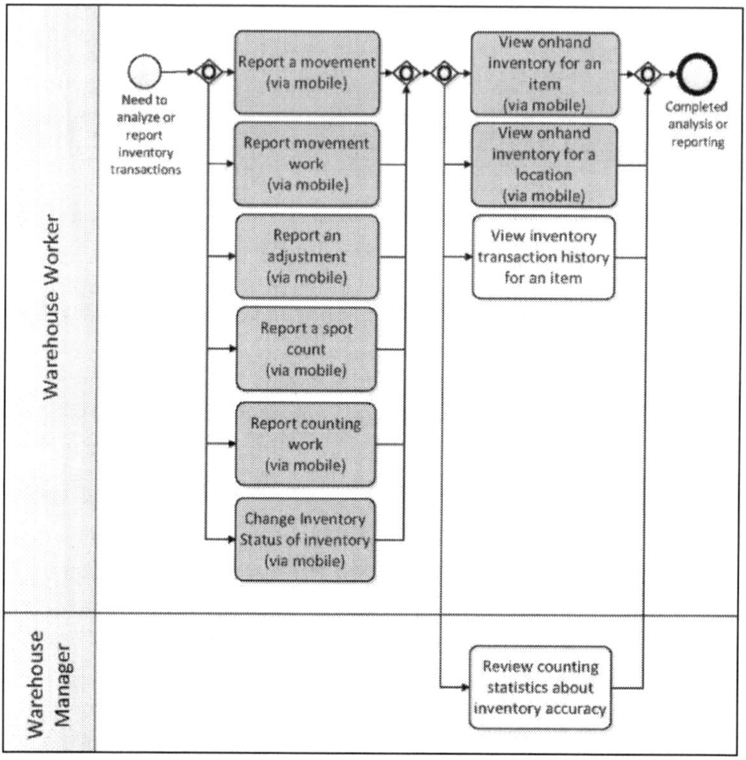

Report a Movement via Mobile Device On the mobile device, the starting point for reporting a move can be a selected license plate ID or a location, and the quantity can reflect a selected unit of measure such as a pallet or each. The resulting transactions have a single Word ID for the pick and put work. The key setup information includes the Mobile Device Menu Item (with a Work Creation Process of *Movement*) and a Work Template (for a Work Order Type of Inventory Movement). The resulting inventory transactions include the pick/put work transactions.

Report Movement Work via Mobile Device Movement work can be automatically created when viewing an inquiry about the inventory within a location, where you access the Create Inventory Movement Work form. The movement work can then be reported via mobile device transactions. The key setup information includes the Mobile Device Menu Item (that uses exist working work for a work order type of *Inventory Movement*) and same Work Template described above. Movement work can also be created using other approaches.

Report an Inventory Adjustment via Mobile Device On the mobile device, you identify a location as the starting point for reporting an inventory adjustment and then provide an additional entry about the selected license plate ID or item. The quantity can reflect a selected unit of measure such as a pallet or each.. You also select the option to report an incremental quantity (via the Adjust In or Adjust Out options) or an updated quantity (via the Count option). The key setup information only involves a Mobile Device Menu Item (with a Work Creation Process for *Adjustment In* or *Adjustment Out*). It does not really matter, because you can select the option when reporting the transaction on the mobile device. The resulting inventory transaction is identified as a count, and does not involve work transactions. Cycle count discrepancies need to be resolved as described in a subsequent chapter (Section 22.4).

Report a Spot Count (aka Quantity Adjustment) via Mobile Device On the mobile device, you identify a location as the starting point for reporting a spot count, and then provide an additional entry about the selected license plate ID or item. The quantity reflects the inventory unit of measure for the item (such as each). The key setup information only involves a Mobile Device Menu Item (with a Work Creation Process for *Spot Cycle Counting*). The resulting inventory transaction is identified as a count, and does not involve work transactions. Cycle count discrepancies need to be resolved as described in a subsequent chapter (Section 22.4).

Report Counting Work via Mobile Device Cycle count work must be created prior to reporting the work via mobile device. The Advanced WMS approach provides three options for creating cycle count work, and cycle count discrepancies may occur in each option. These options involve extended explanations described in a separate chapter (Chapter 22), which also describes how to report counting work via the mobile device.

Change Inventory Status of Inventory via Mobile Device On the mobile device, you identify a license plate ID (or the location and item) in order to display the existing status and select the new status. The status change applies to the entire quantity. The key setup information only involves a Mobile Device Menu Item (with a Work Creation Process for *Quarantine*).

Other Approaches for Reporting the Basic Inventory Transactions The other approaches include the previously-described client transactions for the Basic Inventory approach (Section 3.2). These include the transfer journal, the inventory adjustment journal, quantity adjustments, and the counting journal. They also include the client transaction for changing Inventory Status.

View On Hand Inventory for an Item On the mobile device, you can view the current inventory balance for an selected item. The key setup information only involves a Mobile Device Menu Item for an "indirect" mode and a selected Activity Code of an *Item Inquiry*.

View On Hand Inventory for a Location On the mobile device, you can view the current inventory balance for an selected location. The key setup information only involves a Mobile Device Menu Item for an "indirect" mode and a selected Activity Code of a *Location Inquiry*.

View Inventory Transaction History for an Item You can view standardized inquiries about inventory by item or location, and also view inventory transaction history. When viewing transaction history, a transaction filter can limit the displayed information to "work only" transactions or "omit work" transactions, or you can view "display all" transactions. The next chapter provides further explanation about the impact of work orders on inventory transaction history (Section 14.6).

View Counting Statistics about Inventory Accuracy The warehouse manager can view the Counting Statistics report about the inventory accuracy percentage over a specified date range. The percentage reflects the number of cycle count transactions with a discrepancy divided by the total number of cycle count transactions. The selection criteria for the report typically specify a date range (about counting dates) and summarize the inventory accuracy information by warehouse.

13.4 Significance of Inventory Status (and the Combined Disposition Code)

The significance of Inventory Status was described in a previous chapter (Chapter 4), so this section focuses on the unique aspects of Inventory Status within the Advanced WMS approach to warehouse management. The unique aspects include the following.

- *Inventory Status in the Reservation Hierarchy.* Inventory Status is typically placed above the location within a Reservation Hierarchy.

- *Inventory Status Within the Combined Disposition Code* The advanced approach supports the selection of a "combined disposition code" when reporting purchase order arrival or RMA arrival via mobile device transactions. It is actually termed "disposition code", but I find that confusing.[1] A "combined disposition code" reflects the combination of one value for Inventory Status and one RMA disposition code. However, you can simply define just the corresponding Inventory Status. For example, a combined code of *Needs-Rework* could reflect the Inventory Status value for *Needs-Rework*. An additional combined code would be needed for an Inventory Status of *Return-To-Vendor*. Case 58 illustrates the use of a combined disposition code during purchase order arrival.

The assignment of a combined disposition code can also be used for directed putaway, such as placing *Needs-Rework* material at the desired location for rework. You define the relevant value for the combined disposition code as part of the location directive for the work order types about purchase orders and return orders.

Case 58: Receiving Clerk Assigns Inventory Status During Purchase Order Arrival

The warehouse manager and quality manager at a manufacturing company were considering options for identifying a quality problem at the time of purchase order arrival, where a receiving clerk can immediately report a problem. One approach involved the user-defined values for Inventory Status, with possible values of *Good*, *To-Be-Scrapped*, *Return-to-Vendor*, *Needs-Rework* and *Needs-Inspection*. The default value for inventory status was always identified as *Good* on purchase order lines.

If receiving clerks noticed a quality problem, they would override the Inventory Status when reporting arrival via a mobile device transaction. More specifically, they would select a value of the "combined disposition code" corresponding to the Inventory Status of *Needs-Inspection*. The managers prepared a diagram of the proposed business process shown in Figure 13.3, and grey shading indicates the mobile device transactions. In order to simplify the diagram, it does not include a putaway transaction from the receiving location. They also prepared a similar diagram for the Basic Inventory approach for comparison purposes (Case 14).

[1] As a confusing issue, the same form name of "Disposition Codes" is used for two different forms. You define the RMA disposition codes on the Disposition Codes form (as part of the sales and marketing setup information for sales order returns), and you define the "combined disposition code" on the Disposition Codes form (as part of warehouse management setup information for mobile devices). This "combined disposition code" can also be displayed on the mobile device transactions for purchase order arrivals and RMA arrivals, and it is labeled just "disposition code".

Figure 13.3 Assign Inventory Status During Purchase Order Arrival Using the Advanced WMS Approach

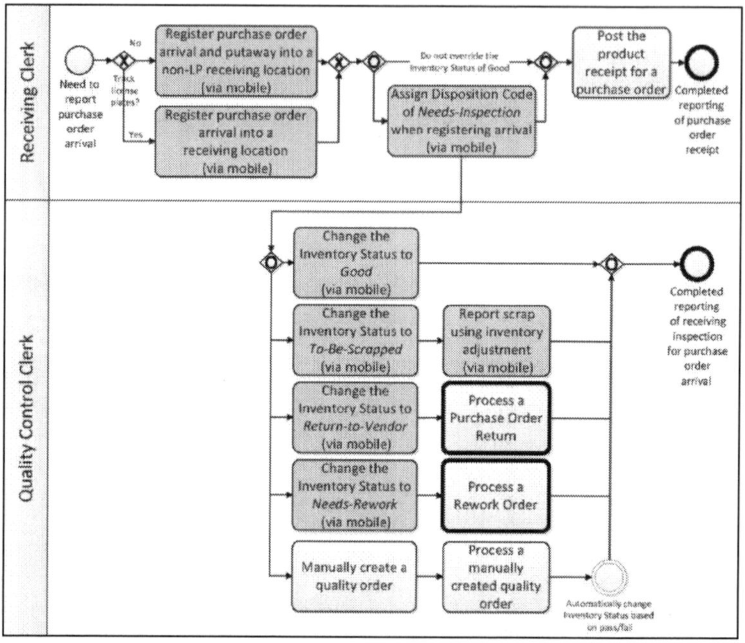

As shown in the figure, the receiving clerk can use the mobile device to "register purchase order arrival and putaway into a non-LP receiving location" in order to minimize use of license plates. Alternatively, when license plates are required, the receiving clerk can "register purchase order arrival into a receiving location" that is license plate controlled. In either case, the receiving clerk can identify a quality problem by selecting the disposition code corresponding to a blocked Inventory Status of *Needs-Inspection.* This results in an entry on the Blocked Inventory form to communicate needed follow-up by a quality control clerk.

Using a mobile device transaction, the quality control clerk can subsequently make a determination by changing the value of Inventory Status to a value of *Good, To-Be-Scrapped, Return-to-Vendor* or *Needs-Rework*. As an additional option, the quality control clerk can manually create and process a quality order. Other roles are typically involved in the additional processing of a purchase order return or a rework order.

As an alternative, the receiving clerks could be responsible for assigning the other values of the Inventory Status. However, the quality manager was reluctant to have receiving clerks report anything more than simply assigning a value of *Needs-Inspection*, and preferred that a quality control clerk make any further determination.

13.5 Define a WMS-Enabled Warehouse and its Locations

Each warehouse has a unique identifier and must be assigned to a site. The warehouse must be enabled for warehouse management by designating the *Use Warehouse Management Processes* policy. This is commonly termed a WMS-enabled warehouse or WMS warehouse for short. The policy works in conjunction with a similar item-related policy for determining whether the Advanced WMS approach will be used, as previously described for the major options for warehouse management (Section 2.1). Other warehouse-related information includes its associated bin locations and their related location profiles, zones and warehouse types.

The analysis of a particular warehouse layout generally starts with the segmentation of various bin locations into similar groups. This segmentation will be reflected in the definition of Location Profiles for each group of similar bin locations, and in the definition of zones and their related bin locations.

Significance of Location Type Location types have a special significance for supporting various capabilities within the Advanced WMS approach. The location types are user-defined, and one location type should be defined for each one of the following purposes. The first two location types (for final shipping and staging) are considered mandatory. The name of each user-defined location type should reflect its purpose.

- *Final Shipping.* This location type supports shipments of sales orders and transfer orders. An example name is Baydoor or Outbound-Dock. You assign a company-wide default for the location type that represents final shipment.

- *Staging.* This location type supports staging of shipments for sales orders and transfer orders. An example name is Stage or Staging. It does not apply to staging material for production. You assign a company-wide default for the location type that represents staging.

- *Pack.* This location type supports manual packing of shipments for sales orders and transfer orders. An example name is Pack or Pack-Station.

- *Picking.* This location type supports picking locations requiring replenishment in order to support sales order picking and shipping. An example name is Pick or Picking. It does not apply to picking raw materials for production orders.

- *Receiving.* This location type supports receiving for purchase orders, transfer orders and customer returns. An example name is Recv or Receiving.

- *Quality.* This location type supports receiving inspection for purchase orders, transfer orders, production orders and customer returns. An example name is Quality or QC or QMS.

- *Production.* This location type supports the production input locations for raw material picking purposes, and the production output locations for reporting finished quantities. An example name is Production or Floorstock.

- *Bulk.* This location type typically applies to general locations within a warehouse, where the locations are not used for any of the above purposes (such as final shipping, receiving and so forth).

- *User.* This location type only has internal significance within AX. The system places inventory into a "user location" whenever a user is in process on the mobile device, thereby eliminating a black hole of inventory visibility. Inventory is ultimately tracked to a bin location. An example name is User.

- *Webshop.* This location type only has internal significance within AX. An example name is Webshop.

Significance of Location Profiles for Bin Locations A location profile defines a set of policies about similar bin locations. The similarities include the naming format, the location type, the requirements for license plate tracking, constraints about mixing inventory, characteristics about bin capacity, and characteristics about putaway logic.

- *Same Naming Conventions for Location Identifiers.* A location format defines how many segments should be included in the identifier and the length of each segment. For example, the segments might represent an aisle, rack, level and location.

- *Same Location Type.* The location type has a special significance within the Advanced WMS approach, as described in the previous subsection.

- *Same Requirements for License Plate Tracking.* Some locations require license plate tracking, such as the locations for receiving and final shipping. These locations are often termed an LP-controlled location. Other locations do not generally require license plate tracking, such as the location associated within an in-transit warehouse and locations representing floorstock inventory within production. These locations are often termed non-LP-controlled locations.

  The choice of license plate tracking represents one of the strategic options for using the Advanced WMS approach, as described at the beginning of the book. A given warehouse can minimize the use of license plates in a simplistic scenario (Case 1) or extensively use license plates (Case 2).

- *Similar Constraints About Mixing Inventory.* Constraints about mixing inventory can prevent different items, inventory statuses and/or batch numbers within the bin location.

- *Similar Characteristics for Volume, Weight, and Location Dimensions.* These optional characteristics can be used with more advanced putaway logic, so that bin locations are not loaded beyond their usable weight/volume or dimensions.

- *Similar Characteristics for Putaway Logic.* The location profile can be used within a location directive much like a zone. For example, the location profile may identify quality locations for location directives related to receiving inspection.

- *Policy on Negative Inventory.* Negative inventory can be allowed or prevented at a given location. This policy represents a refinement of the considerations about negative inventory (Section 24.6).

- *Policy on Cycle Counting.* Cycle counting may not be possible in the bin locations, such as a production floorstock location for partially completed items.

Define Bin Locations Within a Warehouse The identifier for a bin location can be manually assigned, or automatically created for specified range numbers. You can also copy bin locations from another warehouse. You can print barcoded label for each bin location. A bin location must be assigned a location profile, and it can optionally be assigned to a zone.

Identify Zones Within a Warehouse A zone can be assigned to one or more warehouse locations in order to support putaway logic. It typically reflects a characteristic about storage requirements. Examples include a freezer or cooler (Case 59), and separate areas for quality purposes such as storage of different allergens (Case 60).

Warehouse Types for Transit and Quarantine A normal warehouse is designated with a warehouse type of main. A transit warehouse will be required to support transfer orders shipped from a main warehouse. A quarantine warehouse is not typically required.

- *Transit Warehouse.* Each main warehouse requires an associated transit warehouse when using transfer orders to ship material from the warehouse. A transit warehouse has a separate identifier, a warehouse type of transit, and at least one bin location that always acts as a default. The transit warehouse can be designated as WMS-enabled, and its bin location must be a non-LP-controlled location. You need a minimum of one transit warehouse per site, which can be assigned to the main warehouses within the site. Alternatively, a transit warehouse can be defined for each main warehouse that acts as a ship-from location for transfer orders. The different transit warehouses provide more granular visibility of in transit inventory. Chapter 16 explained the use of transfer orders in a multisite operation.

- *Quarantine Warehouse.* A quarantine warehouse and the related quarantine orders are not used in the Advanced WMS approach, because the concept of blocking inventory usage is typically accomplished via the Inventory Status.[2]

Warehouse-Related Policies A warehouse can have a default bin location that applies to all receipts, such as receipts for purchase orders and transfer orders. This default bin location for receipts can also be defined as item-specific within the item's warehouse item information.

[2] A WMS-enabled warehouse may also require transactions for a non-WMS item, which may involve the use of quarantine orders described in the chapter about quality management (Section 26.6).

Additional default locations can also be identified for other types of transactions supported by the Advanced WMS approach. For example, the defaults can be related to production orders (for a production input location and a finished goods location), kanban orders (for a finished good location) and sales orders (for a shipment maintenance location). These defaults will be further explained in the context of each transaction.

A warehouse should have a specified calendar of working hours in order to coordinate supply chain activities.

A warehouse can be designated as non-nettable (via the manual planning flag) so that supplies are ignored by master scheduling logic.

Additional policies support variations in business processes when using the Advanced WMS approach. For example, two policies apply to the variations of the release to warehouse for sales orders, and another policy determines when the bill of lading can be generated for a sales order. The impact of these additional policies will be covered in the relevant chapters.

13.6 Define Item-Related Policies for Warehouse Management

The Storage Dimension Group assigned to an item determines whether it is WMS-enabled, and also determines the related use of Inventory Status and License Plates. The Advanced WMS approach only applies to warehouse transactions for a WMS-enabled item at a WMS-enabled warehouse, as previously described at the beginning of the book (Section 2.1).

Many other aspects of item-related policies represent common information for both the advanced and basic approaches to warehouse management. This includes enterprise versus company-level information for an item, alternate item identifiers, information about purchased and manufactured items, and many of the unit of measure considerations. A subsequent chapter about item definition provides further explanation about the common information (Chapter 24). It also covers several unique aspects of both approaches, and those pertaining to the advanced approach are repeated here. The unique aspects of the Advanced WMS approach involve the following item-related information.

Assign a Reservation Hierarchy to an Item A reservation hierarchy must be assigned to each item. The reservation hierarchy should not include batch numbers or serial numbers unless they are included in an item's Tracking Dimension Group. For example, a serialized item must be assigned a reservation hierarchy which includes the serial number, and a batch-controlled item must be assigned a reservation hierarchy which includes the batch number. The placement of the batch number in the reservation hierarchy determines whether batch numbers are critical to reservation logic or simply used for tracking purposes.

Additional UM Considerations for the Advanced WMS Approach

Several additional unit of measure considerations apply to the advanced approach and the use of license plates. The assignment of a license plate ID often reflects a physical pallet. The term "physical pallet" will be used to simplify the explanation. An item typically has a standard quantity per physical pallet. You must define the UM conversion when the standard quantity is greater than one, such as the number of pieces per pallet. Some items involve additional UM conversion factors, such as pieces per box and boxes per physical pallet.

These UM considerations must be reflected in the Unit Sequence Group assigned to the item, which defines several warehouse policies related to the use of mobile device transactions -- especially for receipts. You typically define several Unit Sequence Groups reflecting the common UM considerations related to your products, and then assign the applicable group to each item. For example, the group should include a UM code that represents an item's inventory UM and another UM code representing a physical pallet, such as "pieces and pallets". The following policies can be identified for the applicable UM codes within the group.

- *Identify the UM Code that Represents a Physical Pallet for the Item.* This UM code is typically designated as the default value for recording receipts and transfers via mobile device transactions, although you can override this suggested UM when recording the transaction. Based on this UM code and the item's standard quantity per physical pallet, the system will suggest the number of license plates when receiving a large number of pieces, including the use of a single pallet when the number of pieces reflects a less-than-pallet quantity.

- *Identify the UM Code(s) Corresponding to Less Than a Pallet Quantity.* You typically assign the "license plate grouping" policy to these UM codes, which avoids a suggested pallet for every one of the units. As already noted, the system will suggest using a single pallet when the number of pieces reflects a less-than-pallet quantity.

- *Identify the Default UM Code for Reporting Cycle Counts.* This default UM code typically reflects the inventory UM, but it can be another UM Code.

- *Identify the Default UM Code for Reporting Finished Quantities of a Manufactured Item.* Depending on the scenario, a mobile device transaction can be used to report an item's finished quantity in pieces, physical pallets or some other UM code. This default UM code can be overridden when you actually report the finished quantity via a mobile device transaction. The default does not apply when reporting finished quantities via the client.

Fixed Locations for an Item An item can be assigned to one or more warehouse locations using the Fixed Locations form, and these are displayed on the Released Products form for the item. Multiple items can have the same fixed location assigned to them. An item's fixed locations will be suggested for putaway when a location directive action includes the policy for "only use item fixed locations". An item's fixed location may also represent a picking location that requires replenishment, so that the same policy for "only use item fixed locations" should be specified on a location directive action for replenishment work.

Filter Code Values for Warehouse Purposes The user-defined values for a filter code can be used for multiple purposes in warehouse management. One purpose involves putaway logic, where the values represent an item characteristic affecting suggested putaway locations. Similar values may also be reflected in the zones within a warehouse. The following case studies illustrate the use of filter code values for putaway logic.

Case 59: Putaway of Items Requiring Cold Storage

At a food products manufacturer, the user-defined filter code values reflected an item characteristic about cold storage requirements -- such as values of *freezer*, *cooler* and *ambient*. The relevant value was assigned to each item as one of the item's filter codes. The user-defined zones for warehouse locations reflected similar values, so that a location directive about the relevant putaway zone could be based on the item characteristic.

Case 60: Putaway of Items with Allergens

At a food products manufacturer, the raw materials containing a certain type of allergen required physical separation within inventory. The user-defined filter code values reflected the item characteristic about allergens -- such as values of *peanuts, walnuts* and *none*. The relevant value was assigned to each item as one or more of the item's filter codes. The user-defined zones for warehouse locations reflected the physical separation of inventory for each type of allergen, so that a location directive about the relevant putaway zone could be based on the item characteristic.

Negative Inventory Policy The negative inventory policies are embedded in the Item Model Group assigned to an item. An additional policy only applies to the Advanced WMS approach, where you can further refine the ability to allow or prevent negative inventory by inventory location. The policy is embedded in the Location Profile assigned to the location. However, locations that use license plate tracking cannot have this negative inventory policy. A subsequent chapter provides further guidelines about negative inventory policies (Section 24.6).

AX Policies About Using Notes The document handling capabilities within AX support the use of notes, and notes can be used to guide selected types of warehouse activities. For example, notes can be defined as part of purchase order header information to provide instructions on mobile device transactions for receiving work. It is often helpful to create user-defined note types that are only applicable to a given type of transaction, such as a note type for purchase order receiving instructions. In this way, a note can be entered (and used) for just the applicable note type. The effective use of notes generally requires different note types, and also takes advantage of note inheritance and the AX policies about the use of notes. A subsequent chapter provides further explanation about the effective use of notes (Section 24.5).

When using the advanced approach, the applicable note type for an order header can be displayed on the mobile device transactions in order to provide (1) receiving instructions when reporting purchase order arrivals and (2) picking/shipping instructions when reporting picking work for sales order shipments. The applicable note type for mobile device transactions is defined by a companywide policy (on the Warehouse Management Parameters form).

The concept of an applicable note type for a sales order header also applies to several other printed documents and screens, including a bill of lading, a load report, a shipment picking list and the packing screen. The applicable note type for each of these is defined by companywide policies (on the Warehouse Management Parameters form).

Assign NMFC Code to a Salable Item The National Motor Freight Code (NMFC Code) provides a classification and description for the Bill of Lading in the Advanced WMS approach.[3] After defining the values for NMFC codes, you can assign the NMFC code to an item as part of its enterprise-level information on the Products form.

Batch and Serial Tracking Policies for an Item Many aspects of item-related policies about batch and serial tracking represent common information for both the advanced and basic approaches to warehouse management. A subsequent chapter provides further explanation about the common information (Chapter 25). It also covers several unique aspects of both approaches, and those pertaining to the advanced approach are repeated here.

When using the Advanced WMS approach with serialized items, the mobile device transactions support manual and automatic assignment of serial numbers. However, they do not support deferred assignment of serial numbers, nor do they support the automatic assignment of serial numbers based on an ad hoc mask.

With batch-controlled items, the mobile device transactions support manual and automatic assignment of batch numbers. However, manual assignment for a finished quantity of a production order requires an additional policy (labeled "override batch number") for the related mobile device transaction. In addition, the location directive actions related to picking material - for sales orders, transfer orders and production orders - require an additional "batch-enabled" policy and its associated strategy (such as FEFO batch reservations). A mobile device can also be used to change the batch disposition code assigned to a batch number.

The mobile device transactions for picking and moving a serialized item or a batch-controlled item can differ based on the use of license plates and the quantities involved. When reporting moves, for example, the mobile device transaction can be reported for the license plate ID containing multiple serial numbers (at a license plate controlled location) or for individual serial numbers. A similar approach applies to picking a license plate containing multiple serial numbers or batch numbers.

[3] The Bill of Lading in the Basic Inventory approach employs item information rather than NMFC code information.

Quality-Related Policies for an Item Almost all aspects of an item's quality-related policies represent common information for both the advanced and basic approaches to warehouse management. This includes the use of quality orders, holds and stop flags, MSDS documents, and inventory blocking. A subsequent chapter provides further explanation about quality management (Chapter 26).

13.7 Executive Summary

Several fundamentals of the Advanced WMS approach provide the foundation for explaining business processes in subsequent chapters. These fundamentals include the key setup information, such as the definition of warehouse locations and the item-related policies for warehouse management. They include the significance of license plates and Inventory Status, as well as basic inventory transactions such as moves and adjustments.

Several case studies illustrated the fundamentals. These included assigning Inventory Status during purchase order arrival (Case 58), putaway of items requiring cold storage (Case 59), and putaway of items with allergens (Case 60). A previously-cited case study about adjacent warehouses also applies (Case 12).

Chapter 14

Overview of Work Orders

The significance of the term "work order" differs widely in different contexts and ERP software packages. The different contexts include work orders for equipment maintenance, field service work orders, a work order as a synonym for production orders, and work orders for warehouse management. This chapter focuses on work orders for warehouse management.

The different types of work orders provide a starting point for further explanation. Work orders support many different types of warehouse transactions—ranging from sales order picking to putaway of purchase order arrivals—and there are different ways to create a work order. For example, some work orders are created by mobile device transactions and other work orders are created by client transactions. The execution of a work order is typically reported via a mobile device transaction. The ability to create and execute work orders via a mobile device transaction requires definition of the corresponding mobile device menu items. These considerations are reflected in the following sections within the chapter.

1. Types of Work Orders
2. Structure of a Work Order (aka Work ID)
3. Creating a Work Order
4. Define the Mobile Device Menu Items Related to Work Orders
5. Define the Mobile Device Menu Items for Indirect Activities
6. Impact of Work Orders on Inventory Transaction History

14.1 Types of Work Orders

Work orders support many different types of warehouse transactions—ranging from sales order picking to putaway of purchase order arrivals—and each work order transaction typically represents one step in a business process. A standard set of work order types are predefined within AX, and additional ones can be developed as a customization. Examples of these predefined work order types are illustrated in Figure 14.1 along with a description. The figure identifies the related business process (and its figure) in which the work order supports a key step. It also introduces the use of a Work Class ID and an example value; its significance will be covered shortly.

In addition to summarizing several examples of different work order types, this section covers the standard inquiries about work orders based on work order type, the work templates and location directives for different work order types, and the significance of the Work Class ID for a work order type.

Figure 14.1 Examples of Work Order Types

	Work Order Type	Description of Work Order	Example Process	Example of a Work Class ID
1	Inventory Movement	Move inventory to location	Figure 13.2	Inventory Move
2	Purchase Order	Putaway inventory of a purchase order arrival at receiving location	Figure 15.1	PO Putaway
3	Sales Order	Pick inventory to an outbound dock for a sales order	Figure 16.1	Sales
4	Transfer Issue	Pick inventory to an outbound dock for a transfer order	Figure 17.1	Transfer Out
5	Transfer Receipt	Putaway inventory of a transfer order arrival at a receiving location	Figure 18.1	Transfer In
6	Raw Material Picking	Pick component inventory to production input location for a production order	Figure 19.2	RM Pick
7	Finished Goods Putaway	Putaway inventory of a finished quantity at a production output location	Figure 20.1	FG Putaway

The examples in Figure 14.1 do not include all possible work order types. Examples of other types include (1) co-product and by-product putaway for a batch order, (2) kanban picking, (3) kanban putaway, (4) RMA putaway, (5) replenishment of picking locations, and (6) cycle counts. Different work order types are also applicable to the variations of a given transaction, such as the work order type for sales order picking to a pack location (for manual or automated packing purposes) versus sales order picking to an outbound dock.

Inquiries About Work Orders based on Work Order Type The different work order types are reflected in several standard inquiries and reports.

- *Inquiries About Work Orders Related to Sales Orders.* Standard inquiries can be used to identify the open, in process, and closed work orders related to sales orders as well as all work orders.

- *Inquiries About Work Orders Related to Purchase Orders.* Standard inquiries can be used to identify the open, in process, and closed work orders related to purchase orders as well as all work orders.

- *Inquiries About Work Orders Related to Cycle Counts.* Standard inquiries can be used to identify the open and closed work orders related to cycle count work, as well as those pending review.

- *Inquiries About Work Orders Related to Replenishment.* Standard inquiries can be used to identify the open, in process, and closed work orders related to replenishment.

- *Inquiries About all Work Orders.* A standard inquiry about all work orders can be used with filtering by work order type. The filtering can also reflect other applicable factors, such as the applicable site/warehouse or the applicable shipment/load for the work orders.

- *Printed Report About Work Orders.* The selection criteria for printed reports can reflect the work order type. The printed report for each work order provides barcoded information about critical fields such as the Work ID, order number and item number.

Work Templates and Location Directives for Different Work Order Types The different work order types are reflected in the definition of work templates and location directives.

- *Work Templates for a Work Order Type.* A work template specifies the pick and put steps for each type of a work order. In a work order for sales order picking, for example, the "pick" step identifies the stocking location for inventory to be picked, and the "put" step identifies the placement location such as an outbound dock. Each pick and put aspect is termed a work type. Other work types can also be specified such as a print step

- *Location Directives for a Work Order Type.* The nature of a location directive depends on the work order type. With putaway of a purchase order arrival, for example, a location directive action (and its edit query) can indicate the rules about a putaway location, and the conditions in which the rules apply. With sales order picking, as another example, a location directive action (and its edit criteria) can indicate rules about where to put the picked material, such as an outbound dock or a staging location. Applicable conditions can also be specified. These applicable conditions are warehouse-specific and often include other characteristics as part of a separate edit query.

The detailed aspects of work templates and location directives, and the associated detailed design of mobile device transactions, are considered by many to be the heart of a good warehouse management system. However, a detailed explanation falls outside the book's scope.

Significance of the Work Class ID for a Work Order Type The right side of Figure 14.1 illustrates examples of the user-definable Work Class ID, which you map to a relevant work order type. You specify the applicable Work Class ID (rather than the work order type) as part of defining mobile device menu items that involve "existing work." For example, the "existing work" may reflect creation of picking work for sales orders or the creation of putaway work for purchase order arrivals. A subsequent section explains the different ways to create work orders.

The Work Class ID provides the basis for suggested "put" locations. That is, as part of defining a Work Class ID, you select the related Location Type that has been assigned to the suggested "put" locations. The Location Type is actually embedded in the Location Profile assigned to locations, as described in the previous chapter about the significance of Location Profiles and Location Types (Section 13.5). The suggested locations are termed "Valid Put Location Types."

The significance of different values for a Work Class ID is sometimes easier to understand via case studies. One example involves sales order picking work to a final prep location prior to moving the inventory to an outbound dock (Case 61). Other examples would apply to other work order types, such as picking or putaway for transfer orders, and raw material picking for production orders or putaway of finished quantities.

At a minimum, one Work Class ID must be defined for each Work Order Type, and the information about a valid put location type does not need to be specified. This minimum definition is reflected in the example values shown in Figure 14.1.

Case 61: Sales Order Picking Work to a Final Prep Location

A manufacturer of promotional items such as coffee mugs and apparel would personalize the item as a final prep step prior to shipment. Examples of personalized apparel included embroidery or printing of text provided by the customer. They were considering the use of different Work Class IDs in order to model the personalization work centers as a final prep location. For example, one work center was called Embroidery and another was called Printing.

As a solution approach, the personalization work centers can be defined as different locations with different Location Types. In addition, the definition of different Work Class IDs can correspond to each work center, and indicate the appropriate location for final prep. In this way, when the sales order picking work is created, the suggested "put" can indicate the relevant location for the work order (such as Embroidery or Printing). A warehouse worker would use a mobile device transaction to report movement to an outbound dock after final prep was completed.

14.2 Structure of a Work Order (aka Work ID)

The information about a work order and its related work lines differs slightly based on the type of work order, but the same structure and life cycle still apply. That is, a work order consists of a work order header and multiple work lines, and its life cycle consists of different values for work status. A work order and its work lines represent a set of interrelated warehouse activities.[1] This set of interrelated warehouse activities is commonly identified as a Work ID within AX. For example, you can enter or scan the Work ID when reporting various mobile device transactions for a work order.

Work Order Header Information A work order is uniquely identified by a system-assigned number called the Work ID. The header information includes the work order type, the work status, the applicable site/warehouse, and the source order (if applicable). It includes other related information when applicable, such as the related shipment, load and wave for a work order about sales order picking.

A work order header also indicates how it was created. The next section explains the various ways to create a work order, and the use of a system-assigned "work creation number" to uniquely identify how a work order was created.

Work Line Information The information for each work line includes the work type (such as pick or put) and the item, location, quantity, UM, and work class ID (that reflects the applicable work order type).

[1] In contrast, the line items for other types of orders – such as purchase orders, sales orders and transfer orders – represent an independent activity, so that transactions for one line can be reported independently from the other lines.

Life Cycle for a Work Order A work order has a work status of *open* when initially created. Subsequent steps to report work will automatically change the status to *in process* and *closed.* The applicable values for work status and their significance are described below.

- *Open.* The status indicates the work order has been initially created, and you can print the work (with bar-coded information) and optionally cancel or block the work.
- *In Process.* The status indicates the work has been reported for one or more work lines for the work order. You cannot cancel the work order at this status, but the reported work can be reversed.
- *Closed.* The status indicates that all work lines have been completely reported.
- *Cancelled.* The status indicates the work order has been cancelled, which also changes the status of all work lines to *cancelled.* A work order cannot be cancelled after work has been reported against it.

Each work line for a work order also has a work status with the same possible values. That is, a work line has a work status of *open* when it is initially created, and subsequent steps to report work will automatically change the status to *in process* and *closed.* A work line can also be cancelled.

The work status is reflected in standard AX inquiries, where you can optionally view closed work orders. In addition, some of the standard AX inquiries are differentiated by work status, such as the inquiries about open, closed and in process work orders related to purchase work, sales work and replenishment work.

Cancelling a Work Order Cancelling a work order represents one aspect of reversing transactions in a business process. Subsequent chapters describe these reversing transactions in the business processes for purchase order receiving (Section 15.4), sales order picking/shipping (Section 16.4), transfer order picking/shipping (Section 17.4), transfer order receiving (Section 18.4), production order picking (Section 19.5) and production order receiving (Section 20.4). A work order can only be cancelled prior to reporting any work for it.

Work Priorities for Work Orders A work priority can be assigned to each work order, thereby helping to prioritize the need for reporting work. For example, the reporting of purchase order arrivals and production order receipts may have a high priority so that inventory will be available for sales order picking. You can define the default value for a work priority as part of the work template information for each work order type.

Blocking (and Unblocking) a Work Order A work order can be blocked in order to prevent further transactions until you remove the blocking.

14.3 Creating a Work Order

There are several ways to create a work order for each work order type. Examples of the work creation process are illustrated in Figure 14.2, along with the result of work creation and a description of the associated work order. The numbering and descriptions reflect the corresponding entries from Figure 14.1. Work orders can be created by mobile device transactions and client transactions. The figure uses grey shading to identify the mobile device transactions that can be used to create a work order and to perform a work order. The following subsections provide further explanation about the examples of creating a work order.

Figure 14.2 Examples of Creating a Work Order

	Example of a Work Creation Process	Result of Work Creation	Description of Work Order
1	Create move for a selected location	Create movement work	Move inventory to location
2	Register purchase order arrival via mobile device	Create putaway work for a purchase order arrival	Putaway inventory of a purchase order arrival at receiving location
3	Release a shipment wave for sales order(s)	Create picking work for a sales order shipment	Pick inventory to an outbound dock for a sales order
4	Release a shipment wave for transfer order(s)	Create picking work for a transfer order shipment	Pick inventory to an outbound dock for a transfer order
5	Register transfer order arrival via mobile device	Create putaway work for a transfer order arrival	Putaway inventory of a transfer order arrival at a receiving location
6	Release a production wave for production order components	Create raw material picking work for a production wave	Pick component inventory to production input location for a production order
7	Report a finished quantity for a production order via client transaction or via mobile device	Create putaway work for a finished quantity of a production order	Putaway inventory of a finished quantity of a production order at a production output location

Legend: ▭ = Perform mobile device transaction

Create Move for a Selected Location Movement work can be automatically created when viewing an inquiry about the inventory within a location, where you access the Create Inventory Movement Work form.

Movement work can also be created using other approaches. For example, movement work can be created as a result of a reversing transaction within the picking process for sales orders (Section 16.4) or transfer orders (Section 17.4). More specifically, when reversing all picking work associated with a work order, the dialogue on the Reverse Work screen enables you to indicate how to handle the material, and one option involves the automatic creation of movement work to a specified location.

As another example, movement work can be created for moving material from one location to another, such as creating work for moving material from a separate QC area to its stocking location. Case 64 and Case 70 provide illustrative examples. This requires a mobile device menu item to create the movement work (with a work creation process of *Movement by Template*), and another one for reporting the movement work (with a work order type of Inventory Movement as the basis for use existing work).

Register Purchase Order Arrival via Mobile Device Registering a purchase order arrival via a mobile device will automatically create putaway work. The putaway work can be executed at a later time, or executed immediately as part of the mobile device transaction. You define this choice – and the basis for identifying an arrival—as part of defining the menu device menu item for reporting purchase order arrivals. The basis for identifying arrivals can be the purchase order number and item number, or the purchase order number and line number. These choices are reflected in subsequent explanations about putaway work in the context of the purchase order receiving process (Section 15.1).

Two other bases for identifying an arrival only apply when using purchase loads or purchase ASNs. That is, you can identify arrivals by load number and item number, or by license plate numbers (defined within the ASN information). Subsequent explanations cover the purchase load receiving process (Section 15.9).

Release a Shipment Wave for Sales Order(s) A shipment wave can contain one or more sales order lines, and releasing the shipment wave will automatically create picking work. The step is actually termed "process" the shipment wave. Subsequent explanations cover picking work in the context of the sales order picking/receiving process (Section 16.1) and wave planning (Section 16.10).

Release a Shipment Wave for Transfer Order(s) Similar to sales orders, a shipment wave can contain one or more transfer order lines, and releasing the shipment wave will automatically create picking work. The step is actually termed "process" the shipment wave. Subsequent explanations cover picking work in the context of the transfer order picking/receiving process (Section 17.1) and wave planning (Section 16.10).

Register Transfer Order Arrival via Mobile Device Registering a transfer order arrival via a mobile device will automatically create putaway work. The putaway work can be executed at a later time, or executed immediately as part of the mobile device transaction. You define this choice—and the basis for identifying an arrival—as part of defining the menu device menu item for reporting purchase order arrivals. The basis for identifying arrivals can be the transfer order number and item number, or the transfer order number and line number. These choices are reflected in subsequent explanations about putaway work in the context of the transfer order receiving process (Section 18.1).

Release a Production Wave for Production Order Components A production wave contains the components for one or more production orders, and releasing the production wave will automatically create raw material picking work. The step is actually termed "process" the production wave. Subsequent explanations cover raw material picking work in the context of the production order picking process (Section 19.1) and wave planning (Section 19.7).

Report a Finished Quantity for Production Order Reporting a finished quantity via a mobile device will automatically create putaway work. The putaway work can be executed at a later time, or executed immediately as part of the mobile device transaction. You select this choice as part of defining the menu device menu item for reporting a finished quantity. The choice is reflected in subsequent explanations about putaway work in the context of the production order receiving process (Section 15.1).

A client transaction can also be used for reporting a finished quantity, and it similarly creates putaway work automatically. The variations of client transactions for reporting production order receipts are covered in a subsequent chapter (Section 20.6).

Other Examples of Creating a Work Order Other examples include the creation of replenishment work for picking locations (Section 16.14) and the creation of cycle count work (Chapter 22).

Work Creation Numbers Information for a work order header indicates how it was created in terms of a system-assigned work creation number. A standard AX inquiry – labeled the Work Creation History Log – displays a list of these work creation numbers, along with related information about the item, quantity, UM, source order and transaction type. It includes other related information when applicable, such as the related shipment and load for work creation about sales order picking. It also provides a message about a failed work creation. The work creation history can be periodically deleted using Work Creation History Purge task, and you indicate the number of days of history to keep.

14.4 Define the Mobile Device Menu Items related to Work Orders

Mobile device transactions are used to create and perform work orders, and each transaction requires definition of a mobile device menu item. With work order creation related to purchase orders, for example, you can define one menu item for reporting purchase order receipts in order to create putaway work for subsequent reporting, and a second menu item for reporting the receipt and putaway work in a single mobile device transaction. As another example, you can define a menu item for reporting sales order picking work. You indicate a mode of "work" when defining each of these mobile device menu items. Each chapter's explanation of key constructs includes a brief summary of the setup information related to mobile device menu items.

The detailed design of mobile device transactions can simplify the end-user experience for handling every possible situation. However, the topic largely falls outside the book's scope. One aspect involving the definition and use of an Audit Template ID is relevant as an alternative approach for reporting inspection.

Define the Need for Capturing Quality-Related Data When Defining a Mobile Device Menu Item Some scenarios need to capture quality-related data when reporting mobile device transactions. This involves the assignment of an Audit Template ID when defining the mobile device menu item. Each user-defined ID must be defined beforehand, and there are several capabilities associated with the definition of an Audit Template ID. At its simplest, you define one or more data capture questions (and the trigger for asking the questions) as part of an Audit Template ID. In this way, the worker that reports the mobile device transaction will be automatically prompted to answer the questions when reporting the mobile device transaction. Illustrative examples include Case 62 and Case 63.

Case 62: Using the Mobile Device to Capture Quality-Related Data about Purchase Receipts

The quality management team at a food products company wanted to capture several aspects of quality-related data at the time of recording purchase receipts of raw materials. Examples include the temperature and condition of a given receipt, and also a checklist of truck inspection criteria for a purchase load (such as cleanliness, odor and valid driver ID). They were considering the "Audit Template ID" capabilities for the mobile device transaction to receive and putaway purchase receipts. They could define the data capture questions (with a trigger based on a different load ID) as part of an Audit Template ID, and then assign the Audit Template ID to the mobile device menu item. In this way, the receiving clerk will be automatically prompted to answer the questions when reporting the mobile device transaction.

Case 63: Using the Mobile Device to Capture LIMS Data about Production Output

The quality management team at a manufacturing company wanted to capture several aspects of quality-related data at the time of recording finished quantities for production orders. Examples include many of the data elements currently required for their Laboratory Information Management System (LIMS). They were considering the "Audit Template ID" capabilities for the mobile device transaction to receive and putaway finished quantities. They could define the data capture questions (with a trigger based on a different order number) as part of an Audit Template ID, and then assign the Audit Template ID to the mobile device menu item. In this way, the worker that reports the mobile device transaction will be automatically prompted to answer the questions when reporting the mobile device transaction.

14.5 Define the Mobile Device Menu Items for Indirect Activities

Mobile device transactions can be used for purposes other than work orders. These are termed indirect activities. You indicate a mode of "indirect" when defining the mobile device menu item, and you select from a predefined list of indirect activities. The list includes the following transactions.

- Inquiry About On-Hand Inventory for an Item or for a Location
- Inquiry About a License Plate

- Reprint the Label for a License Plate
- Create a Nested License Plate, and Break Down a Nested License Plate
- Report the Start of a Production Order
- Report Scrap for a Component of a Production Order
- Change the Batch Disposition Code for a Batch Number

Two indirect activities involving transportation management include driver check in and check out for transportation appointment purposes.

14.6 Impact of Work Orders on Inventory Transaction History

The execution of a work order creates entries for inventory transaction history. When viewing transaction history, a transaction filter can limit the displayed information to "work only" transactions or "omit work" transactions, or you can view "display all" transactions. The "work only" transactions identify the related work order, whereas normal inventory transactions identify the related sales order, purchase order, transfer order, production order or inventory journal. However, the execution of work orders has a significant impact on the volume of inventory transaction history.

A simple example illustrates the increased volume of inventory transaction history. The simple example reflects a distribution scenario, where an item is purchased and then sold—resulting in two normal inventory transactions. This simple example also resulted in eight work order transactions, which represents a significant increase in the volume of inventory transaction history.

The increased volume is also reflected in the Item Tracing form for batch tracking of a batch-controlled item. Relative to the above-mentioned example, the work order transactions result in eight additional levels in the multi-level indented format for batch tracking. The Item Tracing form currently provides an option to display only the normal inventory transactions, but they are not displayed in a multi-level indented format. Another option displays only the batch numbers in the tree, but it has the same shortcoming.

14.7 Executive Summary

This chapter focused on work orders for warehouse management and the different types of work orders—ranging from sales order picking to putaway of purchase order arrivals. It covered the different ways to create a work order, since some work orders are created by mobile device transactions and others are created by client transactions. It explained how to execute a work order via a mobile device transaction, and the definition of the corresponding mobile device menu items.

Several case studies illustrated variations in the use of work orders and mobile device transactions. These included sales order picking work to a final prep location (Case 61), capturing quality-related data about purchase receipts (Case 62), and capturing LIMS data about production output (Case 63).

Chapter 15

Purchase Order Receiving

The Advanced WMS approach supports several variations for purchase order receiving. For explanatory purposes, it is easiest to start with a simple yet typical business process, and explain the related life cycles, reversing transactions and key constructs. The basic process provides a baseline for explaining variations, such as differences in reporting receipts for a purchase load and the different approaches to receiving inspection. These topics are reflected in the following sections within the chapter:

1. Basic Process for Purchase Order Receiving
2. Additional Steps in the Basic Process
3. Life Cycles Related to the Basic Process
4. Reversing Transactions in the Basic Process
5. Key Constructs in the Basic Process for Purchase Order Receiving
6. Major Variations for Purchase Order Receiving
7. Minor Variations
8. Receiving Inspection for Purchase Order Arrivals
9. Receive a Purchase Load
10. Comparing Approaches to Purchase Order Receiving

Effective procurement practices represent a critical consideration for purchase order receiving. The purchase orders should reflect up-to-date S&OP game plans and up-to-date delivery dates and quantities. Additional factors include a manageable level of expediting. These considerations will make life easier for warehouse management.

15.1 Basic Process for Purchase Order Receiving

The business process for purchase order receiving can have many variations. A starting point of a simple yet typical business process provides a baseline for explaining the variations. The basic process shown in Figure 15.1 consists of several steps performed by a receiving clerk and warehouse worker. The figure highlights the mobile device transactions with grey shading, and identifies an automatic step to create putaway work. The process starts with the need to report purchase order arrival and ends with a completed receipt. This section provides an overview of the basic process and describes each step in more detail.

Figure 15.1 Basic Process for Purchase Order Receiving

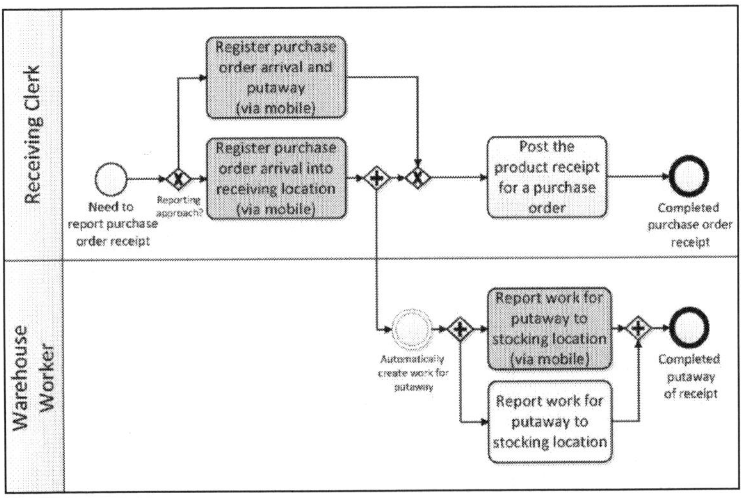

Overview The receiving clerk typically uses the mobile device to register purchase order arrivals into a receiving location (and to assign license plate IDs), which automatically creates putaway work. The warehouse worker uses the mobile device to report putaway from the receiving location to a stocking location. A suggested stocking location can reflect location directives, or the warehouse worker can determine and report the stocking location. Alternatively, the receiving clerk registers the arrival and reports putaway at the same time. In either case, the receiving clerk subsequently identifies the vendor's packing list number when posting the product receipt for the purchase order.

Register Purchase Order Arrival into a Receiving Location (via Mobile Device) The receiving clerk uses the mobile device to register purchase order arrival into a receiving location and to assign license plate IDs.

Register Purchase Order Arrival and Putaway (via Mobile Device) The receiving clerk uses the mobile device to register purchase order arrival (and assign license plate IDs) and immediately report putaway to a stocking location.

In some cases, the received material does not require license plate tracking and the putaway location is not license plate controlled. This may reflect a stocking location, or it may be next to the receiving area so a warehouse worker must report a subsequent move to the stocking location.

Report Work for Putaway to Stocking Location (via Mobile Device) The warehouse worker uses the mobile device to report putaway work for the received material to a stocking location.. A suggested stocking location can reflect location directives, or the warehouse worker can determine and report the stocking location. In some cases, the received material does not require license plate tracking and the putaway location is not license plate controlled.

Review Work for Putaway of a Purchase Order Arrival The warehouse worker can review and optionally print the work for putaway of a purchase order arrival.

Post the Product Receipt for a Purchase Order The receiving clerk posts the product receipt for a purchase order, which updates the financial impact of received material.

Enforcing the Major Steps in a Typical Process The major steps of recording registering arrival and posting the product receipt can be enforced by two policies within the Item Model Group assigned to an item. These policies are labeled the Registration Requirements checkbox and the Receiving Requirements checkbox.

15.2 Additional Steps in the Basic Process

The basic process often includes several additional steps or slight variations which are not shown in Figure 15.1 so that the diagram does not become too complex. The following steps may be needed.

Print Labels for License Plates Labels can be automatically generated and printed when reporting purchase order arrivals via mobile devices, and subsequently reprinted when needed. The label information and layout can reflect company-specific and product-specific requirements, and the nature of the label printer. This involves some technical details that fall outside the book's scope.

Immediate Putaway into a Non-LP-Controlled Location The mobile device transaction for reporting arrival and putaway can be used to place received material into a location that is not license plate controlled. The putaway location may reflect a stocking location or a location near the receiving area. In this way, the license plate IDs do not apply when viewing and tracking inventory.

Alternatives for Posting the Product Receipt The receiving clerk can post the product receipt by directly accessing the Posting Product Receipt form (where selection criteria can be used to populate information), or by accessing it from the Purchase Order form (so that it inherits information from the selected order). Both approaches can reflect a quantity basis of *registered* so that the registered information about item arrivals will be used in posting the product receipt.

An alternative approach involves the use of purchase loads and reporting arrivals against a purchase load, so that a single transaction can be used to post the product receipts for all purchase orders within the load. A subsequent section provides further explanation about the use of purchase loads (Section 15.9).

Receive Short When No Further Receipts are Expected When posting a product receipt for a purchase order, you can optionally indicate that a purchase order line has been received short (relative to the ordered quantity) and that no further receipts are expected. The status of the purchase order line will be updated to *Received.* Use the *Close for Receipt* checkbox for the relevant line when posting the product receipt.

Requirement for a Complete Delivery A purchase order can be flagged for complete delivery, which means the entire order quantity must be identified when posting the product receipt. It does not impact the reporting of partial quantities on the arrival journal.

Perform Posting of Product Receipt by an Accounts Payable Clerk In some scenarios, the accounts payable clerk performs posting of product receipts. One rationale is that posting should be tightly controlled because it updates the financial information about receipts. A second rationale is that the quality order results can be considered in the quantity being posted, as illustrated in a previous case study (Case 18).

Identify Potential Problems in Delivery Dates The delivery date for a purchase order line provides the basis for expected receiving in the warehouse. In particular, the confirmed delivery date for a purchase line (or a line within a delivery schedule) typically indicates the most realistic up-to-date information from the vendor. Several standard inquiries identify potential problems about deliveries. You can identify purchase order lines without confirmed delivery dates or with past due delivery dates. You can also identify purchase-related backorders. These problems typically require action by the purchasing agent and coordination with the vendor, but they are also relevant for expected receiving activities in the warehouse.

Identify Purchase-Related Backorders A purchase-related backorder within AX simply refers to any purchase line with a delivery date prior to a specified date (aka the backorder date).[1] This simple definition includes purchase lines with a partially delivered quantity, where the line has not been closed short when posting the product receipt. A partially delivered quantity is the normal interpretation of a purchase backorder. Standardized inquiries can be used to identify all purchase-related backorders or just those related to a vendor. The purchasing agent typically reviews purchase-related backorders and takes action for a selected backorder. The actions include expediting delivery from the vendor, updating the confirmed delivery date, and/or reducing the quantity for the purchase line.

Inquiries about Work Orders Related to Purchase Orders Standard inquiries can be used to identify the open, in process, and closed work orders related to purchase orders as well as all work orders.

15.3 Life Cycles related to the Basic Process

The basic process involves several related constructs where the status for each construct reflects various steps in the process. Figure 15.2 summarizes this information, and identifies those steps representing the minimum number of touch points for updating status. Shading highlights the key constructs of mobile device transactions and putaway work.

A different approach to the receiving process involves purchase loads, and a subsequent section and diagram explain the different constructs and related life cycles (Section 15.9).

[1] This simple definition is critical for understanding "backordered lines" with a future delivery date when compared to a specified backorder date in the future.

Figure 15.2 Life Cycles Related to Purchase Order Receiving

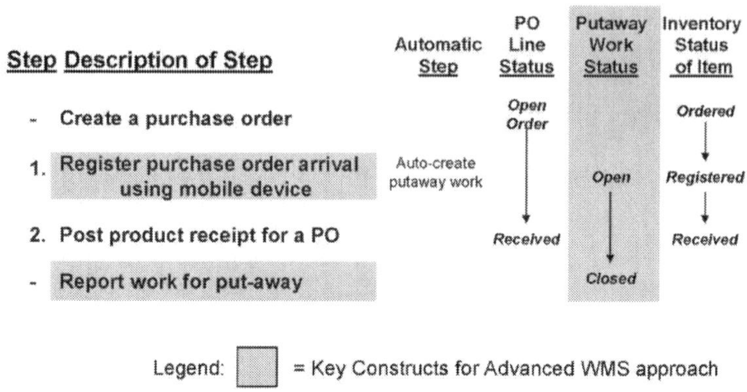

15.4 Reversing Transactions in the Basic Process

Purchase order receiving transactions may need to be reversed for several reasons. However, the ability to reverse transactions is limited with current AX functionality. You can cancel the work order for putaway work, but the options to correct or cancel the product receipt do not currently work. In contrast, these options work for the Basic Inventory approach as described in a previous chapter (Section 5.4).

Borrowing from the previous figure, Figure 15.3 illustrates the steps within the basic process (shown in grey text) and the point at which you can perform a reversing transaction (shown in black text). As identified by the step number in the figure, you can (1X) cancel the work order for putaway work.

Figure 15.3 Reversing Transactions in the Basic Process for Purchase Order Receiving

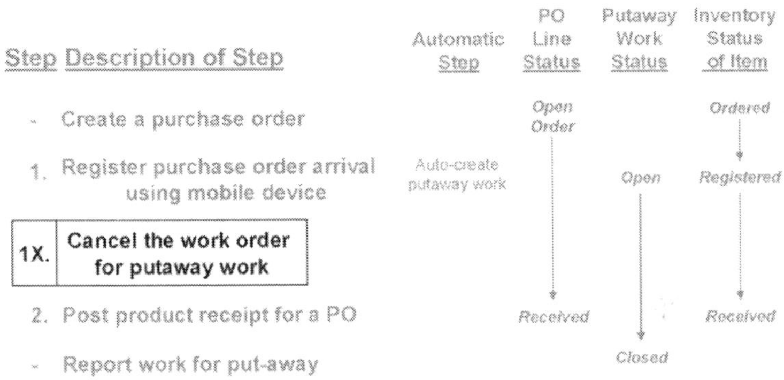

15.5 Key Constructs in the Basic Process for Purchase Order Receiving

The basic process for purchase order receiving employs mobile devices to register receipts at a receiving location, and to report putaway work to a stocking location. Alternatively, the receipt and putaway can be performed as part of the same mobile device transaction. As a final step, you must post the product receipt for the purchase order in order to update the financial information associated with the received material. This section summarizes the key construct of the Mobile Device Menu Item to support the mobile device transactions, and the significance of posting the product receipt.

Mobile Device Menu Items The appropriate Mobile Device Menu Items must be defined in order to report a purchase order arrival and the related putaway work. Different menu items are needed to support the variations of mobile device transactions, as described below.

- *Menu Item for Registering Purchase Order Arrival.* As part of defining the menu item, you select a work creation process that determines the basis for identifying the received material. The options include *Purchase Order Item Receiving* and *Purchase Order Line Receiving*. You also indicate whether a license plate should be manually or automatically assigned, whether to group items on a single license plate (based on the reported unit of measure for the received quantity, and the related policies within Unit Sequence Group assigned to the item), and whether to create/print a label for each license plate.

- *Menu Item for Putaway of Purchase Order Arrival.* As part of defining the menu item, you select the option "Use existing work" and indicate the relevant work order type for *purchase orders*. The related constructs include a Location Directive and Work Template for the work order type of Purchase Orders.

- *Menu Item for Purchase Order Arrival and Putaway.* As part of defining the menu item, you select a work creation process that determines the basis for identifying the received material. The options include *Purchase Order Item Receiving and Putaway* and *Purchase Order Line Receiving and Putaway.* Other aspects are the similar to the above-mentioned setup information, including the related constructs of a Location Directive and Work Template for putaway of the received material.

Viewing Work related to Putaway of Purchase Order Arrivals The Open Purchase Work form displays the putaway work for purchase order arrivals, which have a work status of open. Using this form, you can print the work (with bar-coded information) and optionally cancel or block the work.

Significance of Posting the Product Receipt and the Product Receipt Journal The posting of a product receipt represents the completion of the purchase order receiving process and it serves several purposes as summarized below. You can access the Posting Product Receipt form directly or for a selected purchase order.

As part of posting the product receipt, you identify the vendor's packing list number (aka the product receipt number), and a companywide policy determines how to handle duplicate numbers.[2] You also record the received items, typically based on the previously registered quantities. You can indicate when a purchase order line with a short receipt should be closed, indicating that no further receipts are expected.

After posting the product receipt, the system automatically updates the purchase order (such as updating the line status or order status to *Received*), and creates a Product Receipt Journal containing the receipt information.

The identifier for a Product Receipt Journal reflects the user-assigned product receipt number (aka vendor's packing list number), and consists of a header and line item information. From the header, you can view the related vouchers, distributions and subledger journal entries. Each line item indicates the related

---

[2] The companywide policy (defined in the Procurement and Sourcing Parameters form) determines whether entry of a duplicate number results in a warning or rejection in order to avoid duplication of reported receipts. Alternatively, you can choose to accept entries of a duplicate number without any warning to the user

item, quantity and purchase order. You can access the Product Receipt Journal form for a selected purchase order, or access it directly.

15.6 Major Variations for Purchase Order Receiving

The basic process for purchase order receiving provides the foundation for explaining major variations. The major variations include the use of receiving inspection, purchase loads and purchase order returns, as well as a simple inventory transaction.

Simple Inventory Transaction for Reporting Purchase Order Receipts The receiving clerk can bypass the use of mobile devices and putaway work by using a simple inventory transaction, where you register the item when posting the product receipt for a purchase order. You can also identify registration information for a line item on a purchase order prior to posting the product receipt. This simple inventory transaction applies to both the basic and advanced approaches.

Receiving Inspection for Purchase Order Arrivals There are many variations of receiving inspection for purchased material. For example, the receiving inspection may be performed by receiving clerks at the time of arrival into a receiving location, or by a quality control clerk reporting against an automatically-created quality order. In addition, the test results for a quality order may be reported for a small sample while the material remains in a receiving location, or the received material may be placed in a separate QC area until test results have been reported. A subsequent section provides further explanation about the variations of receiving inspection (Section 15.8).

Receive a Purchase Load A purchase load can contain one or more purchase order line items, and the contents of a purchase load can be defined at the time of arrival. The purchase load typically represents the contents of a vendor's packing list, and you report arrival against the Load ID and the related purchase order number(s). Alternatively, a purchase load can reflect the planning and coordination of transportation for an inbound load and its associated freight charges. A subsequent section provides further explanation about receiving a purchase load (Section 15.9).

Receive a License Plate Defined by ASN Information In some cases, the vendor provides an ASN (Advanced Ship Notice) that defines the contents and related license plate information about the inbound material. This ASN information can be imported into AX, and you report arrival against the predefined license plate IDs.

Returns to Vendor Returning material to a vendor typically involves a different type of purchase order (termed a returned order), so that you can identify the vendor's RMA number (Return Material Authorization). It can also be handled via a purchase order line item with a negative quantity. The return transactions cannot be reported via mobile devices, and a previous chapter explained a typical process for purchase order returns (Section 5.9).

Receive Batch-Controlled Items A batch-controlled item involves the assignment of batch numbers when reporting purchase order arrival via mobile device transactions; it may also involve reporting of vendor batch information and/or a batch disposition code. A subsequent chapter describes the various approaches to batch number assignment, the nature of vendor batch information and batch disposition codes (Chapter 25).

Receive Serialized Items A serialized item involves the assignment of serial numbers when reporting purchase order arrival via mobile device transactions. A subsequent chapter describes the various approaches to serial number assignment (Chapter 25).

15.7 Minor Variations

Several minor variations apply to the basic process for purchase order receiving and its major variations. These include the use of delivery tolerances, safety margins and notes. Other minor variations were identified as part of the additional steps for the basic process, such as receiving short, requirements for a complete delivery, and posting product receipts by an accounts payable clerk.

Impact of Delivery Tolerances on Purchase Order Receiving When delivery tolerances are acceptable, they determine how much the quantities being received can differ from the ordered quantity. Over- and under-delivery tolerances (related to purchase orders) are expressed as a percentage and the values assigned to an item act as defaults for a purchase order line item. Delivery tolerances of zero percent for a purchase order line mean that the received quantity must equal the ordered quantity. A companywide policy (embedded in the Procurement and Sourcing parameters) determines whether over- and under-deliveries will be acceptable for purchase orders. The over-delivery tolerance is enforced when reporting arrivals and both over- and under-delivery tolerances are enforced when posting the packing slip for a purchase order.

Modeling the Required Time for Receiving/Inspection Activities Some scenarios have a significant time requirement for receiving and inspection activities related to an item's receipt such as 1 or more days. A significant time requirement should be included in the supply chain model so that purchase order delivery dates will correctly reflect the required time. The required time can be identified as the receipt safety margin, where you define the number of days as part of the Coverage Group assigned to the item. When using quality orders, a significant time requirement for inspection should also be identified in the expected date for the completion of the quality order.

Effective Use of Notes for Purchase Order Receiving Purposes Notes can be entered for a purchase order header and displayed on the mobile device when reporting purchase order arrival. These notes can indicate special instructions for the receiving clerk. A subsequent chapter provides further explanation about the effective use of notes for warehouse management purposes (Section 24.5).

15.8 Receiving Inspection for Purchase Order Arrivals

There are many variations of receiving inspection for purchased material. For example, the receiving inspection may be performed by receiving clerks at the time of arrival into a receiving location, typically by assigning an inventor status to the received material. Alternatively, receiving inspection can be performed by a quality control clerk reporting against an automatically-created quality order. The test results for a quality order may be reported for a small sample while the material remains in a receiving location, or the received material may be placed in a separate QC area until test results have been reported. Validation results of pass or fail can automatically update the Inventory Status of the received inventory, or the batch disposition code of batch-controlled items.

As an explanatory approach, the different approaches for receiving inspection are more easily explained via case studies. A previous chapter described one case study about receiving inspection by receiving clerks at the time of arrival (Case 58). Other previously-cited cases included receiving inspection and batch disposition codes (Case 19), reporting quality order results after putaway (Case 20) and receiving inspection with delayed testing results (Case 21). A common scenario involves receiving inspection at a separate QC area and the use of quality orders, as described below for Case 64.

Case 64: Receiving Inspection at a Separate QC Area

For certain purchased items at a manufacturing company, the entire quantity of a purchase order arrival was placed in a separate QC location until test results could be reported. The quality control clerk reported these test results for the associated quality order. After the units passed validation, a warehouse worker would create putaway work and then report the putaway work from the QC location to a stocking location. Figure 15.4 illustrates the business process, and grey shading indicates the mobile device transactions.

Figure 15.4 Receiving Inspection at a Separate QC Area

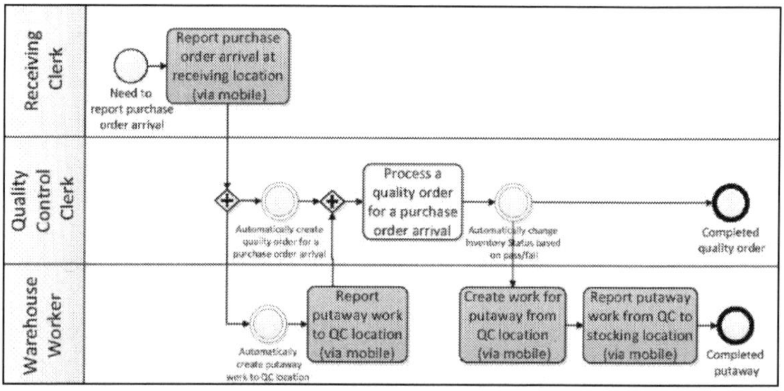

Some setup information was required to support mobile device transactions for creating and reporting putaway work from the QC location. In order to create work, the Mobile Device Menu Item defined a work creation process of *Movement by template*. The putaway work required a Mobile Device Menu Item with the "Use existing work" option and the relevant work order type for *inventory movement*. The related constructs include a Location Directive and Work Template for the work order type of Inventory Movement.

15.9 Receive a Purchase Load

A purchase load can contain one or more purchase order line items. In many cases, the contents of a purchase load are defined at the time of arrival in order to simplify the receiving process. The purchase load typically represents the contents of a vendor's packing list, and you report arrival against the load number. In other cases, the contents of a purchase load reflect the planning and coordination of transportation for the inbound load. This section describes a typical business process for both approaches to define a purchase load, and also summarizes the life cycles related to purchase load receiving.

Receive a Purchase Load Defined at Time of Arrival The process of receiving a purchase load differs from the process for receiving purchase orders. The differences include the definition of a purchase load (by the receiving clerk), registering arrival of the purchase load, and posting the product receipts for purchase orders within the load. These unique aspects are reflected in the simple yet typical process shown in Figure 15.5, which consists of several steps performed by a receiving clerk and warehouse worker. The process starts with the need for receiving a purchase load and ends with completed receipts.

Figure 15.5 Typical Process for Purchase Load Receiving

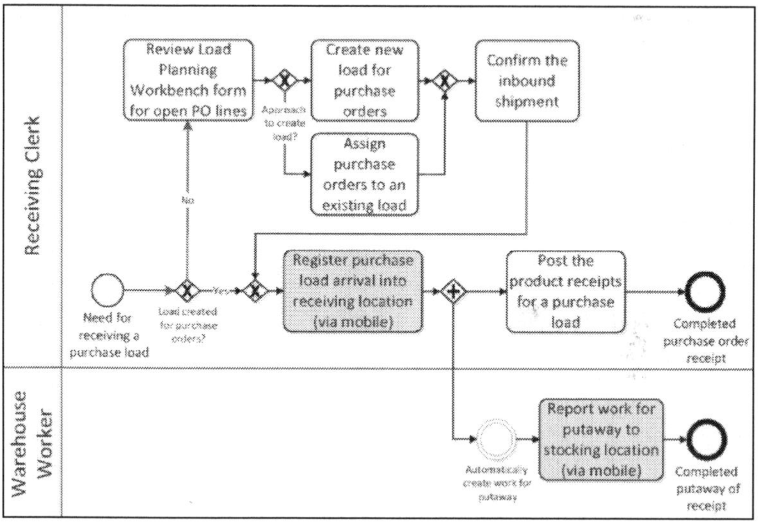

- *Overview.* The receiving clerk uses the Load Planning Workbench to view and select the purchase order line items that represent the contents of newly-arrived material (or anticipated arrivals). The receiving clerk can then create a purchase load for selected lines, or assign them to an existing load. When ready, the receiving clerk confirms the inbound shipment of the purchase load, which enables further reporting about the newly-arrived material.

  The receiving clerk identifies the Load ID and related purchase order number(s) when using the mobile device to register purchase load arrival into a receiving location and to assign license plate IDs. When the received material has been completely reported, the receiving clerk posts the product receipts for all purchase orders in the load. The warehouse worker uses the mobile device to report putaway work for the received material to a stocking location.

- *Review Load Planning Workbench Form for Open Purchase Order Lines.* The receiving clerk uses the Load Planning Workbench to view and select the purchase order line items that represent the contents of newly-arrived material (or anticipated arrivals). The displayed information can reflect selection criteria, such as the ship-to warehouse, vendor and delivery date. The receiving clerk can then create a purchase load for selected lines, or assign them to an existing load.

- *Create New Load for Purchase Orders.* The receiving clerk uses the Load Planning Workbench form to create a new load for selected purchase orders. The total weight and volume of the load can be reviewed prior to creation. The form displays the newly-created load in the Loads section, where each line identifies the Load ID and related information such as the vendor. A Load Details section provides additional information about a selected load, such as the related purchase order number(s), items and quantities.

- *Assign Purchase Orders to an Existing Load.* The receiving clerk uses the Load Planning Workbench form to assign selected purchase orders to an existing load. The total weight and volume of the load can be reviewed prior to creation. The form displays the load in the Loads section, where each line identifies the Load ID and related information such as the vendor. A Load Details section provides additional information about a selected load, such as the related purchase order number(s), items and quantities. If needed, the load lines within one purchase load can be moved to a different load.

- *Confirm the Inbound Shipment* When ready, the receiving clerk confirms the inbound shipment of the purchase load, which enables further reporting about the newly-arrived material. This step normally represents the confirmed shipment of a purchase load from the vendor or carrier.

  Confirming the inbound shipment has an additional impact when using the advanced transportation management functionality to assign a rate to an inbound load for purchase orders. It updates the purchase orders within the load with the related charges.

- *Register Purchase Load Arrival into receiving location (via Mobile Device).* The receiving clerk identifies the Load ID and related purchase order number(s) when using the mobile device to register purchase load arrival into a receiving location and to assign license plate IDs. Alternative options include immediate putaway as part of reporting arrival, including putaway into a location that is not license plate controlled.

- *Post the Product Receipts for a Purchase Load.* When the reporting of purchase load arrival has been completed, the receiving clerk can post the product receipts for all purchase orders within the load. This requires starting from the Load form (or the Load Planning Workbench) for the selected load, and then posting the product receipts for the load. The Load ID (plus a suffix) is displayed as a default value for the product receipt numbers, and it can be overridden prior to posting. Case 65 illustrates the approach.

- *Report Work for Putaway to Stocking Location.* The warehouse worker uses the mobile device to report putaway work for the received material to a stocking location. A suggested stocking location can reflect location directives, or the warehouse worker can determine and report the stocking location. In some cases, the received material does not require license plate tracking and the putaway location is not license plate controlled.

Case 65: Receive a Purchase Load Defined at Time of Arrival

The receiving clerks at a manufacturing/distribution company defined the contents of a purchase load that represented the contents of newly-arrived material (or anticipated arrivals). Each load and its related purchase order lines typically reflected the contents of a vendor's packing list. In this way, a receiving clerk used the mobile device to report arrivals against the Load ID. When arrival information was completely reported for a load, the receiving clerk posted the product receipts for all purchase orders within the load, and entered the vendor's packing list number(s) as part of the posting process.

Receive a Purchase Load Defined by Load Planning The contents of a purchase load may reflect the planning and coordination of transportation for the inbound load. Relative to the previously described business process, the steps associated with defining a purchase load and confirming the inbound shipment are typically performed by a transportation coordinator. Otherwise the business process is the same for receiving a purchase load. A subsequent chapter about transportation management provides further explanation of load planning for an inbound load (Section 23.12).

Life Cycles Related to Purchase Load Receiving The typical process for purchase load receiving involves several related constructs where the status for each construct reflects various steps in the process. Figure 15.6 summarizes this information, and identifies those steps representing the minimum number of touch points for updating status. Shading highlights the key constructs of a load and shipment, the mobile device transactions for reporting arrival and putaway work.

Figure 15.6 Life Cycles Related to Purchase Load Receiving

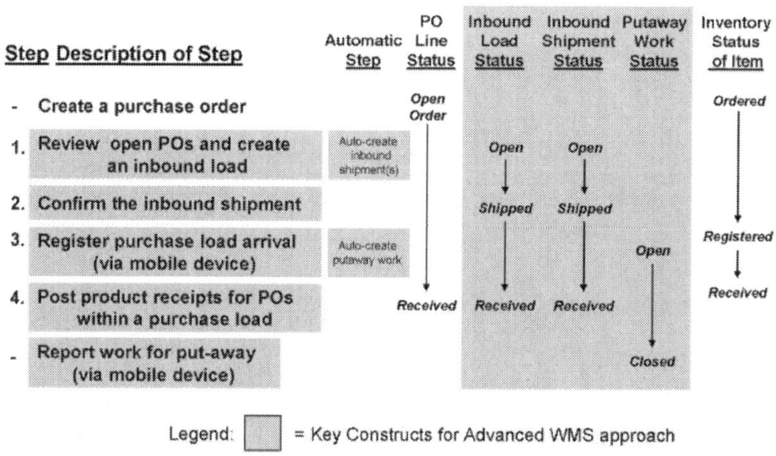

An inbound load consists of one or more shipments, where each shipment consists of the purchase order line items for one vendor. When initially created, the inbound load and shipment have a status of *open*, and subsequent steps change the status to *shipped* and *received.*

15.10 Comparing Approaches to Purchase Order Receiving

The two approaches to warehouse management in AX 2012 R3 can be compared in several different ways. The differences in conceptual models provide one way to make a comparison. It is best illustrated by comparing the two approaches for a simple yet typical business process involving purchase load receiving. This provides the basis for an apples-to-apples comparison of comparable steps, as summarized in Figure 15.7. These steps represent the minimum number of touch points within the business process for updating status, and the figure draws on previously presented information for each approach.

Figure 15.7 Comparing Approaches for Purchase Order Receiving

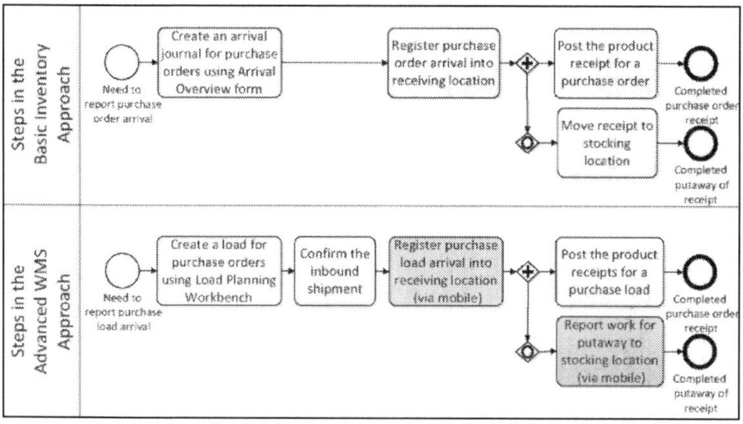

In summary, the comparable steps indicate the differences in conceptual models for the same business process. The starting point differs significantly between the basic approach (which generates an arrival journal for selected orders using the Arrival Overview form) and the advanced approach (which creates a load for selected orders using the Load Planning Workbench form). The advanced approach also employs mobile device transactions for reporting arrival and putaway work (shown with grey shading in the figure). It also requires an additional step to confirm the inbound shipment. Both approaches require a final step of posting the product receipt to update financial information. The basic approach supports posting of all product receipts for purchase orders within an arrival journal, and the advanced approach supports posting of all product receipts for purchase orders within a purchase load.

15.11 Executive Summary

The Advanced WMS approach supports several variations for purchase order receiving. This chapter started with a simple yet typical business process, and explained the related life cycles, reversing transactions and key constructs. The basic process provided a baseline for explaining variations, such as differences in reporting receipts for a purchase load and the different approaches to receiving inspection.

Several case studies illustrated the variations. These included receiving inspection at a separate QC area (Case 64) and receiving a purchase load defined at time of arrival (Case 65). Several previously-cited case studies also apply. These include reporting quality order results after putaway (Case 20), cross docking for special orders (Case 24), modeling the required time for purchase order receiving/inspection (Case 26), purchase orders delivered to a subcontractor warehouse (Case 49), assigning the Inventory Status during purchase order arrival (Case 58), putaway of items requiring cold storage (Case 59) or physical separation (Case 60), and using the mobile device to capture quality-related data about purchase receipts. Several case studies in subsequent chapters also apply, such as vendor batch numbers (Case 80), country of origin for purchased material (Case 81), and nonconformance reports for purchased material (Case 83).

Chapter 16

Sales Order Picking/Shipping

The Advanced WMS approach supports multiple variations in the sales order picking/shipping process. For explanatory purposes, it is easiest to start with a simple yet typical business process, and explain the related life cycles, reversing transactions, key constructs, and related inquiries and reports. The basic process provides a baseline for explaining variations.

Many of the major variations within the Advanced WMS approach involve an extended explanation. For example, the variations often involve extended explanations of a typical process, related life cycles and key constructs, and unique setup information. Hence, the topics related to the basic process and its variations can be segmented into two groups. These considerations are reflected in the following sections within the chapter.

Topics about a Basic Process

1. Basic Process for Sales Order Picking/Shipping
2. Additional Steps in the Basic Process
3. Life Cycles Related to Basic Process
4. Reversing Transactions in Basic Process
5. Key Constructs in the Basic Process for Sales Order Picking/Shipping
6. Major Variations of Sales Order Picking/Shipping
7. Minor Variations
8. Inquiries and Reports About Sales Order Picking/Shipping

Topics about Variations to the Basic Process

9. Variations of Release to Warehouse for Sales Orders
10. Variations of Wave Picking for Sales Shipments
11. Variations of Load Planning for Sales Orders
12. Variations of Manual Packing

13. Variations of Automated Packing
14. Variations in Replenishment of Picking Locations
15. Staging and Loading Steps Prior to Shipment
16. Extended Explanation of Life Cycles Related to Sales Order Picking/Shipping
17. Comparing Approaches to Sales Order Picking/Shipping

Realistic delivery dates on sales orders represent a critical consideration for sales order picking/shipping. Delivery promises should reflect S&OP game plans and the delivery dates should reflect up-to-date information. Other factors may apply such as a manageable level of expediting. These considerations will make life easier for warehouse management.

16.1 Basic Process for Sales Order Picking/Shipping

The business process for sales order picking/shipping can have many variations. The starting point of a simple yet typical process for order-based picking provides a baseline for explaining the variations. The basic process shown in Figure 16.1 consists of several steps performed by a shipping clerk and warehouse worker. The figure uses grey shading to highlight the mobile device transactions, and identifies several automatic steps. The process starts with the need for sales order picking/shipping and ends with completed shipments. This section provides an overview of the basic process and describes each step in more detail.

Figure 16.1 Basic Process for Sales Order Picking/Shipping

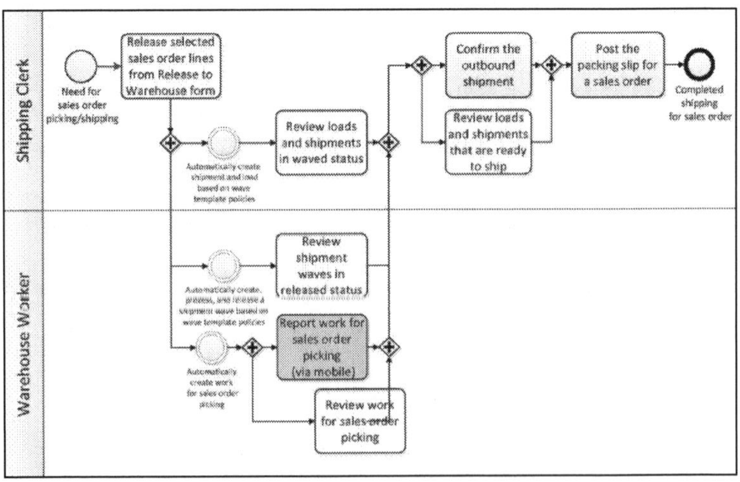

The basic process reflects an order-based picking approach with placement at an outbound dock. In this basic process, the release to warehouse step automatically creates a single shipment, a corresponding load and a released wave for a sales order. The released wave automatically creates the picking work. This basic process employs one variation for the release to warehouse step that requires reserved material prior to release. A subsequent section describes other variations of the release to warehouse step (Section 16.9).

Overview The shipping clerk uses the Release To Warehouse form to review a subset of open sales order lines based on selection criteria, such as the ship-from warehouse, ship date and delivery mode. The shipping clerk selects the desired line items and releases them to the warehouse for picking/shipping. The release-to-warehouse step automatically creates a shipment, load and a released shipment wave for a sales order based on wave template policies. The shipping clerk can review the shipments and loads in a waved status.

The warehouse worker reviews the picking work for the released shipment wave, and uses the mobile device to report work for each pick (from stocking locations) and the put to an outbound dock location. At that point, the shipping clerk can review loads and shipments that are ready to ship. The shipping clerk prints relevant documents such as a bill of lading, confirms the outbound shipment after the goods have actually left, and posts the packing slip against relevant sales orders.

Release Selected Sales Order Lines Using the Release To Warehouse Form The shipping clerk uses the Release To Warehouse form to anticipate sales order shipping requirements by reviewing a subset of open sales order lines based on selection criteria, such as the ship-from warehouse, ship date and delivery mode. The shipping clerk selects the desired lines and adds them to the list for subsequent release to warehouse. Lines can also be removed from the list.

The shipping clerk releases the selected lines to the warehouse for picking/shipping, which updates the released status of a sales order. Given the order-based picking approach (defined by wave template policies), the release to warehouse step will automatically create the following:

- *Automatically Create a Single Shipment and a Corresponding Load and Wave for Each Selected Sales Order.* Additional ones will be automatically created for a sales order when its selected lines reflect a different ship-from site.[1] The wave template policies also result in automatic updates to the status of a wave (to released), which triggers the creation of picking work for the wave.

- *Automatically Create Work for Sales Order Picking.* The work consists of one or more picks for the selected line items and the puts to an outbound dock.

The release to warehouse step will identify errors that prevent actual release (if any), such as the lack of reserved inventory or missing address information.

Review Loads and Shipments in Waved Status The shipping clerk can review information on the Waved Loads form and the Waved Shipments form, and perform the following:

- *Using the Waved Loads Form.* The shipping clerk can view the related wave and work for a selected load, print relevant documents, and optionally assign the load to a different outbound dock.

- *Using the Waved Shipments Form.* The shipping clerk can view the related work and quality order (if applicable) for a selected shipment, print relevant documents, and optionally consolidate shipments or transfer a shipment to a different load.

Review Shipment Waves in Released Status Using the Open Waves form, the warehouse worker can review the related load, shipment and work for a selected wave and optionally print the picking list.

Report Work for Sales Order Picking (via Mobile Device) The warehouse worker uses the mobile device to report the "pick" and "put" transactions for the work order. Each "pick" identifies the stocking location for inventory to be picked, and each "put" identifies the assigned location for an outbound dock.

---

[1] A companywide policy (within the Accounts Receivable Parameters form) determines whether separate picking lists will be generated for different delivery modes on sales lines within a sales order, but this policy only applies to the Basic Inventory approach. It does not apply to the Advanced WMS approach.

Review Work for Sales Order Picking to an Outbound Dock The warehouse worker can print the work for sales order picking to help identify the needed picking. The options for printed documents include the printed picking list for a wave and printed work orders, and both documents provide bar-coded information to simplify recording of the work by mobile devices.

Review Loads and Shipments that are Ready to Ship The shipping clerk can anticipate shipping activities by reviewing information on the Loads Ready To Ship form and the Shipments Ready To Ship form, and print relevant documents such as a bill of lading or load list.

Confirm the Outbound Shipment The shipping clerk confirms the outbound shipment when the goods are actually shipped. The shipping clerk may also post the sales order packing slip prior to confirming the outbound shipment.

Confirming the outbound shipment has an additional impact when using the advanced transportation management functionality to assign a rate to an outbound load for sales orders. It updates the sales orders within the load with the related charges.

Post the Packing Slip for a Sales Order The shipping clerk posts the packing slip for a sales order (based on information from sales order picking), which automatically generates a packing slip journal. The packing slip is typically printed when posted, or it can be printed at a subsequent time.

Enforcing the Major Steps in the Basic Process The major steps of picking and shipping a sales order can be enforced by two policies within the item model group assigned to an item. These policies are labeled Picking Requirements and Deduction Requirements.

16.2 Additional Steps in the Basic Process

The basic process often involves additional steps or slight variations not shown in Figure 16.1 so that the diagram does not become too complex. Examples include the following steps.

Short Pick When Reporting Sales Order Picking Work You can select the Short Pick option as part of reporting the mobile device transaction, and then specify the actual pick quantity. You also need to select a reason for short picking which indicates the applicable action(s).

A reason for short picking reflects a work exception and must be defined beforehand on the Work Exceptions form. You also identify the applicable actions for the short pick reason, such as (1) automatically create cycle count work, (2) treat the quantity difference as an automatic inventory adjustment out, and/or (3) treat the quantity difference as an automatic decrement to the quantity on the shipment or load. You can also identify no applicable actions. Multiple work exceptions (aka reasons) may need to be defined to support different combinations of these applicable actions. After reporting a short pick on the mobile device, the transaction and selected reason can be viewed on the Work Exceptions Log inquiry. The inquiry includes pertinent information such as the sales order, load, and shipment.

Print Labels for License Plates Labels can be automatically generated and printed when reporting sales order picking via mobile devices, and subsequently reprinted when needed. The ability to print labels is identified as a separate step in the work template for sales order picking. The label information and layout can reflect company-specific and product-specific requirements, and the nature of the label printer. This involves some technical details that fall outside the book's scope.

Print Bill of Lading for a Sales Order Shipment The shipping clerk can optionally print a bill of lading for a sales order shipment before or after confirming the outbound shipment. The bill of lading format reflects information about the National Motor Freight Code (NMFC) assigned to each product.

Identify Sales Order Lines Picked but not yet Shipped One indicator of needed actions for warehouse management consists of sales order line items which have been picked but not yet shipped. You can identify these needed actions using the standard inquiries about Shipments Ready to Ship and Loads Ready to Ship.

Identify Sales Order Lines with Past Due Ship Dates One indicator of needed actions for warehouse management consists of sales order line items with past-due ship dates You can identify these needed actions using a standard form (labeled Delayed Shipments, within Sales and Marketing), which lists the sales lines with a promised ship date that is past due relative to a specified backorder date.

Identify Sales-Related Backorders A sales-related backorder within AX simply refers to any sales line with a ship date prior to a specified date (aka the backorder date).[2] This simple definition also applies to a sales line with an unshipped or partially shipped quantity, where the line has not been closed short when reporting actual shipment. This represents the more common interpretation of a sales-related backorder. Some scenarios need to identify the quantity for an unshipped or partially shipped line as "backordered" on sales order documents.[3] A standard inquiry provides information about sales-related backorders (labeled Backorder Lines, within Sales and Marketing).

The customer service rep typically reviews sales-related backorders and takes action for a selected backorder, but the information is also critical for the warehouse manager. The actions include updating the promise date or reducing the quantity for the sales order line, or a request to expedite a supply order.

Inquiries About Work Orders Related to Sales Orders Standard inquiries can be used to identify the open, in process, and closed work orders related to sales orders as well as all work orders.

Impact of an Order Hold on Sales Order Picking/Shipping The assignment of a Hold Code to a sales order will prevent any picking/shipping transactions until the Hold Code has been cleared. It results in a corresponding infolog when attempting to enter transactions.

Review Performance Metrics for On Time Delivery and Full Quantity Two performance metrics include on time delivery and full quantity delivery, typically measured over a specified time interval. Each performance metric reflects several underlying assumptions, as described below.

- *On Time Delivery.* On-time delivery for a sales line reflects a comparison between the actual and promised ship date. The basis of the promised date can be the requested or confirmed date for the sales line, and either option should reflect consistent assignment of the promised date. In addition, achievement of on-time delivery typically reflects an exact match between dates or early delivery, so that only late shipments indicate a performance problem.

- *Full Quantity Delivery.* Full quantity delivery for a sales line reflects a comparison between the ordered quantity and the actual shipped quantity.

---

[2] This simple definition is critical for understanding "backordered lines" with a future ship date when compared to a specified backorder date in the future.

[3] The treatment of unshipped and partially shipped line items is defined by the Backorder Tracking policy for printing packing slips and invoices (within the Forms Setup form in Accounts Receivable).

The achievement of full delivery typically requires an exact match between quantities, so that quantity differences indicate a performance problem. Some would argue that delivery tolerances for over- and under-shipment quantities on a sales line (expressed as a percentage) should be considered in the performance metric.

You can identify these two performance metrics and their underlying assumptions using a standard report (labeled Top Sales Order Lines Not Shipped in Full or Not Shipped on Time, within Inventory Management), where the report dialogue also specifies the applicable time interval and warehouses(s). The standard report does not account for delivery tolerances.

A standard inquiry provides a similar performance metric for on-time delivery (labeled Deviations Between Actual and Expected Shipments, within Sales and Marketing). The displayed information identifies sales lines with late shipments, and reflects a selected basis for the promised ship date and time interval (expressed as a number of look-back days).

16.3 Life Cycles related to the Basic Process

The basic process involves several related constructs, where the status for each construct reflects various steps in the process. Figure 16.2 summarizes this information for the basic process, and only displays those steps representing the minimum number of touch points for updating status. Grey shading highlights the key constructs related to the Advanced WMS approach. These key constructs include reservations, the release status of a sales order and the related shipments, loads, waves and picking work.

The release to warehouse step represents a key part of any business process for sales order picking/shipping. For the basic process, this step automatically creates a shipment and corresponding load for each sales order, and automatically creates and releases the corresponding wave (as reflected in a waved status for the shipment and load). The released wave also results in the automatic creation of picking work for the wave. Additional steps in the basic process—for reporting work and confirming the outbound shipment—will automatically update the status of each construct. A subsequent section provides an extended explanation about each construct's life cycle and its status values (Section 16.16).

Figure 16.2 Life Cycles Related to the Basic Process for Sales Order Picking/Shipping

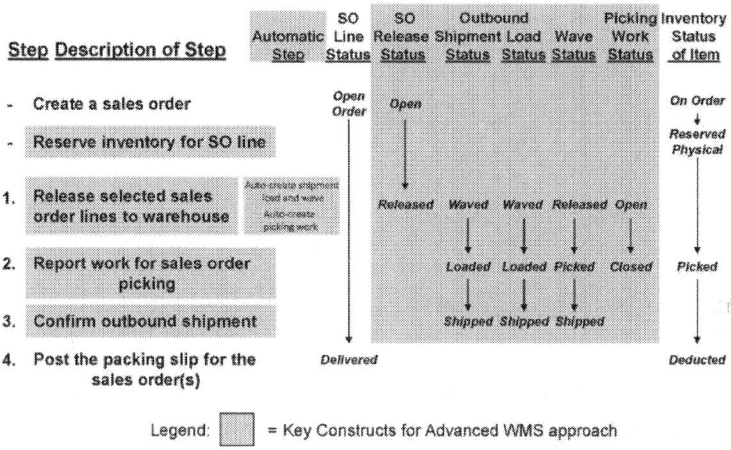

The inventory status for the item on a sales order line is also shown on the right side of Figure 16.2. Steps in the basic process will automatically change this status from *on order* to *reserved physical*, *picked* and *deducted.*

16.4 Reversing Transactions in the Basic Process

The ability to reverse transactions requires an understanding of the current point within the business process, and the associated status of key constructs. Borrowing from the previous figure, Figure 16.3 illustrates the steps within the basic process (shown in grey text) and the various points at which you can perform reversing transactions (shown in black text). The figure also illustrates the impact of a reversing transaction on status, and the arrows indicate the resulting point in the business process. As identified by step numbers in the figure, you can reverse transactions (1X) after initially creating the picking work for the released wave, (2X) after reporting actual picking and (4X) after reporting actual shipment.

Figure 16.3 Reversing Transactions in the Basic Process for Sales Order Picking/Shipping

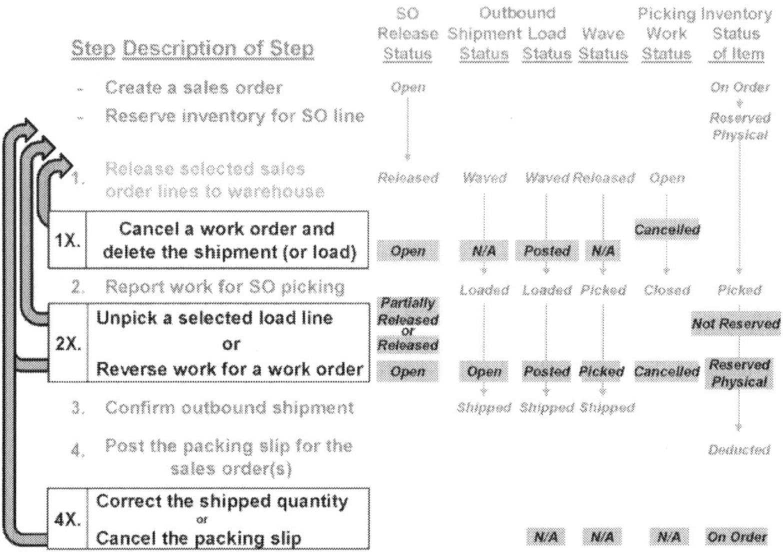

Step 1X: Cancel Work Order and Delete the Shipment (or Load) You can cancel a work order prior to reporting any work line, which changes the release status to *open*. In addition, after cancelling the work, you can delete the associated shipment (or load) which also deletes the corresponding wave. The deletion typically means that a status no longer applies, as shown by a value of "N/A" within the figure, although the load status is updated to *posted.* At this point, you can start over with the release to warehouse step, which will create a new shipment, load, wave and work order. Alternatively, you can also modify or cancel the sales order at this point in time.

Step 2X: Unpick a Selected Load Line The completed work for sales order picking can be unpicked by starting from the relevant load and a selected load line, and then accessing a separate form (labeled Load Line Unpicking) to reduce the picked quantity. You specify the quantity to reverse and the move to location (which cannot be a LP-controlled location), and also indicate whether the quantity should be removed from the shipment or load. The specified quantity can reflect the entire quantity or partial quantity that has been picked. This reversing transaction will update the released status of the sales order (to open or partially released) and remove the reservations.

Step 2X: Reverse the Work for a Work Order As an alternative to unpicking individual transactions, you can reverse all picking work associated with a work order prior to confirming the outbound shipment. When initiating this transaction, the dialogue on the Reverse Work screen enables you to indicate how to handle the material. For example, it can remain at the current location (such as an outbound dock), it can be automatically moved to a specified location (such as a stocking location), or you can automatically create movement work to a specified location. The remaining work for a partially completed work order will be cancelled.

Step 4X: Correct the Shipped Quantity or Cancel the Packing Slip Information can be corrected or cancelled after posting the sales order packing slip but before you generate the invoice. You perform the correction or cancellation from the Packing Slip Journal form, as described below.

- *Correct the Quantity for a Packing Slip.* When you select the Correct function, you access the Correct Packing Slip form in order to enter a different shipped quantity. The quantity difference (with the previously entered quantity) will be reversed.

- *Cancel a Packing Slip.* When you select the Cancel function, you will cancel the sales order packing slip.

16.5 Key Constructs in the Basic Process for Sales Order Picking/Shipping

The Advanced WMS approach for sales order picking/shipping involves several key constructs in addition to the sales order. These key constructs include reservations, the release status of a sales order, and the related shipments, loads, waves and work orders for picking work. Previous figures and explanations have already illustrated these key constructs.

Reservation Policies for a Sales Order and its Line Items The reservation policy assigned to a sales order line item indicates whether inventory will be reserved automatically or manually. The options for this reservation policy include *Automatic* and *Manual.* A third option is termed *Explosion* and it also supports automatic reservations, but further explanation focuses on just the two options for simplicity's sake. When initially adding a line item, its reservation policy can be inherited from the item or from the sales order header.

- *Inherit Reservation Policy From the Item.* The item's reservation policy (*Automatic* versus *Manual*) is embedded in the Item Model Group assigned to the item.

- *Inherit Reservation Policy From the Sales Order Header.* The option for the item's reservation policy is termed Default, and it is embedded in the Item Model Group assigned to the item. This approach represents functionality within previous AX versions. The reservation policy for a sales order header can be inherited from the companywide policy (embedded in the A/R Parameters) and overridden.

After line items have been added to a sales order, a change to the reservation policy in the sales order header can update the policy for every line item.

Release Status of a Sales Order The release status indicates whether the sales order's line items have been released to the warehouse, with possible values of *Open, Released,* and *Partially Released.* In the basic process, the release to warehouse step requires reservations for each sales order line, otherwise they cannot be released to the warehouse. Other variations of the release to warehouse step do not require reservations beforehand, and they can result in reservations (Section 16.9).

Shipments, Loads, Waves and Work Orders for Sales Order Picking/Shipping Order-based picking represents one variation of the business process. With order-based picking, the release to warehouse step automatically creates a shipment and corresponding load for each sales order, and automatically creates and releases the corresponding wave (as reflected in a waved status for the shipment and load). The released wave also results in the automatic creation of picking work for the wave. Additional steps in the basic process—for reporting work and confirming the outbound shipment—automatically update the status of each construct, as illustrated in Figure 16.2.

Each of the major variations for sales order picking/shipping has slightly different steps which involve differences in the life cycles and status for shipments, loads and waves. Subsequent sections describe these major variations and similar figures illustrate the related life cycles.

16.6 Major Variations of Sales Order Picking/Shipping

The basic process for sales order picking/shipping provides the baseline for explaining major variations. Several variations involve a brief explanation. Others involve an extended explanation that will be provided in subsequent sections. This section lists all of the major variations and includes brief explanations when applicable. The list indicates the relevant section for topics requiring an extended explanation.[4]

- Simple Inventory Transaction for Sales Order Picking/Shipping
- Picking Batch-Controlled Items
- Picking Serialized Items
- Shipping Serialized Items with Deferred Assignment of Serial Numbers
- Variations of Release to Warehouse for Sales Orders (Section 16.9)
- Variations of Wave Picking for Sales Shipment (Section 16.10)
- Variations of Load Planning for Sales Orders (Section 16.11)
- Variations of Manual Packing (Section 16.12)
- Variations of Automated Packing (Section 16.13)
- Variations in Replenishment of Picking Locations (Section 16.14)
- Staging and Loading Steps Prior to Shipping (Section 16.15)

Simple Inventory Transaction for Sales Order Picking/Shipping The shipping clerk can bypass the use of loads, shipments, waves and picking work by using a simple inventory transaction, where you report actual picking when posting the packing slip for a sales order. This simple inventory transaction applies to both the basic and advanced approaches.

Picking Batch-Controlled Items The picking work for batch-controlled items is impacted by reservation logic. That is, the Reservation Hierarchy assigned to an item determines whether its batch numbers will be reserved or not. Reservations of specific batch numbers are critical in many scenarios, such as shelf-life items involving FEFO reservations and customer requirements for remaining shelf life. As a result, the relevant batch will be displayed and printed on the work line for the work order, and also displayed on the mobile device when reporting the picking work.

[4] One other major variation involves cluster picking for sales shipments. It is not included because the prior research and case studies could not be completed prior to publication deadlines.

Two additional policies about sales order picking work must be defined for correctly supporting reservations of batch-controlled items. These policies are defined as part of the Location Directive Actions related to the work order type for sales orders, where you indicate the pick should be "Batch-Enabled" and also select the relevant "Strategy" for locating material. For example, the strategy should be "FEFO Batch Reservations" in order to correctly support picking of shelf-life items.

Other aspects of picking batch-controlled items can differ based on the use of license plates and the quantities involved. For example, the picking work may identify specific license plates (at an LP-controlled location), or the target license plate for picking work may contain multiple items and batch numbers. In addition, the picking work reflects the restricted usage policies for batch disposition codes that can be assigned to batch numbers. A subsequent chapter provides further explanation of batch-controlled items (Section 25.3).

Picking Serialized Items The picking work for a serialized item is not typically impacted by reservation logic because of the item's Reservation Hierarchy, where serial numbers are below the location. The picking work can differ based on the use of license plates and the quantities involved. For example, the picking work may identify a specific license plate containing multiple serial numbers of an item, or the target license plate for picking work may contain multiple items and serial numbers. A subsequent chapter provides further explanation of serialized items (Section 25.1).

Shipping Serialized Items with Deferred Assignment of Serial Numbers With the deferred approach, the information must be reported as part of a simple inventory transaction because it cannot be reported by a mobile device transaction. That is, you register the item's serial number(s) when posting the sales order packing slip by accessing the Serial Numbers form for the line item.

16.7 Minor Variations

Several minor variations apply to the basic process for sales order picking/shipping and its major variations. These include the use of quality orders, customer pickups, delivery tolerances, expedite policies, safety margins and notes. Other minor variations were identified as part of the additional steps for the basic process, such as identifying needed actions for warehouse management and the impact of sales order holds. This section covers the following list of topics and their explanations.

- Quality Orders for Sales Order Picking/Shipping
- Impact of a Customer Pickup
- Significance of Ship Complete Policies
- Impact of Delivery Tolerances
- Impact of the Fulfillment Rate for Sales Orders
- Significance of Expedite Policies
- Modeling the Required Time for Picking/Shipping Activities
- Relevance of Order Entry Deadlines for Picking/Shipping Activities
- Effective Use of Notes for Sales Order Picking/Shipping Purposes

Quality Orders for Sales Order Picking/Shipping A quality order can be automatically generated when you create picking work related to a sales line, or post the packing slip for a sales order, as defined by Quality Associations related to sales orders for an item. For example, the validation of test results may be required before you can actually report the picking work (as a result of blocking), and the mobile device will prevent entry and display a message about the blocking until the quality order has been closed. Alternatively, without blocking, you can report the picking work without the quality order validation. A subsequent chapter about quality management provides further explanation of quality orders (Section 26.3).

Impact of a Customer Pickup A customer pickup can be reported by a simple inventory transaction and generation of an invoice. Otherwise, it requires the reporting of picking work to an outbound dock (via mobile device), and then you can use the Sales Pickup form as a short-cut approach for posting the packing slip and invoice.

Significance of Ship Complete Policies A sales order line can be flagged as "ship complete," so that you will receive an error unless you ship the entire quantity when posting the sales order packing slip. An additional "ship complete" flag for the entire sales order has a slightly different significance, since it prevents the generation of a sales order picking list until all lines have sufficient inventory to be reserved for the ordered quantity. Hence, using both policies will help ensure that all lines will be picked and that order quantities for individual lines will be shipped complete.

As an alternative approach, the concept of "ship complete" can be enforced using the delivery tolerance functionality, since delivery tolerances of zero percent for a sales line mean that the shipped quantity must equal the ordered quantity. It is also possible to enforce a companywide policy so that any over- and under-delivery quantities are not acceptable. The next point provides further explanation of delivery tolerances.

Impact of Delivery Tolerances on Sales Order Picking/Shipping When delivery tolerances are acceptable, they determine how much the quantities being picked and shipped for a sales line can differ from the ordered quantity. Over- and under-delivery tolerances are expressed as a percentage and the values assigned to an item act as defaults for a sales order line item. Delivery tolerances of zero percent for a sales line mean that the shipped quantity must equal the ordered quantity. A companywide policy (embedded in the A/R parameters) determines whether over- and under-deliveries will be acceptable for sales orders.

An over-delivery tolerance applies to both the picked quantity and the shipped quantity for a sales line. For example, the system displays an error message infolog and prevents over-picking (beyond the over-delivery tolerance) when reporting the quantity picked, as well as over-shipping (beyond the delivery tolerance) when posting the sales order packing slip.

An under-delivery tolerance only applies to the shipped quantity for a sales line. For example, you cannot post the packing slip for an under-shipped quantity (beyond the under-delivery tolerance) in conjunction with the "close short" flag, and the displays an error message infolog.

Impact of the Fulfillment Rate for Sales Orders A fulfillment rate indirectly impacts sales order picking. It only applies to the release to warehouse step, which precedes any sales order picking activity. A set of rules about a fulfillment rate allows a sales order to be released to the warehouse with partial reservations rather than being fully reserved. Exceptions about meeting the fulfillment rate can prevent the release to warehouse for a sales order, or simply provide a warning. The rules about a fulfillment rate can be defined as a companywide policy and optionally overridden as a customer-specific set of rules. The rules apply to all four variations of the release to warehouse step, as described in a subsequent section (Section 16.9).

Significance of Expedite Policies An expedite shipment flag can be assigned to a sales order header, and it provides one of the selection criteria for the release to warehouse step (described in Section 16.9). It does not directly impact picking/shipping activities.

Modeling the Required Time for Picking/Shipping Activities Some scenarios have a significant time requirement for picking/shipping activities related to a sales order (such as 1 or 2 days). A significant time requirement should be included in the supply chain model so that (1) promised ship dates will reflect the required time and (2) picking will be scheduled prior to the ship date.

- *Identify the Picking/Shipping Time as a Safety Margin.* The required time can be identified as the issue safety margin for a salable item, where you define the number of days as part of the Coverage Group assigned to the item. For example, when demands exist for an item with one day prep time, master scheduling logic will generate planned orders to arrive one day before the demand date. As another consideration, the release to warehouse step should be performed one day prior to the ship date.

- *Include the Picking/Shipping Time in Delivery Promises* The required time (expressed as the issue safety margin, described above) can be included in delivery promises based on ATP logic, where you assign a delivery date control policy of "ATP plus issue margin" to the saleable item as part of its default order policies. For example, when entering a sales line for a stocked item with one day prep time, the earliest possible promised date will be one day later.

  Some scenarios do not use ATP logic as the basis for delivery promises, such as using CTP logic for delivery promises about make-to-order items. In many of these scenarios, the required time can be modeled by the sales lead time assigned to an item as part of its default order policies.

Relevance of Order Entry Deadlines for Picking/Shipping Activities Some scenarios involve same day shipments for sales orders that have been entered by a specified deadline. This order entry deadline frequently represents a prerequisite for meeting the departure time of a shipping vehicle, so that adequate time is available for picking/shipping activities. An order entry deadline also means that an order entered after the specified time will be treated as if it were received the next day, thereby affecting the assignment of a promised ship date. You define a set of deadlines for each day within a week (termed an order entry deadline group), and then assign the deadline group to each customer and site.

Effective Use of Notes for Sales Order Picking/Shipping Purposes The mobile device transaction for sales order picking work can display notes to guide picking/shipping activities. These notes can be entered on the sales order header. The related shipment(s) will inherit the notes and you can also directly define a note for a shipment. A subsequent chapter provides further explanation about the effective use of notes for warehouse management purposes (Section 24.5).

16.8 Inquiries and Reports about Sales Order Picking/Shipping

Some of the relevant inquiries and reports have already been identified as part of the additional steps for the basic process. For example, the standard inquiries can identify the sales order lines with partial picking, sales order lines picked but not yet shipped, sales order lines with past due ship dates, sales-related backorders, and performance metrics for on time delivery and full quantity. Other standard inquires apply to shipments, loads, waves and work orders related to sales orders.

Inquiries about Outbound Shipments and Loads Several standard inquiries apply to the shipments and loads related to sales orders. Some were previously mentioned in the basic process for sales order picking/shipping (Figure 16.1), such as shipments and loads in waved status or ready to ship. These examples indicate the significance of different steps in the business process, since the status of the shipment or load determines the relevant inquiry. Figure 16.4 summarizes the variations of inquiries about shipments and loads in the context of different steps in the picking/shipping process.

Figure 16.4 Inquiries about Shipments and Loads Related to Sales Orders

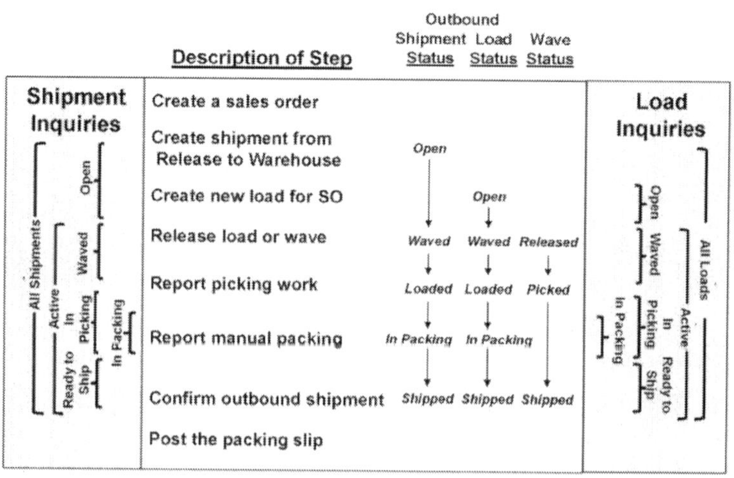

One of the steps and the associated value of *In Packing* only apply to the use of manual packing, as described in a subsequent section (Section 16.12). A separate inquiry applies to shipments and loads that have a status of *In Packing*.

Inquiries About Shipment Waves Standard inquiries can be used to identify the pending, open and closed shipment waves as well as all waves. These inquiries will be described as part of a subsequent section about wave planning (Section 16.10). A shipment wave can apply to sales orders or transfer orders. It is different than a production wave for the components of production orders.

Inquiries About Work Orders Related to Sales Orders Standard inquiries can be used to identify the open, in process, and closed work orders related to sales orders as well as all work orders. The various inquiries about work orders were also covered in a previous chapter about work orders (Chapter 14).

16.9 Variations of Release to Warehouse for Sales Orders

The release to warehouse step represents a key part of any business process for sales order picking/shipping, and it automatically updates the "Release Status" for a sales order. There are multiple options for performing the release to warehouse and the use of selection criteria. An additional factor termed the fulfillment rate applies to each option. The considerations are reflected in the following topics within the section.

- Options for Release to Warehouse
- Selection Criteria About Sales Orders for Release to Warehouse
- Significance of the Fulfillment Rate for Release to Warehouse
- Identify Errors related to the Release to Warehouse step

Options for Release to Warehouse The release to warehouse step has four options which reflect two basic factors. One factor involves the prerequisite for reserved inventory, and two options allow you to defer reservations until release to warehouse. In addition, the rules concerning a fulfillment rate allow a sales order to be released to the warehouse with partial reservations of the ordered quantities. The second factor involves the approach for performing the release to warehouse step, and the various approaches are reflected in the following four options.

- *Perform Release to Warehouse for a Sales Order.* The release to warehouse step can be performed from the Sales Order form, typically at the completion of the order entry process by the customer service rep. The release step applies to all lines on the sales order and inventory must be fully reserved for all lines.

- *Perform Release to Warehouse for Selected Sales Order Lines Using the Release to Warehouse Form.* The Release To Warehouse form can be used to view a subset of open sales order lines based on selection criteria (such as the ship-from warehouse, ship date and delivery mode) and then release selected lines which have been fully reserved beforehand. It is typically used by the shipping clerk to anticipate shipping requirements and to initiate required picking activities, and it only supports the release to warehouse step. This option was employed in the basic process for sales order picking/shipping.

- *Perform Automatic Release to Warehouse with Selection Criteria for Sales Order Lines.* The Automatic Release To Warehouse task can be performed on a periodic basis, where selection criteria determine the applicable sales order lines. Inventory for each line item must be fully reserved beforehand unless a warehouse-specific policy (labeled "Reserve when orders are released by a batch job") allows deferred reservations at the time of the release to warehouse step. Different sets of selection criteria can support variations in decisions about the release to warehouse.

- *Perform Release to Warehouse for a Selected Load Using the Load Planning Workbench.* The Load Planning Workbench form can be used to view a subset of open sales order lines based on selection criteria (such as the ship-from warehouse, ship date and delivery mode), typically by a transportation coordinator. Selected sale order lines can then be assigned to a new load, or to an existing load, and information about loads are displayed in the bottom half of the form. When applicable, the transportation coordinator will assign a rate/route to the outbound load.

  The transportation coordinator can view and filter the loads, and then release a selected load to the warehouse. Inventory for each sales order line within the load must be fully reserved beforehand unless a warehouse-specific policy (labeled "Reserve inventory at load posting") allows deferred reservations at the time of the release to warehouse step.

Selection criteria about open sales lines (and also loads) can be identified by filtering options at the top of the form (such as the ship-from warehouse and ship date) or by using grid filters. In addition, you can optionally predefine filters about sales orders and loads with the user-defined Load Planning Filters.

Selection Criteria About Sales Orders for the Release to Warehouse Step Selection criteria about sales order lines can be used with three of the options for the release to warehouse step. Examples of these selection criteria are summarized in Figure 16.5 and described below. The figure indicates the applicable constructs for each selection criteria, such as the sales order line or header. It also highlights several selection criteria (via shading) which provide the basis for prioritizing picking/shipping activities, such as the ship date and mode of delivery for a sales line.

Figure 16.5 Example Selection Criteria for Release to Warehouse for Sales Orders

<table>
<tr><th rowspan="2"></th><th rowspan="2">Field Name</th><th colspan="3">Applicable Construct</th></tr>
<tr><th>SO Line</th><th>SO Header</th><th>Customer</th></tr>
<tr><td></td><td>Ship from site/warehouse</td><td rowspan="4">Yes</td><td rowspan="5">Yes</td><td rowspan="5">N/A</td></tr>
<tr><td rowspan="5">Basis for Prioritizing SO Picking/Shipping</td><td>Ship date</td></tr>
<tr><td>Mode of delivery</td></tr>
<tr><td>Shipping carrier/service</td></tr>
<tr><td>Expedited shipment flag</td><td rowspan="3">N/A</td></tr>
<tr><td>Customer classification group</td><td>N/A</td><td>Yes</td></tr>
<tr><td></td><td>Customer</td><td rowspan="2">Yes</td><td rowspan="2">N/A</td></tr>
<tr><td></td><td>Ship-to address information</td><td>Yes</td></tr>
</table>

- *Ship-From Site and Warehouse.* The ship-from site and warehouse provide an organizing focus for picking/shipping activities.

- *Ship Date.* The ship date provides the primary basis for scheduling and prioritizing the picking/shipping activities, and is frequently used in conjunction with other prioritization criteria. The confirmed ship date is typically used, although the requested ship date may be used in some cases.

- *Mode of Delivery.* The mode of delivery provides another organizing focus for picking/shipping activities, especially when preparing shipments for a scheduled pickup time. A sales order may have multiple picking lists that reflect different delivery modes on sales lines. A delivery mode may reflect faster or expedited delivery, and can be associated with an Expedite Code.

- *Shipping Carrier and Carrier Service.* The shipping carrier and carrier service can be used as an organizing focus of picking/shipping activities, especially when preparing shipments for a scheduled pickup time by the carrier.

- *Expedited Shipment Flag.* The expedite shipment flag can only be assigned to a sales order header, and it provides an additional basis for expediting. As the primary purpose, it works in conjunction with the shipping carrier assigned to a sales order in order to include the carrier's shipping charges (for expedited shipment) when they are normally considered as free for orders exceeding a specified total amount.

- *Customer Classification Group.* A user-defined customer classification group can be assigned to a customer, and it provides one basis for selecting sales lines when using the Automatic Release To Warehouse approach.

- *Customer.* A selected customer provides another organizing focus for picking/shipping activities, such as generating picking lists for shipping sales orders to a customer.

- *Ship-to Address Information.* Various elements of the address can be used as an organizing focus of picking/shipping activities, such as shipping sales orders (or loads) to the same address.

Significance of the Fulfillment Rate on the Release to Warehouse Step A set of rules about a fulfillment rate allows a sales order to be released to the warehouse with partial reservations of the ordered quantities rather than being fully reserved. The rules apply to all four options of release to warehouse. For example, a fulfillment rate of 90% means that the total of reserved quantities for all sales lines must be 90% or greater that the total of the ordered quantities. The fulfillment rate can apply to the total quantity or total value (quantity times price) of a sales order's lines. In either case, it is possible that the reservations for a given line on a multiline sales order may not meet the fulfillment rate but the overall sales order does.

A related policy (labeled the "fulfillment violations message") determines whether an exception for the fulfillment rate will prevent the release to warehouse for a sales order, or simply provide a warning (or no message) while still allowing the release. When prevented, an example infolog message would be "A fulfillment rate of 90 was not met for sales order 12345," which is displayed after attempting to release to warehouse.

The set of rules about a fulfillment rate can be defined as a companywide policy (as part of the Accounts Receivable Parameters), and optionally overridden as a customer-specific set of rules. The set of rules do not apply when using a fulfillment rate of 0% and/or a fulfillment violation message policy of "none."

Identify Errors Related to the Release to Warehouse Step Several types of errors can be identified by the release to warehouse step, and they must be corrected in order to successfully perform the release. The lack of reserved inventory represents a common error. Other types of errors include missing address information for the customer and missing a load template when releasing a load. When using the Load Planning Workbench, you can first validate a load and then review any errors prior to releasing the load to the warehouse.

16.10 Variations of Wave Picking for Sales Shipments

A wave picking approach commonly refers to a grouping of sales order shipments with the same delivery requirements, such as the same ship date and carrier for a ship-from warehouse. The grouping is termed a shipment wave or wave for short.[5] The contents of a shipment wave can be released and picked together to meet a planned departure time of a shipping vehicle.

There are many variations of a wave picking approach. At its simplest, a shipment wave reflects the sales lines for a single sales order, so that the wave picking approach is frequently termed order-based picking. This variation was employed in the basic process for sales order picking/shipping, where each wave was automatically created and released by the release to warehouse step. Other variations involve wave picking for a grouping of sales order shipments, which represents the more common reference for a wave picking approach.

[5] A wave picking approach can also apply to the components for a grouping of production orders or kanban orders in a manufacturing scenario, where the grouping is termed a production wave and kanban wave respectively. A subsequent chapter describes wave picking for production waves (Section 19.7).

The planning aspects of wave picking for a group of shipments consist of several steps typically performed by a warehouse planner. Some of the steps can be performed automatically to reflect the planner's normal decision making about wave planning, as modeled by policies within a wave template. For example, a wave template might be defined for each variation of a carrier that serves a given warehouse, and you define the applicable carrier as part of the query criteria for each wave template. In this way, performing the release to warehouse step will automatically create sales shipments and also assign them to an applicable wave. These automatic steps can be illustrated in a typical process for wave planning.

An extended explanation about wave planning can be segmented into several topics, and this section includes the following topics.

- Typical Process for Wave Planning of Sales Shipments
- Life Cycles Related to Manual Wave Planning
- Reversing Transactions in Manual Wave Planning
- Order-Based Picking as a Wave Picking Variation

Typical Process for Wave Planning of Sales Shipments A typical process for wave planning consists of several steps, as illustrated in Figure 16.6 and described below. The need for wave planning starts with the automatic generation of sales order shipments by the release to warehouse step. Some of these steps can be automated to reflect the planner's normal decision making about wave planning, and these automatic steps are shown in the figure. As an explanatory approach, it is easiest to first describe the manual steps shown in the figure and then describe the more common use of automatic steps.

Figure 16.6 Typical Process for Wave Planning of Sales Order Shipments

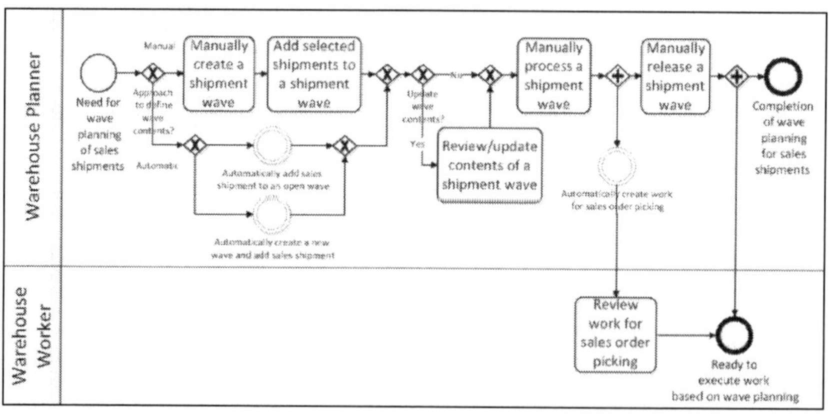

With the manual approach to defining wave contents, the warehouse planner manually creates a shipment wave for a selected wave template, and then reviews the unassigned sales shipments by accessing the Maintain Shipments form. The warehouse planner can view totals for selected shipments (such as total weight, volume and pieces), add selected shipments to the wave lines, and then view totals again for all wave lines. The grouping of selected shipments typically reflects similar delivery requirements, such as the same ship date and shipping carrier for a ship-from warehouse. These similar delivery requirements can be identified (as query criteria) for user-defined Wave Filter Codes, thereby facilitating the display and selection of shipments. If needed, the planner updates the wave contents (such as adding or deleting wave lines) prior to processing and releasing the shipment wave.

With an automatic approach to defining wave contents, the warehouse planner defines warehouse templates that reflect normal decision making. In the previously mentioned example, a wave template might be defined for each variation of a carrier that serves a given warehouse, and you define the applicable carrier as part of the query criteria for each wave template. Two additional policies within a wave template determine how to automatically assign sales order shipments to a wave (after they have been automatically created by the release to warehouse step). These two policies work in conjunction to define wave contents, as described below for the shipping carrier example.

- *Automatic Additions to an Existing Wave.* This policy results in automatic additions of newly-created shipments to an open wave for the applicable shipping carrier (if an open wave exists). Sales shipments will continue to be added automatically to an open wave until the wave has been released.

  Many scenarios have a cutoff time for automatic additions to an existing wave, such as a cutoff time of 1:00 pm in order to perform wave picking prior to a 3:00 pm departure time of the shipping vehicle. The shipments created after the cutoff time will result in automatic creation of a new wave that represents a next day shipment. The applicable cutoff time can be defined within the query criteria for a wave template. This cutoff time should also be reflected in the order entry deadlines for a site.

  As related policies, you can optionally define several maximum limits for a wave so that automatic additions will be made until a maximum has been reached and then a new wave will be automatically created. The limits include a maximum weight, a maximum number of shipments, and/or a maximum number of wave lines. These limits can help scale the amount of work or weight for a given wave.

The same maximum limits can also be used to automatically process a wave when its values reach the maximum limits (aka thresholds), which involves the additional wave template policy for "*process wave automatically at threshold*."

- *Automatic Creation of a New Wave.* This policy applies to newly-created shipments when an open wave does not already exist for the applicable shipping carrier, so that a new wave will be automatically created for the shipment. Subsequent creation of sales shipments with the same shipping carrier will be automatically added to the open wave because of the automatic addition policy.

Some wave picking scenarios involve replenishment of picking locations, as described in a subsequent section (Section 16.14).

After identifying the selected shipments in the wave, the warehouse planner indicates "process the wave" which automatically (1) updates the wave status to held and (2) creates work for sales order picking. The picking work reflects the warehouse-specific work template (about how to create the picking work) and location directive (about the pick and put locations). This step will also (3) create a load containing the selected shipments if one has not already been created. At this point in time, the warehouse worker can review the work for sales picking, and optionally print a picking list for the wave or print the associated picking work. However, the picking work cannot be reported until the wave has been released by the warehouse planner.

Life Cycles Related to a Manual Wave Planning Process As an explanatory approach, it is easiest to describe the life cycles and steps related to a manual wave planning process. These steps are illustrated in Figure 16.7 and highlighted by grey shading. The figure also displays the key constructs and the corresponding status for each step. The left side of the figure identifies the standard inquiries relative to wave status. These standard inquiries identity the subsets of pending, open and closed waves, and one inquiry identifies all waves.

As the starting point of the process, the release to warehouse step automatically creates sales shipments with a shipment status of *open*. These can be viewed on the Open Shipments form, and you consolidate multiple sales shipments into a single shipment.

Figure 16.7 Life Cycles Related to Manual Wave Planning for Sales Shipments

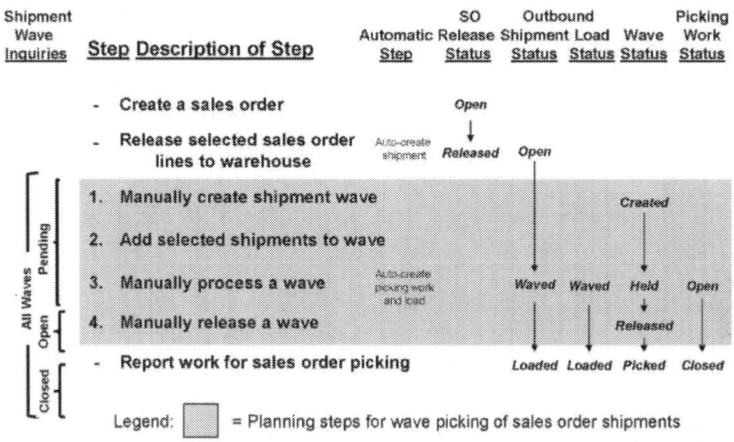

The warehouse planner manually creates a shipment wave (with a wave status of *created*), and then adds selected shipments to the wave. At the appropriate time, the warehouse planner indicates "process the wave" which automatically updates the wave status (to *held*) and the shipment status (to *waved*), and also creates work for sales order picking. This step will also create a load containing the selected shipments if one has not already been created. At this point in time, the warehouse worker can review the work for sales picking, but the picking work cannot be reported until the wave has been released by the warehouse planner.

Reversing Transactions in Manual Wave Planning for Sales Shipments The ability to reverse transactions requires an understanding of the current point within the business process, and the associated status of key constructs. Borrowing from the previous figure, Figure 16.8 illustrates the steps within the wave planning process (shown in grey text) and the various points at which you can perform reversing transactions (shown in black text). The figure also illustrates the impact of a reversing transaction on status, and the arrows indicate the resulting point in the business process. As identified by step numbers in the figure, you can reverse transactions (3X) after processing a wave and (4X) after releasing a wave.

Figure 16.8 Reversing Transactions in Manual Wave Planning for Sales Shipments

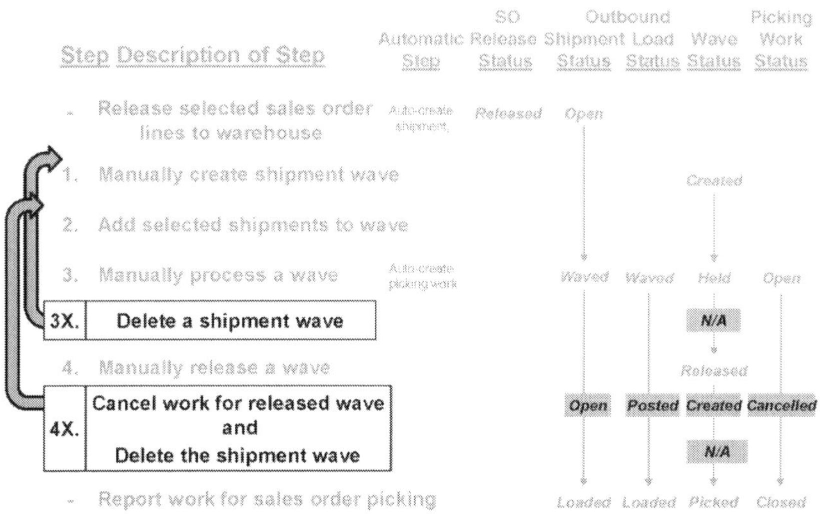

Step 3X: Delete a Shipment Wave You can delete a shipment wave after updating its status to held. The deletion means that a status no longer applies, as shown by a value of "N/A" within the figure.

Step 4X: Cancel Work for a Released Shipment Wave You can cancel work for a released shipment wave prior to reporting the associated work, which also updates the status for the associated work order(s), shipment(s) and load(s).

Step 4X: Delete a Released Shipment Wave You can only delete a released shipment wave after first cancelling all associated work.

Order-Based Picking as a Wave Picking Variation An order-based picking approach requires the appropriate wave template policies. In particular, a wave should be automatically created for each newly-created sales shipment stemming from the release to warehouse step. And these newly-created shipments should not be added to an existing wave. In many scenarios, the additional steps to process and release the wave will also be automatically performed as a result of the release to warehouse step.

16.11 Variations of Load Planning for Sales Orders

Load planning for sales orders can serve multiple requirements related to warehouse and transportation management. From a transportation viewpoint, for example, each load provides an organizing focus for a transportation coordinator to assign the appropriate route and rate, and arrange the transportation appointments. From a warehouse viewpoint, the scheduled departure date/time for a load provides an organizing focus to coordinate sales order picking for a shipment wave. This section focuses on the warehouse viewpoint, and a subsequent chapter covers the transportation viewpoint (Section 23.4).

This section describes the steps in a typical load planning process for sales orders and illustrates the life cycles related to this process. Each of the steps employs the Load Planning Workbench form, so that the section concludes with a summary of this form. A separate section also describes the significance of a load template for representing a shipping vehicle or container. These considerations are reflected in the following topics within the section.

- Typical Load Planning Process for Sales Orders
- Load Planning for Sales Order Shipments
- Life Cycles Related to the Typical Load Planning Process
- Reversing Transactions in the Load Planning Process
- Significance of a Load Template
- Summary of the Load Planning Workbench

Typical Load Planning Process for Sales Orders A typical load planning process consists of several steps performed by a transportation coordinator using the Load Planning Workbench. The steps are sometimes performed by a warehouse planner or by multiple roles. The load planning process can focus on open sales orders or shipments. The typical process shown in Figure 16.9 focuses on load planning of open sales lines with all steps performed by the transportation coordinator. Completion of the process can trigger several automatic steps.

Figure 16.9 Typical Load Planning Process for Sales Orders

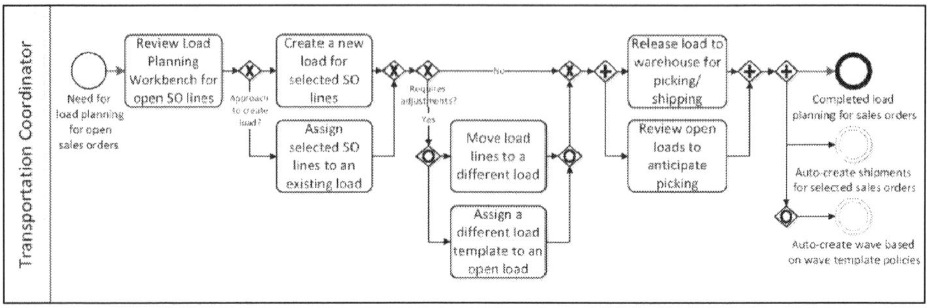

The transportation coordinator uses the Load Planning Workbench to anticipate picking/shipping activities by viewing a subset of open sales lines. The displayed subset can reflect selection criteria within the header (such as the ship-from warehouse and ship date) or filtering on displayed fields. The desired sales lines can then be selected from the displayed subset.

The transportation coordinator can assign selected sales lines to an existing load by first selecting the applicable load, or assign them to a new load. For assignment to a new load, the coordinator identifies the applicable load template about the shipping vehicle or container (which defines a maximum allowed weight and volume). In either case, the proposed assignment includes a comparison of the weight/volume for selected lines to the maximum allowed. The transportation coordinator can cancel or accept the proposed assignment to a load. When accepted, an infolog warning will be displayed if the maximum weight or load has been exceeded by the proposed assignment.

Adjustments may be necessary. For example, appropriate adjustments should be taken when the maximums have been exceeded for a load template. In this case, you can move load lines to a different load, or assign a different load template to the load (with larger maximums), otherwise you obtain an error when attempting to release the load to the warehouse.

At the appropriate time, the transportation coordinator releases the load to the warehouse. The release to warehouse step will automatically create shipments for the sales orders comprising the load lines, and also create the deferred reservations. In addition, this step can automatically create a shipment wave based on wave template policies.

Subsequent steps for a load can also be performed on the Load Planning Workbench. These subsequent steps include confirming the outbound shipment for a load and posting the packing slips for all sales orders within a load.

Typical Load Planning Process for Sales Order Shipments The previous description of a typical load planning process focused on a starting point of open sales lines. In contrast, some processes focus on a starting point of sales order shipments already released to the warehouse. The Load Planning Workbench supports both starting points, and there are several minor differences. First, the filtering criteria for displayed shipments are slightly different than for sales lines, since the shipment information does not include some aspects of sales orders (such as the mode of delivery and the Expedited Shipment flag). Second, releasing the load to the warehouse does not create a shipment because the shipment already exists.

The Open Shipments form displays sales shipments with an open status, and supports consolidation of multiple sales shipments into a single shipment. You can also transfer a sales shipment to a new or existing load.

Life Cycles related to the Typical Load Planning Process The typical load planning process involves several related constructs, where the life cycle and status of each construct reflect steps in the process. Figure 16.10 summarizes this information for the major constructs and steps within the process, where shading highlights some of the key steps. The inventory status reflects deferred reservations occurring when the load has been released to the warehouse. The figure includes several other aspects of loads, such as the subsequent steps to confirm the outbound shipment for a load and post the packing slips for all sales orders within a load.

Figure 16.10 Life Cycles Related to Typical Load Planning Process for Sales Orders

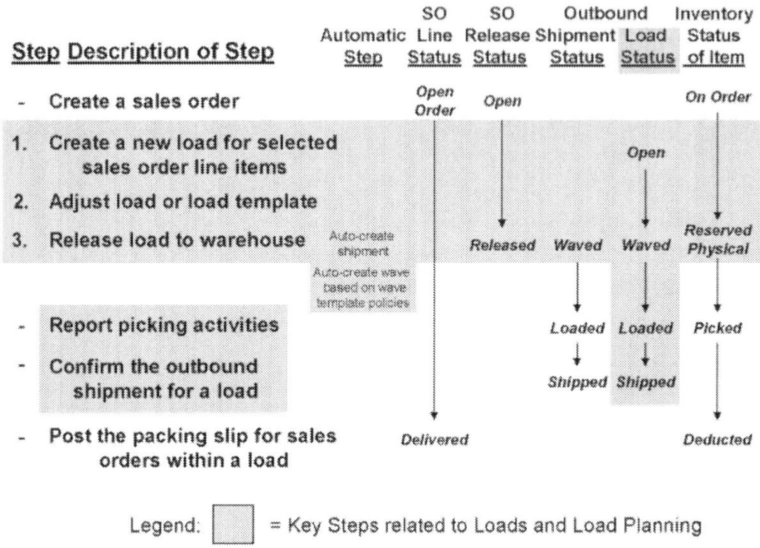

Significance of a Load Template A load template often represents a shipping vehicle or a container with a maximum allowed weight and volume, and the term *shipping vehicle/container* will be used here for explanatory purposes. You define each applicable vehicle/container as a load template, and also define its characteristics such as the maximum allowed weight and volume.[6]

As previously mentioned, you can assign a proposed vehicle/container when creating a new load for selected sales lines, and the proposed assignment includes a comparison of the weight/volume for selected lines to the maximum allowed. An infolog warning will be displayed if the maximum weight or volume has been exceeded by the proposed assignment. In addition, when a maximum has been exceeded, you will obtain an error when attempting to release the load to the warehouse. You can assign a different vehicle/container to a load prior to release to warehouse.

In some cases, the considerations about maximum allowed weight and volume do not apply to a load, so that you should define and assign a load template that represents the "unlimited" option (with zero values for these fields).

---

[6] Using the Equipment form in the Transportation Management module, you can optionally define various types of transportation equipment (along with maximum allowed weight and volume) and assign the equipment to a load, but this only provides reference information.

Since each load must be assigned a load template, you can initially assign the load template representing the unlimited option, and then change the assignment to meet the weight/volume requirements for the load.

Summary of the Load Planning Workbench Form The Load Planning Workbench form supports a wide range of actions and inquiries at different steps within a business process for sales order picking/shipping. For example, it supports all of the steps in the typical load planning process as well as subsequent steps to the point of confirming the outbound shipment and packing slip posting for sales orders within a load. As a result, it is difficult to summarize all aspects of the Load Planning Workbench. However, the three major sections within the form provide a starting point for summarizing and understanding its usage.

The Load Planning Workbench form consists of three sections labeled Supply and Demand, Loads and Line Details, and each section serves different purposes as described below.

- *Supply and Demand Section.* This section provides multiple tabs identifying different sources of supply and demand, and two of these tabs (labeled Sales Lines and Shipments) identify the sales order lines and shipments for our context of load planning. The displayed information can reflect selection criteria within the header such as the ship-from warehouse and ship date, or filtering on displayed fields. You can optionally predefine the filters for sales lines or for shipments (as Load Planning Filters), and then select the filter as part of the header information.

- *Sales Lines Tab.* This tab displays open sales lines that have not yet been released to warehouse, and the displayed fields provide the basis for filtering applicable lines. The filtering criteria about sales order lines were illustrated in a previous figure (Figure 16.9).

- *Shipments Tab.* This tab displays open shipments that have already been released to warehouse but not yet assigned to a load, and the displayed fields provide the basis for filtering applicable lines. The filtering criteria for shipments are slightly different than for sales lines, since the shipment information does not include some aspects of sales orders (such as the mode of delivery and the Expedited Shipment flag).

  The desired sales lines (or shipments) can then be selected, and assigning them to a new load will create a new entry in the Loads section. Alternatively, you can assign them to an existing load by first selecting the relevant load in the Loads section. In either case, the lines are no longer displayed in the Supply and Demand section.

- *Loads Section.* This section can display just the unshipped outbound loads for our context of load planning (based on selection criteria in the header). Each line in the Loads section identifies the Load ID and related information such as the customer, the ship-from warehouse, the total weight (and remaining unused weight for the load template), the shipping carrier (if assigned), and load status.

  When viewing a selected load in the Loads section, the Line Details section displays information about each load line such as the related sales order number, item and quantity.

  The Loads section supports several actions and inquiries at different steps within the business process. For example, the actions include moving load lines from an open load to another load, assigning a rate or route to the load, and releasing the load to the warehouse.[7] At the appropriate time, you can print the bill of lading, confirm the outbound shipment for a load, and post the packing slips for sales orders within the load. Example inquiries include accessing the related wave and work details after they have been created for the load.

- *Lines Details Section.* When viewing a selected load in the Loads section, the Line Details section displays information about each load line such as the related sales order number, item and quantity. You can optionally delete a selected load line, or perform a reversing transaction (to reduce the picked quantity) after reporting picking work.

16.12 Variations of Manual Packing

Some scenarios require manual packing into containers prior to actual shipment. A container represents the physical structure in which products are packed. Common examples of container types include various sizes of a cardboard box, and a packed container has a unique identifier termed the container ID. However, a container may also reflect other structures or even a reusable object with a permanent container ID. One or more container IDs may be required for a given sales order shipment.

[7] A previous section described the variations for releasing a load to the warehouse, where a warehouse-specific policy determines whether reservations can be deferred until the release step (Section 16.9).

There are many variations of manual packing. For example, the identifier for a packed container that represents a cardboard box is typically assigned automatically at the time of packing, whereas manual assignment often applies to reusable containers. Most scenarios require a printed version of the container contents, and a packed container may require the assignment of shipping charges. Some scenarios will place a packed container at a designated outbound dock for subsequent shipping, whereas others will immediately report shipping after closing the container. Within AX, all of the above-mentioned factors can be incorporated into one or more user-defined processes for manual packing, where each variation is termed a packing profile. However, additional factors can also lead to variations of manual packing.

As an explanatory approach, it is easiest to review a simple yet typical process in a common scenario for manual packing. The common scenario involves the use of cardboard boxes (in several sizes) as containers, placement of a packed container at an outbound dock location for subsequent shipment, and no assignment of shipping charges. The typical process provides the foundation for explaining related setup information, life cycles and reversing transactions in subsequent subsections. These considerations are reflected in the following topics within the section.

- Typical Process for Manual Packing of Sales Order Shipments
- Report Manual Packing Steps Using the Close Container Form
- Life Cycles Related to Manual Packing of Sales Order Shipments
- Unique setup Information to Support the Manual Packing Process

Typical Process for Manual Packing of a Sales Order Shipment The typical process starts with a warehouse worker picking material for placement at a location representing a packing station, and consists of several steps performed by a warehouse worker or shipping clerk. The typical process is illustrated in Figure 16.11, and shading indicates the only step performed by mobile devices. The process starts with the creation of a work order for sales order picking to a pack location, and ends with completion of manual packing and placement of the container in a destination location (such as an outbound dock).

Figure 16.11 Typical Process for Manual Packing of a Sales Order Shipment

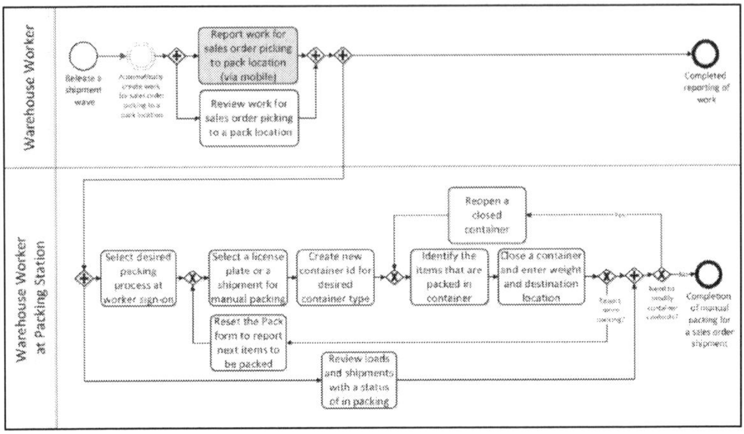

- *Overview.* After material has been delivered to a packing station, the warehouse worker selects a shipment (or license plate) for manual packing, creates a new container id for the desired container type, and identifies the items that are packed in the container. When completed, the shipping clerk reports the container as closed, and identifies the weight and destination location as part of the closing process. All of these transactions are performed using the Pack form. At that point, the shipping clerk can review shipments that are ready to ship.

- *Report Work for Sales Order Picking to a Pack Location (via Mobile Device).* A warehouse worker moves the material to a location that represents a packing station, which provides the starting point for reporting manual packing via the Pack form.

- *Review Loads and Shipments With a Status of In Packing.* The warehouse worker uses the standard inquiries about shipments (or loads) that currently have a status of in packing, which provides a coordinating mechanism for packing activities.

- *Select Desired Packing Process at Time of Worker Sign-On.* As the first step, the warehouse worker accesses the Pack form in order to sign on and select the applicable process for manual packing (aka the packing profile).

- *Select a License Plate or a Shipment for Manual Packing.* After accessing the Pack form, the warehouse worker identifies what will be packed by selecting a shipment ID or license plate ID currently at a pack location. After this selection, the Pack form displays header and line item information. The header information includes the customer and related shipment ID, and notes from the sales order header that may guide packing (if specified). Each line item identifies the item and quantity to be packed. You can also access detailed information about the related shipment.

- *Create New Container ID for the Desired Container Type.* The warehouse worker creates a new container ID (which is automatically assigned in this typical process) and selects the appropriate container type (which reflects a box size). If needed, the container type can be changed to a larger or smaller box size. It is worth noting that manual packing does not support nested containers.

- *Identify the Items that are Packed in the Container.* After creating a new container ID, the warehouse worker identifies each item and quantity placed in the container by selecting from the list of items associated with the license plate (or shipment) that was initially identified for manual packing. The display information includes the items and quantities remaining to be packed and those already packed. The system prevents entry of an over packed quantity, and provides a warning when the container's maximum allowable weight has been exceed. No warnings are provided about other physical dimensions (such as volume or width) in order to allow flexibility during packing. For example, you might be able to squeeze or fold items into the container.

  As you report items packed in containers, the Pack form displays the total weight and quantity of items in the current container, and also the total number of containers for the selected shipment.

  After a container has been packed, you can view the structure of the selected container to identify its contents.

- *Close a Container and Enter Weight and Destination Location.* The warehouse worker uses the Pack form to close a container, and the associated dialogue to enter the destination location and weight (which can be automatically calculated based on the weights for items within the container). The close step will automatically move the container to the destination location, and prevent any additions to the container. The close step may entail the following two options when they have been included in the packing profile that was initially selected. These two options are not shown in Figure 16.11.

- *Automatically Print the Container Pack List.* The printed version consists of header and line information, where the header identifies the customer and ship-to address, and the relevant identifiers for the sales order, shipment and container. Each line identifies the item and quantity within the container. Alternatively, you can subsequently print the report for a selected container.

- *Display the Posting Packing Slip Form.* You can optionally post the sales order packing slip for a closed container, or simply cancel the step and perform posting at a subsequent time. Posting the packing slip will deduct inventory and update the sales order.

- *Reset the Pack Form to Report Next Items to be Packed.* Using the Pack form, the warehouse worker can reset the form in order to start reporting the next license plate or shipment to be packed.

- *Reopen a Closed Container.* The warehouse worker can reopen a closed container by first accessing the Containers form directly or from the Pack form (by clicking the Available Containers button). Several different actions can be undertaken after a container has been reopened. For example, you can change the packed quantity of an item, or even delete the container and start over with the step to create a new container ID.

- *Assign a Tracking Number to a Container.* The shipping clerk use the Container form to assign a tracking number (and a master tracking number, if applicable) to a container.

- *View the Container Structure for a Packed Container.* The container structure identifies the items and quantities within a container. The container structure can be viewed from Container form, either by accessing it directly or from the Shipment Details form.

Report Manual Packing Steps Using the Close Container Form

Almost all of the steps in the typical process can be reported using the Pack form. The Close Container form provides an alternative reporting approach for several of the steps. For example, you can perform the close step for a selected container, or perform the step to create a new container id for a selected shipment.

Life Cycles Related to Manual Packing of Sales Order Shipments

The typical process for manual packing involves several related constructs, where the life cycle and stats for each construct reflect the various steps in the process. Figure 16.12 summarizes this information and the shading highlights key aspects of manual packing.

Figure 16.12 Life Cycles Related to Manual Packing of Sales Order Shipments

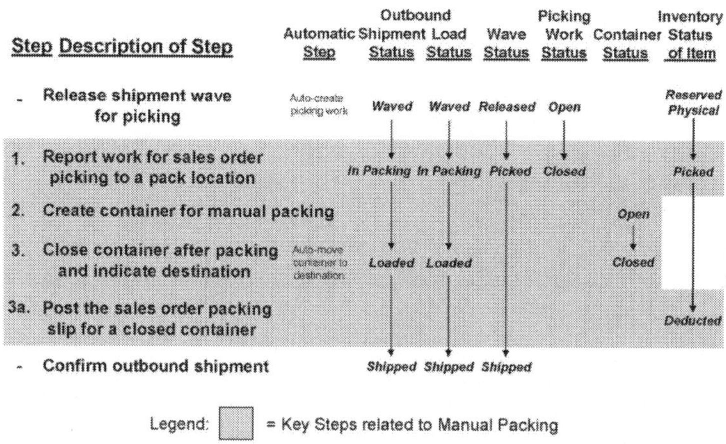

Releasing a shipment wave will automatically create the work for picking sales orders to a pack location, as defined by the criteria for work templates and location directions. After reporting work for picking to a pack location, the status of the associated shipment and load will be automatically updated to *in packing*, and you can view the standard inquiries about shipments and loads that are currently in packing. The creation and closing of a container will automatically update the container status, and a closed container will be automatically moved to the designated destination location. As part of the closing step, you can optionally include an additional step for posting the packing slip for the closed container, which updates the inventory status to *deducted.* This optional additional step is shown as Step 3a in the figure.

The reversing transactions include the previously described approaches for cancelling or reversing the picking work (Section 16.3). They also include deletion of a container ID prior to actual shipment, and reopening a closed container ID to make corrections.

Unique Setup Information to Support a Manual Packing Process
Relative to the basic process, the unique setup information includes the pack locations, the mobile device transaction for picking to a pack location, container types and packing profiles.

- *Pack Locations.* Each packing station is identified as a pack location with a location profile ID that reflects a location type for Pack and no license plate tracking. This location profile ID is also identified as a companywide policy for a pack location (on the Warehouse Parameters form).

- *Mobile Device Transactions for Picking to a Pack Location.* The warehouse-specific work template and location directive for sales orders identify the "put" to a pack location (or the location profile ID for pack locations). They also identify the query criteria about a sales order characteristic indicating the need for manual packing.

- *Container Types.* The user-defined container types consist of several sizes of cardboard boxes, and each container type has a maximum allowable weight.

- *Packing Profiles.* Each variation of the manual packing process within a given warehouse should be defined as a packing profile. In the typical process described above, the packing profile employed automatic numbering for container IDs and identified a warehouse-specific closing profile about the default destination location, the weight unit of measure, and automatic printing of the container pack list.

- *Displaying Sales Order Notes About Manual Packing Requests.* Displaying notes from the sales order header on the Pack form.

Case 66: Packing Structure Documentation for the Carrier and Customer

A manufacturer needed to provide documentation to the carrier and the customer about the packing structure of the shipped items within a case. As a proposed solution approach, they will define a container per case (rather than a license plate per case) and print a label per case.

16.13 Variations of Automated Packing

Some scenarios have standardized the decision making logic about how to pack items into containers. Example decisions include the required number and size of physical containers for the lines within a sales order shipment based on product and container physical dimensions, and an optimized packing structure within a container. This standardized decision making can be incorporated into an automated packing process (also termed a containerization process within AX), where the suggestions are embedded in the picking work triggered by a released shipment wave. More specifically, each work order contains the work lines identifying the suggested container as well as each item and quantity to place in the container. For example, a shipment requiring five containers would have five work orders. In this way, the warehouse worker can pick the goods directly into the containers with optimal picking routes, and place the material directly at an outbound dock.

The use of an automated packing process assumes that the resulting suggestions are 100% correct because they cannot be overridden, and the mobile device transaction simply reports that the work was completed. Compared to manual packing, it eliminates the need for reporting container selection, item assignment, and container closing at the packing station. However, the number of work orders may involve more reporting.

The two different approaches to packing—automated packing versus manual packing—employ mutually exclusive approaches to containers. Containers created from the automated packing process cannot be used or modified in the manual packing process. For example, you will not be able to use the Pack form to pack items into these containers, or use the Container form to reopen a closed container or change item quantities. However, the two approaches can be used in tandem, as illustrated in Case 67.

This remainder of this section summarizes the automated packing logic and the unique setup requirements.

Summary of the Automated Packing Logic Much of the automated packing logic consists of multiple policies embedded within a container build template. Each template defines one variation of the containerization process, and its applicability is defined by the associated query criteria. For example, a given containerization process may only apply to specific customers, products and/or warehouses. This section summarizes the logic.

The basic logic will create a new container for each new shipment ID. It can optionally create a new container for each different item so that different items will not be packed in the same container. Alternatively, the mixing logic rules can allow different items in one container. The basic logic will suggest the smallest possible container that meets the item's physical dimensions. The sequence in which containers should be considered is defined by a container group consisting of a sequence of container types. It also defines the maximum fill percentage of each container type within the group. A given shipment ID may contain multiple lines requiring multiple containers, and you can view the created container structure for a shipment. You can also view the contents of a container.

The reversing transactions include the previously described approaches for cancelling or reversing the picking work (Section 16.4). The picking work reflects the automated packing logic. Canceling the work will also delete the automatically created containers so that you can start over as if the wave has not been released. You cannot manually delete these containers.

In certain situations, the automated packing process can fail in suggesting a container. For example, it will fail when a single item cannot fit into a container, or when an item's quantity cannot fit into a single container and the quantity cannot be split into multiple containers.

Unique Setup Information to Support an Automated Packing Process The setup information for automated packing differs from manual packing, since it does not involve packing locations and the associated picking work to a packing location. Rather, the picking work is placed at an outbound dock and it is assumed that the suggested packing will be completed as part of the picking process. It still requires the definition of container types, and the unique additional aspects include the definition of an item's physical dimensions, a container build template and a containerization step within the shipment wave template.

- *Define all Physical Dimensions of an Item.* All of the physical dimensions for an item must be correctly defined in order to support the automated packing logic. For each applicable unit of measure, the dimensions must be specified for the item's weight and volume as well as width, length and height. .

- *Container Build Templates.* A container build template includes multiple policies that provide the core logic for an automated packing process, as previously mentioned in the summary of automated packing logic.

- *Containerization Step Within the Shipment Wave Template.* Releasing a shipment wave will automatically create picking work that reflects the automated packing logic, but only when the shipment wave includes a containerization step as a selected method. Multiple containerization steps may be needed to reflect variations that have been identified as wave steps.

Case 67: Combined use of Manual and Automated Packing

A distributor stocked an item in both pallets and pieces, with the two different UM stocked in two different locations. A sales order quantity sometimes required pallets or pieces or both. They employed an automated packing process for pallets, and manual packing of pieces into an appropriate container, in order to deliver the goods to the outbound dock.

Case 68: Multi-Level Container Structure

A manufacturing/distribution company had a multi-level container structure that reflected nested containers. In a typical scenario, a warehouse worker would pack the goods into cartons (first level containers), and then put several of those cartons on a pallet (second level containers). They were considering the use of automated packing to calculate the required containers at different levels and build up the nested structure.

16.14 Variations in Replenishment of Picking Locations

Some scenarios employ one or more picking lines that contain the most popular items, thereby reducing the time to retrieve inventory from bulk locations. The need for replenishing these picking locations can be manually determined, and the move transactions can be reported via mobile devices. However, the needs can also be automatically determined using three different approaches that also create replenishment work for reporting via mobile devices.

Approaches to Create Replenishment Work One approach is termed the min/max approach because it employs min/max quantities for selected items/locations and a separate calculation creates replenishment work when the quantity falls below the minimum. This approach typically applies to scenarios with stable demand and corresponding min/max quantities. The other two options apply to more dynamic scenarios, where suggested replenishment can reflect constant changes in demand.

The second approach reflects demand stemming from selected loads. This "load demand approach" also employs a separate calculation to create replenishment work when the existing quantity for the selected items/locations cannot satisfy the demand for the specified load.

The third approach reflects the demand stemming from waves, and does not employ a separate calculation. With the "wave demand approach," the replenishment work can be created when you process a wave as part of a wave picking process.

Typical Process to Create and Perform Replenishment Work The three approaches to create replenishment work provide the starting point for a typical process, as summarized in Figure 16.13 and described below. Shading indicates the mobile device transaction common to all three approaches, and the figure includes the setup activity for just one approach to keep the diagram simple.

Figure 16.13 Typical Process to Create and Perform Replenishment

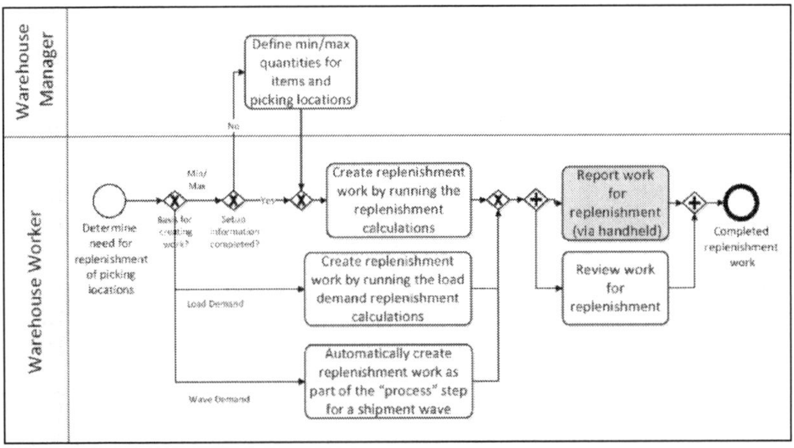

- *Define Min/Max Quantities for Items and Picking Locations*. The warehouse manager defines the min/max logic within a replenishment template (with a replenishment type of Min/Max), where each template line defines the minimum and maximum quantity for a selected item and picking location. In most scenarios, the picking location reflects a fixed location for the item, so that the replenishment calculations will suggest replenishment even when the fixed location is empty. Related policies include the applicable unit of measure for the min/max quantities and for the replenishment quantity, the applicable rule for rounding, and the applicable work template for replenishment (which defines the pick and put transactions).

Different scenarios can be modeled with multiple replenishment templates, such as modeling multiple picking lines (with different picking locations and items) or changes within a given picking line.

The source of inventory for replenishing the picking locations must be identified in a location directive for replenishment picking, as defined by its query criteria. For example, the source of inventory could be a selected warehouse and/or a location profile representing bulk storage. In addition, the query criteria must indicate the applicable replenishment template described above.

- *Create Replenishment Work by Running the Replenishment Calculations.* Running the periodic task of a replenishment calculation (for a specified replenishment template for min/max) will create replenishment work when the quantity falls below the minimum for the item and picking location. The suggested quantity will achieve the maximum quantity for the item and picking location, and the location directive for replenishment indicates the source of replenishment (such as bulk locations). Replenishment work will not be generated when the source has insufficient inventory to satisfy suggested quantity. The replenishment calculations based on min/max logic (labeled Replenishment for short) can be performed as needed, or scheduled as part of a batch job.

- *Create Replenishment Work by Running the Load Demand Replenishment.* Running the periodic task of a load demand replenishment calculation (for a specified load) will create replenishment work when the existing quantity for the item and location cannot satisfy the demand for the load. The suggested quantity will meet the demand, and the location directive for replenishment indicates the source of replenishment (such as bulk locations). Replenishment work will not be generated when the source has insufficient inventory to satisfy suggested quantity. The replenishment calculations based on load demand can be performed as needed or scheduled as part of a batch job.

  The unique setup information includes a replenishment template (with a replenishment type of Load Demand) that defines the applicable items and locations. Other setup includes a work template for replenishment, and a location directive for replenishment (with query criteria about the applicable replenishment template for load demand).

- *Automatically Create Replenishment Work as Part of "Process" Step for a Shipment Wave.* With the wave demand approach, the inventory at picking locations can be replenished to meet just the demand stemming from shipment waves, so that a separate calculation is not required. The replenishment work can be automatically created as part of the process step for a shipment wave.

The unique setup information includes a replenishment template (with a replenishment type of Wave Demand) that defines the applicable items. Other setup includes a work template for replenishment and a location directive for replenishment (with query criteria about the applicable replenishment template for wave demand). The unique setup also involves a wave template that includes the replenishment method, and the policy to "automate replenishment work" when you process a shipment wave.

- *Report Work for Replenishment.* The warehouse worker uses the mobile device to report the "pick" and "put" transactions for a Work ID containing replenishment work lines. Each "pick" identifies the stocking location for inventory to be picked, and each "put" identifies the picking location.

- *Review Work for Replenishment.* The warehouse worker can print the replenishment work to help identify the needed picking for a Work ID. The printed document provides bar-coded information to simplify recording of the work.

16.15 Staging and Loading Steps Prior to Shipping

Staging and loading steps are sometimes necessary within the process for sales order picking/shipping. A typical example involves staging material for delivery via truck, and then loading the material on the truck prior to reporting actual shipment. In this case, you report the work for sales order picking to a staging location and then report the work for sales order loading. At that point, you can review shipments and loads that are ready to ship.

The staging and loading steps represent an alternative approach to simply picking to an outbound location, which was employed in the basic process for sales order picking/shipping. Figure 16.14 illustrates these two alternatives to reporting work for a shipment wave, and highlights the mobile device transactions via shading.

Figure 16.14 Staging and Loading Steps Prior to Shipping

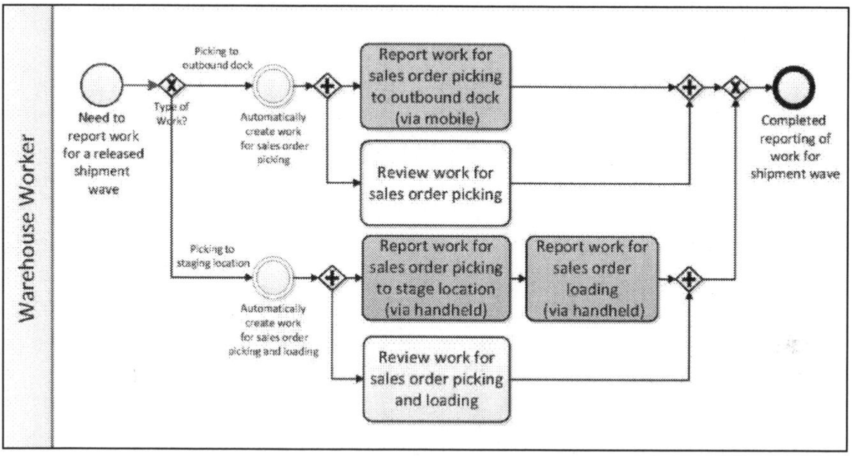

16.16 Extended Explanation of Life Cycles Related to Sales Order Picking/Shipping

The Advanced WMS approach for sales order picking/shipping involves several key constructs in addition to the sales order. These key constructs include the release status of a sales order, and the related shipments, loads, and waves for picking work. Their life cycles were previously illustrated for the basic process (Figure 16.2). The same constructs and life cycles are also employed in transfer order picking/shipping (Figure 17.2). This section provides an extended explanation of the status for each construct, and it applies to both sales orders and transfer orders.

Release Status of a Sales Order The release to warehouse step represents a key part of any business process for sales order picking/shipping, and the release status of a sales order has the following significance.

- *Open.* The status indicates the sales order has not yet been released to warehouse.

- *Released.* The status indicates that all sales order line items have been released to the warehouse.

- *Partially Released.* The status indicates that some of the sales order lines items have been released to warehouse.

Several types of reversing transactions can change the status from *released* back to *partially released* or even *open*. For example, the reversing transactions include unpicking a selected load line or reversing the reported picking work (Figure 16.3).

Status of a Sales Shipment The life cycle of a sales shipment can vary in different processes. Previous examples include the basic process and its reversing transactions (Figures 16.2 and 16.3), the manual wave planning process and its reversing transactions (Figures 16.7 and 16.8), the load planning process (Figure 16.10), and the manual packing process (Figures 16.12). The life cycle was also illustrated for the inquiries about sales shipments (Figure 16.5). A shipment status applies to each sales shipment, and the applicable values and their significance are described below.

- *Created.* The status typically indicates the shipment has been created as a result of the release to warehouse step. Alternatively, a shipment can be created automatically at the time of entering a sales order and line item (based on a companywide policy).

- *Waved.* The status indicates that the shipment has been assigned to a shipment wave and that picking work has not yet started. The shipment wave must be released before picking work can be reported.

- *In Process.* The status indicates that picking work for the shipment has been started but not yet completed. The completed picking work is typically indicated by a *Loaded* status, or by an *In Packing* status when using a manual packing approach.

- *In Packing.* The status indicates that picking work has moved the shipment to a pack location, and manual packing of containers has not yet been reported as closed with delivery to an outbound dock destination.

- *Loaded.* The status indicates that the picking work has been completely reported for all lines within the shipment, typically by placing the material at an outbound dock. It can also indicate that all containers have been closed when using a manual packing approach.

- *Shipped* The status indicates that the outbound shipment has been confirmed for the shipment.

Status of an Outbound Load The life cycle of an outbound load can vary in different processes. Previous examples include the basic process and its reversing transactions (Figures 16.2 and 16.3), the manual wave planning process and its reversing transactions (Figures 16.7 and 16.8), the load planning process (Figure 16.10), and the manual packing process (Figures 16.12). The life cycle was also illustrated for the inquiries about loads (Figure 16.5). A load status applies to each outbound load containing sales orders, and the applicable values and their significance are described below.

- *Open.* The status typically indicates that the load has been created with one or more load lines reflecting sales shipments. Alternatively, a load can be created automatically at the time of entering a sales order and line item (based on a companywide policy).
- *Waved.* The status indicates that shipments associated with the load have been assigned to a shipment wave, and that picking work has not yet started. The shipment wave must be released before picking work can be reported.
- *In Process.* The status indicates that picking work associated with the load has been started but not yet completed. The completed picking work is typically indicated by a *Loaded* status, or by an *In Packing* status when using a manual packing approach.
- *In Packing.* The status indicates that picking work has moved related load lines to a pack location, and manual packing of containers has not yet been reported as closed with delivery to an outbound dock destination.
- *Loaded.* The status indicates that the picking work has been completely reported for all lines within the load, typically by placing the material at an outbound dock. It can also indicate that all containers have been closed when using a manual packing approach.
- *Shipped* The status indicates that the outbound shipment has been confirmed for the load.
- *Posted.* The status has more than one meaning. It can indicate that the release-to-warehouse step has been performed for the load and related load lines have been assigned to shipments, where the shipments may or may not be on a shipment wave. As another meaning, it can indicate the load has been deleted as part of reversing transactions (illustrated in Figure 16.3 and Figure 16.8).

Status of a Sales Shipment Wave The life cycle of a shipment wave can vary in different processes. Previous examples include the basic process and its reversing transactions (Figures 16.2 and 16.3) and the manual wave planning process and its reversing transactions (Figures 16.7 and 16.8). A wave status applies to each shipment wave containing sales orders, and the applicable values and their significance are described below.

- *Created.* The status indicates that the wave has been created, and shipments may or may not have been assigned to the wave. Based on wave template policies, the system can automatically "create the wave" as a result of another step in the business process, such as the release to warehouse step for an order-based picking approach. Alternatively, a wave can be created automatically at the time of creating a sales order and its first line (based on a companywide policy).

- *Executing.* The status indicates the wave is in the process of being executed, and typically reflects a long duration of wave picking.

- *Held.* The status indicates reporting of "process the wave," which automatically creates picking work for all shipments assigned to the wave. Picking work cannot be reported until the wave has been released. Based on wave template policies, the system can automatically "process the wave" as a result of another step in the business process, such as the release to warehouse step.

- *Released.* The status indicates that the wave has been released so that picking work can be reported for all shipments assigned to the wave. Based on wave template policies, the system can automatically "release the wave" as a result of another step in the business process, such as the release to warehouse step.

- *Picked.* The status indicates that the picking work has been completely reported for all lines within the wave.

- *Shipped* The status indicates that the outbound shipment has been confirmed for the corresponding load.

16.17 Comparing Approaches for Sales Order Picking/Shipping

The two approaches to warehouse management in AX 2012 R3 can be compared in several different ways. The differences in conceptual models provide one way to make a comparison. It is best illustrated by comparing the two approaches for a simple yet typical business process involving order-based picking for sales orders. This provides the basis for an apples-to-apples comparison of comparable steps, as summarized in Figure 16.15. These steps represent the minimum number of touch points within the business process for updating status, and the figure draws on previously presented information for each approach.

Figure 16.15 Comparing Approaches for Sales Order Picking/Shipping

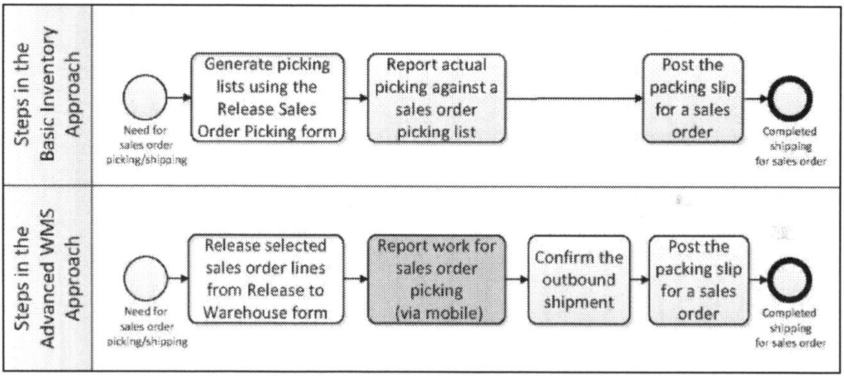

In summary, the comparable steps indicate the differences in conceptual models for the same business process. The starting point differs between the basic approach (which generates picking lists for selected orders using the Release Sales Order Picking form) and the advanced approach (which releases selected orders using the Release to Warehouse form). The advanced approach also employs a mobile device transaction for reporting picking work (shown with grey shading in the figure). It also requires an additional step to confirm the out bound shipment. Both approaches require a final step of posting the packing slip to update financial information.

There are other aspects of comparable functionality. For example, both approaches support the wave picking concept and the generation of a bill of lading, but they are implemented differently.

16.18 Executive Summary

The Advanced WMS approach supports multiple variations in the sales order picking/shipping process. This chapter started with a simple yet typical business process, and explained the related life cycles, reversing transactions, key constructs, and the related inquiries and reports. The basic process provided a baseline for explaining variations, such as variations of the release to warehouse, wave picking, load planning, manual packing, staging and loading steps, and the replenishment of picking locations.

Several case studies illustrated the variations. These included the packing structure documentation for the carrier and customer (Case 66), the combined use of manual and automated packing (Case 67), and defining a multi-level container structure (Case 68). Several previously-cited cases also apply. These include selling off-spec or blemished products (Case 15), performance metrics for on-time delivery and full quantity (Case 31), sales order shipments from a remote warehouse (Case 28) or a subcontractor warehouse (Case 50), printing an MSDS document to accompany a sales order shipment (Case 54), and sales order picking work to a final prep location (Case 61). Several case studies from subsequent chapters also apply, such as RMAs for serialized items (Case 77), deferred assignment for a serialized end-item and its serialized components (Case 78), and certificates of analysis for sales order shipments (Case 82).

Chapter 17

Transfer Order Picking/Shipping

The Advanced WMS approach supports multiple variations in the transfer order picking/shipping process. For explanatory purposes, it is easiest to start with a simple yet typical business process, and explain the related life cycles, reversing transactions, key constructs, and related inquiries and reports. The basic process provides a baseline for explaining variations.

Many of the major variations for transfer order picking/shipping involve an extended explanation. Hence, the topics related to the basic process and to its variations can be segmented into two groups. These considerations are reflected in the following sections within the chapter.

Topics about a Basic Process

1. Basic Process for Transfer Order Picking/Shipping
2. Additional Steps in the Basic Process
3. Life Cycles Related to the Basic Process
4. Reversing Transactions in the Basic Process
5. Key Constructs in the Basic Process for Transfer Order Picking/Shipping
6. Major Variations of Transfer Order Picking/Shipping
7. Minor Variations
8. Inquiries and Reports about Transfer Order Picking/Shipping

Topics about Variations to the Basic Process

9. Variations of Release to Warehouse for Transfer Orders
10. Variations of Wave Picking for Transfer Order Shipments
11. Variations of Load Planning for Transfer Orders
12. Staging and Loading Steps Prior to Shipment
13. Comparing Approaches to Transfer Order Picking/Shipping

Effective distribution planning represents a critical consideration for transfer order picking/shipping and receiving. The requirements for transfer orders should reflect S&OP game plans, a reasonable model of the supply chain, up-to-date information about shipment and delivery dates. Other factors may apply such as a manageable level of expediting. These considerations will make life easier for warehouse management.

17.1 Basic Process for Transfer Order Picking/Shipping

The business process for transfer order picking/shipping can have many variations. The starting point of a simple yet typical process for order-based picking provides a baseline for explaining the variations. The basic process shown in Figure 17.1 consists of several steps performed by a shipping clerk and warehouse worker. The figure uses grey shading to highlight the mobile device transaction for picking work, and it identifies several automatic steps. The process starts with the need for transfer order picking/shipping and ends with completed shipments. This section provides an overview of the basic process and describes each step in more detail.

Figure 17.1 Basic Process for Transfer Order Picking/Shipping

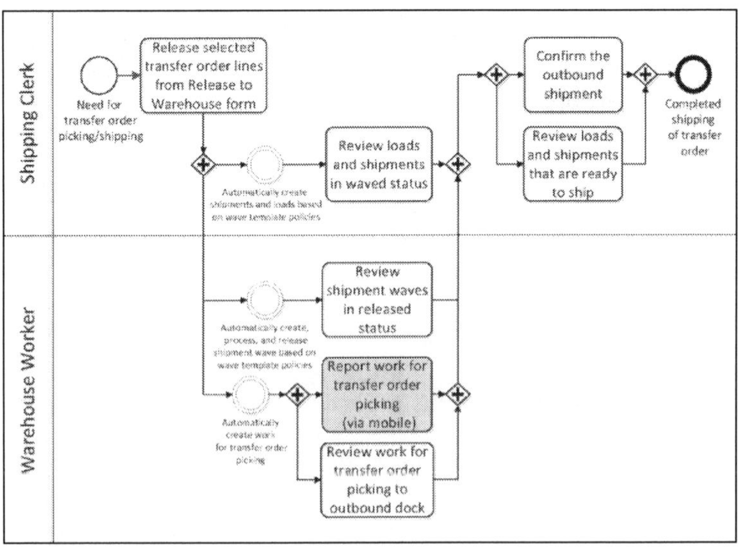

The basic process reflects an order-based picking approach with placement at an outbound dock. In this basic process, the release to warehouse step automatically creates a single shipment, a corresponding load and a released wave for a transfer

order. The released wave automatically creates the picking work. This basic process employs one variation for the release to warehouse step that requires reserved material prior to release. A subsequent section describes other variations of the release to warehouse step (Section 17.9).

Overview The shipping clerk uses the Release To Warehouse form to review a subset of open transfer order lines based on selection criteria, such as the ship-from warehouse, ship date and delivery mode. The shipping clerk selects the desired line items and releases them to the warehouse for picking/shipping. The release to warehouse step automatically creates a shipment, load and a released shipment wave for a transfer order based on wave template policies. The shipping clerk can review the shipments and loads in a waved status.

The warehouse worker reviews the picking work for the released shipment wave, and uses the mobile device to report work for each pick (from stocking locations) and the put to an outbound dock location. At that point, the shipping clerk can review loads and shipments that are ready to ship. The shipping clerk prints relevant documents and confirms the outbound shipment after the goods have actually left.

Release Selected Transfer Order Lines Using the Release To Warehouse Form The shipping clerk uses the Release To Warehouse form to anticipate transfer order shipping requirements by reviewing a subset of open transfer order lines based on selection criteria, such as the ship-from warehouse, ship date and delivery mode. The shipping clerk selects the desired lines and adds them to the list for subsequent release to warehouse. Lines can also be removed from the list.

The shipping clerk releases the selected lines to the warehouse for picking/shipping, which updates the released quantity on the transfer order line items. Given the order-based picking approach (defined by wave template policies), the release to warehouse step will automatically create the following:

- *Automatically Create a Single Shipment and a Corresponding Load and Wave for Each Selected Transfer Order.* The wave template policies also result in automatic updates to the status of a wave (to released), which triggers the creation of picking work for the wave.

- *Automatically Create Work for Transfer Order Picking.* The work consists of one or more picks for the selected line items and the puts to an outbound dock.

The release to warehouse step will identify errors that prevent actual release (if any), such as the lack of reserved inventory or missing address information for the ship-to warehouse.

Review Loads and Shipment in Waved Status The shipping clerk can review information on the Waved Loads form and the Waved Shipments form, and perform the following:

- *Using the Waved Loads Form.* The shipping clerk can view the related wave and work for a selected load, print relevant documents, and optionally assign the load to a different outbound dock.

- *Using the Waved Shipments Form.* The shipping clerk can view the related work and quality order (if applicable) for a selected shipment, print relevant documents, and optionally consolidate shipments or transfer a shipment to a different load.

Review Shipment Waves in Released Status Using the Open Waves form, the warehouse worker can review the related load, shipment and work for a selected wave and optionally print the picking list.

Report Work for Transfer Order Picking (via Mobile Device) The warehouse worker uses the mobile device to report the "pick" and "put" transactions for the work order. Each "pick" identifies the stocking location for inventory to be picked, and each "put" identifies the assigned location for an outbound dock.

Review Work for Transfer Order Picking to an Outbound Dock The warehouse worker can print the work for transfer order picking to help identify the needed picking. The options for printed documents include the printed picking list for a wave and printed work orders, and both documents provide bar-coded information to simplify recording of the work by mobile devices.

Review Loads and Shipments that are Already to Ship The shipping clerk can anticipate shipping activities by reviewing information on the Loads Ready To Ship form and the Shipments Ready To Ship form, and print relevant documents such as a load list.

Confirm the Outbound Shipment The shipping clerk confirms the outbound shipment for the selected load or shipment when the goods are actually shipped. It can be confirmed from several different forms, including a form related to loads (such as Loads Ready to Ship) or shipments (such as Shipments

Ready to Ship). It can also be confirmed from the related work order, or from the Load Planning Workbench.

Confirming the outbound shipment has an additional impact when using the advanced transportation management functionality to assign a rate to an outbound load for transfer orders. It updates the transfer orders within the load with the related charges.

17.2 Additional Steps in the Basic Process

The basic process often involves additional steps or slight variations not shown in Figure 17.1 so that the diagram does not become too complex. Examples include the following steps.

Short Pick When Reporting Transfer Order Picking Work You can select the Short Pick option as part of reporting the mobile device transaction, and then specify the actual pick quantity. You also need to select a reason for short picking which indicates the applicable action(s).

A reason for short picking reflects a work exception and must be defined beforehand on the Work Exceptions form. You also identify the applicable actions for the short pick reason, such as (1) automatically create cycle count work, (2) treat the quantity difference as an automatic inventory adjustment out, and/or (3) treat the quantity difference as an automatic decrement to the quantity on the shipment or load. You can also identify no applicable actions. Multiple work exceptions (aka reasons) may need to be defined to support different combinations of these applicable actions. After reporting a short pick on the mobile device, the transaction and selected reason can be viewed on the Work Exceptions Log inquiry. The inquiry includes pertinent information such as the transfer order, load, and shipment.

Print Labels for License Plates Labels can be automatically generated and printed when reporting transfer order picking via mobile devices, and subsequently reprinted when needed. The ability to print labels is identified as a separate step in the work template for transfer order picking. The label information and layout can reflect company-specific and product-specific requirements, and the nature of the label printer. This involves some technical details that fall outside the book's scope.

Print Bill of Lading for a Transfer Order Shipment The shipping clerk can optionally print a bill of lading for a transfer order shipment after confirming the outbound shipment. The bill of lading format reflects information about the National Motor Freight Code (NMFC) assigned to each product.

Identify Transfer Order Lines Picked but not yet Shipped One indicator of needed actions for warehouse management consists of transfer order line items which have been picked but not yet shipped as of today's date. You can identify these needed actions using a standard report labeled Inventory Picked not Delivered.

View In-Transit Inventory The inventory for an in-transit warehouse can be viewed from any of the on-hand inquiries.

Print Shipment Document for a Transfer Order You can print a Transfer Order Shipment document from the Transfer Order form, or by using the Transfer Order Shipment report and its associated dialogue about selection criteria. The document identifies the transfer order number and related information (such as the ship-to address, mode of delivery, posting date, and tracking number (if specified), as well as information about its line items.

One-Step Transaction for a Transfer Order Some scenarios employ a one-step shipment process for a transfer order which means there is no tracking of in-transit inventory and no receipt transaction. You indicate this policy (termed the auto-receive policy) when posting a transfer order shipment. The one-step approach can be used with short transportation times.

Other Inquiries and Reports Other sources of information include an inquiry about transfer order history and inquiries about outbound shipments and loads related to transfer orders, as summarized in a subsequent section (Section 17.8).

17.3 Life Cycles Related to the Basic Process

The basic process involves several related constructs, where the status for each construct reflects various steps in the process. Figure 17.2 summarizes this information for the basic process, and only displays those steps representing the minimum number of touch points for updating status. Grey shading highlights the key constructs related to the Advanced WMS approach. These key constructs include reservations, the release status of a transfer order and the related shipments, loads, waves and picking work.

Figure 17.2 Life Cycles Related to Basic Process for Transfer Order Picking/Shipping

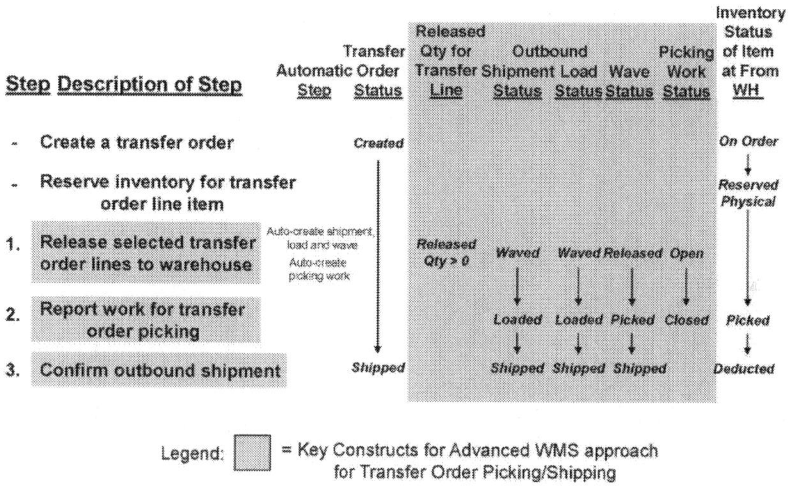

The release to warehouse step represents a key part of any business process for transfer order picking/shipping. For the basic process, this step automatically creates a shipment and corresponding load for each transfer order, and automatically creates and releases the corresponding wave (as reflected in a waved status for the shipment and load). The released wave also results in the automatic creation of picking work for the wave. Additional steps in the basic process—for reporting work and confirming the outbound shipment—will automatically update the status of each construct.

The inventory status for the item on a transfer order line is also shown on the right side of Figure 17.2. With respect to the ship-from warehouse, steps in the basic process will automatically change this status from *on order* to *reserved physical*, *picked* and *deducted.*

17.4 Reversing Transactions in the Basic Process

The ability to reverse transactions requires an understanding of the current point within the business process, and the associated status of key constructs. Borrowing from the previous figure, Figure 17.3 illustrates the steps within the basic process (shown in grey text) and the various points at which you can perform reversing transactions (shown in black text). The figure also illustrates the impact of a reversing transaction on status, and the arrows indicate the resulting point in the business process. As identified by step numbers in the figure, you can reverse transactions (1X) after initially creating the picking work for the released wave and (2X) after reporting actual picking.

Figure 17.3 Reversing Transactions in the Basic Process for Transfer Order Picking/Shipping

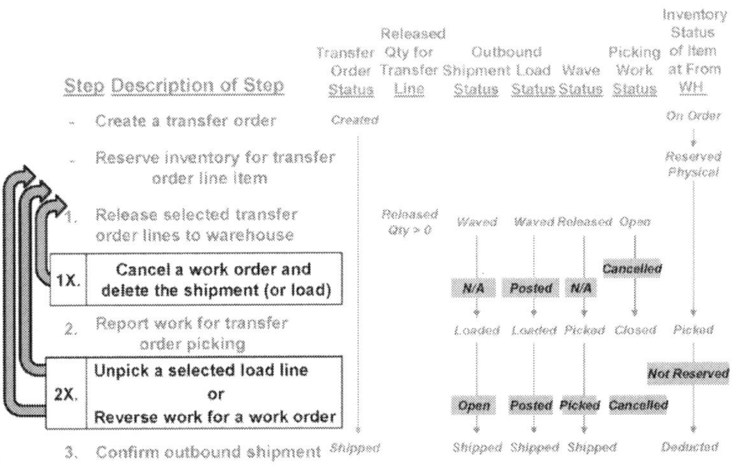

Step 1X: Cancel Work Order and Delete the Shipment (or Load) You can cancel a work order prior to reporting any work line, which changes the released quantity for a transfer order line. In addition, after cancelling the work, you can delete the associated shipment (or load) which also deletes the corresponding wave. The deletion typically means that a status no longer applies, as shown by a value of "N/A" within the figure, although the load status is updated to *posted*. At this point, you can start over with the release to warehouse step, which will create a new shipment, load, wave and work order.

Step 2X: Unpick a Selected Load Line The completed work for transfer order picking can be unpicked by starting from the relevant load and a selected load line, and then accessing a separate form (labeled Load Line Unpicking) to reduce the picked quantity. You specify the quantity to reverse and the move to location (which cannot be a LP-controlled location), and also indicate whether the quantity should be removed from the shipment or load. The specified quantity can reflect the entire quantity or partial quantity that has been picked, which will remove the reservations.

Step 2X: Reverse the Work for a Work Order As an alternative to unpicking individual transactions, you can reverse all picking work associated with a work order prior to confirming the outbound shipment. When initiating this transaction, the dialogue on the Reverse Work screen enables you to indicate how to handle the material. For example, it can remain at the current location (such as an outbound dock), it can be automatically moved to a specified location (such as a stocking location), or you can automatically create movement work to a specified location. The remaining work for a partially completed work order will be cancelled.

Reversing Options After Confirming the Outbound Shipment Transactions cannot be reversed after confirming the outbound shipment.

17.5 Key Constructs for Transfer Order Picking/Shipping

The Advanced WMS approach for transfer order picking/shipping involves several key constructs in addition to the transfer order. These key constructs include reservations, the release status of a transfer order, and the related shipments, loads, waves and work orders for picking work. Previous figures and explanations have already illustrated these key constructs.

Reservation Policies for a Transfer Order and its Line Items The reservation policy assigned to a transfer order line item indicates whether inventory will be reserved automatically or manually. When initially adding a line item, this policy—labeled the "Reserve items automatically" checkbox—is inherited from the transfer order header, and it can be overridden. The policy for the transfer order can be inherited from a companywide policy (embedded in the Inventory and Warehouse Management parameters).

Release Status of a Transfer Order Line Item The concept of a separate "release status" applies to sales orders but not to transfer orders. For transfer orders, the release to warehouse step automatically updates the Release Quantity for the applicable line items.

In the basic process, the release to warehouse step requires reservations for each transfer order line otherwise the line items cannot be released to the warehouse. Other variations of the release to warehouse step do not require reservations beforehand, and they can result in reservations (Section 17.9).

Shipments, Loads, Waves and Work Orders for Transfer Order Picking/Shipping Order-based picking represents one variation of the business process. With order-based picking, the release to warehouse step automatically creates a shipment and corresponding load for each transfer order, and automatically creates and releases the corresponding wave (as reflected in a waved status for the shipment and load). The released wave also results in the automatic creation of picking work for the wave. Additional steps in the basic process—for reporting work and confirming the outbound shipment—automatically update the status of each construct.

Each of the major variations for transfer order picking/shipping has slightly different steps which involve differences in the life cycles and status for shipments, loads and waves. Subsequent sections describe these major variations.

17.6 Major Variations of Transfer Order Picking/Shipping

The basic process for transfer order picking/shipping provides the foundation for explaining major variations. Several variations involve a brief explanation. Others involve an extended explanation that will be provided in subsequent sections. This section lists all of the major variations and includes brief explanations when applicable. The list indicates the relevant section for topics requiring an extended explanation.

- Simple Inventory Transaction for Transfer Order Picking/Shipping
- Picking Batch-Controlled Items
- Picking Serialized Items
- Variations of Release to Warehouse for Transfer Orders (Section 17.9)
- Variations of Wave Picking for Transfer Order Shipment (Section 17.10)
- Variations of Load Planning for Transfer Orders (Section 17.11)
- Staging and Loading Steps Prior to Shipping (Section 17.12)

Several of the major variations for transfer orders are almost exactly the same as those for sales orders, such as the variations for wave picking, load planning and staging/loading steps. A full explanation about the variations for transfer orders is largely redundant. This chapter covers the topic briefly and refers to the extended explanations in the previous chapter.

Some of the major variations for sales orders do not apply to transfer orders, such as manual packing, automated packing, and cluster picking.

Simple Inventory Transactions for Transfer Order Picking/Shipping
The shipping clerk can bypass the use of loads, shipments, waves and work by using a simple inventory transaction to post a transfer order shipment using the

Transfer Order form. In order to perform the simple transaction, you must specify the relevant license plate and location (for the picked material) on each transfer order line item prior to posting the transfer order shipment. You can optionally indicate (via the Auto Receive checkbox) that the material should be automatically reported as received at the ship-to warehouse. This simple inventory transaction applies to both the basic and advanced approaches.

Picking Batch-Controlled Items The picking work for batch-controlled items is impacted by reservation logic. That is, the Reservation Hierarchy assigned to an item determines whether its batch numbers will be reserved or not. Reservations of specific batch numbers are critical in many scenarios, such as shelf-life items involving FEFO reservations and customer requirements for remaining shelf life. As a result, the relevant batch will be displayed and printed on the work line for the work order, and also displayed on the mobile device when reporting the picking work.

Two additional policies about transfer order picking work must be defined for correctly supporting reservations of batch-controlled items. These policies are defined as part of the Location Directive Actions related to the work order type for transfer issue, where you indicate the pick should be "Batch-Enabled" and also select the relevant "Strategy" for locating material. For example, the strategy should be "FEFO Batch Reservations" in order to correctly support picking of shelf-life items.

Other aspects of picking batch-controlled items can differ based on the use of license plates and the quantities involved. For example, the picking work may identify specific license plates (at an LP-controlled location), or the target license plate for picking work may contain multiple items and batch numbers. In addition, the picking work reflects the restricted usage policies for batch disposition codes that can be assigned to batch numbers. A subsequent chapter provides further explanation of batch-controlled items (Section 25.3).

Picking Serialized Items The picking work for a serialized item is not typically impacted by reservation logic because of the item's Reservation Hierarchy, where serial numbers are below the location. The picking work can differ based on the use of license plates and the quantities involved. For example, the picking work may identify a specific license plate containing multiple serial numbers of an item, or the target license plate for picking work may contain multiple items and serial numbers. A subsequent chapter provides further explanation of serialized items (Section 25.1).

17.7 Minor Variations

Several minor variations apply to the basic process for transfer order picking/shipping and its major variations. These include the use of delivery tolerances and safety margins. Other minor variations were identified as part of the additional steps for the basic process, such as a one-step transaction for transfer orders.

Impact of Delivery Tolerances on Transfer Order Picking/Shipping When delivery tolerances are acceptable, they determine how much the quantities being picked and shipped for a transfer order line can differ from the ordered quantity. Over- and under-delivery tolerances (related to transfer orders) are expressed as a percentage and the values assigned to an item act as defaults for a transfer order line item. Delivery tolerances of zero percent for a transfer line mean that the shipped quantity must equal the ordered quantity. A companywide policy (embedded in the Inventory Management parameters) determines whether over- and under-deliveries will be acceptable for transfer orders.

A picked quantity that exceeds the delivery tolerances will prevent confirmation of the outbound shipment, and the system displays a corresponding infolog about the problem.

Modeling the Required Time for Picking/Shipping Activities Some scenarios have a significant time requirement for picking/shipping activities related to a transfer order (such as 1 or 2 days) A significant time requirement should be included in the supply chain model so that (1) promised ship dates will reflect the required time and (2) picking will be scheduled prior to the ship date.

- *Identify the Picking/Shipping Time as a Safety Margin* The required time can be identified as the issue safety margin, where you define the number of days as part of the Coverage Group assigned to the item. It is normally assigned as part of the Item Coverage information for the item and ship-to warehouse, where you identify the source warehouse for planned transfer orders and also override the normal Coverage Group assigned to the item.

  For example, when demands exist for an item with one day prep time, master scheduling logic will generate planned orders to arrive one day before the demand date. As another consideration, when using the Release to Warehouse form to anticipate picking activities, you should release orders for picking one day prior to the ship date.

- *Include Picking/Shipping Time in Delivery Promises* The required time (expressed as the issue safety margin, described above) can be included in delivery promises based on ATP logic, where you assign a delivery date control policy of "ATP plus issue margin" to the item as part of its default order policies for inventory. For example, when manually entering a transfer order line for an item with one day prep time, the earliest possible ship date will be one day later.

  Some scenarios do not use ATP logic as the basis for delivery promises. In many of these scenarios, the required time can be modeled by the sales lead time assigned to an item as part of its default order policies for inventory.

17.8 Inquiries and Reports About Transfer Order Picking/Shipping

Some of the relevant inquiries and reports have already been identified as part of the additional steps for the basic process. For example, the standard inquiries can identify the transfer order lines with partial picking. Other standard inquires apply to shipments, loads, waves and work orders related to transfer orders.

Transfer Order History The Transfer Order History form displays all transfer orders with separate lines for the related shipment and receipt transactions, and the related line items for a selected transaction. It displays the posting date and voucher for each transaction line, and the tracking ID (if specified) for a shipment transaction.

Transfer Overview Report This report provides a one line summary of each transfer order, including its status, the ship-from and ship-to warehouses, and the ship and receipt dates. It also identifies the item and quantity for each line item on a transfer order. You can specify selection criteria as part of the associated report dialogue—such as the relevant ship-from warehouse, ship date and order status—in order to view the desired subset of transfer orders. The report can also be generated from the Transfer Order form, so that the selection criteria inherit the order information.

Inquiries About Outbound Shipments and Loads Several standard inquiries apply to the outbound shipments and loads related to transfer orders. Some were previously mentioned in the basic process for transfer order picking/shipping (Figure 17.1), such as shipments and loads in waved status or ready to ship. These examples indicate the significance of different steps in the business process, since the status of the shipment or load determines the relevant inquiry. Figure 17.4 summarizes the variations of inquiries about shipments and loads in the context of different steps in the picking/shipping process.

Figure 17.4 Inquiries About Shipments and Loads Related to Transfer Orders

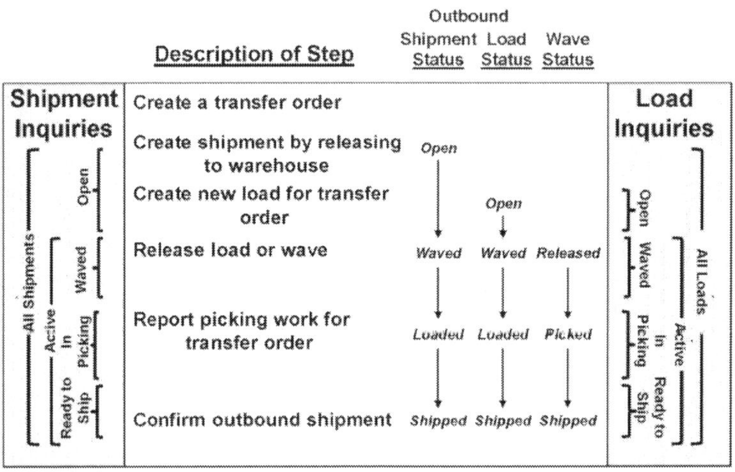

17.9 Variations of Release to Warehouse for Transfer Orders

The release to warehouse step represents a key part of any business process for transfer order picking/shipping, and it automatically updates the released quantity on transfer lines. There are multiple options for performing the release to warehouse and the use of selection criteria.

Options for Release to Warehouse The release to warehouse step has four options which reflect two basic factors. One factor involves the prerequisite for reserved inventory, and two of the options support deferred reservations until release to warehouse. The second factor involves the approach for performing the release to warehouse step, and the various approaches are reflected in the following four options.

- *Perform Release to Warehouse for a Transfer Order.* The release to warehouse step can be performed from the Transfer Order form. It applies to all lines on the transfer order and inventory must be fully reserved for all lines.

- *Perform Release to Warehouse for Selected Transfer Order Lines Using the Release to Warehouse Form* The Release To Warehouse form can be used to view a subset of open transfer order lines based on selection criteria (such as the ship-from warehouse, ship date and delivery mode) and then release selected lines which have been fully reserved beforehand. It is typically used by the shipping clerk to anticipate shipping requirements and to initiate required picking activities, and it only supports the release to warehouse step. This option was employed in the basic process for transfer order picking/shipping.

- *Perform Automatic Release to Warehouse with Selection criteria for Transfer Order Lines.* The Automatic Release of Transfer Orders can be performed on a periodic basis, where selection criteria determine the applicable transfer order lines. Inventory for each line item must be fully reserved beforehand unless a warehouse-specific policy (labeled "Reserve when orders are released by a batch job") allows deferred reservations at the time of the release to warehouse step. Different sets of selection criteria can support variations in decisions about the release to warehouse.

- *Perform Release to Warehouse for a Selected Outbound Load Using the Load Planning Workbench.* The Load Planning Workbench form can be used to view a subset of transfer order lines based on selection criteria (such as the ship-from warehouse, ship date and mode of delivery), typically by a transportation coordinator. Selected transfer order line items can then be assigned to a new load, or to an existing load, and information about loads are displayed in the bottom half of the form. When applicable, the transportation coordinator will assign a rate/route to the outbound load.

  The transportation coordinator can view and filter the loads, and then release a selected load to the warehouse. Inventory for each transfer order line within the load must be fully reserved beforehand unless a warehouse-specific policy (labeled "Reserve inventory at load posting") allows deferred reservations at the time of the release to warehouse step.

  Selection criteria about open transfer order line items (and also loads) can be identified by filtering options at the top of the form (such as the ship-from warehouse and ship date) or by using grid filters. In addition, you can optionally predefine filters about transfer orders and loads with the user-defined Load Planning Filters.

Selection Criteria About Transfer Orders for the Release to Warehouse Step Selection criteria about transfer order lines can be used with three of the options for the release to warehouse step. Examples of these selection criteria are summarized in Figure 17.5. The figure indicates the applicable constructs for each selection criteria, such as the transfer order line or header. It also highlights several selection criteria (via shading) which provide the basis for prioritizing picking/shipping activities, such as the ship date and mode of delivery for a transfer order.

Figure 17.5 Example Selection Criteria for Release to Warehouse for Transfer Orders

<table>
<tr><th rowspan="2">Field Name for a Transfer Order</th><th colspan="2">Applicable Construct</th></tr>
<tr><th>Order Header</th><th>Order Line</th></tr>
<tr><td>Ship-from Warehouse</td><td rowspan="6">Yes</td><td rowspan="2">N/A</td></tr>
<tr><td>Mode of Delivery</td></tr>
<tr><td>Ship Date</td><td>Yes</td></tr>
<tr><td>Transfer Order Number</td><td rowspan="2">N/A</td></tr>
<tr><td>Ship-to Warehouse</td></tr>
<tr><td>Receive Date</td><td>Yes</td></tr>
</table>

Basis for Prioritizing Picking/Shipping: Mode of Delivery, Ship Date

Identify Errors related to the Release to Warehouse Step Several types of errors can be identified by the release to warehouse step, and they must be corrected in order to successfully perform the release. The lack of reserved inventory represents a common error. Other types of errors include missing address information for the ship-to warehouse and missing a load template when releasing a load. When using the Load Planning Workbench, you can first validate a load and then review any errors prior to releasing the load to the warehouse.

17.10 Variations of Wave Picking for Transfer Order Shipments

A wave picking approach commonly refers to a grouping of transfer order shipments with the same delivery requirements, such as the same ship date and carrier for a ship-from warehouse. The grouping is termed a shipment wave or wave for short. The contents of a shipment wave can be released and picked together to meet a planned departure time of a shipping vehicle.

The planning and execution of wave picking for transfer orders are almost exactly the same as those for sales orders. A full explanation about wave planning for transfer orders is largely redundant. This section provides an abbreviated explanation and refers to the extended explanations in the previous chapter.

There are many variations of a wave picking approach. At its simplest, a shipment wave reflects the line items for a single transfer order, so that the wave picking approach is frequently termed order-based picking. This variation was employed in the basic process for transfer order picking/shipping described earlier (Section 17.1), where each wave was automatically created and released by the release to warehouse step. Other variations involve wave picking for a grouping of transfer order shipments, which represents the more common reference for a wave picking approach.

The planning aspects of wave picking for a group of shipments consist of several steps typically performed by a warehouse planner. Some of the steps can be performed automatically to reflect the planner's normal decision making about wave planning, as modeled by policies within a wave template. For example, a wave template might be defined for each variation of a carrier that serves a given warehouse, and you define the applicable carrier as part of the query criteria for each wave template. In this way, performing the release to warehouse step will automatically create shipments and also assign them to an applicable wave. These automatic steps can be illustrated in a typical process for wave planning.

A typical process for wave planning consists of several steps, as illustrated in Figure 17.6. The need for wave planning starts with the automatic generation of transfer order shipments by the release to warehouse step. Some of these steps can be automated to reflect the planner's normal decision making about wave planning.

The starting point indicates two approaches to defining wave contents – labeled a manual approach and an automatic approach – that also apply to sales orders. The details of these two approaches, and additional considerations about the life cycles and reversing transactions related to wave planning, were explained in the previous chapter about sales orders (Section 16.10).

Figure 17.6 Typical Process for Wave Planning of Transfer Order Shipments

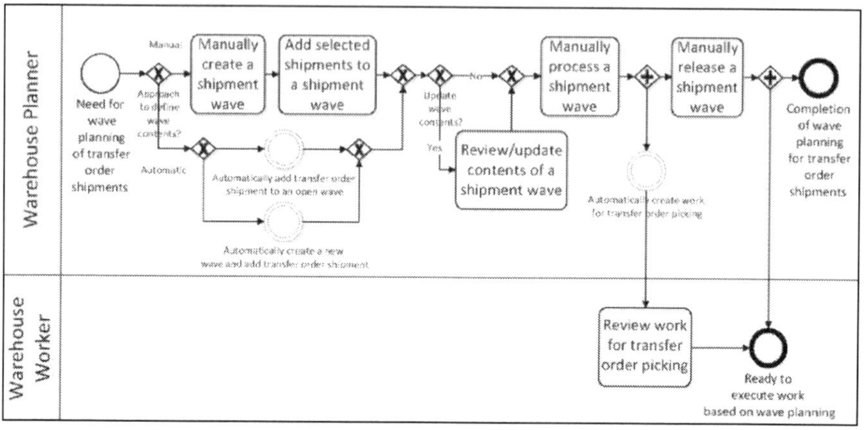

17.11 Variations in Load Planning for Transfer Orders

Load planning for transfer orders can serve multiple requirements related to warehouse and transportation management. From a transportation viewpoint, for example, each load provides an organizing focus for a transportation coordinator to assign the appropriate route and rate, and arrange the transportation appointments. From a warehouse viewpoint, the scheduled departure date/time for a load provides an organizing focus to coordinate picking for a shipment wave. This section focuses on the warehouse viewpoint, and a subsequent chapter covers the transportation viewpoint (Section 23.11).

The load planning process for transfer orders is almost exactly the same as that for sales orders. It employs the same constructs, life cycles and reversing transactions, and builds on the same use of load templates and the Load Planning Workbench form. A full explanation about load planning for transfer orders is largely redundant. This section provides an abbreviated explanation and refers to the extended explanations in the previous chapter.

A typical load planning process consists of several steps typically performed by a transportation coordinator using the Load Planning Workbench. The steps are sometimes performed by a warehouse planner or by multiple roles. The typical load planning process shown in Figure 17.7 focuses on load planning of open transfer order line items with all steps performed by the transportation coordinator.

Figure 17.7 Typical Load Planning Process for Transfer Orders

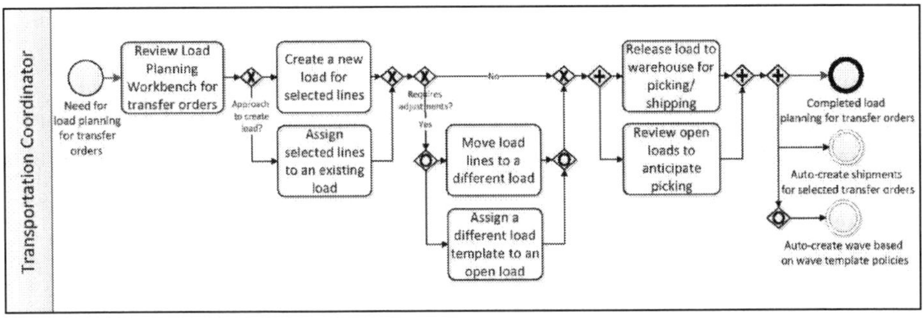

The starting point of reviewing transfer orders on the Load Planning Workbench is the only major difference in comparison to load planning for sales orders. The details about other steps in the process and the related life cycles were explained in the previous chapter about sales orders (Section 16.11).

17.12 Staging and Loading Steps prior to Shipping

Staging and loading steps are sometimes necessary within the process for transfer order picking/shipping. A typical example involves staging material for delivery via truck, and then loading the material on the truck prior to reporting actual shipment. In this case, you report the work for transfer order picking to a staging location and then report the work for transfer order loading. At that point, you can review shipments and loads that are ready to ship.

The staging and loading steps represent an alternative approach to simply picking to an outbound location, which was employed in the basic process. Figure 17.8 illustrates these two alternatives to reporting work for a shipment wave. The figure highlights the mobile device transactions via shading, and identifies the automatic steps.

The unique setup information for staging/loading steps includes the mobile device menu items for staging and for loading of transfer orders, and the related work templates and location directives for transfer issues. For example, the work template for transfer issues should specify the relevant query criteria about when staging/loading steps are required (such as a mode of delivery via truck), and the location directive should specify a valid put location type of Stage (for the related pick and put to a staging location).

Figure 17.8 Staging and Loading Steps Prior to Transfer Order Shipping

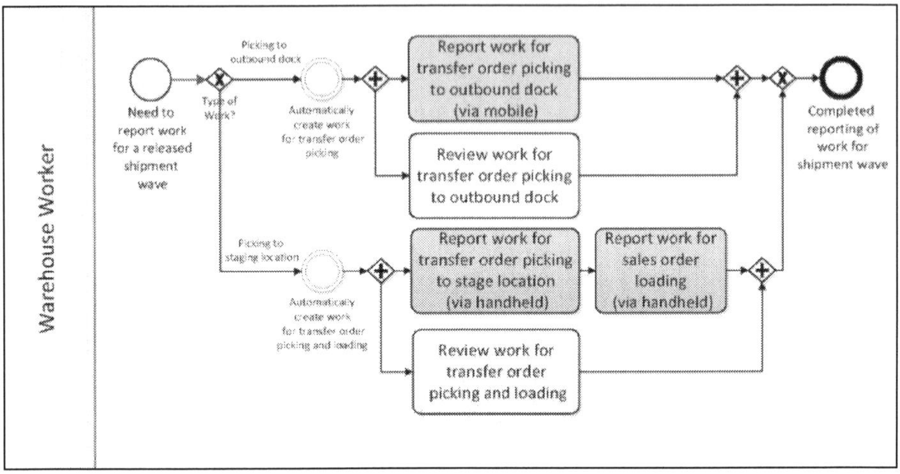

17.13 Comparing Approaches for Transfer Order Picking/Shipping

The two approaches to warehouse management in AX 2012 R3 can be compared in several different ways. The differences in conceptual models provide one way to make a comparison. It is best illustrated by comparing the two approaches for a simple yet typical business process involving order-based picking for transfer orders. This provides the basis for an apples-to-apples comparison of comparable steps, as summarized in Figure 17.9. These steps represent the minimum number of touch points within the business process for updating status, and the figure draws on previously presented information for each approach.

In summary, the comparable steps indicate the differences in conceptual models for the same business process. The starting point differs significantly between the basic approach (which generates picking lists for selected orders using the Release Transfer Order Picking form) and the advanced approach (which releases selected orders using the Release to Warehouse form). The advanced approach also employs a mobile device transaction for reporting picking work (shown with grey shading in the figure). The last step to "confirm the outbound shipment" replaces the need to "report actual shipment of a transfer order."

Figure 17.9 Comparing Approaches for Transfer Order Picking/Shipping

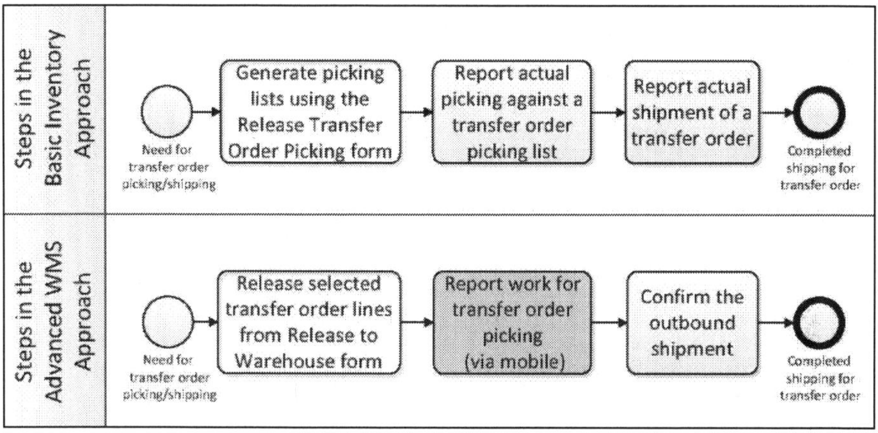

17.14 Executive Summary

The Advanced WMS approach supports multiple variations in the transfer order picking/shipping process. This chapter started with a simple yet typical business process, and explained the related life cycles, reversing transactions, key constructs, and the related inquiries and reports. The basic process provided a baseline for explaining variations, such as variations of the release to warehouse, wave picking, load planning, and staging and loading steps.

Chapter 18

Transfer Order Receiving

The Advanced WMS approach supports a few variations in the transfer order receiving process and they are largely dependent on information about the shipped material. For example, the material shipped from a WMS-enabled warehouse must be received in terms of the license plate IDs that were shipped. In contrast, the material shipped from a non-WMS warehouse must be received by transfer order number since they do not have a license plate ID. For explanatory purposes, it is easiest to start with the former scenario and a simple yet typical business process, and explain the related life cycles, reversing transactions and key constructs. This basic process provides a baseline for explaining variations. These considerations are reflected in the following sections within the chapter:

1. Basic Process for Transfer Order Receiving
2. Additional Steps in the Basic Process
3. Life Cycles Related to the Basic Process
4. Reversing Transactions in the Basic Process
5. Key Constructs for Transfer Order Receiving
6. Variations of Transfer Order Receiving
7. Comparing Approaches for Transfer Order Receiving

18.1 Basic Process for Transfer Order Receiving

A common scenario involves transfer order receiving when picking/shipping has been reported by the Advanced WMS approach, so that you report receipts against each license plate included in a transfer order shipment. The starting point of a simple yet typical process provides a baseline for explaining the variations. The basic process shown in Figure 18.1 consists of several steps performed by a receiving clerk and warehouse worker. The figure uses grey shading to highlight the mobile device transactions. The process starts with the need to report transfer order receiving and ends with completed receipts. This section provides an overview of the basic process and describes each step in more detail.

Figure 18.1 Basic Process for Transfer Order Receiving

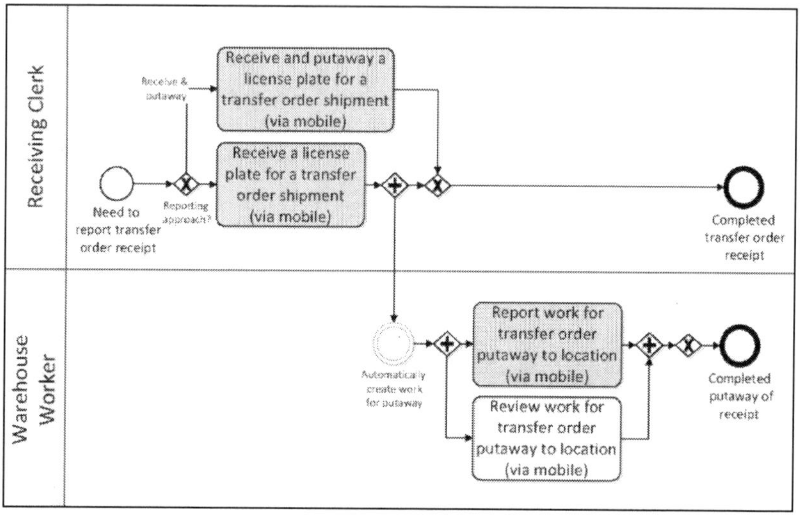

Overview The receiving clerk uses the mobile device to receive a license plate for a transfer order shipment, which updates inventory balances and automatically creates putaway work. The warehouse worker uses the mobile device to report putaway from the receiving location to a stocking location. A suggested stocking location can reflect location directives, or the warehouse worker can determine and report the stocking location. As an alternative reporting approach, the receiving clerk can report receipt and putaway as part of the mobile device transaction.

Receive a License Plate for a Transfer Order Shipment (via Mobile Device) The receiving clerk uses the mobile device to report receipt of the license plate within a transfer order shipment, and identify the item being received. This receipt transaction updates inventory and also posts the transfer order receipt to update financial information.

Receive and Putaway a License Plate for a Transfer Order Shipment (via Mobile Device) The receiving clerk uses the mobile device to report receipt of the license plate within a transfer order shipment, and identify the item being received. This receipt transaction updates inventory and also posts the transfer order receipt to update financial information. The receiving clerk also reports putaway as part of the mobile device transaction.

Report Work for Transfer Order Putaway to Stocking Location (via Mobile Device) The warehouse worker uses the mobile device to report putaway work for the received material. A suggested stocking location can reflect location directives, or the warehouse worker can determine and report the stocking location. In some cases the received material does not require license plate tracking and the putaway location does not need to be license plate controlled.

Review Work for Transfer Order Putaway to a Stocking Location The warehouse worker can review and optionally print the work for transfer order putaway.

18.2 Additional Steps in the Basic Process

The basic process often involves additional steps or slight variations not shown in Figure 18.1 so that the diagram does not become too complex. Examples include the following steps.

Print Labels for License Plates Labels can be automatically generated and printed when reporting transfer order picking via mobile devices, and subsequently reprinted when needed. The ability to print labels is identified as a separate step in the work template for transfer order picking. The label information and layout can reflect company-specific and product-specific requirements, and the nature of the label printer.

View In-Transit Inventory The inventory for an in-transit warehouse can be viewed from any of the on-hand inquiries.

Report a "Lost in Transit" Quantity or a "Scrap" Quantity The shipped quantity for a transfer order must be reported as completely received; it cannot be left in transit. In order to report a quantity that represents "lost in transit" or scrap, the quantity can be reported as received and then immediately reported as an inventory adjustment out.

Print Receipt Document for a Transfer Order You can print a Transfer Order Receipt document from the Transfer Order form, or by using the report for Transfer Order Receipts and its associated dialogue about selection criteria. The document identifies the transfer order number and related information such as the ship-from warehouse, mode of delivery, posting date and tracking number as well as information about its line items.

Other Inquiries and Reports Other sources of information include an inquiry about transfer order history and inquiries about the shipments and loads related to transfer orders, as summarized in the previous chapter (Section 17.8).

18.3 Life Cycles Related to the Basic Process

The basic process for transfer order receiving involves several related constructs, where the status for each construct reflects various steps in the process. Figure 34.2 summarizes this information for the basic process, where shading highlights the key constructs related to the Advanced WMS approach.

Figure 18.2 Life Cycles Related to the Basic Process for Transfer Order Receiving

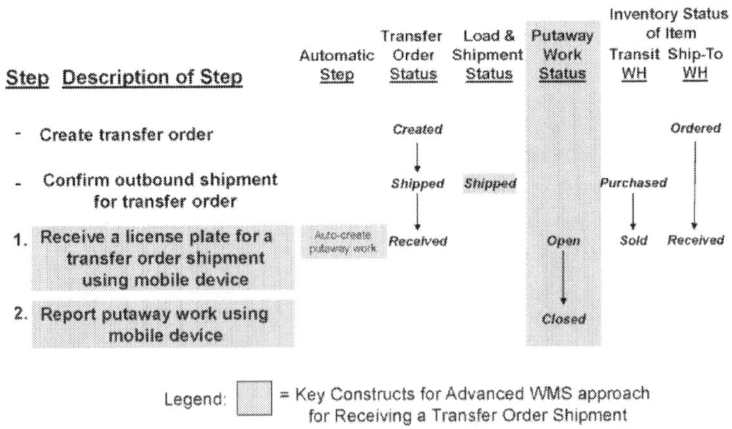

As shown in the figure, after an outbound shipment has been confirmed for a transfer order, you can use the mobile device transaction for receiving a license plate within the shipment. This mobile transaction will automatically update inventory balances, post the transfer order receipt and create putaway work. The transfer order status will also be updated (to *Received*) after reporting all line items as received. The right side of Figure 18.2 shows the inventory status for an item on a transfer order line. At the ship-to warehouse, for example, the steps will change this status from *Ordered* to *Received.*

18.4 Reversing Transactions in the Basic Process

Information cannot be corrected or cancelled after reporting actual shipment of a transfer order. In addition, the entire shipped quantity must ultimately be reported as received; it cannot remain in transit. As noted earlier, there are options for reporting a "lost in transit" quantity or a "scrap" quantity, where you report the quantity as received and then immediately report an inventory adjustment out.

18.5 Key Constructs for Transfer Order Receiving

The basic process for transfer order receiving employs mobile devices to report receipts at a receiving location, and to report putaway work to a stocking location. Alternatively, the receipt and putaway can be performed as part of the same mobile device transaction. This section summarizes the key construct of the Mobile Device Menu Item to support the mobile device transactions.

Mobile Device Menu Items The appropriate Mobile Device Menu Items must be defined in order to report transfer order receipts of license plates and the related putaway work. Two different Mobile Device Menu Items must be defined in order to report a transfer order receipt and the related putaway work.

- *Menu Item for Transfer Order Receipt of a License Plate.* As part of defining the menu item, you select a work creation process for "license plate receiving." As a result, when reporting receipt using the mobile device, you start by entering the license plate and the item number being received. Completing the receipt transaction will automatically create putaway work for the license plate. The mobile device transaction assumes you will also report the putaway work immediately, so that you must cancel out of the transaction in order to report putaway as a separate transaction.

- *Menu Item for Putaway of a Transfer Order Receipt.* As part of defining the menu item, the policy for *use existing work* and the selected work class (for transfer receipt) enable you to report putaway work as a separate mobile device transaction policy.

Review Putaway Work Related to a Transfer Order Receipt You can review the putaway work for a selected work order on the All Work form, or by accessing the work order information from a selected line on the Transfer Order form. In either case, you can print the work (with bar-coded information) and optionally cancel the work.

18.6 Variations of Transfer Order Receiving

The basic process for transfer order receiving provides the foundation for explaining variations, such as reporting receipts from a non-WMS warehouse.

No Simple Inventory Transaction for Reporting Transfer Order Receipts A simple inventory transaction (such as simply posting a transfer order receipt) becomes quite complicated, so that it does not represent a major alternative. However, it is mentioned here for completeness sake.

Report Transfer Order Receiving When Items Have Been Shipped From a Non-WMS Warehouse A slightly different receiving process is required when transfer order shipments have been reported using the Basic Inventory approach, since the receipts cannot be identified by a license plate. Common scenarios include transfer order shipments from a subcontractor warehouse or a remote warehouse, which typically do not employ the Advanced WMS approach for reporting shipments.

The receipts must be identified by the transfer order number, which requires a different menu item to support the different basis of identification. Otherwise, the receiving steps are exactly the same as the basic process, as illustrated in Figure 18.3.

Figure 18.3 Receiving Transfer Orders From a Non-WMS Warehouse

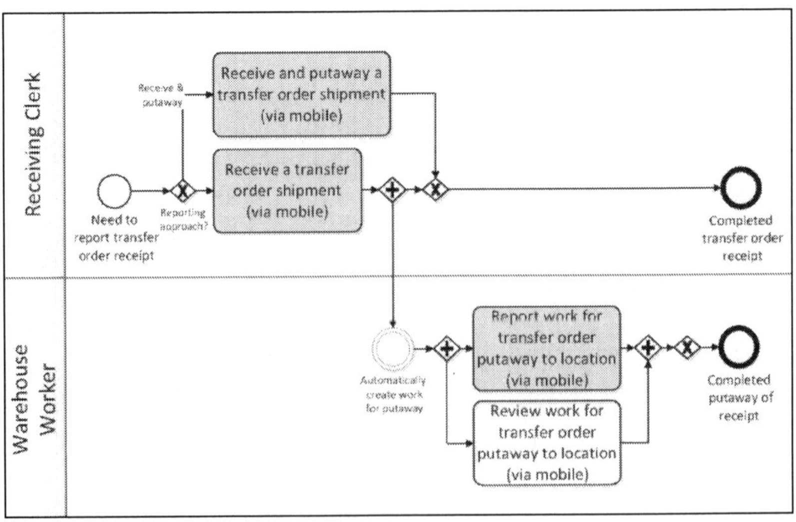

The appropriate Mobile Device Menu Items must be defined in order to report transfer order receipts (without license plates) and the related putaway work.

- *Menu Item for Transfer Order Receipt.* As part of defining the menu item, you select a work creation process that determines the basis for identifying the received material. The options include *Transfer Order Item Receiving* and *Transfer Order Line Receiving.* You also indicate whether a license plate should be manually or automatically assigned, whether to group items on a single license plate (based on the reported unit of measure for the received quantity, and the related policies within Unit Sequence Group assigned to the item), and whether to create/print a label for each license plate.

- *Menu Item for Putaway of a Transfer Order Receipt.* As part of defining the menu item, you select the option "Use existing work" and indicate the relevant work order type for *transfer receive.* The related constructs include a Location Directive and Work Template for the work order type of Transfer Receipt.

- *Menu Item for Transfer Order Receipt and Putaway.* As part of defining the menu item, you select a work creation process that determines the basis for identifying the received material. The options include *Transfer Order Item Receiving and Putaway* and *Transfer Order Line Receiving and Putaway.* Other aspects are the similar to the above-mentioned setup information, including the related constructs of a Location Directive and Work Template for putaway of the received material.

Receiving Batch-Controlled Items There is no specialized reporting of batch numbers since they are already identified for the shipped items.

Receiving Serialized Items There is no specialized reporting of serial numbers since they are already identified for the shipped items.

Modeling the Required Time for Transfer Order Receiving Activities Some scenarios have a significant time requirement for receiving activities related to a transfer order (such as 1 or 2 days), while many others have a much shorter preparation time of minutes. A significant time requirement should be included in the supply chain model so that receiving will be scheduled prior to the ship date.

The required time can be identified as the receipt safety margin, where you define the number of days as part of the Coverage Group assigned to the item. It is normally assigned as part of the Item Coverage information for the item and ship-to warehouse, where you identify the source warehouse for planned transfer orders and also override the normal Coverage Group assigned to the item.

18.7 Comparing Approaches for Transfer Order Receiving

The two approaches to warehouse management in AX 2012 R3 can be compared in several different ways. The differences in conceptual models provide one way to make a comparison. It is best illustrated by comparing the two approaches for a simple yet typical business process involving transfer order receiving, as summarized in Figure 18.4. These steps represent the minimum number of touch points within the business process for updating status, and the figure draws on previously presented information for each approach.

Figure 18.4 Comparing Approaches for Transfer Order Receiving

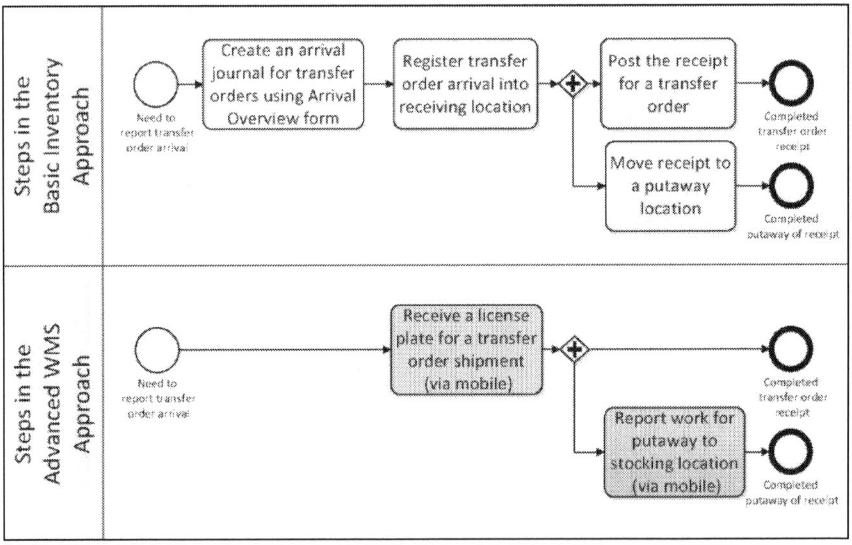

In summary, the comparable steps indicate the significant differences in conceptual models for the same business process. The basic approach involves a different starting point (to create an arrival journal which acts as the basis for registering arrivals), an additional ending step (for posting the receipt), and a transfer journal for reporting putaway. In contrast, the advanced approach simply employs mobile devices for reporting receipt and putaway. The figure illustrates transfer order receipts from a WMS enabled warehouse (and the use of license plates), but the figure would be similar for receipts from a non-WMS warehouse.

18.8 Executive Summary

The Advanced WMS approach supports a few variations in the transfer order receiving process and they are largely dependent on information about the shipped material. For example, the material shipped from a WMS-enabled warehouse must be received in terms of the license plate IDs that were shipped. In contrast, the material shipped from a non-WMS warehouse must be received by transfer order number. This chapter started with a simple yet typical business process involving license plate IDs, and explained the related life cycles, reversing transactions and key constructs. This basic process provided a baseline for explaining variations, such as receiving items from a non-WMS warehouse.

Several previously-cited case studies apply. These include reporting "Lost in Transit" for a transfer order (Case 32), updating the transfer order receipt date for overseas deliveries (Case 34), transportation constraints about transfer orders to/from a subcontractor (Case 55), and coordinating transportation for Asian subcontractors (Case 56). Another case study involves subcontracted production with full visibility of in-transit inventory (Case 72).

Chapter 19

Production Order Picking

The Advanced WMS approach supports multiple variations in picking and receiving material for production orders. In particular, it provides new capabilities for raw material picking which also supports production wave picking, although it still uses the production order picking list for reporting actual material usage. This chapter covers topics related to picking and the next chapter covers topics related to receiving. The explanation focuses on production orders (for BOM items) but also covers batch orders (for formula items) as one of the major variations of the business process.

A simple production scenario provides the context for explaining the basic processes for picking and receiving, especially the differing viewpoints of engineering, production reporting and warehouse management. Given this context, it is easiest to start with a simple yet typical business process that represents order-based picking for production orders, and then explain the related life cycles, reversing transactions and key constructs. The basic process provides a baseline for explaining major variations. These topics are reflected in the following sections within the chapter:

1. Production Scenario #2 for Internal Production
2. Basic Process for Production Order Picking
3. Additional Steps in the Basic Process
4. Life Cycles Related to the Basic Process
5. Reversing Transactions in the Basic Process
6. Key Constructs for Production Order Picking
7. Major Variations of Production Order Picking
8. Variations of Production Wave Planning
9. Comparing Approaches to Production Order Picking

Effective production scheduling represents a critical consideration for production order picking and receiving. In order to be effective and realistic, a production schedule should reflect up-to-date S&OP game plans, capacity and material constraints, near term stability, and other factors such as production sequencing and a manageable level of expediting. One key factor involves the time granularity of production orders, where large time increments (such as orders representing a month's worth of production) do not provide sufficient granularity for coordinating warehouse activities, or provide the visibility of expected receipts. These considerations will make life easier for warehouse management.

19.1 Production Scenario #2 for Internal Manufacturing

A simple production scenario provides a baseline for explaining the Advanced WMS approach to production order picking and receiving. It can be called Production Scenario #2 to differentiate it from the simple Production Scenario #1 that was used for explaining the Basic Inventory approach (Section 9.1). The slight differences in Scenario #2 will be used to highlight the unique aspects of raw material picking work to a production input location, the use of a production output location, and the alternatives for reporting finished quantities via mobile device and client transactions.

There are several viewpoints of this simple production scenario. From an engineering viewpoint, the scenario consists of a single level bill of material (BOM) to produce an end-item from raw material components, and a single operation within the routing. From a production reporting viewpoint, the key constructs consist of a production order and its picking list journal. The production order quantity represents a single production run with a single picking list journal in this simple scenario. Production is responsible for reporting actual component usage against the picking list journal, and oftentimes for reporting the finished quantity for the production order.

From a warehouse viewpoint, the key constructs consist of different warehouse locations for raw materials, production floorstock, and finished goods. The key transactions involve delivering raw materials to production input locations and putaway of finished goods to stocking locations. Oftentimes, warehouse workers are responsible for reporting the finished quantity, or for reporting the finished quantity as part of reporting putaway. Figure 19.1 summarizes these different viewpoints of engineering, production reporting and warehouse management, especially the responsibilities for reporting transactions.

Figure 19.1 Production Scenario #2 for Internal Manufacturing

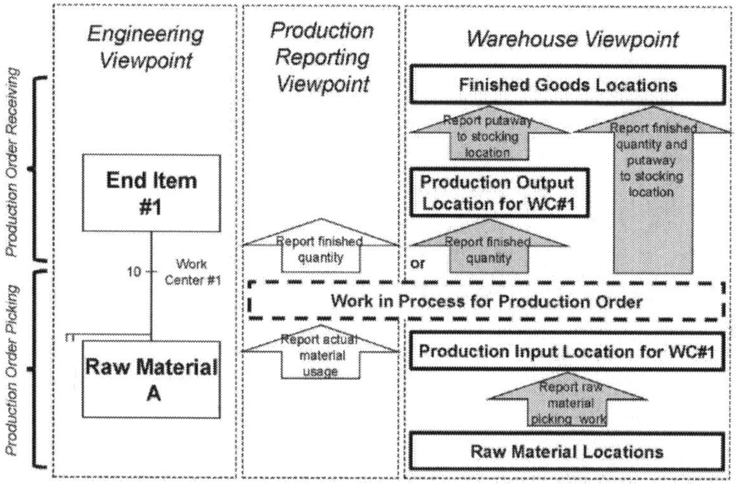

The figure identifies the single-level bill of material and routing for the simple scenario, where End-Item #1 is produced from Raw Material A (and other components) by a routing operation at Work Center #1 (aka a resource). A resource group identifies several similar work centers, and the resource group has a common production input location (located at the start of production) and a common output location (located at the end of production). These are commonly termed floorstock or lineside locations, and reflect the lean principle of stocking at the point of use.

The arrows indicate key transactions for production reporting and warehouse reporting, and the figure identifies the mobile device transactions via grey shading. The figure indicates the different alternatives for reporting the finished quantity via screen or a mobile device, or as part of reporting putaway via a mobile device. The figure also identifies the relevant warehouse locations for raw material and finished goods, and the production input and output locations for the work center. The left side of the figure indicates the segmentation of book chapters about production order picking and receiving. This chapter covers production order picking and the next chapter covers production order receiving.

19.2 Basic Process for Production Order Picking

The basic process reflects the previously-described baseline of a simple production scenario and the related transactions. It also reflects order-based picking (rather than wave picking) and normal material (rather than serialized or batch-controlled material). Subsequent sections describe these variations to the basic process.

The basic process shown in Figure 19.2 consists of several steps typically performed by a machine operator and warehouse worker, but there are many variations about the role responsibilities. It highlights the mobile device transaction for raw material picking with grey shading, and identifies several automatic actions within the system. The process starts with the need to issue goods to production and ends with the completed issues to production.

Figure 19.2 Basic Process for Production Order Picking

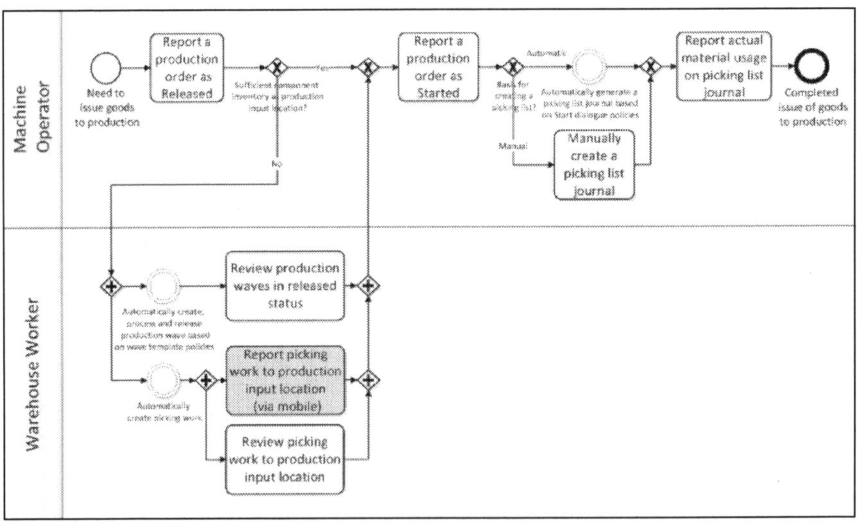

Overview The machine operator reports a production order as Released, which acts as the trigger for several automatic actions to support actual production. This includes creating and releasing a production wave for the order, which triggers creation of picking work for delivering components to a production input location when it has insufficient component inventory.

The warehouse worker reviews the released production waves and the associated picking work. Using the mobile device, the warehouse worker reports the picking work (consisting of picks and puts) for delivering components to the designated production input location.

When ready, the machine operator reports a production order as Started, which automatically generates a picking list journal (based on the Start dialogue policies). The machine operator reports actual material usage on the picking list journal. In some cases, the machine operator will manually generate a picking list as an alternative to automatic generation, or to identify unexpected component requirements. In either case, the machine operator posts the picking list journal after reporting actual material usage.

Report a Production Order as Released The machine operator reports a production order as Released, which acts as the trigger for several automatic actions to support actual production. The release step automatically reserves the component inventory (based on the reservation policy for the production order). It will automatically create, process and release a production wave for the production order (based on policies within the applicable production wave template). The "process" step for a production wave can also trigger creation of raw material picking work for delivering components to a production input location.

Review Production Waves in Released Status The warehouse worker reviews released production waves to identify which production orders require delivery of components to production input locations, and optionally prints a picking list for a production wave..

Report Picking Work to the Production Input Location (via Mobile Device) Using the mobile device, the warehouse worker reports work for picking components from stocking locations and delivering them to production input locations.

Review Picking Work for Production Input Location The warehouse worker can review and print the work order for delivering components to the production input location. The printed document provides bar-coded information to simplify recording of the work.

Report a Production Order as Started The machine operator reports a production order as Started, which automatically generates a picking list journal based on the Start dialogue policies. As part of the Start dialogue, for example, the machine operator will start the entire order quantity and generate the picking list journal for components with a forward flushing principle.

Based on the reservation policy for the production order, the component inventory can be automatically reserved (at the time of releasing or starting the order), so that the printed picking list indicates the reserved quantity for each component.

Manually Create a Picking List Journal In some cases, the machine operator will manually generate a picking list as an alternative to automatic generation, or to identify reversing transactions for previously reported material usage. It may serve other purposes, such as identifying unexpected requirements so that the warehouse worker can use the printed picking list to pick and deliver additional material.

Report Actual Material Usage on Picking List Journal The machine operator reports actual material usage on the picking list journal. For a given component, the machine operator can indicate when material usage has been completely reported so that remaining requirements (if any) will be ignored. The machine operator posts the picking list journal when completed. .

19.3 Additional Steps in the Basic Process

The basic process often includes several additional steps or slight variations which are not shown in Figure 19.2 so that the diagram does not become too complex. For explanatory purposes, the additional steps can segmented based on when they occur relative to starting a production order. The first additional step can occur before starting, the second acts as an alternative approach for reporting an order as started, and the others occur after the order has started.

Assign (and Remove) a Stop Flag to a Production Order Prior to Started Status The Stop flag primarily serves warehouse management purposes and prevents changes in order status prior to starting a production order. For example, assigning the Stop flag to a scheduled order prevents a change in order status to Released (which prevents creation of raw material picking work) or Started (which prevents reporting of actual material usage). The Stop flag also prevents resetting order status. You assign and remove the Stop flag as an explicit step on the Production Orders form, and a Stop checkbox is also displayed as part of the warehouse management information for the order. The Stop flag has no impact when raw material picking work already exists, or when assigned after a production order has been started.

Report a Production Order as Started Using the Mobile Device This transaction assumes actual material usage from the production input location will be 100% correct, since it automatically creates and posts the picking list journal. The transaction ignores the Start dialogue policies, and all components in the Production BOM (regardless of flushing principle) will be deducted from inventory.

Report Component Scrap Using the Mobile Device Reporting component scrap via a mobile device transaction will automatically create and post a separate picking list journal for the specified production order, component item, quantity, and production input location.

Report Component Scrap When Reporting Actual Material Usage on the Picking List Journal You can report component scrap for a line item on the picking lust journal; where you identify a separate scrap quantity and an optional reason code.

Report Actual Usage of Additional Components You can report usage of an additional component by adding it as a line item on the picking lust journal.

Identify Material Shortages for a Production Order A material shortage represents the remaining requirements for a component in the Production BOM for a started production order. The system ignores the components' remaining required quantity under several conditions: when a specific component has been flagged as completely picked; when picking for all components has been flagged as complete; when an operation linked to the material has been flagged as complete; or when the production order status becomes reported-as-finished. Shortages can be viewed on the Material Stock-out List inquiry.

Move Unused Raw Material Back to Stocking Location Using the Mobile Device In many scenarios, the unused inventory at the production input location needs to be returned to a stocking location. For example, the quantity for an entire license plate (such as an entire pallet or barrel) can be delivered to the input location by raw material picking work, so that you need to move the item's unused inventory back to stock. Some scenarios will leave the unused inventory at the production input location to support subsequent production orders, thereby reducing or eliminating creation of raw material picking work.

Enforcing the Sequence of Major Steps in the Basic Process Some scenarios need to limit the ability to change production order status, such as preventing a jump to a Started status so that orders must be reported as released before they can be started. These companywide policies (defined on the Production Control Parameters form) consist of a matrix about the allowed changes from one status to another.

19.4 Life Cycles Related to the Basic Process

The basic process involves several related constructs, where the status for each construct reflects various steps in the process. Figure 19.3 summarizes this information for the basic process, and only displays those steps representing the minimum number of touch points for updating status. Grey shading highlights the key constructs related to the Advanced WMS approach. In addition to the production order, these key constructs include the production wave and related raw material picking work, the production input locations, and the picking list journal.

Figure 19.3 Life Cycles Related to the Basic Process for Production Order Picking

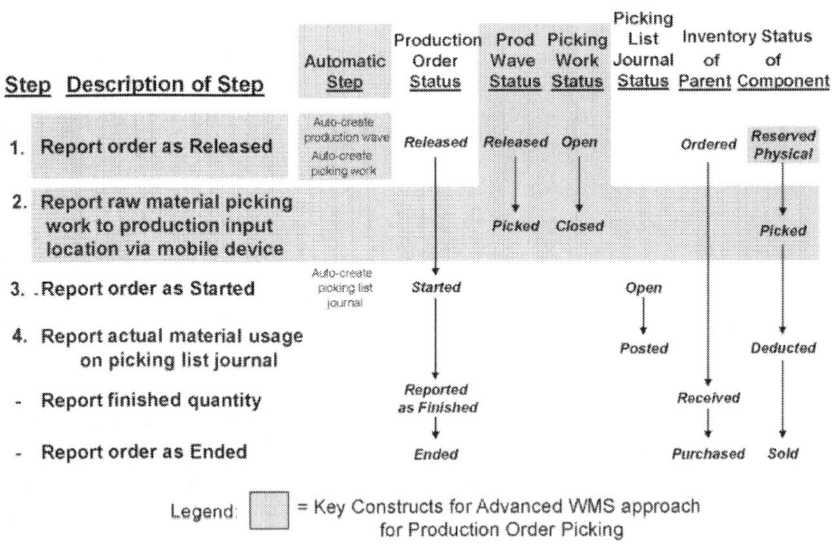

The release to warehouse step provides the starting point of the process, where you report a production order as released. For the basic process of order-based picking, this step will automatically create, process and release a production wave for the production order (based on wave template policies), and the released wave creates the picking work for delivering components to the production input location. The step also reserves component inventory (based on the reservation policy for the order).

As you report picking work, the component's inventory status changes to *picked* and the on-hand inquiries no longer display this inventory. The production wave's status changes to *Picke*d after reporting all related picking work. Reporting the production order as Started will automatically create the picking list journal, and reporting actual component usage (and posting the journal) changes the component's inventory status to *Deducted.* The inventory status of a component and the parent item are shown on the right side of Figure 19.3, and their status will be updated by the additional steps to report the finished quantity and end the production order.

Each of the major variations for production order picking and receiving has slightly different steps which involve differences in the life cycles and status for the key constructs. Subsequent sections describe the major variations and similar figures illustrate the related life cycles.

19.5 Reversing Transactions in the Basic Process

The ability to reverse transactions requires an understanding of the current point within the business process, and the associated status of key constructs. Borrowing from the previous figure, Figure 19.4 illustrates the steps within the basic process (shown in grey text) and the various points at which you can perform reversing transactions (shown in black text). The figure also illustrates the impact of a reversing transaction on status, and the arrows indicate the resulting point in the business process. As identified by step numbers in the figure, you can reverse transactions (1X) after initially creating the raw material picking work for a released production wave, (4X) after reporting actual material usage on the picking list journal, and (AnyX) at any time prior to ending the production order.

Step 1X: Cancel Work Order for Raw Material Picking You can cancel a Work Order prior to reporting any work, which changes the work order status to *cancelled* and the wave status to *created.* At this point, you can modify the production order (such as a changed quantity), and release the order again to create the picking work again for the wave. Alternatively, you can manually process and release the wave again, which will also create the picking work again. If applicable, you can even delete the order after resetting its order status to *created.*

Figure 19.4 Reversing Transactions in the Basic Process for Production Order Picking

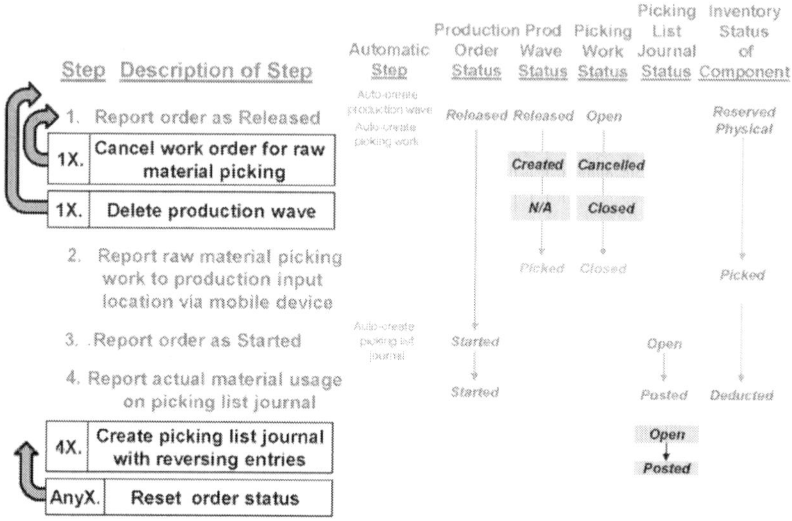

Step 1X: Delete the Production Wave After cancelling the related work orders, you can delete a production wave. The figure displays a status of "N/A" to indicate the deletion. At this point, releasing the order again will create another production wave and its associated work orders.

Step 3X: Delete the Picking List Journal for a Production Order You can delete a picking list journal prior to posting it. This step is not shown in the figure.

Step 4X: Create a Picking List Journal with Reversing Entries You can reverse one or more transactions from a previously posted picking list. As the starting point, you manually generate a picking list journal with lines created from a previously posted picking list. The lines (with a negative quantity) can be adjusted prior to posting the picking list. For example, some of the transactions can be deleted (because they do not need to be reversed) or the negative quantity can be reduced to indicate a partial reversal.

Step AnyX: Reset Order Status for a Production Order A production order can be reset to a previous status at any time prior to the *Ended* status. You indicate the desired order status on the reset order dialogue. For example, order status may be changed to *Created* to allow deletion, or changed to *Released* from *Started* so that the system automatically reverses all transactions about actual production activities.

19.6 Key Constructs for Production Order Picking

The Advanced WMS approach for issuing goods to production involves several key constructs in addition to the production order and its Production BOM/routing. These key constructs include reservations, production input locations, the production wave and related raw material picking work, and the picking list journal.

Reservation Policies for a Production Order The reservation policy assigned to a production order determines when components will be reserved relative to order status. In most scenarios, you select a reservation policy so that components will be automatically reserved at the time of releasing the production order. A related reservation policy determines whether components must be fully reserved or partially reserved when releasing a production order to the warehouse.

The reservation policy for an order is initially inherited as a companywide or site-specific policy and it can be overridden. Some scenarios employ a reservation policy of Manual. You can view and update reservations for components in the Production BOM or the Picking List Journal by accessing the Reservations form.

Production Input Locations A production input location is identified on raw material picking work as the "put" location. It is typically defined as a non- LP-controlled location to avoid additional details in reporting actual material usage. In addition, the production input location is normally assigned to raw material picking work based on the resource (or resource group) that needs the raw material, as described shortly. However, some scenarios do not employ routings, so that the assignment can reflect a warehouse-specific default value.

The production input location can be defined for a resource group (such as a common location for multiple machines) and optionally overridden for a resource with the group (such as a machine-specific location). The automatic assignment of a production input location to raw material picking work reflects the resource or resource group performing a routing operation, which is determined by scheduling logic for production orders.

The linkage between a routing operation and its production input location involves several interrelated considerations. First, the operation sequence number of the routing operation provides the basis for identifying required BOM components with the same operation number. Second, each BOM component must be defined with the relevant operation number and a "resource consumption" policy. The resource consumption policy ensures that component requirements will be linked to the assigned resource (or resource group), which ultimately provides the basis for assignment of an input location to raw material picking work. A previous figure illustrated these interrelated considerations about the assignment of production input locations (Figure 9.6).

Work Orders for Raw Material Picking and the Inventory at Production Input Locations Several factors impact the creation of work orders for raw material picking and the related consideration about inventory at production input locations.

- *Insufficient Component Inventory at the Production Input Location.* Raw material picking work will only be created when the production input location has insufficient inventory to meet requirements.

- *Consideration of all Components in the Production BOM.* The creation of raw material picking work reflects all Production BOM components (regardless of flushing principle) at the time of creation. The Production BOM typically reflects the parent item's bill of material but it can be modified.

- *Delivery of Entire Quantity for a License Plate (versus Exact Quantity).* When a raw material item is stocked in a location that is not license plate controlled, the raw material pick work will suggest the exact quantity to meet requirements.

  In contrast, the raw material picking work will suggest delivery of the entire quantity on a license plate when the material is stocked in a license plate controlled location, even though it is greater than the required quantity for a component. In addition, multiple occurrences of the same component in a BOM can result in raw material picking work for multiple license plates, which further compounds the concerns.

- *Visibility of Component Inventory at the Production input Location.* After reporting raw material picking, an inventory status of "picked" applies to the component's required quantity. This means it is not visible in on-hand inquiries. However, inventory that represents an over-issued quantity remains visible in on-hand inquiries. As a final point, as a result of under-reporting actual material usage and then reporting a production order as finished, the "picked" status no longer applies and the unused inventory becomes visible.

Significance of a Production Wave Template The wave template determines whether wave planning steps will be performed manually or automatically after reporting a production order as released. For example, many wave planning scenarios will employ automatic assignment of components to an existing production wave, and manual steps to process and release the wave. A subsequent section provides further explanation about production wave planning (Section 19.8).

Mobile Device Transactions The primary mobile device transaction consists of raw material picking to a production input location. As part of defining the menu item, you select the policy for *use existing work* and the work order type for *raw material picking*. A work template and a location directive are also defined for the work order type of *raw material picking*. Once created, you can review this picking work by accessing it for the related production order (on the Production Order form), for the related production wave (on the Production Wave form), or for a selected work order (on the All Work form).

Additional mobile device transactions include starting a production order, reporting component scrap, and moving unused material from the production input location to a stocking location.

Picking List Journals The production order and its related picking list journal(s) represent critical tools for coordination and reporting of production and warehouse activities. Their significance can differ widely depending on the scenario. In the simple scenario, for example, the production order represents a single production run and the picking list journal contains all components and reflects the entire order quantity. An extended explanation of these constructs was provided in a previous chapter (Section 9.9).

19.7 Major Variations of Production Order Picking

The basic process for production order picking provides the foundation for explaining major variations. The major variations are listed below and covered in separate explanations.

- Simple Inventory Transaction for Production Order Picking
- Report Production Order Picking via Auto-Deduction
- Picking Batch-Controlled Items
- Picking Serialized Items

- Report Batch Order Picking
- Process a Rework Order for a Finished Quantity
- Variations of Production Wave Planning

Simple Inventory Transaction for Production Order Picking The use of raw material picking work is optional, so that you can simply report actual usage on the picking list journal. This means that releasing a production order does not create raw material picking work. It also means that the production input location for a resource group (or resource) should be blank, so that the reserved inventory reflects the stocking location of a component. The simple inventory transaction of the picking list journal applies to both the basic and advanced approaches.

Report Production Order Picking via Auto-Deduction Reporting a production order as Started can trigger automatic deduction of components based on policies in the Start dialogue. For example, as a result of starting an order, the picking list journal can be generated and posted immediately for components with a flushing principle of *Start.*

Reporting a production order as Started via the mobile device will automatically create and post the picking list journal. The transaction ignores the Start dialogue policies, and all components in the Production BOM (regardless of flushing principle) will be deducted from inventory.

Reporting the finished quantity for a production order can also trigger automatic deduction of components based on policies in the Report as Finished dialogue. For example, as a result of reporting a finished quantity, the picking list journal can be generated and posted immediately for components with a flushing principle of *Finish.*

Picking Batch-Controlled Items The picking work for batch-controlled items is impacted by reservation logic. That is, the Reservation Hierarchy assigned to an item determines whether its batch numbers will be reserved or not. Reservations of specific batch numbers are critical in many scenarios, such as shelf-life items involving FEFO reservations. As a result, the relevant batch will be displayed and printed on the work line for the work order, and also displayed on the mobile device when reporting the picking work.

Two additional policies about raw material picking work must be defined for correctly supporting reservations of batch-controlled items. These policies are defined as part of the Location Directive Actions related to the work order type for raw material picking, where you indicate the pick should be "Batch-Enabled" and also select the relevant "Strategy" for locating material. For example, the strategy should be "FEFO Batch Reservations" in order to correctly support picking of shelf-life items.

Other aspects of picking batch-controlled items can differ based on the use of license plates and the quantities involved. For example, the picking work may identify specific license plates (at an LP-controlled location), or the target license plate for picking work may contain multiple items and batch numbers. In addition, the picking work reflects the restricted usage policies for batch disposition codes that can be assigned to batch numbers. A subsequent chapter provides further explanation of batch-controlled items (Section 25.3).

Picking Serialized Items The picking work for a serialized item is not typically impacted by reservation logic because of the item's Reservation Hierarchy, where serial numbers are below the location. The picking work can differ based on the use of license plates and the quantities involved. For example, the picking work may identify a specific license plate containing multiple serial numbers of an item, or the target license plate for picking work may contain multiple items and serial numbers. A subsequent chapter provides further explanation of serialized items (Section 25.1).

Report Batch Order Picking The same warehouse management considerations of production order picking also apply to batch orders. For example, the use of raw material picking work and the picking list journal apply to both types of orders.

Report Production Order Picking for a Rework Order Rework may be necessary for the finished quantity of a production order that has not been reported as scrapped. The approach for generating and reporting raw material picking work, and the approach for reporting actual material usage, is the same for a rework order.

Variations of Wave Picking for Production A wave picking approach commonly refers to a grouping of released production orders with the same start date, so that a single wave contains the raw material picking work for multiple orders. The grouping is termed a production wave or wave for short. There are many variations of a wave picking approach. At its simplest, a production wave reflects the raw material picking work for a single production order, so that the wave picking approach is frequently termed order-based picking. This variation was employed in the basic process for production order picking described earlier (Section 35.1), where each wave was automatically created and released by reporting a production order as Released. Other variations involve wave picking for a grouping of production orders, which represents the more common reference for a wave picking approach. The planning aspects of wave picking for a group of released production orders consist of several steps typically performed by a warehouse planner. Some of the steps can be performed automatically to reflect the planner's normal decision making about wave planning, as modeled by policies within a wave template. For example, a production wave template might be defined so that releases of different production orders at different times will be automatically added to an existing wave.

The next section provides further explanation about the variations in production wave planning.

19.8 Variations of Production Wave Planning

A wave picking approach commonly refers to a grouping of released production orders with the same start date, so that a single wave contains the raw material picking work for multiple orders. The grouping is termed a production wave or wave for short.[1] The contents of a production wave can be released and picked together to meet production requirements.

There are many variations of a wave picking approach. At its simplest, a production wave reflects the raw material picking work for a single production order, so that the wave picking approach is frequently termed order-based picking. This variation was employed in the basic process for production order picking described earlier, where each wave was automatically created and released by reporting a production order as Released. Other variations involve wave picking for a grouping of production orders, which represents the more common reference for a wave picking approach.

The planning aspects of wave picking for a group of released production orders consist of several steps typically performed by a warehouse planner. Some of the steps can be performed automatically to reflect the planner's normal decision making about wave planning, as modeled by policies within a wave template. For example, a production wave template might be defined so that releases of different production orders at different times will be automatically added to an existing wave. These automatic steps can be illustrated in a typical process for wave planning. The typical process is one of several topics covered within the section, as listed below.

---

[1] A wave picking approach can also apply to a grouping of sales order shipments, where the grouping is termed a shipment wave. A previous chapter described wave picking for shipment waves (Section 16.10).

- Typical Process for Production Wave Planning
- Life Cycles Related to a Manual Wave Planning Process
- Reversing Transactions in Manual Wave Planning
- Order-Based Picking as a Wave Picking Variation
- Status of a Production Wave

Typical Process for Production Wave Planning A typical process for production wave planning consists of several steps, as illustrated in Figure 19.5 and described below. The business process starts with the need for wave planning based on released production orders, and ends with the completion of wave planning so that warehouse workers can execute the related work. As shown in the figure, some of the steps can be automated to reflect the planner's normal decision making about wave planning. As an explanatory approach, it is easiest to first describe the manual steps shown in the figure and then describe the more common use of automatic steps.

Figure 19.5 Typical Process for Production Wave Planning

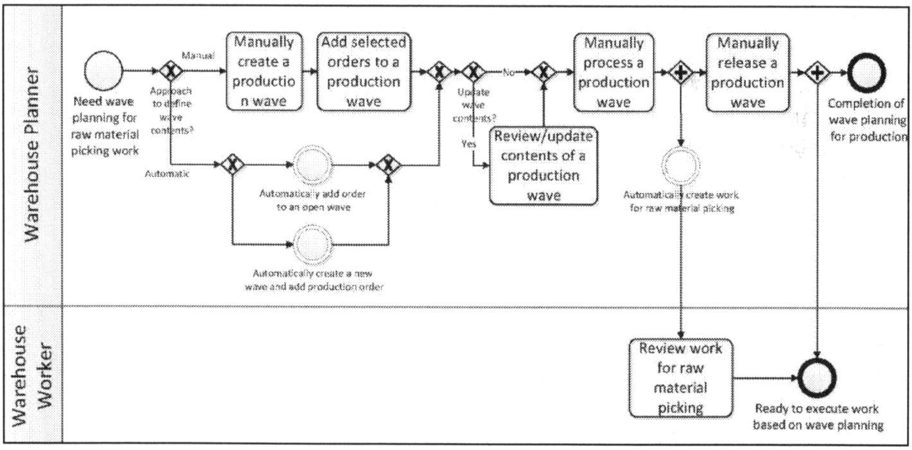

With the manual approach to defining wave contents, the warehouse planner manually creates a production wave for a selected wave template, and then reviews the unassigned production order components (aka production BOM lines) by accessing the Maintain Productions form. The warehouse planner can view totals for selected components (such as total weight, volume and pieces), add selected components to the wave lines, and then view totals again for all wave lines. The grouping of selected components typically reflects similar delivery requirements, such as the same production start date and site. If needed, the planner updates the wave contents (such as adding or deleting wave lines) prior to processing and releasing the production wave.

With an automatic approach to defining wave contents, the warehouse planner defines warehouse templates that reflect normal decision making. In the previously mentioned example, a wave template might be defined for each production site, and you define the applicable site as part of the query criteria for a wave template. Two additional policies within a wave template determine how to automatically assign components to a wave (after reporting a production order as released). These two policies work in conjunction to define wave contents, as described below for the shipping carrier example.

- *Automatic Additions to an Existing Wave.* This policy results in automatic additions of the components for newly released production orders. The automatic additions occur until the wave status has been changed from open to held or released.

- *Automatic Creation of a New Wave.* This policy applies to a newly released production order when a production wave does not already exist, so that a new wave will be automatically created for its components.

After identifying the selected components in the wave, the warehouse planner indicates "process the wave" which automatically (1) updates the wave status to *Held* and (2) creates work for raw material picking. The picking work reflects the warehouse-specific work template (about how to create the picking work) and location directive (about the pick and put locations).

At this point in time, the warehouse worker can review the work for raw material picking, and optionally print a picking list for the wave or print the associated work. However, the raw material picking work cannot be reported until the wave has been released by the warehouse planner.

Life Cycles Related to a Manual Wave Planning Process As an explanatory approach, it is easiest to describe the life cycles and steps related to a manual wave planning process. These steps are illustrated in Figure 19.6 and highlighted by grey shading. The figure only displays those steps representing the minimum number of touch points for updating status. The figure also displays the key constructs and the corresponding status for each step. The left side of the figure identifies the standard inquiries relative to wave status. These standard inquiries identity the subsets of pending, open and closed waves, and one inquiry identifies all production waves.

Figure 19.6 Life Cycles Related to Manual Wave Planning for Production

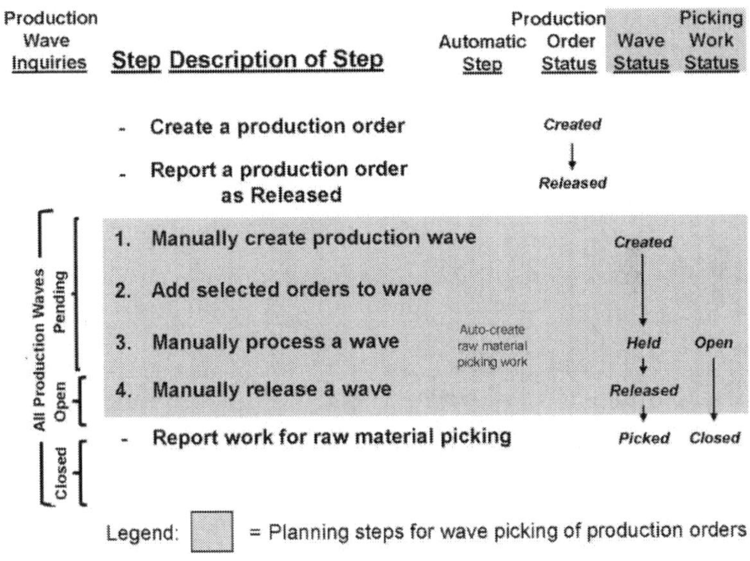

As the starting point, the warehouse planner manually creates a production wave (with a wave status of *Created*), and then adds selected components from released production orders to the wave. At the appropriate time, the warehouse planner indicates "process the wave" which automatically updates the wave status (to *Held*) and also creates work for raw material picking. At this point in time, the warehouse worker can review the work for raw material picking, but the picking work cannot be reported until the wave has been released by the warehouse planner.

Reversing Transactions in Manual Wave Planning The ability to reverse transactions requires an understanding of the current point within the business process, and the associated status of key constructs. Borrowing from the previous figure, Figure 19.7 illustrates the steps within the wave planning process (shown in grey text) and the various points at which you can perform reversing transactions (shown in black text). The figure also illustrates the impact of a reversing transaction on status, and the arrows indicate the resulting point in the business process. As identified by step numbers in the figure, you can reverse transactions (3X) after processing a wave and (4X) after releasing a wave.

Figure 19.7 Reversing Transactions in Manual Wave Planning for Production

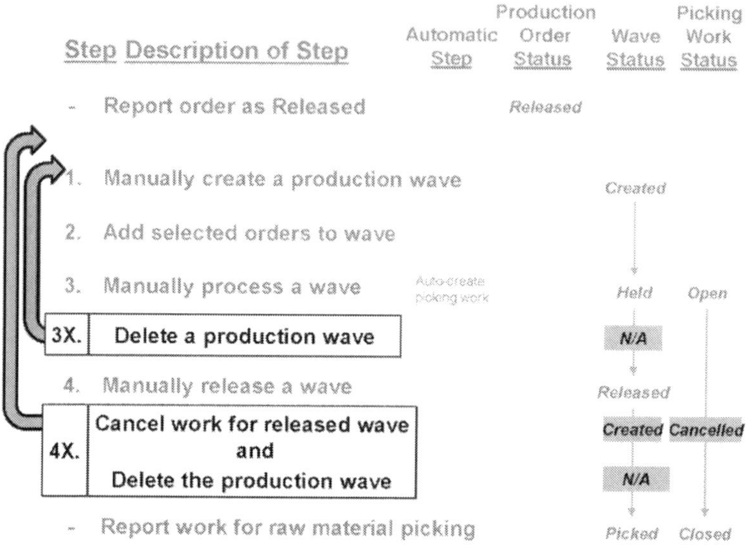

Step 3X: Delete a Production Wave You can delete a production wave after updating its status to held. The deletion means that a status no longer applies, as shown by a value of "N/A" within the figure.

Step 4X: Cancel Work for a Released Production Wave You can cancel work for a released production wave prior to reporting the associated work, which also updates the status for the associated work order.

Step 4X: Delete a Released Production Wave You can only delete a released wave after first cancelling all associated work.

Order-Based Picking as a Wave Picking Variation An order-based picking approach requires the appropriate wave template policies. In particular, a wave should be automatically created for each newly released production order. In many scenarios, the additional steps to process and release the wave will be performed manually, while other scenarios will use automatic steps.

Status of a Production Wave The life cycle of a production wave can vary in different processes. Previous examples of the wave status included the basic process and its reversing transactions (Figures 19.2 and 19.3) and the manual wave planning process and its reversing transactions (Figures 19.6 and 19.7). A wave status applies to each production wave containing components of released production orders, and the applicable values and their significance are described below.

- *Created.* The status indicates that the wave has been created, and production BOM components may or may not have been assigned to the wave. Based on wave template policies, the system can automatically "create the wave" as a result of another step in the business process, such as reporting a production order as released in an order-based picking approach.

- *Held.* The status indicates reporting of "process the wave," which automatically creates raw material picking work for all components shipments assigned to the wave. Picking work cannot be reported until the wave has been released. Based on wave template policies, the system can automatically "process the wave" as a result of another step in the business process, such as reporting a production order as released.

- *Released.* The status indicates that the wave has been released so that picking work can be reported for all components assigned to the wave. Based on wave template policies, the system can automatically "release the wave" as a result of another step in the business process, such as reporting a production order as released.

- *Picked.* The status indicates that the picking work has been completely reported for all lines within the wave.

19.9 Comparing Approaches for Production Order Picking

The two approaches to warehouse management in AX 2012 R3 can be compared in several different ways. The differences in conceptual models provide one way to make a comparison. It is best illustrated by comparing the two approaches for a simple yet typical business process involving order-based picking for production orders. The nature of this business process varies slightly based on the scenario, as illustrated by Production Scenario #1 (Section 9.1) and Production Scenario #2 (Section 19.1) for each approach. This provides the basis for an apples-to-apples comparison of comparable steps, as summarized in Figure 19.8. These steps represent the minimum number of touch points within the business process for updating status, and the figure draws on previously presented information for each approach.

Figure 19.8 Comparing Approaches for Production Order Picking

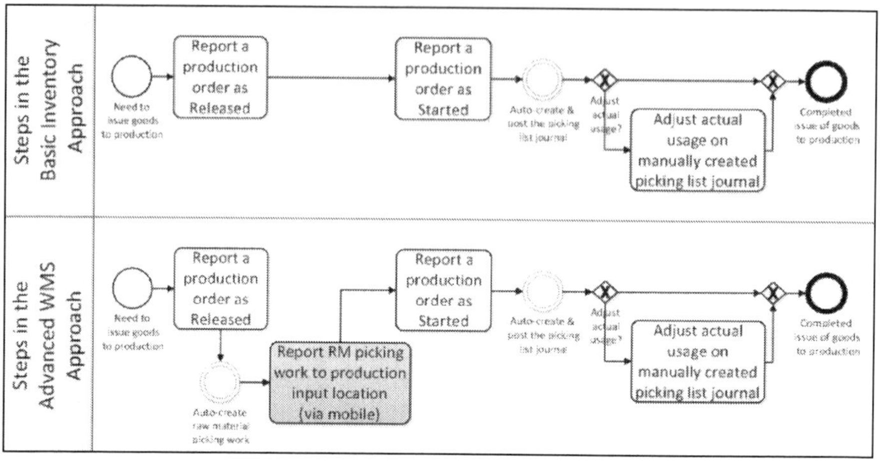

In summary, the comparable steps indicate one key difference in conceptual models for essentially the same business process. The advanced approach supports an additional step and mobile device transaction for raw material picking to a production input location. However, the basic approach could employ withdrawal kanbans to similarly support this step. The figure illustrates the similar steps of backflushing material usage (triggered by starting a production order) and possible adjustments to the reported usage.

19.10 Executive Summary

The Advanced WMS approach supports multiple variations in picking and receiving material for production orders. As a starting point, a simple production scenario for internal manufacturing provided the context for explaining the basic processes for picking and receiving. This chapter focused on picking and the next chapter covers receiving. Given this context, the chapter described a simple yet typical business process for production order picking, and then explained the related life cycles, reversing transactions and key constructs. The basic process provided a baseline for explaining variations, such as the significance of a picking list journal, auto-deduction of components, and variations in production wave planning.

Chapter 20

Production Order Receiving

The Advanced WMS approach supports multiple variations in picking and receiving material for production orders. This chapter covers topics related to receiving and the previous chapter covered topics related to picking. The explanation focuses on production orders (for BOM items) but also covers batch orders (for formula items) as one of the major variations of the business process.

A simple production scenario—described in the previous chapter—provides the context for explaining a basic process for receiving. It is easiest to start with a simple yet typical process and then explain the related life cycles, reversing transactions and key constructs. The basic process provides a baseline for explaining several major variations, such as alternatives for reporting finished quantities and production inspection. These topics are reflected in the following sections within the chapter:

1. Basic Process for Production Order Receiving
2. Additional Steps in the Basic Process
3. Life Cycles Related to the Basic Process
4. Reversing Transactions in the Basic Process
5. Key Constructs for Production Order Receiving
6. Major Variations of Production Order Receiving
7. Alternatives for Reporting Finished Quantities
8. Production Inspection of Finished Quantities
9. Comparing Approaches for Production Order Receiving

20.1 Basic Process for Production Order Receiving

A simple production scenario described in the previous chapter provides a baseline for explaining the basic business processes related to production order receiving, especially the viewpoints of production and warehouse reporting. For example, the finished quantity may be reported by warehouse or production workers into a production output location, with reporting via mobile devices or client transactions. Using the mobile device, the putaway work may be reported separately or in combination with reporting the finished quantity. In some cases, the finished quantity may not require putaway, since it is placed in the production input location for the next production step.

The basic process shown in Figure 20.1 consists of several steps typically performed by a machine operator and warehouse worker, but there are many variations about the role responsibilities and reporting approaches. The business process starts with the need to receive a finished quantity and ends with completed receipts. The starting point shows three alternatives for reporting the finished quantity. The figure uses grey shading to highlight the mobile device transactions, and it identifies the automatic step for creating putaway work. This section provides an overview of the basic process and describes each step in more detail.

Figure 20.1 Basic Process for Production Order Receiving

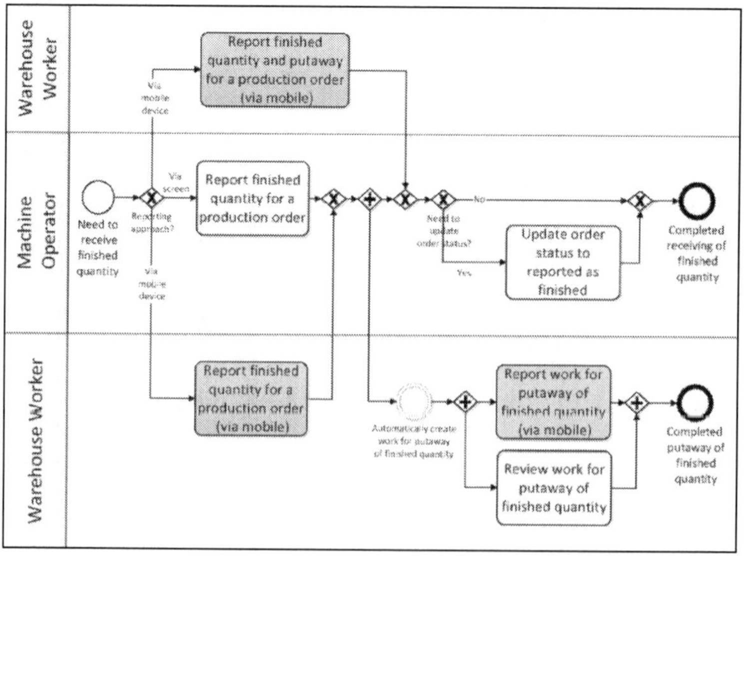

Overview The finished quantity of a production order can be reported by different approaches, as illustrated by the three alternatives in Figure 20.1. The finished quantity can be reported by the machine operator (using the client) in one approach, or it can be reported by the warehouse worker (using the mobile device) in another approach. In many cases, the finished quantity is placed in a production output location and a warehouse operator (using the mobile device) can report putaway work to a stocking location. Alternatively, the warehouse or production worker can report both finished quantity and putaway using a mobile device transaction. The finished quantity may be reported multiple times for a given order, or reported once when it represents the entire order quantity. The machine operator updates the order status to *Reported as Finished* after all production activities have been reported.

Report the Finished Quantity for a Production Order (via the Client) The machine operator use the client to report the finished quantity into a production output location. The finished quantity can be reported for the entire order quantity, or it may be reported for multiple receipts. Each receipt triggers automatic creation of putaway work. Reporting a finished quantity that represents the last of the production output can be flagged, so that the order status will be updated to *Reported as Finished.*

When applicable, the machine operator reports the trashed quantity (aka error quantity) for a production order and an optional reason code. The trashed quantity is not tracked in inventory, and the value of the scrapped inventory is charged to an inventory loss account.

Report the Finished Quantity for a Production Order (via Mobile Device) The warehouse worker uses the mobile device to report the finished quantity into a production output location. The finished quantity can be reported for the entire order quantity, or it may be reported for multiple receipts. Each receipt triggers automatic creation of putaway work. The system automatically prints a label as part of reporting the finished quantity so that the label can be attached to each license plate.

Report the Finished Quantity and Putaway for a Production Order (via Mobile Device) The warehouse worker uses the mobile device to report both the finished quantity and putaway to a stocking location. The finished quantity can be reported for the entire order quantity, or it may be reported for multiple receipts. The system automatically prints a label as part of reporting the finished quantity so that the label can be attached to each license plate.

Update Order Status to Reported as Finished (via the Client) When reporting finished quantities via the client, the last of the production output can be flagged so that the order status will be updated to *Reported as Finished.* However, when reporting via mobile devices, a separate "report as finished" transaction must be reported via the client. A zero quantity can be reported in order to update the order status. An order status of *Reported as Finished* means that any remaining requirements for material or capacity will be ignored, and any difference between the ordered quantity and received quantity will also be ignored.

Report Work for Putaway of Finished Quantity (via Mobile Device) The warehouse worker uses the mobile device to report putaway work for a finished quantity.

Review Work for Putaway of Finished Quantity The warehouse worker can review and print the work for putaway of the finished quantity. The printed document provides bar-coded information to simplify recording of the work.

20.2 Additional Steps in the Basic Process

The basic process often includes several additional steps or slight variations which are not shown in Figure 20.1 so that the diagram does not become too complex. The following additional steps may be needed.

Report the Trashed Quantity for a Production Order (via Client) The trashed quantity (aka error quantity) can be reported when reporting a finished quantity via the client. It cannot be reported via the mobile device. The trashed quantity represents an incremental output (in addition to good quantity). It may reflect the entire order quantity, and a quality order will still be generated. The trashed quantity is not tracked in inventory, and the value of the scrapped inventory is charged to an inventory loss account.

Report the Last Pallet for a Production Order (via Mobile Device) The need for reporting "last pallet" stems from the AX functionality related to delivering inventory to production input locations via raw material picking work. The required quantity of inventory has a status of *Picked* at the production input location. When less inventory is actually consumed (on the picking list journal), it is important to revert the unconsumed inventory to a status of *On Order* so that it can be returned to stock or used for other orders. You revert this status by reporting the last pallet for a production order, which also updates a checkbox field (labeled Last Pallet) for a production order.

The "last pallet" transaction is only needed for scenarios with unconsumed inventory at the production input location. It is typically performed after reporting all production activities. The "last pallet" transaction serves no other purpose. It does not update production order status, so that an additional client transaction may be needed to change status to *Reported as Finished.* In addition, other types of related transactions do not have the same impact as the "last pallet" transaction, such as flagging a component as completely picked or changing order status to *Reported as Finished.*

Move Unused Raw Material Back to Stocking Location (via Mobile Device) In many scenarios, the unused inventory at the production input location needs to be returned to a stocking location. For example, the quantity for an entire license plate (such as an entire pallet or barrel) gets delivered to the input location by raw material picking work, so that you need to move the item's unused inventory back to stock. In addition, performing the "last pallet" transaction resets the status of unconsumed inventory (if any) so that it can be returned to stock or used by other orders. Some scenarios will leave the unused inventory at the input location to support subsequent production orders, thereby reducing or eliminating creation of raw material picking work.

20.3 Life Cycles Related to the Basic Process

The basic process involves several related constructs, where the status for each construct reflects various steps in the process. Figure 20.2 summarizes this information for the basic process, and shading highlights the key constructs related to the Advanced WMS approach. The major constructs include the use of mobile devices for the reporting of a finished quantity and related putaway work, with a status automatically updated by the different steps.

Reporting a finished quantity provides the starting point of the process, and Figure 20.2 illustrates the steps associated with a reporting approach via mobile devices. A subsequent section explains the other alternatives for reporting finished quantities (Section 20.7). Reporting a finished quantity via a mobile device will automatically create and post a report as finished journal (termed an RAF journal for short), which updates the item's inventory status to *Received.* It can also automatically create the putaway work for the finished quantity.

The figure includes the separate step for updating order status (via the client), which represents a required step when using mobile devices as the reporting approach for finished quantities. The right side of the figure illustrates the inventory status associated with the parent item and a component for the production order.

Figure 20.2 Life Cycles Related to the Basic Process for Production Order Receiving

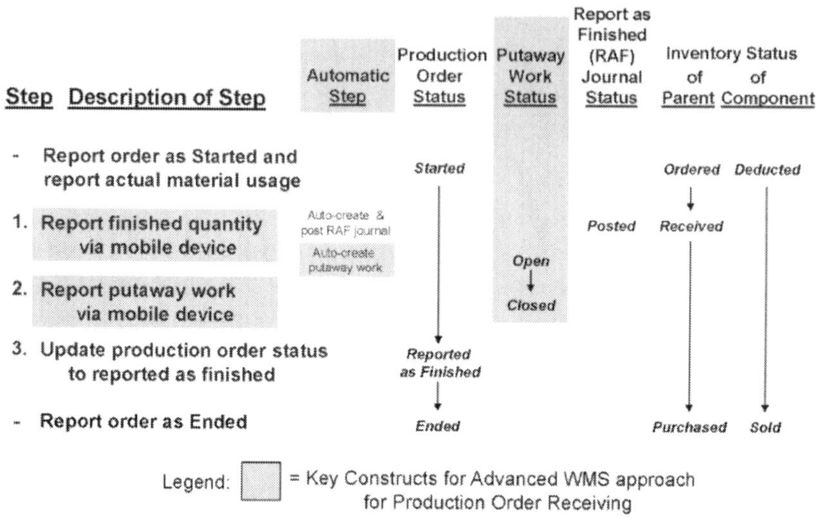

20.4 Reversing Transactions in the Basic Process

The ability to reverse transactions requires an understanding of the current point within the business process, and the associated status of key constructs. Borrowing from the previous figure, Figure 20.3 illustrates the steps within the basic process (shown in grey text) and the various points at which you can perform reversing transactions (shown in black text). The figure also illustrates the impact of a reversing transaction on status, and the arrows indicate the resulting point in the business process. As identified by step numbers in the figure, you can reverse transactions (1X) after initially creating the putaway work for a finished quantity and (AnyX) at any time prior to ending the production order.

Step 1X: Cancel Work Order for Putaway of Finished Quantity You can cancel a work order prior to reporting any work, which changes the work order status to *Cancelled*. In this case, the finished quantity simply remains in the production output location, and you decide further steps such as moving or scrapping the inventory.

Figure 20.3 Reversing Transactions in the Basic Process for Production Order Receiving

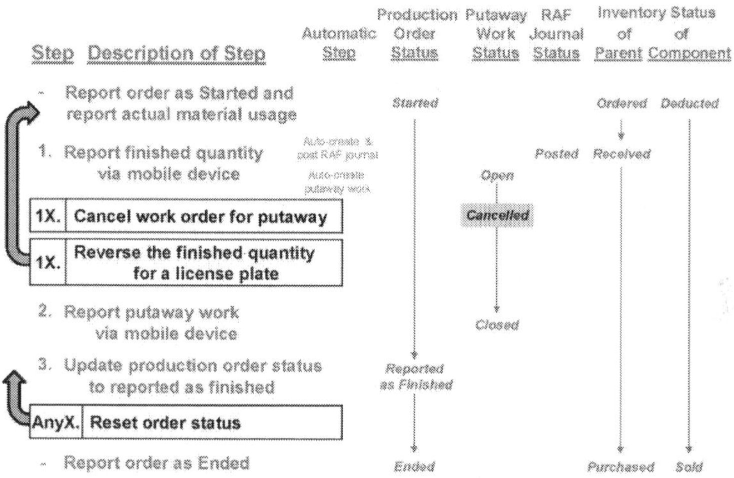

Step 1X: Reverse the Finished Quantity for a License Plate You can reverse the finished quantity for a specified license plate by accessing the Reverse License Plate dialogue for a selected production order. The transaction will back out the item's inventory and the appropriate amount of raw materials will be placed back into the production input location. The arrow in Figure 20.3 indicates the impact of this reversing transaction, since you can start over with reporting actual material usage and finished quantities. The reversed quantity can reflect all or part of the license plate quantity. The transaction is typically performed when you over-report the finished quantity and need to make a correction.

Step AnyX: Reset Order Status for a Production Order A production order can be reset to a previous status at any time prior to the *Ended* status. You indicate the desired order status on the reset order dialogue. The finished quantities will not be reversed by resetting the order status from *Reported as Finished* to *Started*. However, based on my testing, resetting to an earlier status typically encounters difficulties so that the order status cannot be changed.

20.5 Key Constructs for Production Order Receiving

The Advanced WMS approach for production order receiving involves several key constructs in addition to the production order. These include production output locations and setup information for several mobile device transactions.

Production Output Locations You identify a production output location when reporting the finished quantity for a production order (using either a mobile device or the client). It must be defined as an LP-controlled location to support automatic creation of putaway work. However, the mobile device transaction can be used to report both the finished quantity and putaway, where the putaway location does not need to be a license plate controlled location.

The production output location is normally inherited based on routing information, as described shortly. However, some scenarios do not employ routings, so that the inherited location can reflect a warehouse-specific default value. In either case, the inherited value can be overridden when reporting the finished quantity.

The production output location is defined for a resource group, such as common location for multiple machines. When reporting a finished quantity, the inherited value reflects the output location for the resource group associated with the item's final routing operation. This resource group (and a resource) is determined by scheduling logic for production orders.

Mobile Device Transactions Several mobile device transactions apply to production order receiving. The primary transactions include reporting the finished quantity for a production order and the related putaway, and a combination of these two steps. With each variation, you start by entering the production order number when reporting the receipt.

- *Menu Item for Reporting Finished Quantity* As part of defining the menu item, you select a work creation process for *report as finished.* The receipt must be placed in an LP-controlled location and assigned a license plate number. Completing the transaction will automatically create putaway work for the license plate. You can review this putaway work by accessing it for the related production order (on the Production Order form), for a selected work order (on the All Work form).

- *Menu Item for Putaway of a Finished Quantity* As part of defining the menu item, you select the policy for *use existing work* and the work class for *finished goods putaway.* A work template and a location directive are also defined for the work type of *finished goods putaway.*

- *Menu Item for Reporting Finished Quantity and Putaway* As part of defining the menu item, you select a work creation process for *report as finished and putaway.* A work template and a location directive are also defined for the work type of *finished goods putaway.*

Another mobile device transaction involves reporting the last pallet received, which was explained as an additional step in the basic process (Section 20.2).

20.6 Major Variations of Production Order Receiving

The basic process for production order picking provides the foundation for explaining major variations. The major variations are listed below and covered in separate explanations. The last two topics involve an extended explanation, as identified by the related section numbers.

- Simple Inventory Transaction for Production Order Receiving
- Receiving Batch-Controlled Items
- Receiving Serialized Items
- Report Batch Order Receiving
- Report Batch Order Receiving of Co/By-Products
- Alternatives for Reporting Finished Quantities (Section 20.7)
- Production Inspection of Finished Quantities (Section 20.8)

Simple Inventory Transaction for Production Order Receiving The concept of a simple inventory transaction is already embedded within the alternative approaches for reporting a finished quantity via client transactions. These simple inventory transactions apply to both the basic and advanced approaches.

Receive Batch-Controlled Items The assignment of a batch number to a finished quantity reflects several policies described in a subsequent chapter about quality management (Section 25.2). The impact of these policies differs slightly when reporting finished quantities via a mobile device versus the client, especially for automatic versus manual assignment of a batch number. The system supports automatic and manual assignment of a batch number in transactions reported via the client. Automatic assignment is also supported by mobile device transactions, but manual assignment requires an additional policy (labeled "override batch number") in the definition of the mobile device menu item.

Receive Serialized Items The assignment of serial numbers to a finished quantity reflects several policies described in a subsequent chapter about quality management (Section 25.1). The impact of these policies differs slightly when reporting finished quantities via a mobile device versus the client, especially for automatic versus manual assignment of a batch number. The system supports automatic and manual assignment of a serial number in transactions reported via the client. Automatic assignment is also supported by mobile device transactions, but manual assignment is not supported.

Report Batch Order Receiving The same approaches for reporting finished quantities of a production order also apply to a batch order. Hence, it does not represent a major variation but is included for completeness sake.

Report Batch Order Receiving of Co/By-Products The same mobile device transactions for reporting finished quantities of a production order also apply to the finished quantities for a batch order with co-products and/or by-products. You identify the relevant batch order number and item number when reporting a finished quantity. However, an additional mobile device menu item must be defined to support the putaway of co/by-products.

As part of defining the menu item, you select the policy for *use existing work* and the work class associated with the work order type of *co-product and by-product putaway*. A work template and a location directive are also defined for the work order type *co-product and by-product putaway*. You select this menu item for reporting putaway of a co/by-product.

20.7 Alternatives for Reporting Finished Quantities of Production Orders

The finished quantity of a production order can be reported in different ways, as illustrated in the basic process (Section 20.1). This section summarizes the alternatives for reporting finished quantities, segmented by the use of mobile devices versus the client. As a related topic, it also explains the approaches for updating order status to *Reported as Finished.*[1]

Mobile Device Transactions for Reporting a Finished Quantity The mobile device transactions include reporting a finished quantity and reporting both a finished quantity and putaway. A previous section described the definition of these mobile device menu items. Both approaches will automatically create and post an inventory journal (labeled the Report as Finished Journal). The transactions do not update order status to *Reported as Finished*, so that an additional "report as finished" transaction must be reported on the client.

[1] The term reported-as-finished has several contexts within Dynamics AX that can lead to confusion. These contexts include the update task for a production order, a journal for reporting unit completions by operation, report-as-finished flags when reporting production activities, and the status of a production order.

Client Transactions for Reporting a Finished Quantity There are several client transactions for reporting a finished quantity, which can also be used to update order status to *Reported as Finished.* Each client transaction will automatically create putaway work for the finished quantity, just like the mobile device transactions.

- *Report as Finished form.* The Report as Finished form can be accessed by starting from the Production Order form so that it inherits information from the selected order. When applicable, you indicate the finished quantity represents the last of the remaining production output (by selecting the checkbox labeled End Job) so that the order status will be updated to *Reported as Finished.* Processing this task will automatically create and post an inventory journal for the finished quantity (labeled the Report as Finished Journal).

  The Report as Finished form can also be accessed directly in order to report the finished quantity for multiple orders. Information about multiple orders can be populated using selection criteria, such as the order's scheduled delivery date/time or the item's production pool.

- *Route Card Journal for Reporting Unit Completions at the Last Operation.* When routing data exists, reporting the unit completions at the last operation can automatically create and post the Report as Finished Journal.

- *Report as Finished Journal.* Each transaction for reporting a finished quantity will automatically create and post an inventory journal labeled the Report as Finished journal. The journal consists of header information (identifying the production order) and one or more line items, where each line identifies an item and its finished quantity. The journal can be accessed by starting from the Production Order form so that it only displays information about the selected order. It can also be accessed directly in order to display information about all orders. In either case, you can manually create a new journal and line item in order to report a finished quantity.

The client transactions for reporting a finished quantity were also covered for the Basic Inventory approach to production order receiving (Section 10.6).

Update the Order Status to Reported as Finished All of the above-mentioned client transactions can update order status to *Reported as Finished.* You indicate the finished quantity represents the last of the remaining production output by selecting the checkbox labeled End Job. When applicable, you can also report a zero quantity in order to update the order status.

It is assumed no more transactions need to be reported after updating order status, so that any remaining component requirements or expected receipts will be ignored. However, transactions can still be reported until order status has been updated to Ended.

Conditions Preventing Updates to Order Status Missing feedback or errors can prevent an order status update, and a warning infolog identifies the conditions when attempting to update order status. You can override these warnings by using the *Accept Errors flag* when reporting the finished quantity. Examples of missing feedback or errors include the following.

- Each component must be completely issued or flagged as completed in the picking list journal.
- Each operation must be flagged as completed.
- The total finished quantity must be less than or equal to the started quantity.

20.8 Production Inspection of Finished Quantities

There are many variations of production inspection for manufactured items. For example, production inspection may be performed by machine operators when reporting a finished quantity, typically by assigning an Inventory Status to the received material. Alternatively, production inspection can be performed by a quality control clerk reporting against an automatically-created quality order. The test results for a quality order may be reported for a small sample while the material remains in a production location, or the material may be placed in a separate QC area until test results have been reported. Validation results of pass or fail can automatically update the Inventory Status of the inventory, or the batch disposition code of batch-controlled items. The test results may also be reported during production by automatically creating quality orders for selected routing operations.

As an explanatory approach, the different approaches for production inspection are more easily explained via case studies. Production inspection can be reported by machine operators (Case 69), or by quality control clerks at a separate QC area (Case 70).

Case 69: Production Inspection by Machine Operators The production manager at a manufacturing company wanted the machine operators to report inspection of finished quantities for production orders. A machine operator could immediately report a trashed quantity (aka the error quantity) when reporting a good quantity on the Report as Finished form, thereby bypassing the need for additional steps. Alternatively, the machine operator could assign an inventory status of *To-Be-Scrapped*, *Needs-Rework* or *Needs-Inspection* to a received quantity, thereby indicating the need for an additional step. The corresponding steps involved an inventory adjustment, a rework order, or a quality order.

Case 70: Production Inspection at a Separate QC Area For certain electronic items at a manufacturing company, the entire finished quantity of a production order was placed in a separate QC location for so that each unit could go through a burn in process. Several test results were monitored for the burn in process. The quality control clerk reported these test results for the associated quality order with sample sizes of one unit. After the units passed validation, a warehouse worker would create putaway work and then report the putaway work from the QC location to a stocking location. Figure 20.4 illustrates the business process, and grey shading indicates the mobile device transactions.

Figure 20.4 Production Inspection at a Separate QC Area

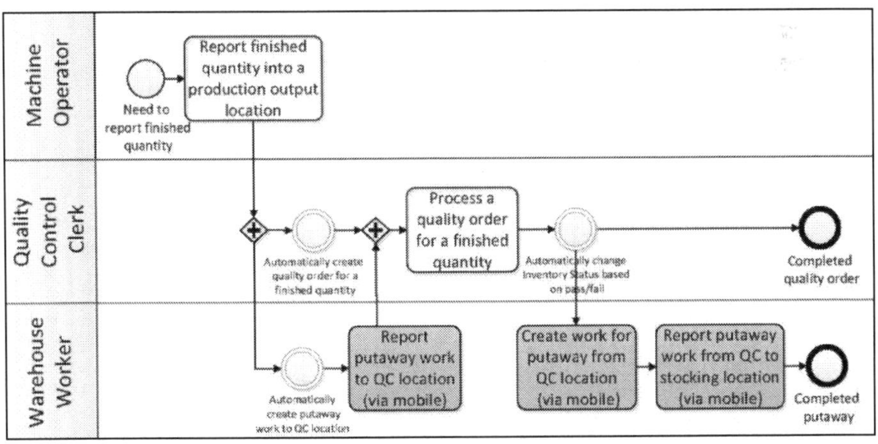

20.9 Comparing Approaches for Production Order Receiving

The two approaches to warehouse management in AX 2012 R3 can be compared in several different ways. The differences in conceptual models provide one way to make a comparison. It is best illustrated by comparing the two approaches for a simple yet typical business process for production order receiving. This provides the basis for an apples-to-apples comparison of comparable steps, as summarized in Figure 20.5. These steps represent the minimum number of touch points within the business process for updating status, and the figure draws on previously presented information for each approach.

Figure 20.5 Comparing Approaches for Production Order Receiving

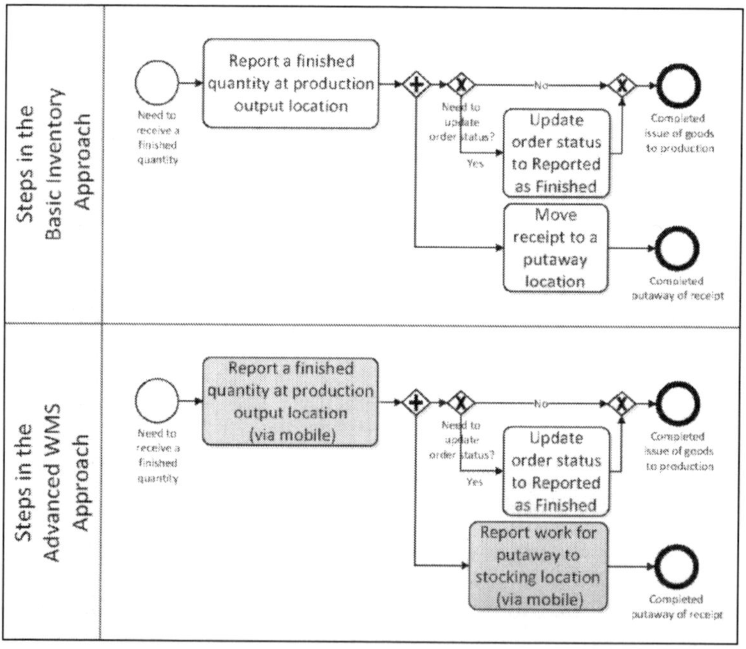

In summary, both approaches employ a similar process and client transactions for reporting finished quantities and updating order status to *Reported as Finished.* However, the advanced approach supports mobile device transactions for reporting finished quantities and putaway, as highlighted by grey shading in the figure.

20.10 Executive Summary

The Advanced WMS approach supports multiple variations in picking and receiving material for production orders. This chapter covered topics related to receiving, and employed the simple production scenario—described in the previous chapter—as the context for explaining a basic process for receiving. The chapter started with a simple yet typical process and then explained the related life cycles, reversing transactions and key constructs. The basic process provided a baseline for explaining several major variations, such as alternatives for reporting finished quantities and production inspection.

Several case studies illustrated the variations. These included production inspection by machine operators (Case 69) and production inspection at a separate QC area (Case 70). Related case studies in other chapters include using the mobile device to capture LIMS data about production output (Case 63), deferred assignment for a serialized end-item and its serialized components (Case 78), merging physical batches into a new batch (Case 79), and destructive testing of finished quantities (Case 84).

Chapter 21

Subcontracted Production

Subcontracted production often involves inventory tracking at a non-WMS warehouse representing the subcontractor, which means the Advanced WMS approach does not apply to many of the warehouse-related transactions. However, there are several variations of subcontracted production which do involve transactions at a WMS-enabled warehouse. This includes production order picking and receiving, and also transfer order shipping and receiving. These selected transactions are covered within this chapter since a previous chapter provided an overall explanation of subcontracted production (Chapter 11).

Subcontracted production can have many variations of the supplied material and handling of the finished quantities. These variations provide an organizing focus for covering the relevant warehouse transactions supported by the Advanced WMS approach. These considerations are reflected in the following sections within the chapter.

1. Variations of Supplied Material for Subcontracted Production
2. Variations of Finished Quantities for Subcontracted Production
3. Key Constructs for Subcontracted Production
4. Case Studies for Subcontracted Production

Several aspects of supply chain management represent critical considerations for subcontracted production. The requirements should reflect S&OP game plans, a reasonable model of the supply chain, and up-to-date information about the subcontracted production order and its supplied material. In many cases, up-to-date information is also needed for purchase order or transfer order deliveries of supplied material, as well as transfer order deliveries of finished quantities. Other factors may apply such as a manageable level of expediting.

21.1 Variations of Supplied Material for Subcontracted Production

Subcontracted production involves supplied material—either completely supplied or partially supplied—and there are several delivery options as well as options for reporting usage. Borrowing from a previous diagram (Figure 11.1) about variations of subcontracted production, Figure 21.1 illustrates these options and grey shading identifies those supported by mobile device transactions and the Advanced WMS approach. The two applicable variations include raw material picking work for the supplied material and transfer order shipments of the supplied material.

Figure 21.1 Variations of Supplied Material

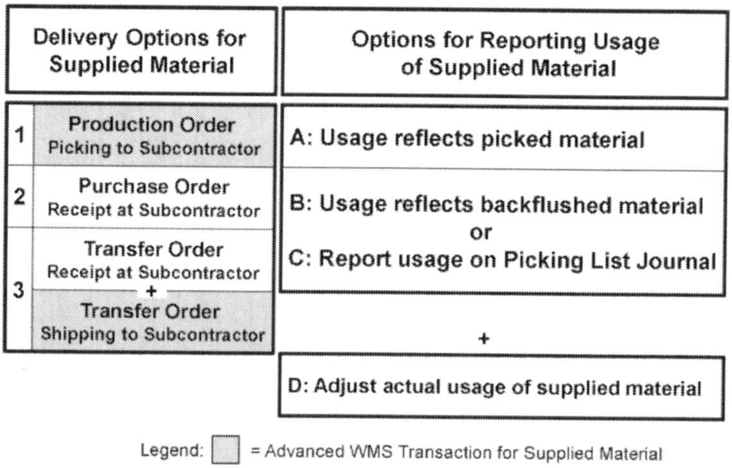

Report Raw Material Picking Work for the Supplied Material (via Mobile Device) Raw material picking is not really required for subcontracted production, but it does offer some advantages for supplied components. Mobile device transactions can report raw material picking to a production input location. The production input location represents "send to subcontractor." Since the subcontractor is typically identified as a resource within the routing information, the production input location can be vendor-specific (for a specific resource) or it could reflect multiple subcontractors (for a resource group). You can optionally use wave picking for components of multiple production orders produced at a subcontractor.

Report Transfer Order Picking Work for the Supplied Material (via Mobile Device) A mobile device transaction can report transfer order picking, or staging and loading steps. Additional capabilities within the Advanced WMS approach can also be used, such was wave picking and load planning.

21.2 Variations of Receiving a Finished Quantity for Subcontracted Production

There are several variations in subcontracted production which can be supported by mobile device transactions and the Advanced WMS approach. Borrowing from a previous diagram (Figure 11.2) about variations of subcontracted production, Figure 21.2 illustrates these options and grey shading identifies the applicable ones for an internal WMS-enabled warehouse. The applicable options include reporting the finished quantity of a production order, and receiving a transfer order that was shipped from a non-WMS warehouse.

Figure 21.2 Variations of Receiving a Finished Quantity

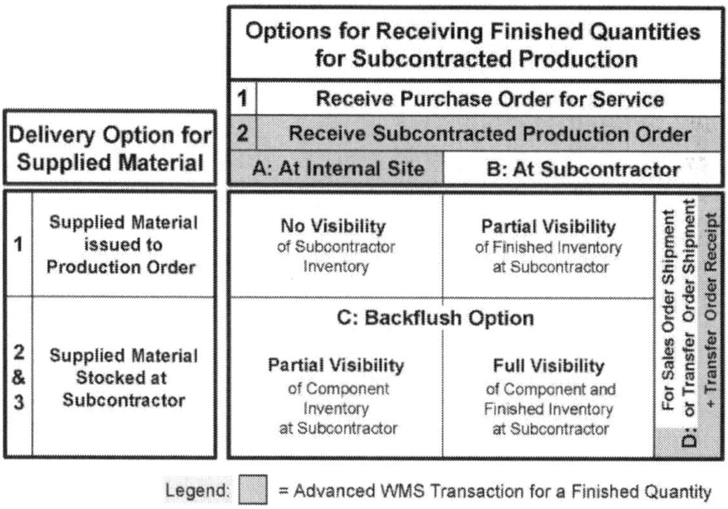

Report a Finished Quantity for a Production Order (via Mobile Device) The inventory can be received into a receiving location (with a subsequent putaway transaction), or you can report receipt and putaway as part of one transaction.

Receive a Transfer Order Shipment from a Non-WMS Warehouse (via Mobile Device) The inventory can be received into a receiving location (with a subsequent putaway transaction), or you can report receipt and putaway as part of one transaction.

Visibility of Inventory at Subcontractor Site A basic issue in subcontracted production concerns the visibility of inventory at the subcontractor site and the in-transit inventory. Figure 21.2 also summarizes the three major variations of inventory visibility at the subcontractor site—consisting of no visibility, partial visibility and full visibility. The use of transfer orders to send supplied material, and to receive a finished quantity, can provide additional visibility of in-transit inventory.

21.3 Key Constructs for Subcontracted Production

Subcontracted production and internal production share many similarities in the use of basic constructs like production orders and picking list journals. However, subcontracted production involves significant differences and several variations. In particular, the dual constructs of a production order and its related purchase order (for the subcontracted service) can be received separately, or a single purchase order receipt can be employed for updating both orders.

Key Constructs Related to a Production Order Previous chapters covered the key constructs related to production orders when using the basic approach or the advanced approach. When using the basic approach, for example, these key constructs include the production order and its picking list journal (Section 9.9), the warehouse source of components (Section 9.10), the alternatives for reporting production order receipts (Section 10.8), and production inspection for a finished quantity (Section 10.9). The life cycles and reversing transactions were also explained for production order picking (Sections 9.4 and 9.5) and receiving (Sections 10.3 and 10.4). Similar analyses about key constructs were provided for the advanced approach.

Other Warehouse-Related Transactions for Subcontracted Production Subcontracted production sometimes involves transfer order shipments of supplied material (Chapters 7 and 17) and also transfer order receipts of a finished product from a non-WMS warehouse (Chapters 9 and 18). Subcontracted production may also involve purchase order receipts of supplied material at the subcontractor location (Chapter 5) and/or sales order shipments from the subcontractor location (Chapter 6).

Simple Inventory Transactions A simple inventory transaction is typically employed for reporting transactions occurring at the subcontractor site.

Receive a Purchase Order for the Subcontracted Service The dual constructs of a production order and its related purchase order can be received separately, or a single receipt transaction (for the purchase order) can update both orders. However, you cannot use the mobile device transaction for reporting a purchase order receipt of a subcontracted service.

21.4 Case Studies for Subcontracted Production

Case studies can be used to illustrate the variations of subcontracted production that can be supported by mobile device transactions and the Advanced WMS approach. For example, the simplest scenario involves production order picking and receiving with no visibility of inventory at the subcontractor or in transit (Case 71). Another scenario involves complete visibility of this inventory (Case 72).

Case 71: Subcontracted Production with No Visibility

A manufacturing company produced several products at nearby subcontractors. For a given production order, the raw material picking work delivered a kit of supplied material to a production input location (representing the specific vendor) and sent to the subcontractor. Mobile device transactions were also used for receiving the finished quantity at the originating warehouse. The subcontractor provided a quick turnaround for each production order, thereby minimizing the need for inventory visibility at the subcontractor.

Case 72: Subcontracted Production with Full Visibility

A manufacturing company produced several products at subcontractors located in other states and countries. The supplied material was transferred and stocked at each subcontractor, and the finished quantities were reported prior to transferring the goods to an internal warehouse. This approach provided full visibility of inventory at the subcontractor site and in transit, and also modeled the associated transportation time. Figure 21.3 illustrates the bill of material information and the warehouse-related transactions. \

Figure 21.3 Subcontracted Production With Full Visibility

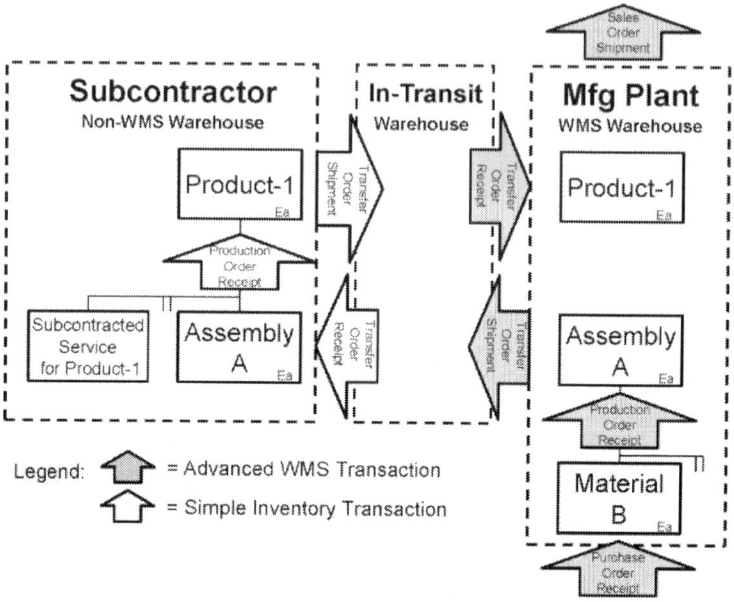

21.5 Executive Summary

Subcontracted production and internal production share many similarities. However, there are many variations of subcontracted production scenarios which involve significant differences about inventory visibility and multisite coordination, and supply chain coordination via the dual constructs of a production order and a corresponding purchase order. The chapter explained the variations associated with supplied material and finished quantities and highlighted the key constructs

Several case studies illustrated the variations. These included subcontracted production with no visibility (Case 71) and with full visibility on inventory (Case 72). Relevant case studies from other chapters include identifying BOM components provided by the subcontractor (Case 42), multiple subcontractors build the same item (Case 43), purchase orders delivered to a subcontractor warehouse (Case 49), and sales order shipments from a subcontractor warehouse (Case 50).

Chapter 22

Additional Options for Cycle Counting

The Advanced WMS approach supports several options for cycle counting. One option involves the use of a cycle count plan for a complete physical inventory or for cycle count purposes. A second option supports the ad hoc generation of a cycle count for selected items or locations. The third option involves cycle counting as part of the sales order picking process, so that cycle count work will be automatically created when picking reduces an item's inventory below a specified quantity (aka the cycle counting threshold). Cycle counting discrepancies may occur in each variation. These topics are reflected in the following sections with the chapter.

1. Perform Cycle Counting Based on a Cycle Count Plan
2. Perform Cycle Counting on ad hoc Basis
3. Perform Cycle Counting When Sales Order Picking Reduces Inventory Below a Threshold Quantity
4. Cycle Counts that are Triggered by Other Transactions
5. Report Cycle Count Work via Mobile Devices
6. Resolve a Cycle Counting Discrepancy

Each variation requires some basic setup information. This includes a mobile device menu item for cycle counting and a Location Profile policy to allow cycle counting within the related locations.

22.1 Perform Cycle Counting Based on a Cycle Count Plan

A cycle count plan may reflect a complete physical inventory or a selected subset for cycle count purposes. For example, the selected subset could be based on counting frequency and the ABC code for items, a control group or empty locations. As illustrated in Figure 22.1, the typical process for using a cycle count plan consists of several steps performed by the warehouse manager and worker. Grey shading highlights the step involving mobile device transactions. The process starts with the need for a planned cycle count and ends with a completed count.

Figure 22.1 Perform Cycle Counting Based on a Cycle Count Plan

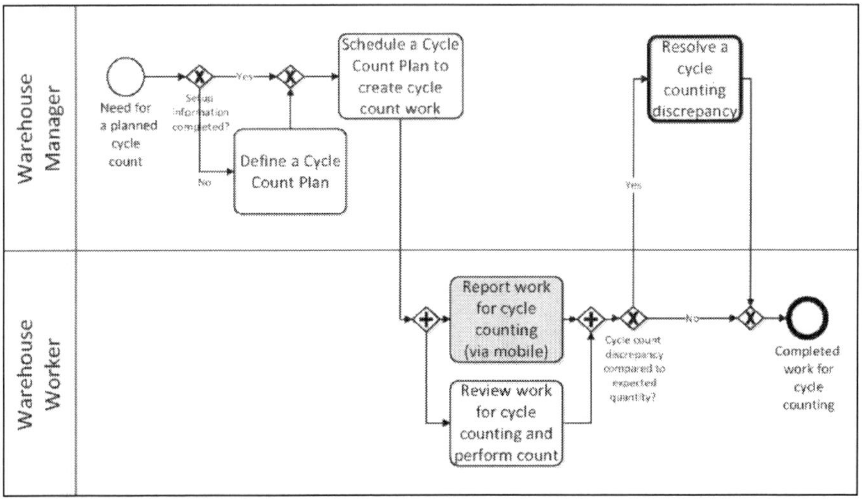

Overview The warehouse manager defines each cycle count plan (and its related selection criteria about items and locations), and also schedules a cycle count plan to create cycle count work. The warehouse worker reports work for cycle counting via the mobile device. Cycle count discrepancies can be resolved by the warehouse manager, as described in a subsequent section.

Define a Cycle Count Plan The warehouse manager defines a cycle count plan and the related selection criteria about items and locations. Different plans can represent different approaches to planned cycle counting, as illustrated by the following examples.

- *Counting Frequency and ABC Code for Items.* A cycle count plan often reflects counting frequency and ABC analysis. For example, three plans would be required for a 30, 60 and 90 day frequency, where you specify the corresponding number of "days between cycle counting" for each plan. You also specify the item's ABC value as part of the selection criteria for each plan. A cycle count plan may also be warehouse- or site-specific, which can be specified as part of the selection criteria about locations.

- *Control Group for Cycle Counting.* With a control group method, you count the same items (or locations) every day in order to identify inventory errors immediately, and fix the source of inventory accuracy problems. In this example, you define a separate plan with a zero for the number of "days between cycle counting," and specify the relevant items (or locations) as part of its selection criteria.

- *Complete Physical Inventory.* A separate plan can be defined for a complete physical inventory, where you specify zero for the number of "days between cycle counting." You also indicate whether to include or exclude empty locations. The selection criteria about locations can be used to indicate a warehouse- or site-specific physical inventory.

- *Count Empty Locations.* One approach to cycle counting focuses on just empty locations, since they are the easiest to count. For this cycle count plan, you specify a policy for "only empty" locations and a zero for the number of "days between cycle counting."

Schedule a Cycle Count Plan to Create Cycle Count Work The warehouse manager schedules a cycle count plan to create cycle count work, so that cycle counting can be reported via mobile devices. This step is also termed "process a cycle count plan."

22.2 Perform Cycle Counting on ad hoc Basis

Cycle counting can be performed on an ad hoc basis, such as counting selected items or locations, or a performing spot count. The use of ad hoc cycle counting consists of several steps performed by the warehouse manager and worker, as illustrated in Figure 22.2 and explained below. Grey shading highlights the steps involving mobile device transactions.

Overview The warehouse manager can execute a periodic task to create cycle count work on an ad hoc basis. There are two different periodic tasks reflecting selection criteria about item or location characteristics. The warehouse worker reports work for cycle counting via the handheld device. The warehouse worker can also report work for a spot count of a location via the handheld device. Cycle count discrepancies can be resolved by the warehouse manager, as described in a subsequent section.

Figure 22.2 Perform Cycle Counting on ad hoc Basis

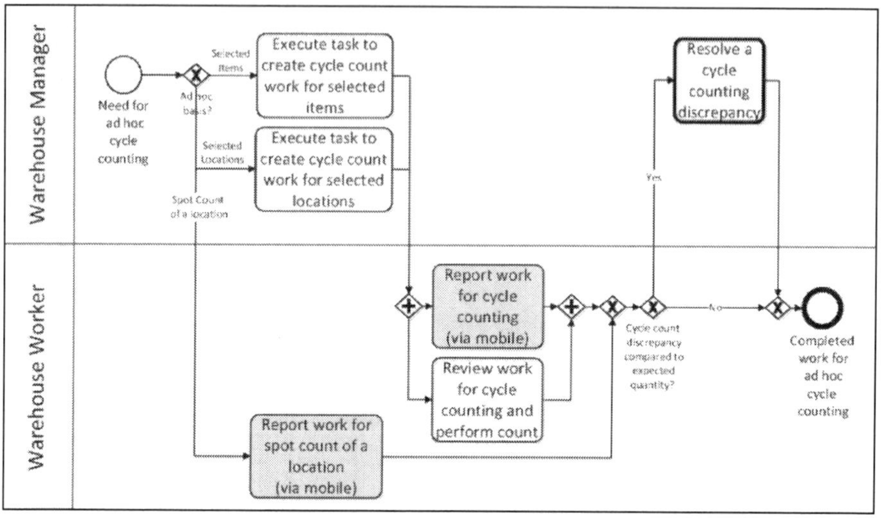

Execute Task to Create Cycle Count Work for Selected Items The warehouse manager executes a periodic task to "create cycle count work by item," where the selection criteria for the task reflect characteristics of the item (such as ABC code) or inventory (such as the location or batch number).

Execute Task to Create Cycle Count Work for Selected Locations The warehouse manager executes a periodic task to "create cycle count work by location," where the selection criteria for the task reflect characteristics of the locations (such as the location identifier, a zone or a warehouse).

Report Work for Spot Count of a Location (via Handheld) The warehouse worker reports work for a spot count of a location via the handheld device. A Mobile Device Menu Item must be defined for Spot Counting, where you select "spot cycle counting" as the work creation process.

22.3 Perform Cycle Counting When Sales Order Picking Reduces Inventory Below a Threshold Quantity

Some scenarios involve cycle counting as part of the sales order picking process, so that cycle count work will be automatically created when picking reduces an item's inventory below a specified quantity (aka the cycle counting threshold). The warehouse manager defines the cycle counting threshold for relevant items and locations. Figure 22.3 illustrates a typical process, starting with the sales order picking step. Grey shading highlights the steps involving mobile device transactions.

Figure 22.3 Perform Cycle Counting When Sales Order Picking Reduces Inventory Below a Threshold Quantity

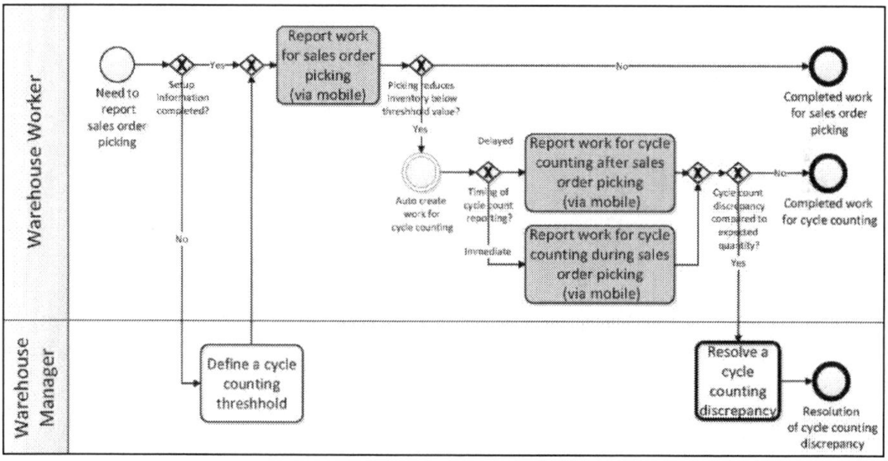

As part of setup information, the warehouse manager defines a cycle counting threshold, which can be defined as the quantity and UM for relevant items and locations (identified by selection criteria). Alternatively, the threshold can be defined as a percentage of the existing inventory quantity. An additional policy indicates whether cycle count work should be reported immediately or delayed until completion of sales order picking.

As another part of setup information, you can optionally disable the use of cycle counting thresholds for a menu item about cycle counting.

22.4 Cycle Counts that are Triggered by Other Transactions

Cycle counts can be triggered as a result of reporting other transactions. One example involves the "Short Pick" transaction for sales order picking or for transfer order picking. You can select the Short Pick option as part of reporting the mobile device transaction, and then specify the actual pick quantity. You also need to select a reason for short picking which indicates the applicable action(s).

A reason for short picking reflects a work exception. As part of defining a work exception, you identify the applicable actions for the short pick reason, such as automatic creation of cycle count work. Hence, reporting a short pick and selecting a reason can automatically create cycle count work.

22.5 Report Cycle Count Work via Mobile Devices

The ability to report cycle count work via a mobile device requires some setup information. For example, the appropriate Mobile Device Menu Items must be defined in order to support various cycle count transactions. As a related issue, the default value for an item's unit of measure can be identified for cycle counting purposes (as part of the Unit Sequence Group assigned to the item).

- *Menu Item for Reporting a Spot Count.* As part of defining the menu item, you select a work creation process for *Spot Cycle Counting*.

- *Menu Item for Reporting Cycle Count Work.* As part of defining the menu item, you select the option "Use existing work" and indicate the relevant work order type for *cycle counting.* The "Directed By" option determines how the work will be reported on the mobile device. For example, by selecting the *System Directed* option, information about the work will be automatically displayed on the mobile device, so you simply enter the quantity and then proceed to the next work (which is automatically displayed). Alternatively, by selecting the *Cycle Count Grouping* option, you identify a location as the starting point for reporting cycle count work, and then provide an additional entry about the selected license plate or item before entering the quantity.

Additional setup information is required for identifying work users with cycle count supervisor authority, as described in the next section.

22.6 Resolve a Cycle Counting Discrepancy

Each variation of cycle counting can result in a count discrepancy, where the counted quantity differs from the expected quantity. The process of resolving discrepancies consist of several steps performed by the warehouse manager, as illustrated in Figure 22.4 and described below.

Figure 22.4 Typical Process for Resolving a Cycle Counting Discrepancy

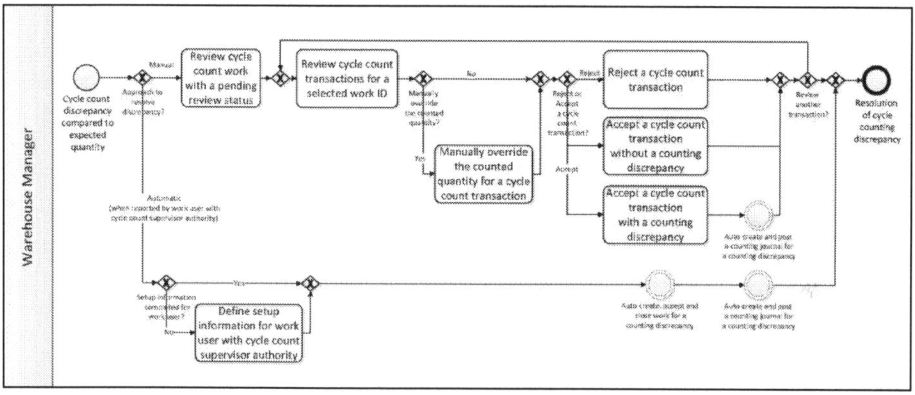

Overview The warehouse manager can resolve a cycle count discrepancy with a manual approach or an automatic approach. With a manual approach, the warehouse manager reviews the cycle count work with a pending review status. The "pending review" status is automatically assigned when there is a discrepancy compared to the expected quantity. After selecting a work ID, the manager reviews the cycle count transactions related to the Work ID. The manager can reject a cycle count transaction (resulting in no impact on inventory) or accept a cycle count transaction with a discrepancy (resulting in automatic creation and posting of a counting journal for the discrepancy).

An automatic approach to resolving a cycle count discrepancy only applies when the cycle count has been reported by a work user with cycle count supervisor authority for the relevant warehouse. In this scenario, the discrepancy will be automatically accepted when it is within the maximum limits for the work user (such as limits for a quantity or value discrepancy), and the system will automatically create and post a counting journal for the discrepancy.

Review Cycle Count Work with a Pending Review Status The warehouse manager reviews the cycle count work with a pending review status. The "pending review" status is automatically assigned when there is a discrepancy compared to the expected quantity.

Review Cycle Count Transactions for a Selected Work ID The warehouse manager reviews the cycle count transactions related to a selected Work ID.

Manually Override the Counted Quantity for a Cycle Count Transaction When applicable, the warehouse manager can manually override the counted quantity for a selected cycle count transaction. As a result, there may be no discrepancy with the expected quantity.

Reject a Cycle Count Transaction The warehouse manager rejects a selected cycle count transaction, so that the transaction does not update inventory.

Accept a Cycle Count Transaction Without a Counting Discrepancy The warehouse manager accepts a selected cycle count transaction without a counting discrepancy, and there is no impact on inventory.

Accept a Cycle Transaction with a Counting Discrepancy The warehouse manager accepts a selected cycle count transaction with a counting discrepancy. As a result, the system will automatically create work (with a work order type of "counting discrepancies accepted"), and also accept and close this work.

Auto-Create and Post a Counting Journal for a Counting Discrepancy As a result of accepting a cycle count transaction, the system immediately auto-creates and posts a counting journal for the counting discrepancy.

Define Setup Information for Work User With Cycle Count Supervisor Authority As part of identifying a work user and their applicable warehouse(s), the warehouse manager can designate their cycle count supervisor authority and the related maximum limits for automatically accepting a cycle count discrepancy from the expected quantity. A maximum limit can be expressed as a quantity, a percentage or a value. For example, the work user may have a maximum value limit of $100 for one of their applicable warehouses, and a value limit of $50 for another warehouse.

The warehouse manager can review and add work users on the Work User screen. For a selected work user, the warehouse manager identifies each applicable warehouse and menu name, and also the user ID and password for accessing the handheld device.

Auto-Create, Accept and Close Work for a Counting Discrepancy When a counting discrepancy has been reported by a work user with cycle count supervisor authority, and the discrepancy is within their maximum limits, the system will automatically create work (with a work order type of "counting discrepancies accepted"), and also accept and close this work.

22.7 Executive Summary

The Advanced WMS approach supports several options for cycle counting and this chapter summarized the options. One option involves the use of a cycle count plan for a complete physical inventory or for cycle count purposes. A second option supports the ad hoc generation of a cycle count for selected items or locations. The third option involves cycle counting as part of the sales order picking process, so that cycle count work will be automatically created when picking reduces an item's inventory below a specified quantity (aka the cycle counting threshold). Cycle counting discrepancies may occur in each variation and the discrepancies require manual or automatic resolution. .

Chapter 23

Integration with Advanced Transportation Management

Transportation management is arguably the most critical and complex component of global supply chains.[1] Even with more local supply chains, the transportation costs and speed of delivery are often significant factors for manufacturing and distribution companies. These considerations need to be supported by integrated transportation management capabilities within a firm's ERP system.

The use of AX software capabilities to support transportation management represents a broad topic with numerous aspects—both technical and managerial—that probably merit a separate book. However, many aspects of transportation planning for outbound loads and shipments involve the previously-described business processes for sales order picking/shipping and transfer order picking/shipping. In a similar fashion, the transportation management for inbound loads and shipments involve the business processes about purchase order receiving. This chapter builds on these previously-described business processes, and focuses on the unique and additional software capabilities for transportation management.

The additional software capabilities within AX include the assignment of a rate and route to a load, and the related ability to enter and reconcile the actual freight charges. Other capabilities include the scheduling and reporting of transportation appointments, and the use of transportation tenders. Newer software capabilities are constantly being added by Microsoft (such as load-building strategies) and by third-party vendors. This chapter provides an introduction to the additional capabilities for transportation management, and consists of the following sections.

---

[1] The implications of a global supply chain on transportation management are covered in the recently published textbook "Transportation: A Global Supply Chain Perspective" by John Coyle and others.

1. Designate an Item that can use the Transportation Management Processes
2. Build on the Basics of Transportation within AX
3. Build on the Advanced WMS Capabilities
4. TMS Capabilities for Outbound Loads
5. Integration Points with the Advanced WMS approach
6. Define an Outbound Load for Sales Orders
7. Assign a Rate and Route to an Outbound Load
8. Transportation Tenders
9. Schedule and Report Transportation Appointments
10. Perform Freight Entry and Reconciliation
11. TMS Capabilities for Outbound Loads for Transfer Orders
12. TMS Capabilities for Inbound Loads for Purchase Orders
13. Additional Case Studies

Several aspects of supply chain management represent critical considerations for transportation management. The requirements for transportation should reflect S&OP game plans, a reasonable model of the supply chain, and up-to-date information about purchase orders (for inbound loads) as well as sales orders and transfer orders (for outbound loads). Other factors include realistic delivery promises for sales orders and a manageable level of expediting.

23.1 Designate an Item That Can Use the Transportation Management Processes

An item-specific policy determines whether an item can "use transportation management processes," and it is automatically assigned to a WMS-enabled item.[2] It can be optionally assigned to an item that is not WMS-enabled, as described in a previous case (Case 53). In either case, these items can be termed a TMS-enabled item for short, and the shortened term will be used going forward.

---

[2] The designation of a WMS-enabled item has been covered in previous chapters. For example, it was explained as part of the major options for warehouse management (Section 2.1) and the fundamentals of the Advanced WMS approach (Section 13.6). It is also described in a subsequent chapter about the significance of the Storage Dimension Group for an item (Section 24.6).

This chapter focuses on the unique and additional software capabilities for supporting transportation management. These additional capabilities have been called different names, but they can be termed TMS capabilities for short. The shortened term will be used going forward.

The additional TMS capabilities are highlighted within the AX user documentation, which differentiates various topics as applicable to "features in the transportation management module" versus "features in the inventory management module." The additional capabilities are also reflected in the menu structure topics for the Transportation Management module. The vast majority of the topics focus on the additional TMS capabilities and related setup information. The other topics about loads and shipments have been covered from a warehouse viewpoint even though they primarily reflect a transportation viewpoint.

Actual use of the additional TMS capabilities is optional. Some scenarios will not use any of the capabilities. Other scenarios may use part of the additional capabilities, such as the manual assignment of a rate/route to a load and the related ability to enter and reconcile freight charges. More sophisticated scenarios may need all of the capabilities as part of their strategic options for using the Advanced WMS approach. These strategic options were illustrated by several case studies at the beginning of the book (Case 2 and Case 3).

23.2 Build on the Basics of Transportation within AX

Several basic aspects of transportation apply to sales orders, transfer orders and purchase orders regardless of the use of software capabilities for transportation management. Examples include the expected transportation times and the significance of delivery dates used in master scheduling logic. These transportation basics reflect key aspects of how a company models and manages its supply chain, especially in terms of the detailed game plans that everybody is working to. The additional TMS capabilities need to support these detailed game plans or update the details if they change—such as changing a ship date or a delivery date. These basics of transportation are summarized here and were covered in a previous chapter (Chapter 12).

Transportation Basics for Sales Orders The key aspects include sales order dates for shipment and delivery, the transportation time to a customer, the sales order promise dates, the need for expediting a sales order shipment, the sales order charges for freight/handling, and shipping documents such as a bill of lading.

Transportation Basics for Transfer Orders The key aspects include transfer order dates for shipment and delivery, the transportation time between warehouses, and the transfer order promise dates.

Transportation Basics for Purchase Orders The key aspects include the significance of a confirmed delivery date, the mode of delivery for a purchase order, and purchase order charges for freight/handling.

23.3 Build on the Advanced WMS Capabilities

Transportation requirements are often the driving factor for many of the previously-described Advanced WMS approaches to warehouse management, especially in the definition and management of loads and shipments. The overlapping requirements about loads and shipments are reflected in the common menu structures for the Transportation Management module and the Warehouse Management module.

The transportation management requirements for outbound loads and shipments can build on the business processes about sales order picking/shipping and transfer order picking/shipping. With sales orders, for example, these business processes include the load planning process for sales orders (Section 16.11). Related business processes include manual packing (Section 16.12) and automated packing of containers (Section 16.13) and staging and loading steps (Section 16.15).

In a similar fashion, the transportation management requirements for inbound loads and shipments can build on the business processes about purchase order receiving, such as load planning (Section 15.9) and an ASN from the vendor.

23.4 TMS Capabilities for Outbound Loads

The TMS capabilities build on the business processes for load planning of outbound loads, and impact several steps for defining and confirming an outbound load. In addition, they support new business processes about the assignment of a rate and route to a load, and the related ability to enter and reconcile the actual freight charges. They also support several new optional business processes. These options include the use of transportation tenders, and the scheduling and reporting of transportation appointments.

The outbound load can reflect sales orders or transfer orders, but further explanation focuses on sales orders. A subsequent section covers outbound loads for transfer orders (Section 23.11). The business processes affected by the TMS capabilities are summarized in Figure 23.1 and described below. The figure indicates the new business processes with grey shading and also identifies the optional processes. Subsequent sections provide further explanation of the business processes shown in Figure 23.1.

Figure 23.1 TMS Capabilities for an Outbound Load for Sales Orders

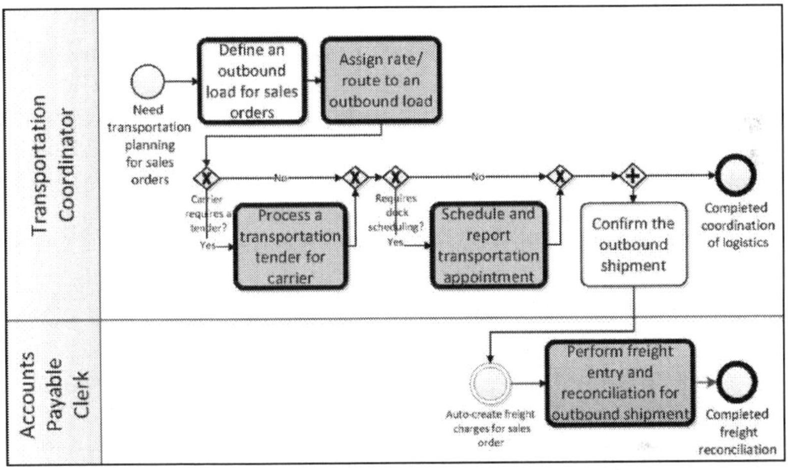

Define an Outbound Load for Sales Orders. The transportation coordinator reviews the Load Planning Workbench for open sales order lines, and arranges the outbound transportation for selected sales orders. The selected sales orders can be assigned to an existing load or to a newly-created load, and the weight/volume can be compared to the capacity of the selected shipping vehicle (aka load template). Previous chapters provided further explanation about this business process, including the basic process for sales order picking/shipping (Section 16.1) and the load planning process for sales orders (Section 16.11). Related business processes include manual packing (Section 16.12) automated packing of containers (Section 16.13), staging and loading steps (Section 16.15) and other variations of the picking/shipping process (Section 16.6).

Assign Rate/Route to an Outbound Load The transportation coordinator assigns a rate and route to an outbound load, either via manual assignment or selection of an automatically-calculated rate and route. The coordinator typically starts from the Load Planning Workbench, and accesses the Rate Route Workbench form to select the rate and route. Alternatively, the coordinator can simply assign a carrier and manually assign the rate (by accessing the Rate Route Detail form).

Process a Transportation Tender for Carrier The transportation coordinator processes a transportation tender when required by the carrier. The process consists of several steps identified by the status of the transportation tender. The transportation tender must be created and submitted to the carrier, the vendor's response (for the confirmed rate and dates) must be confirmed, and then either accepted or denied. The tender must be confirmed prior to confirming the outbound shipment, or the system provides a warning about the need for a transportation tender.

Schedule and Report a Transportation Appointment The transportation coordinator can create and firm a transportation appointment for the outbound (and inbound) docks at a warehouse. In terms of reporting, you can record the actual driver check-in and check-out for the transportation appointment using mobile devices or client transactions. You can also cancel the appointment. The status of the appointment indicates multiple steps in the process, where the initial status (*tentative*) is updated to *firm*, *checked-in* and *completed.*

Confirm an Outbound Load (aka Confirm an Outbound Shipment) The coordinator typically reports the "confirm an outbound load" step before the shipping vehicle is about to leave, and indicates the scheduled date/time. When an outbound shipment is confirmed, you can generate shipping documents—such as a packing list or bill of lading—so they can be sent with the load. Other documents may be needed in some scenarios, such as a commercial invoice, an MSDS document or a Certificate of Analysis (COA). You can also send an ASN (Advanced Ship Notice) to the customer.

When freight charges apply to the sales order, the confirm step will result in the following automatic updates:

- *Auto-Create Freight Charges for the Sales Order Lines.* The freight charges for a load (or shipment) will be automatically allocated to sales order lines within the load (or shipment).

- *Auto-Create Freight Detail for Load.* The freight detail provides the starting point for the freight entry and reconciliation process.

Perform Freight Entry and Reconciliation for an Outbound Shipment The accounts payable clerk performs a multi-step process to enter and reconcile a carrier's invoice. The first step involves selection of the applicable load and then viewing the freight bill details. These freight bill details reflect the rates assigned to the load, and automatic creation after confirming the outbound shipment (based on the freight terms policy). The second step involves generation of an internal freight invoice based on the freight bill details. The third step involves entering information against the internal freight invoice, including the carrier's invoice number, invoice amount(s), the payee vendor, and the payment due date. At this point, the accounts payables clerk performs a matching of the two amounts—for the carrier's invoice against the freight bill details—and submits it for approval. Differences in the amounts must be reconciled prior to approval, which requires a reconciliation reason code and a decision about whether to pay the carrier's invoice. An approved carrier's invoice will automatically create an accounts payable invoice for the payee vendor.

23.5 Integration Points with the Advanced WMS Approach

Several integration points are worth noting relative to the Advanced WMS approach described in previous book chapters. The first key integration point involves the load planning process. The coordinator reviews and selects sales orders on the Load Planning Workbench to create a new load or to assign the selected orders to an existing load. The coordinator evaluates the total weight and volume for the load compared to the capacity of the selected vehicle (aka the selected load template). The coordinator may assign a different vehicle or move load lines from one load to another. At that point, the coordinator assigns a freight rate and route to the load, but these freight charges are not yet assigned to the sales orders within the load.

A similar process applies to outbound loads for transfer orders and related freight charges. This represents new functionality within AX because previous AX versions did not support freight charges for transfer orders.

A second integration point occurs as a result of confirming the outbound shipment, since this step automatically creates and assigns the freight charges to the sales orders within the load.

A third integration point occurs when the actual freight invoice must be entered, since it requires a freight reconciliation process.

Other potential areas of integration involve the use of transportation tenders and/or transportation appointments, since these define the date/time for actual shipping activities related to a load. However, this information does not currently update the shipping dates on the related sales orders.

23.6 Define an Outbound Load for Sales Orders

An outbound load is a single shipment or group of shipments that are shipped from a warehouse location to a customer or intermediate location. You can create an outbound load for sales orders automatically or manually, where manual creation typically starts with load planning and use of the Load Planning Workbench form (Section 16.11). You can consolidate multiple shipments into a load, typically for those shipments going from the same ship-from warehouse to the same destination. Another consolidation example involves shipments to different destinations in the same route that use the same hub(s).

As part of using the Load Planning Workbench form, you can access the Load Building Workbench form to create proposed loads based on load building strategies. For example, this is useful if you want to maximize efficiency by avoiding half full loads, or if you frequently use the same shipping carrier and all the considerations for the loads are known, such as size or weight restrictions. A load building strategy named the "volume-based load building strategy" is provided as an out-of-the-box solution, and you can add your own load-building strategies.

23.7 Assign a Rate and Route to an Outbound Load

The manual assignment of a rate and carrier to an outbound load represents the simplest use of the TMS capabilities. It requires minimal setup information about the carrier and no other additional setup. More sophisticated approaches to the assignment of a transportation rate and route involve considerably more setup information. This section summarizes the manual assignment of a rate/route, and describes some of the setup information for more sophisticated approaches.

Manual Assignment of a Carrier and Rate You can manually assign a carrier to a load on the Load Planning Workbench form, and then manually assign a rate by accessing the Rate Route Details form. A rate can also be manually assigned to a shipment or container within a load, or to a route or route segment. In addition to a rate, you can also manually assign hub charges or accessorial charges, and indicate whether the charges apply to the load, shipment or container.

Setup Information for Shipping Carriers The required setup information for a shipping carrier ranges from the simple to the complex depending on how you want to assign the carrier to a load. For example, more complex setup information is required when assigning a carrier based on criteria such as the least expensive carrier rate, rate shopping, route plan or mode of shipment. At its simplest, you simply define a shipping carrier ID, and specify the shipping carrier ID as part of manually assigning a rate to a load.

Setup Information for Transportation Rates The setup information includes rate masters, the applicable accessorial charges for a shipping carrier or hub, the transportation management engines, and rating profiles.

- *Rate Masters.* Rate masters are part of the rating setup for a shipping carrier. You can use rate masters to determine the available rates for the shipping carrier and to determine whether the rates justify considering the shipping carrier for an assignment.

- *Accessorial Charges for a Shipping Carrier or Hub.* An accessorial assignment associates a carrier with a surcharge configuration, which is used when you rate a shipment.

- *Transportation Management Engines.* Transportation management engines define the logic that is used to calculate the rates for a shipping carrier; they reflect a particular carrier contract. You can manually create one or more engines or automatically initialize the base engine data.

- *Rating Profiles.* A rating profile is unique for a shipping carrier, and it determines whether the shipping carrier's rate matches the customer's requirements.

Setup Information for Transportation Routes The setup information includes the transportation mode and transportation method for a shipping carrier. Some optional information can also be defined about constraints and/or multiple route segments.

- *Transportation Mode for a Shipping Carrier.* The transportation mode represents the form of transport that the carrier uses for freight deliveries, such as less than truckload (LTL), truckload (TL), or parcel. A carrier can be associated with one or more transportation modes.

- *Transportation Method for a Shipping Carrier.* A transportation method represents the form of transport that the carrier uses for freight deliveries, such as air, ground, ocean, or rail. A carrier can be associated with an unlimited number of transportation methods.

- *Optional Constraints.* You can assign transportation constraints for items, shipments, or shipping carriers. One example involves constraints about a hazardous chemical so that the item is not transported using a particular shipping carrier.

- *Optional Multiple Route Segments.* Complex transportation processes often require a route plan with route segments that provide information about freight delivery. A route plan identifies the routing guide that defines the transportation route.

23.8 Transportation Tenders

The use of transportation tenders represents an optional capability. The business process consists of multiple steps typically performed by the transportation coordinator, as summarized in Figure 23.2 and described below.

Figure 23.2 Process a Transportation Tender

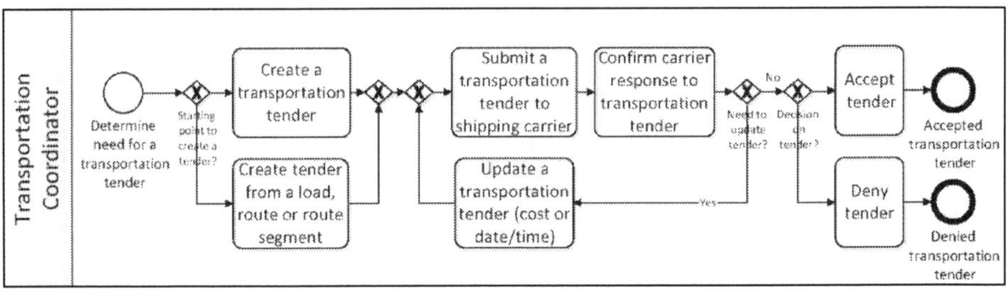

A transportation tender can be created directly, but it is typically created for a selected load, route or route segment. The transportation coordinator submits a tender to a shipping carrier—typically by printing and sending the booking request. The coordinator enters and confirms the vendor's response for the cost and date/time (which can update the tender information), and then indicates whether the tender was accepted or denied.

23.9 Schedule and Report Transportation Appointments

The use of transportation appointments represents an optional capability. The business process consists of multiple steps typically performed by the transportation coordinator, as summarized in Figure 23.2 and described below. Some of the steps may be performed by shipping or receiving clerks via mobile device transactions, such as driver check-in and check-out. These transactions are highlighted by grey shading in the figure.

Figure 23.3 Schedule and Report a Transportation Appointment

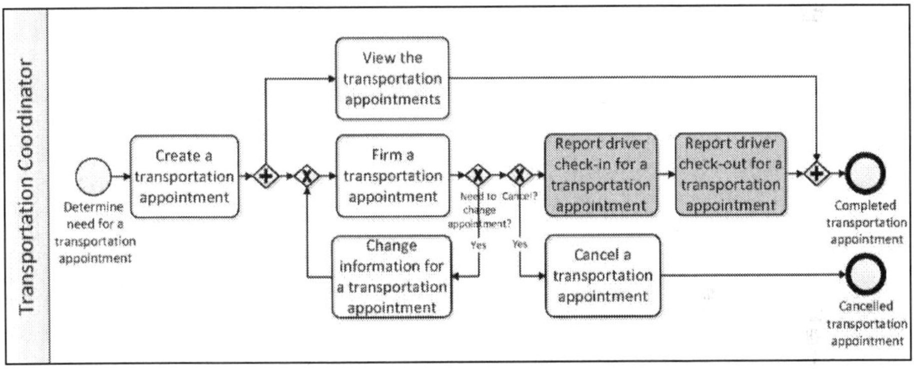

23.10 Perform Freight Entry and Reconciliation

After confirming the outbound shipment of a load, the assigned rate provides the basis for automatic creation of freight charges for sales orders within the load. Freight entry and reconciliation starts with the receipt of the freight invoice. The typical process involves multiple steps and decision points, such as how to handle problems in freight bill matching or approval. Figure 23.4 illustrates some of these decision points in a simplified process for freight entry and reconciliation performed by an accounts payable clerk.

Figure 23.4 Perform Freight Entry and Reconciliation

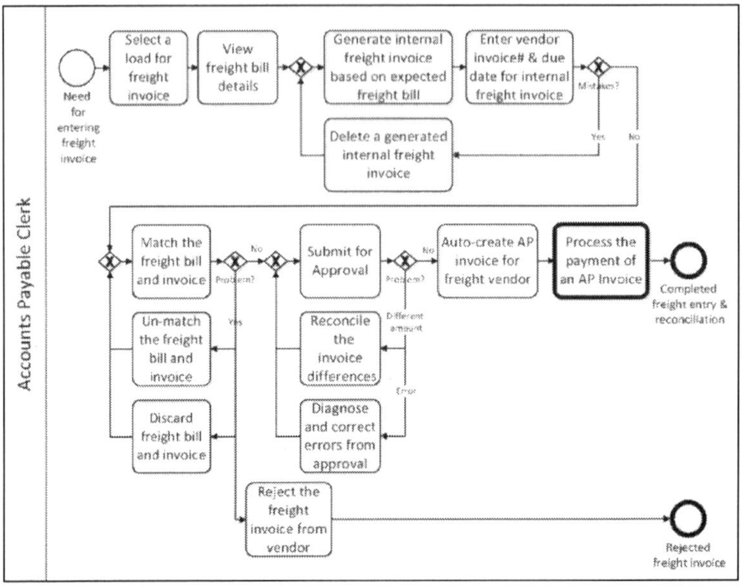

As the first step in the process, the payables clerk selects a load corresponding to the invoice and views the freight bill details about the originally-assigned charges. This information provides the basis for generating an internal freight invoice about the expected freight bill. The payables clerk then matches the actual invoice to the expected freight bill and submits it for approval. If approved, the system automatically creates an accounts payable invoice for the freight vendor so a payment can be processed. If not approved, problems such as errors or different amounts need to be corrected before the clerk can submit it again for approval. The freight invoice can also be rejected.

23.11 TMS Capabilities for Outbound Loads for Transfer Orders

The TMS capabilities for an outbound load were previously described for sales orders (Section 23.6). This section focuses on the capabilities for an outbound load for transfer orders. These capabilities share many similarities with those for sales orders, but there are several major differences in some of the business processes. The business processes with major differences are identified in Figure 23.5 with grey shading and described below.

Figure 23.5 TMS Capabilities for an Outbound Load for Transfer Orders

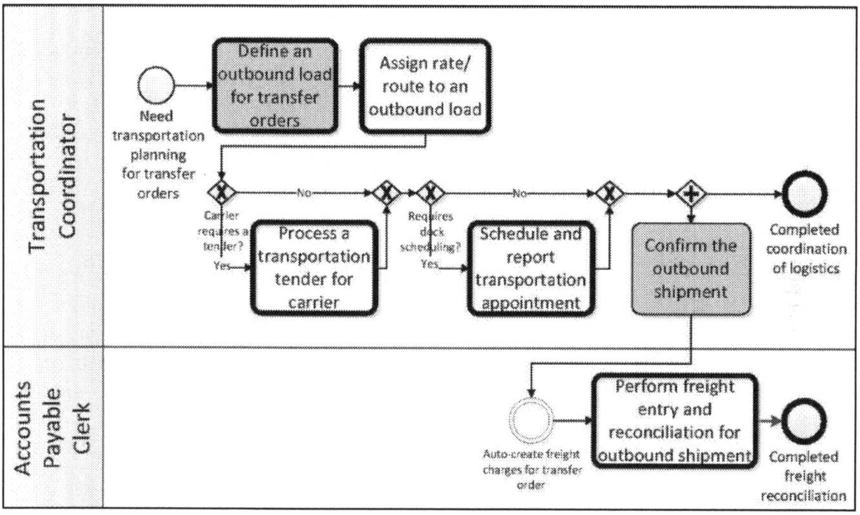

Define an Outbound Load for Transfer Orders The transportation coordinator reviews the Load Planning Workbench for open transfer order lines, and arranges the outbound transportation for selected transfer orders. The selected transfer orders can be assigned to an existing load or to a newly-created load, and the weight/volume can be compared to the capacity of the selected shipping vehicle (aka load template). Previous chapters provided further explanation about this business process, including the basic process for transfer order picking/shipping (Section 17.1) and the load planning process for transfer orders (Section 17.11). Related business processes include staging and loading steps (Section 17.12), and other variations of the process for picking/shipping (Section 17.6).

Confirm an Outbound Load (aka Confirm an Outbound Shipment) The coordinator typically reports the "confirm an outbound load" step before the shipping vehicle is about to leave, and indicates the scheduled date/time. When an outbound shipment is confirmed, you can generate shipping documents—such as a bill of lading or packing list—so they can be sent with the shipment. Other documents may be needed in some scenarios, such as a certificate of origin.

When freight charges apply to the transfer order, the confirm step will result in the following automatic updates:

- *Auto-Create Freight Charges for the Transfer Order Lines.* The freight charges for a load (or shipment) will be automatically allocated to transfer order lines within the load (or shipment).

- *Auto-Create Freight Detail for Load.* The freight detail provides the starting point for the freight entry and reconciliation process.

23.12 TMS Capabilities for Inbound Loads for Purchase Orders

The TMS capabilities for an inbound load share many similarities with those for outbound loads. The capabilities for an outbound load were previously described for sales orders (Section 23.6) and transfer orders (Section 23.11). However, there are several major differences in some of the business processes for inbound loads. The business processes with major differences are identified in Figure 23.6 with grey shading and described below.

Figure 23.6 TMS Capabilities for an Inbound Load for Purchase Orders

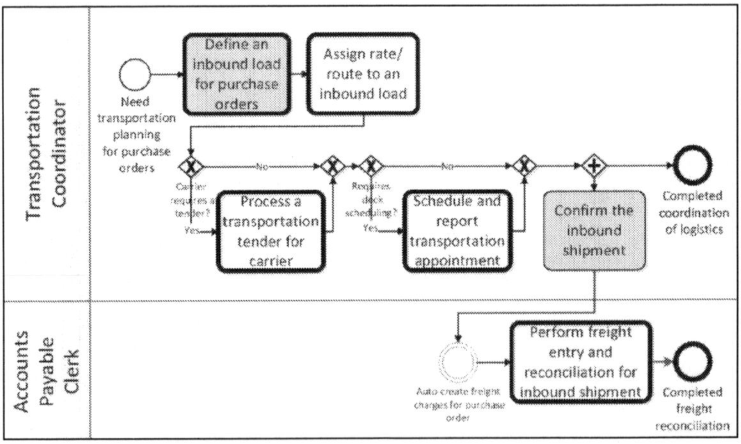

Define an Inbound Load for Purchase Orders The transportation coordinator reviews the Load Planning Workbench for open purchase order lines, and arranges the inbound transportation for selected purchase orders. The selected purchase orders can be assigned to an existing load or to a newly-created load, and the weight/volume can be compared to the capacity of the selected shipping vehicle (aka load template). Previous chapters provided further explanation about this business process, including the load planning process for purchase orders (Section 15.9) and other variations of the receiving process (Section 15.6).

Confirm an Inbound Load (aka Confirm an Inbound Shipment) The coordinator typically reports the "confirm an inbound load" step before the shipping vehicle is about to leave the vendor location, and indicates the scheduled date/time. When an inbound shipment is confirmed, you can generate shipping documents—such as a packing list or bill of lading—so they can be sent with the shipment. Other documents may be needed in some scenarios, such as a certificate of origin.

When freight charges apply to the purchase order, the confirm step will result in the following automatic updates:

- *Auto-Create Freight Charges for the Purchase Order Lines.* The freight charges for a load (or shipment) will be automatically allocated to purchase order lines within the load (or shipment).

- *Auto-Create Freight Detail for Load.* The freight detail provides the starting point for the freight entry and reconciliation process.

23.13 Additional Case Studies

Case 73: Assign Freight Costs to an Outbound Load for a Sales Order A manufacturing/distribution company was using an order-based picking approach to sales orders, where a single shipment and corresponding load were created for each sales order. A transportation coordinator manually assigned the freight charges to each load. As a result of confirming the outbound shipment, the freight charges were automatically allocated to sales order lines, and they were used to automatically create freight detail information for subsequent steps to enter and reconcile actual freight costs.

Case 74: Manage the Transportation of Inbound Loads for Purchase Orders The transportation coordinator and purchasing agent at a manufacturing/distribution company worked closely with several of their key suppliers to identify which purchase order lines should be shipped together as an inbound load. The dynamic nature of the business required many last minute adjustments in the contents and delivery timing of a load. The load ID provided the starting point for recording receipts at the receiving area.

23.14 Executive Summary

The additional TMS capabilities build on the foundation of load planning within the advanced approach to warehouse management, which has been described in previous chapters. They impact the previously described business process for defining and confirming outbound loads and inbound loads. In addition, they support new business processes about the assignment of a rate and route to a load, and the related ability to enter and reconcile the actual freight charges. They also support several new optional business processes. These options include the use of transportation tenders, and the scheduling and reporting of transportation appointments.

The TMS capabilities build on several transportation basics within AX. These transportation basics apply to sales orders, transfer orders, and purchase orders, such as the expected transportation times and the significance of delivery dates used in master scheduling logic.

Several case studies involving transportation management have been cited in previous chapters. Examples included reporting lost in transit for a transfer order (Case 32), transfer orders to/from a subcontractor warehouse (Case 33), updating the transfer order receipt date for overseas deliveries (Case 34), identify truck routes for regional customer deliveries (Case 51), transportation constraints about transfer orders to/from a subcontractor (Case 55), coordinate transportation for Asian subcontractors (Case 56), and the packing structure documentation for the carrier and customer (Case 66).

Chapter 24

Definition of an Item

Information about material items provides the foundation for managing supply chain activities in distribution and manufacturing environments. A comprehensive common database about item information must satisfy requirements stemming from multiple stakeholders to avoid the problems associated with multiple nonintegrated files. The stakeholders include sales, purchasing, warehouse management, quality and accounting, as well as product design/engineering and production for manufactured items. Other stakeholder considerations include customers, vendors, industry standards, intercompany coordination, international operations and web-based applications. The multiple stakeholders often have differing requirements concerning the definition of an item.

This chapter focuses on item definition from a warehouse management perspective. It covers common topics for both the basic and advanced approaches, and highlights some differences when applicable. Previous chapters about the fundamentals for each approach covered their unique aspects. Examples of common topics include unit of measure considerations, alternative identifiers and effective use of notes. Some common topics have been summarized, such as the definition of purchased and manufactured items, and inventory valuation and financial reporting. Other aspects of item definition related to batch/serial tracking and testing requirements are covered in the next two chapters. These topics are reflected in the following sections within this chapter.

1. Enterprise vs Company-Level Information for an Item
2. Unit of Measure Considerations
3. Alternative Item Identifiers
4. Item identifiers using an Item Number and Variant Codes
5. Effective Use of Notes for Warehouse Management Purposes
6. Negative Inventory Policies

7. Information about Purchased Items
8. Information about Manufactured Items
9. Inventory Valuation and Financial Reporting
10. Significance of the Storage Dimension Group

24.1 Enterprise vs Company-Level Information for an Item

Item definition requires an understanding of enterprise-level versus company-level information, whether you employ AX to manage one or multiple companies. In summary, the concept of enterprise- versus company-level information has been implemented within AX using two different constructs and their identifiers—termed the product number and the item number. The product number provides a unique identifier for enterprise-level information about products, whereas the item number provides the unique identifier for company-level information about items. The enterprise-level information consists of just a few key policies and some descriptive information, whereas all other item information is defined at the company-level. Several warehouse-related aspects of the enterprise- and company-level information are summarized Figure 24.1 and described below.

Figure 24.1 Enterprise vs Company-Level Information for an Item

Type of Item Information	Level of Information	
	Enterprise	Company
Item Identifier	Specify Product Number ⇨	Inherit Item Number
Product Name	Specify Product Name	N/A
Storage Dimension Group for an Item	Specify Global Policy ⇨ or	Inherit as a Global Policy or
Tracking Dimension Group for an Item	Leave Blank ⇨	Specify Company Policy
UM Conversions for an Item	Treated as Global	
NMFC Code for an Item	Specify NMFC Code	N/A
Search Name (aka Alias)	Specify Search Name	Specify Search Name

Legend: ⇨ = Release product to a company when using a multicompany approach to item definition

Item Identifier The product number and item number are created at the same time when using a single company approach to item definition. In a multi-company approach, you define the product number and its product name at the enterprise-level, and then create the item number by releasing the product number to selected companies. The item number inherits the same value as the product number, although it can be optionally overridden.

Product Name You define and maintain the product name at the enterprise level, along with optional language-specific translations. The product name applies to the product number as well as related item numbers.

Storage Dimension Group for an Item The policies with a Storage Dimension Group identify a WMS-enabled item and also define the applicability of information about site, warehouse, and bin location. When assigned to an item at the enterprise level in a multi-company scenario, it represents a global policy that will be inherited and mandated for the item at all applicable companies. Otherwise, a blank value means each company can assign their own Storage Dimension Group to the item, which is the most common approach.

Tracking Dimension Group for an Item The policies within a Tracking Dimension Group identify the need for tracking batch numbers or serial numbers (or both) for an item. Most multi-company scenarios will assign it to an item at the enterprise level so that mandated for all applicable companies. In any case, each company can have a different basis for assignment of batch numbers or serial numbers. Chapter 25 provides further explanation of batch and serial tracking considerations.

UM Conversions for an Item The UM conversions for an item are treated as enterprise-level information, and they can be entered and maintained from the Products or the Released Products form. A subsequent section provides further explanation about unit of measure considerations (Section 24.2).

NMFC Code for an Item The National Motor Freight Code (NMFC Code) represents enterprise-level information for an item. It provides a classification and description for the Bill of Lading in the Advanced WMS approach.

Search Name (aka Alias) The value within the search name field can be defined independently for a product number and its related item numbers. The field is commonly displayed in drop-down information, and it can serve as an alternate identifier. Creative uses of the field include the identifier previously used in a legacy system.

Additional Enterprise-Level Information about an Item Several additional types of enterprise-level information can be defined for an item, such as the product image and related products.

- *Product Image.* The product image may be important for warehouse purposes, such as illustrating what a product should look like.

- *Related Products.* The user-defined types of related products must be defined within AX, so that you can assign one or more related products to a product. This only provides reference information, and does not affect any logic within standard AX functionality.

Case 75: Enterprise-Level Policies for Warehouses in a Multi-company Supply Chain A manufacturing/distribution business modeled their multi-company operation using multiple companies within AX, and goods flowed between different AX sites/warehouses in the different companies. As part of the enterprise-level policies, they standardized their item identification and product names, the UM conversion factors and NMFC code for each item, and enforcement of batch number tracking and the use of storage dimensions. Other policies impacting warehouse management were considered to be the responsibility of each company.

Case 76: Customer Supplied Material An item representing customer supplied material was defined as an item and used as a component in a manufactured product. The item was treated just like any other purchased material, except that its site-specific standard costs were assigned a zero value. This approach supported BOM information about the component, and also provided visibility of requirements, coordination via purchase orders, and tracking of receipts, inventory and material usage.

24.2 Unit of Measure Considerations

Considerations about an item's unit of measure (or UM for short) are important for multiple groups within a manufacturing or distribution operation, including purchasing, sales, engineering, production, cost accounting and warehousing. Each group sometimes has unique requirements for an item's UM, and the advanced approach to warehouse management involves special considerations. The unit of measure codes and the assignment of an item's authorized UM (and weight/volume per UM) represent enterprise-level information, whereas other UM aspects represent company-level information. These considerations are reflected in the following topics within the section.

- Definition of Unit of Measure Codes
- Inventory UM for an Item
- Authorized UM for an Item
- Weight/Volume and Physical Dimensions for an Item's UM
- Default UM for Sales and Purchases of an Item
- UM Considerations for the Advanced WMS Approach

Definition of Unit of Measure Codes The unit of measure codes represent enterprise-level information that is language specific. The codes for two different systems of units – metric units and US standard units – are automatically loaded into AX, along with the unit conversion factors (such as grams per kilogram). Additional units of measure must be defined (such as box and case), and the UM conversion factors are often item specific (such as the number of boxes per case).

Inventory UM for an Item Each item requires one UM for costing and inventory purposes. This is termed the inventory UM or base UM. An item's inventory UM is reflected in its inventory balances, replenishment calculations, product costs, and many of the inventory transactions. It is also reflected in the definition of BOM and routing information for a manufactured item. The inventory UM for an item cannot be changed after you report inventory transactions, so the assignment of an inventory UM requires careful consideration.

Authorized UM for an Item The item's inventory UM represents an authorized UM for the item. Any other UM must be authorized before it can be used for the item. An authorized UM means it has a UM conversion factor that ties it back to the item's base UM. Standard UM conversions apply to UM codes representing metric or US standard units, such as conversions between kilograms, grams, and milligrams. Additional UM codes such as box and case may need to be defined, along with their UM conversion factors for an item. When entering transactions for an item, you can view an item's authorized UM in the drop-down list for the UM field.

Weight/Volume and Physical Dimensions for an Item's UM An item's weight/volume and physical dimensions can be defined via two options. As the preferred option, you define this information for one or more of the item's authorized UM (including the item's inventory UM) using the Physical Dimensions form. The volume is automatically calculated based on the physical dimensions. Alternatively, you can define this information for just the item's inventory UM using the Released Products form. The first option represents a greater level of specificity for the source of information used by the system, and it can automatically populate the fields maintained by the second option. The weight, volume and dimensions have an implied unit of measure (such as pounds, cubic inches and inches), which means that a consistent interpretation should be applied to the values.

Default UM for Sales and Purchases of an Item You can optionally specify an item's default UM for sales orders and purchase orders. These represent companywide defaults for the item with the following impacts.

- *Default UM for Sales Orders.* An item's default sales UM applies to the definition of its order quantity modifiers (for a minimum, multiple, maximum, and standard order quantity) for sales orders. The item's default sales UM and order quantity modifiers are normally reflected in a manually entered sales order line. However, when you specify a sales agreement for the sales order, the item's sales UM will default to the sales agreement.

- *Default UM for Purchase Orders.* An item's default purchase UM applies to the definition of its order quantity modifiers (for a minimum, multiple, maximum, and standard order quantity) for purchase orders. The item's default purchase UM and order quantity modifiers are normally reflected in a manually entered purchase order line. However, when you specify a purchase agreement for the purchase order, the item's purchase UM will default to the purchase agreement.

Many items only require a single unit of measure. In these cases, you can simplify system usage by assigning the same UM to the item's inventory UM and to the item's default UM for purchase orders and sales orders.

UM Considerations for the Advanced WMS Approach The advanced approach employs license plates, where the assignment of a license plate ID often reflects a physical pallet. The term "physical pallet" will be used to simplify the explanation. An item typically has a standard quantity per physical pallet. You must define the UM conversion when the standard quantity is greater than one, such as the number of pieces per pallet. Some items involve additional UM conversion factors, such as pieces per box and boxes per physical pallet.

These UM considerations must be reflected in the Unit Sequence Group assigned to the item, which defines several warehouse policies related to the use of mobile device transactions – especially for receipts. You typically define several Unit Sequence Groups reflecting the common UM considerations related to your products, and then assign the applicable group to each item. For example, the group should include a UM code that represents an item's inventory UM and another UM code representing a physical pallet, such as "pieces and pallets" or "gallons and barrels." The following policies can be identified for the applicable UM codes within the group.

- *Identify the UM Code that Represents a Physical Pallet (or Physical License Plate) for the Item.* This UM code is typically designated as the default value for recording receipts and transfers via mobile device transactions, although you can override this suggested UM when recording the transaction. Based on this UM code and the item's standard quantity per physical pallet, the system will suggest the number of license plates when receiving a large number of pieces, including the use of a single pallet when the number of pieces reflects a less-than-pallet quantity.

- *Identify the UM Code(s) Corresponding to Less Than a Pallet Quantity.* You typically assign the "license plate grouping" policy to these UM codes, which avoids a suggested pallet for every one of the units. As already noted, the system will suggest using a single pallet when the number of pieces reflects a less-than-pallet quantity.

- *Identify the Default UM Code for Reporting Cycle Counts.* This default UM code typically reflects the inventory UM, but it can be another UM Code.

- *Identify the Default UM Code for Reporting Finished Quantities of a Manufactured Item.* Depending on the scenario, a mobile device transaction can be used to report an item's finished quantity in pieces, physical pallets or some other UM code. This default UM code can be overridden when you actually report the finished quantity via a mobile device transaction. The default does not apply when reporting finished quantities via the client.

24.3 Alternative Item Identifiers

Several approaches can support an alternative identifier for an internal item number. These approaches include an alternative item number to support bar coding, external item numbers for a customer or vendor, and an external code that represents the identifier for UPC, GTIN or EAN purposes. The item's search name (aka alias) can also be used as an alternative identifier.

Alternative Item Identifier for Bar Coding Purposes The bar code for an item requires an explicit mapping between the internal item number and the bar code digits, even when the bar code digits are exactly the same. The mapping also defines the bar code size and type (such as EAN13 or EAN128/UCC128). If required, the system supports two different bar code identifiers for the same item: one for scanning and one for printing purposes.

Customer or Vendor Item Numbers (aka External Item Number) An internal item number can be associated with other item identifiers for sales and purchasing purposes. These are termed external item numbers. Each external item number can be mapped to one internal item number and have a separate description.

- *Customer Item Number.* The external item number is specified for a single customer to reflect a customer item number. In some cases, it can be specified for a group of customers (or all customers) to reflect a catalog item number or an industry standard.

- *Vendor Item Number.* The external item number is specified for a single vendor to reflect a vendor item number.

GTIN or UPC Number for an Item (aka External Code) Different types of external codes can be defined to represent an industry standard such as the UPC (Universal Product Code) number, EAN (European Article Number) or GTIN (Global Trade Item Number) identifier. You can then define the mapping between an internal item number and the associated identifier for a selected external code.

Alternative Item Identifier for Electronic Transactions Electronic exchange of documents with customers and vendors is supported by various methods such as Microsoft Biztalk. These documents include sales orders and purchase orders. As part of the setup for each type of document, the item identification can be based on the internal item number, the external item number (described above), or the external code (described above).

Search Name (aka Alias) for an Item The search name is displayed in many of the drop-down lookups for an item, and represents an alternative identifier.

Potential problems in the use of alternative identifiers with mobile device transactions were described in a blog about "Product Scanning Confirmation."

24.4 Item Identifiers Using Item Numbers and Variant Codes

Some scenarios can benefit from item identification based on the combined identifiers of an item number and one or more additional fields, where each additional field is termed a variant code. Standard AX includes four possible variant codes named size, color, style and configuration. A variant code can be easily renamed. If needed, you can also create and name additional variant codes. You define the possible values of a variant code for a given item, such the values for an item's color or size. The use of multiple variant codes for a given item also requires definition of the valid combinations of these values. The use of a variant code (and its possible values) represents enterprise-level information of an item.

Several aspects of item information can only be defined for an item number, so that they apply to all of its variants. These item-related fields include the following.

- Inventory UM, and the Defaults for Sales UM and Purchase UM
- UM Conversions
- Item Group and the Associated G/L Accounts
- Approved Vendor
- Assignment to a Product Category
- Batch Tracking and the Policies for Assigning a Batch Number
- Batch Attributes
- MSDS Document
- Item Characteristics for Production Sequencing Purposes

Other aspects of item information can be defined for each combination of values for applicable variant codes, as illustrated below.

- Vendor Item Number
- Customer Item Number
- UPC Code or Other External Code
- Sales Prices, Based on a Policy Within the Product Dimension Group
- Purchase Prices, Based on a Policy Within the Product Dimension Group

- Standard Costs, Based on an Item-Specific Policy (Termed the "Use Combination Cost Price" Policy) That Enables Variants to Have a Different Cost
- Item Coverage Policies, Such as Planned Order Type, P{referred Vendor and Lead Time
- Attachments
- Routing Information for a Manufactured Item
- BOM Information for a Manufactured Item
- Supplies and Demands Identified by Variant

As part of the prior research, the use of item numbers and variant codes were partially tested for both the basic and advanced approaches to warehouse management. For simplicity's sake, the book's explanations focus on using item numbers for item identification purposes.

24.5 Effective Use of Notes for Warehouse Management Purposes

The document handling capabilities within AX support the use of notes, and notes can be used to guide selected types of warehouse activities. For example, notes can be defined as part of the sales order header information in order to provide picking/shipping instructions. It is often helpful to create user-defined note types that are only applicable to a given type of transaction, such as a note type for picking/shipping instructions. In this way, a note can be entered (and used) for just the applicable note type. The effective use of notes generally requires different note types, and also takes advantage of note inheritance and the AX policies about the use of notes.

Inheritance of Notes Notes have a special significance for customers and vendors because they can be inherited by a sales order and purchase order respectively. And a note on a sales order header can be inherited by its related shipment when using the advanced approach to warehouse management. In addition, item-related notes can be inherited by a line item on these orders. These levels of inheritance are illustrated in the top half of Figure 24.2.

Figure 24.2 Effective Use of Notes

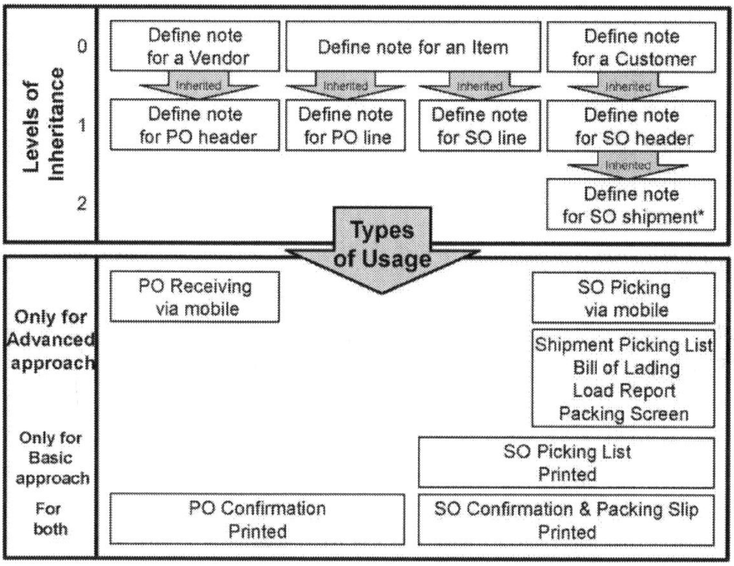

AX Policies About Using Notes The AX policies about using notes differ slightly between the basic and advanced approaches to warehouse management. The different types of usage are identified in the bottom half of Figure 24.2 and explained below.

- *Using Notes in the Basic Approach.* The applicable note type can be printed on sales order picking lists to provide picking/shipping instructions. Applicable note types can also be printed on other sales-related documents (such as confirmations, packing slips and invoices) as well as purchase-related documents (such as confirmations and invoices). The applicable note type for each type of document is defined by several companywide policies (on several parameter forms).

- *Using Notes in the Advanced Approach.* The applicable note type can be displayed on the mobile device transactions in order to provide (1) receiving instructions when reporting purchase order arrivals and (2) picking/shipping instructions when reporting picking work for sales order shipments. As shown in Figure 24.2, the notes about a sales order shipment can be inherited from its related sales order header, or entered manually. The applicable note type for mobile device transactions is defined by a companywide policy (on the Warehouse Management Parameters form).

The concept of an applicable note type also applies to several other printed documents and screens, including a bill of lading, a load report, a shipment picking list and the packing screen. The applicable note type for each of these is defined by companywide policies (on the Warehouse Management Parameters form).

A note can be designated as either external or internal, but this may or may not be useful for the different types of usage.

Notes can be defined for a transfer order and its lines, but they are not included in standard formats for printed documents (such as picking lists, shipment documents and receipt documents) or mobile device transactions. In addition, note inheritance does not apply to the notes for a warehouse and item. Notes can also be defined for a production order and its components, but they are not included in standard formats for printed documents (such as picking list journals) or mobile device transactions related to raw material picking or finished quantities.

In some cases, the effective use of notes will require customized formats for printed documents or for the displayed information on mobile device transactions.

24.6 Negative Inventory Policies

The ability to handle negative inventory has two perspectives. One perspective involves the physical on-hand inventory for an item—termed the "negative physical inventory" policy. The other perspective involves financial considerations for an actual cost item—termed the "negative financial inventory" policy. These two policies are embedded in the Item Model Group assigned to an item.

With most approaches to actual costing for an item, a general guideline would be to prevent negative physical inventory, since this condition creates problems in calculation of actual costs. Negative financial inventory should be allowed, since this allows inventory usage after receipt but prior to financial updates such as posting a vendor's invoice for purchased material. This consideration does not apply to a standard cost item or to an item with moving average costs.

An additional policy only applies to the Advanced WMS approach, where you can further refine the ability to allow or prevent negative inventory by inventory location. The policy is embedded in the Location Profile assigned to the location. However, locations that use license plate tracking cannot have this negative inventory policy.

Other policies can also affect the use of negative inventory. For example, a companywide policy (defined on the Production Control Parameters form) determines whether the posting of the picking list journal can result in negative inventory.

24.7 Information About Purchased Items

A purchased item is typically indicated by its primary source of supply. This is identified by a default order type for planned purchase orders, which can be defined as part of the item's default order policies or as part of the item's coverage planning policies for a specific site/warehouse. However, purchase orders can be created for any material item. The information about a purchased item typically involves several activities performed by different roles, such as the purchasing agent, cost accountant and quality manager. Various aspects of defining a purchased item are summarized below, along with references to applicable chapters of the book.

- Define and enforce the approved vendors for an item
- Define purchase prices and discounts for an item using trade agreements or blanket purchase orders
- Define planning data for a purchased item
- Assign a cost group to a purchased item
- Define standard costs for a purchased item
- Define serial or batch tracking policies for a purchased item (Chapter 25)
- Define testing requirements for a purchased item (Chapter 26)

24.8 Information about Manufactured Items

A manufactured item is typically indicated by its primary source of supply. This is identified by a default order type for planned production orders, which can be defined as part of the item's default order policies or as part of the item's coverage planning policies for a specific site/warehouse. However, production orders can be created for any material item with an approved BOM for the site. The information about a manufactured item involves several activities performed by different roles, such as the product designer, process engineer, production planner, cost accountant and quality manager. Various aspects of defining a manufactured item are summarized below, along with references to applicable chapters within this book.

- Define the bill of material (or formula) for a manufactured item
- Define the routing for a manufactured item
- Define the BOM and routing for a subcontract manufactured item
- Calculate standard costs for a manufactured item
- Calculate planned costs for a manufactured item
- Define planning data for a manufactured item
- Define the product configuration model for a configured item
- Define serial or batch tracking policies for a manufactured item (Chapter 25)
- Define testing requirements for a manufactured item (Chapter 26)

A detailed explanation about most aspects of manufacturing falls outside the book's scope.[1] For example, these topics include the definition of resources and resource groups, master operations, master routings and route versions for internal production purposes and for subcontracted production purposes.

A few aspects of manufacturing are covered within the book because of their relevance to warehouse management. One aspect involves the use of a production unit for indicating the warehouse source of components for a resource group (Section 9.10). Another aspect involves the Production Input Location for a resource or resource group and the Production Output Location for a resource group.

24.9 Inventory Valuation and Financial Reporting

Several item-related policies impact inventory valuation and financial reporting for items. These policies include the inventory valuation method, the item group, and the financial dimension assigned to an item, as described below.

Inventory Valuation Method Item costs provide the basis for valuing inventory transactions. An item's costs can be based on a standard costing or actual costing method (such as FIFO, LIFO, and weighted average cost), as defined by the costing method embedded in the Item Model Group assigned to the item.

[1] Further explanation of these topics has been provided in previous books about Discrete Manufacturing (pages 63-150) and Food Products Manufacturing (pages 53-96 and 123-152).

G/L Accounts and the Item Group The Item Group defines the G/L account numbers impacted by the item's inventory transactions. For example, some of the key G/L accounts include inventory, revenue, cost of goods sold (COGS), and purchase price variances. The item groups and their G/L account numbers do not need to reflect product lines when using a financial dimension for items. For example, the value for the item's financial dimension supports revenue, COGS and inventory by product line.

The item groups assigned to purchased items typically have a parallel with the cost groups assigned to these same items. Cost groups serve a slightly different purpose, since they provide cost group segmentation in the calculated costs of manufactured items. The cost groups also provide an alternative approach for assigning G/L account numbers related to standard cost variances.

The item group can serve several other purposes in addition to the assignment of G/L account numbers, such as similar salable items or similar manufactured items. These other purposes often result in multiple item groups with the same G/L account numbers.

Financial Dimension Assigned to Items The combination of a financial dimension value and G/L account number provide the basis for financial reporting. With a product line dimension, for example, you define the possible values for different product lines. The applicable value for a product line can then be assigned to an item, which will be inherited by any item-related transaction. On a sales line, for example, the financial dimensions could reflect the customer type and product line, where the product line value gets inherited from the item and the customer type gets inherited from the customer.

The assignment of a financial dimension for a business unit has special significance when assigned to an item, since it supports financial reporting by business unit.

Financial dimensions can also be assigned to other entities such as customers, vendors, and sites to support multidimensional reporting. For example, the financial dimension assigned to sites (with a different value for each site) supports financial reporting site by site.

24.10 Significance of the Storage Dimension Group

A user-defined Storage Dimension Group has several policies which can be broadly segmented into two groups. One group of policies is related to the basic versus advanced approach to warehouse management. The second group determines the use of site, warehouse and bin locations.

Policies Related to Basic versus Advanced Warehouse Management
The policy "use warehouse management processes" indicates a WMS-enabled item, and automatically results in use of the Inventory Status and License Plates. These two constructs are not available for any option which does not include the "use warehouse management process" policy.

In terms of the strategic options (described in Section 2.1), a single value can be defined for Inventory Status so that it has no special capabilities, and it can be used in the basic or advanced approaches. The license plate for an item only applies for a WMS-enabled warehouse; it is ignored for a non-WMS warehouse.

Policies Related to the Use of Site, Warehouse and Bin Location
Most scenarios will track an item's inventory by site, warehouse and bin location, while other scenarios simply require site and warehouse. The related policies can reflect the following considerations.

- Policies about Warehouse Specific Setup. One policy indicates whether the warehouse is a mandatory entry on inventory transactions, thereby avoiding use of the "fallback warehouse" concept when it is not entered. The second policy (termed Primary Stocking) indicates whether you want to lock the specified warehouse when reserving the item's inventory, otherwise the system allows overrides for reserving from a different warehouse.

- Indicate the need for physical tracking of inventory by site and warehouse (and bin location).

- Indicate the need for financial tracking of the item's inventory by site and warehouse, or simply by site.

- Indicate whether the item's coverage planning policies apply to the site or the site/warehouse.

24.11 Executive Summary

This chapter focused on item definition from a warehouse management perspective. It covered common topics for both the basic and advanced approaches, and highlighted some differences when applicable. Examples of common topics included unit of measure considerations, alternative identifiers, and the effective use of notes. Some common topics were summarized, such as the definition of purchased and manufactured items, and inventory valuation and financial reporting. Other aspects of item definition related to batch/serial tracking and testing requirements are covered in the next two chapters.

Issues about item definition were covered by several case studies, including enterprise-level policies for warehouses in a multi-company supply chain (Case 75) and customer supplied material (Case 76). Relevant case studies in other chapters include the use of item characteristics for putaway of items requiring cold storage (Case 59) and putaway of items with allergens (Case 60).

Chapter 25

Batch Number and Serial Number Tracking

Some warehouse management scenarios require tracking of serial numbers or batch numbers for a material item, or both. The term batch number is used because Dynamics AX employs the term *lot number* as a system-assigned internal identifier for inventory transactions. A serial number or batch number is typically assigned upon receipt, such as the receipt of a purchase order or the finished quantity of a production order. Subsequent transactions identifying these numbers automatically create tracking history. Several additional capabilities apply to batch tracking for an item, including vendor batch information, shelf life information, batch attributes and/or batch disposition codes to indicate restricted usage. The following sections of the chapter reflect these topics.

1. Serial Number Tracking
2. Deferred Assignment of Serial Numbers
3. Basics of Batch Number Tracking
4. Vendor Batch Information
5. Products with Shelf Life
6. Merging Batches
7. Batch Attributes
8. Batch Disposition Codes and Restricted Usage
9. Additional Case Studies

Many of these topics also involve quality management considerations such as product testing and quality orders. For example, the test results associated with a quality order can apply to a serial number or batch number. The next chapter provides further explanation of quality management.

25.1 Serial Number Tracking

Serial number tracking traditionally refers to a unique serial number for each unit of inventory. AX also supports a single serial number for multiple units of an item (conceptually similar to lot tracking), but this section focuses on serial numbers for individual units. In addition, AX supports inventory tracking of a serialized item or deferred assignment until the item is sold. This section explains the inventory tracking option, and the next section explains the deferred assignment option.

The explanation starts with the identification of a serialized item, the assignment of serial numbers to received material, and the picking and moving of serialized items. Several of these topics involve dual explanations because of differences in the two approaches to warehouse management.

Identify a Serialized Item A serialized item is identified by several policies embedded in the Tracking Dimension Group assigned to the item. One policy indicates that each serial number identifies an individual unit, and additional policies determine whether the serial number assignment must be tracked throughout inventory (the *Active* policy), or deferred until the product is actually sold (the *Active in Sales Process* policy). The deferred assignment approach is further explained in the next section, so that further explanation focuses on tracking inventory of a serialized item. The Tracking Dimension Group has several other policies not typically used for a serialized item, such as sales pricing or coverage planning for specific serial numbers.

The Advanced WMS approach involves an additional consideration, since a serialized item must be assigned an appropriate Reservation Hierarchy that includes the serial number. It is typically placed below the location because it is not relevant for reservation logic.

Typical Inventory Transactions Requiring Assignment of a Serial Number The typical transactions include purchase order receipts, production order receipts, RMA receipts and inventory adjustments when tracking inventory by serial number. The transactions differ slightly between the basic and advanced approaches to warehouse management.

- *Basic Approach:* A purchased item's serial numbers are typically assigned when reporting purchase order arrival using the Arrival Journal form, although they can also be reported (via a simple inventory transaction) by registering the serial numbers when posting the product receipt for a purchase order. A manufactured item's serial numbers are typically assigned when reporting a production order receipt using the Report as Finished form or its alternatives (described in Section 10.7).

- *Advanced Approach:* A purchased item's serial numbers are typically assigned when reporting purchase order arrival via a mobile device transaction, although they can also be reported via a simple inventory transaction (as described above). A manufactured item's serial numbers are typically assigned when reporting the finished quantity via a mobile device transaction, or by using the Report as Finished form or its alternatives.

Several different approaches can be used for assigning a serial number to each unit of an item's inventory, as described in the following points.

Manual Assignment of a Serial Number You can manually assign a serial number to inventory transactions with a quantity of one, so that receipts for a larger quantity must first be split into quantities of one. Manual assignment allows you to enter the existing serial number on received material.

Automatic Assignment Using the item's Serial Number Mask A mask can help enforce internal guidelines about assignment of serial numbers to an item, where you place your internal serial number on received material. It represents one policy within the serial number group assigned to the item. The mask may simply reflect a prefix and counter, or include the date, order number, and/or the system-assigned lot id. A second policy determines when to assign the serial number; it is typically assigned when recording arrivals that update inventory balances.

Automatic Assignment using an Ad Hoc Serial Number Mask The existing serial numbers for received material often reflect a pattern. For example, the pattern might consist of the same 10 characters and three unique digits in a numerical sequence, where the three unique digits differentiate the serial numbers. This pattern and automatic numbering for a range of three digit numbers can be defined as part of the ad hoc serial number mask. However, the ability to use an ad hoc mask differs between the basic and advanced approaches to warehouse management.

- *Basic Approach*: The ad hoc mask and its associated "Create Serial Numbers" dialogue can only be accessed when reporting purchase order arrivals using the Arrival Journal form or when reporting production order receipts using the Report as Finished form or its alternatives. When needed, the serial numbers for the finished item can be assigned beforehand in order to track testing results by serial number during the production process.

- *Advanced Approach*: The assignment of serial numbers using an ad hoc mask is not supported by the mobile device transactions for purchase order arrival, RMA arrival or production order receipt. However, the ad hoc mask can be used as part of a client transaction such as the Report as Finished form or its alternatives.

Picking and Moving Serialized Items Serialized items can be picked for sales orders, transfer orders, production orders and returns to vendor, and also moved to different locations. The reporting differs between the basic and advanced approaches for warehouse management.

- *Basic Approach:* The serial number(s) can be identified when reporting actual picking against a sales order picking list, a transfer order picking list, or a production order picking list. When reporting moves, each serial number requires a separate move transaction.

- *Advanced Approach*: The mobile device transactions for picking a serialized item can differ based on the use of license plates and the quantities involved. For example, when a pallet contains multiple serial numbers (say 100 pieces), and the required quantity represent one pallet, you simply report picking of the one license plate. Alternatively, when the required quantity represents a subset of the serial numbers on a pallet (say 3 pieces), you must identify each serial number when reporting the picking work via the mobile device.

  A special case applies to raw material picking work for a production order, since an entire pallet or an exact number can be picked to meet the required quantity. It depends on whether the inventory is being picked from a license plate controlled location or not.

  When reporting moves, the mobile device transaction for a move can be reported for the license plate ID containing multiple serial numbers (at a license plate controlled location), or for individual serial numbers.

Information About a Serial Number Information about each serial number for an item consists of descriptive text and a manufacturing date. This information can be viewed and maintained on the Serial Numbers form.

Historical Information About Serial Number Tracking The tracking history is automatically maintained based on receipt and issue transactions. This historical information is typically viewed and analyzed using the Item Trace form. It can also be viewed using the Serial Number form, but the simplified format reflects prior AX versions and does not support the analysis capabilities of the Item Trace form. You can view historical information about a selected item or batch number, such as forward or backward tracking information using a multilevel indented format. Each entry in the indented format indicates a receipt or issue. An entry can also reflect a transfer.

Serial Tracking on Intercompany Orders When using intercompany orders in a multi-company operation, the serial numbers assigned to the shipped material (on the intercompany sales order) can automatically apply to the received material (on the intercompany purchase order).

Printing Serial Numbers on Documents The serial numbers can be printed on sales and purchase documents based on the form setup policies. For example, the serial numbers can be printed on the sales order packing slip and invoice.

Case 77: RMAs for Serialized Items A manufacturing company required RMA processing on customer returns of their serialized electronic items. Each serialized number had a 12 month warranty period (from date of sale) for free replacement. The customer identified an item's serial number when requesting an RMA, which was used to verify the applicability of its warranty period. The customer shipped the returned item after receiving an electronic copy of the printed RMA. Items were shipped to a repair facility, which verified the serial number and sent a free replacement (when it was within warranty) or charged for the replacement (when it was not within warranty). The repair facility assigned a disposition to each returned item during an inspection process, which determined whether the item was usable, scrapped, or repairable. A scrapped item could also be stripped down for reusing the high value components.

25.2 Deferred Assignment of Serial Numbers

The concept of deferred assignment of serial numbers applies to many different scenarios, where it avoids detailed tracking of serialized inventory but still supports requirements about serial number information. A simple scenario involves deferred assignment at the time of shipment of an end-item. This represents the current capabilities within AX described in this section. A more complex scenario in a manufacturing company involves deferred assignment for a serialized end-item and its serialized components, as illustrated in Case 78.

A serialized item is identified by several policies embedded in the Tracking Dimension Group assigned to the item. In particular, the policies provide an option about whether the serial number assignment must be tracked throughout inventory (the *Active* policy), or deferred until the end-item is actually sold (the *Active in Sales Process* policy). This section explains the deferred assignment option, and the previous section explained the inventory tracking option.

With deferred assignment, you register the end-item's serial number(s) when posting the sales order packing slip or invoice by accessing the Serial Numbers form for the line item. You can then scan the serial numbers or manually enter a value. You can also indicate an unreadable serial number (resulting in a null value) and change the assignment of a serial number.

The serial numbers can be printed on packing slips or invoices (just like the inventory tracking option), but the lack of inventory information means that serial number tracking is limited to the related sales order. This also means that a previously shipped serial number cannot be identified on a customer return.

Mobile device transactions for sales order picking cannot be used for reporting deferred assignment (when using the Advanced WMS approach). Deferred assignment must be reported via a client transaction for posting the sales order packing slip.

Case 78: Deferred Assignment for a Serialized End-Item and its Serialized Components A manufacturing company produced printed circuit boards that were serialized, and then placed in a cabinet that represented a serialized end-item. The boards were continually changed out during the testing process for the end-item. When the fully-tested end-item was completed, the quality manager wanted to record the serial numbers of the actual boards within a serialized cabinet. This information was critical for warranty and quality tracking purposes. As part of a proposed customization, a new option for deferred assignment would be added to the Storage Dimension Group policies, and a new screen and related database would be developed. The new screen would display a multi-level indented BOM format for the end-item and only those components with the deferred assignment option, so that the actual serial numbers could be recorded after production was completed. This serial number information would be retained in a related database. It could also be used to create "objects" for the serialized items (after the product was shipped) in order to support service and warranty purposes.

25.3 Basics of Batch Number Tracking

Batch number tracking is a critical requirement in many companies, especially those involved in food products or certain types of process manufacturing. The use of batch tracking starts with the identification of a batch-controlled item and several related policies. Different approaches can be used to assign an internal batch number to an item's inventory, and to report picking and moves of the inventory. Several of these topics involve differences in the two approaches to warehouse management.

This section focuses on the basics of batch number tracking and subsequent sections cover the following extensions.

- Vendor batch information (Section 25.4)
- Products with shelf life (Section 25.5)
- Merging batches (Section 25.6)
- Batch attributes (Section 25.7)
- Batch disposition codes and restricted usage (Section 25.8)

Identify a Batch-Controlled Item A batch-controlled item is identified by a the Tracking Dimension Group assigned to the item, which must include the batch number. The batch number dimension has several policies that enforce batch tracking for issues and receipts, and optionally support unique requirements such as batch-specific costing and pricing.

A second set of policies (termed the Batch Number Group) determines how the item's batch numbers are created and when they are assigned to inventory transactions for received material. A batch number can be created manually or automatically, and it is typically assigned upon arrival which updates inventory balances.

Additional policies must be defined for a batch-controlled item when it requires shelf-life considerations or batch attributes, as described in subsequent sections (Sections 25.5 and 25.7)

The Advanced WMS approach involves an additional consideration, since a batch-controlled item must be assigned an appropriate Reservation Hierarchy that includes the batch number. It should be placed above the location when batch numbers are critical for reservations, such as shelf life items or items with attributes used in batch searching logic. It should be placed below the location when the batch number is not relevant for reservation logic.

Typical Inventory Transactions Requiring Assignment of a Batch Number The typical transactions include purchase order receipts, production order receipts, RMA receipts and inventory adjustments. The transactions differ slightly between the basic and advanced approaches to warehouse management.

- *Basic approach:* A purchased item's batch numbers are typically assigned when reporting purchase order arrival using the Arrival Journal form, although they can also be reported (via a simple inventory transaction) by registering the batch numbers when posting the product receipt for a purchase order. A manufactured item's batch numbers are typically assigned when reporting a production order receipt using the Report as Finished form or its alternatives (described in Section 10.7).

- *Advanced approach:* A purchased item's batch numbers are typically assigned when reporting purchase order arrival via a mobile device transaction, although they can also be reported via a simple inventory transaction (as described above). A manufactured item's batch numbers are typically assigned when reporting the finished quantity via a mobile device transaction. An additional policy for the mobile device transaction (labeled "override batch number") allows manual assignment. A manufactured item's batch number can also be assigned by a client transaction using the Report as Finished form or its alternatives.

Several different approaches can be used for assigning an internal batch number as described in the following points. Some scenarios will use manual assignment while others will use automatic assignment, and there are several variations of automatic assignment.

Manually Assign an Internal Batch Number When Reporting Receipt Manual assignment is typically used when the internal batch number can be easily scanned or involves significance that cannot be modeled as a batch number mask.

Automatically Assign an Internal Batch Number When Reporting Receipt Automatic assignment can be based on a batch number mask, such as a prefix and counter. Alternatively, the mask could reflect the date, order number, and/or system-assigned lot id. Other approaches to a batch number mask may need to be customized to meet requirements for a meaningful batch number.

Automatically Assign Different Batch Numbers When Reporting Multiple Receipts for an Order Some scenarios require a unique internal batch number for each receipt of the same order. One example involves partial receipts of the same purchase order line, where the same vendor batch number may apply but the material needs to be tracked by different internal batch numbers. Another example involves multiple receipts of the same production order where each receipt represents a different physical batch (Case 79). A batch numbering policy (within the Batch Number Group) determines whether to assign the same batch number or a different batch number to each partial receipt.[1]

Automatically Assign Different Batch Numbers Based on Fixed Increments Some scenarios require a unique batch number for fixed increments of a receipt quantity, such as assigning unique batch numbers for every 100 units received when receiving a quantity of 1000. This requirement may reflect the item's packaging characteristics, production characteristics or a quality management consideration. The "per quantity" increment is one of the policies within the Batch Number Group.

Pre-Assign a Batch Number to a Production Order or a Purchase Order Line Some scenarios involve a pre-assigned batch number. You can manually assign a batch number to a purchase order line or a batch production order, and the batch number will apply to all receipt transactions.

Picking and Moving Batch-Controlled Items Batch-controlled items can be picked for sales orders, transfer orders, production orders and returns to vendor, and also moved to different locations. The reporting differs between the basic and advanced approaches for warehouse management.

- *Basic Approach:* The batch number(s) can be identified when reporting actual picking against a sales order picking list, a transfer order picking list, or a production order picking list.

- *Advanced Approach*: The mobile device transactions for picking a batch-controlled item can differ based on the use of license plates and the quantities involved. For example, you can report picking of one license plate when it is stocked in a license plate controlled location.

  A special case applies to raw material picking work for a production order, since an entire pallet or an exact number can be picked to meet the required quantity. It depends on whether the inventory is being picked from a license plate controlled location or not.

---

[1] The same batch number will be assigned to partial receipts when the numbering policy (within the Batch Number Group) is simply "assignment on inventory transaction." Different batch numbers will be assigned by specifying the additional policy "assignment upon physical update."

When reporting moves, the mobile device transaction can be reported for a license plate ID containing multiple batches (when stocked at a license plate controlled location).

Viewing the Internal Batch Numbers The key form for batch information—termed the Batch Details form or Batch form for short—provides a list of all internal batch numbers and the related items. It also displays the batch-related information such as shelf life dates and batch attributes.

Changing Batch Numbers of an Item's Inventory You can change the batch number for an inventory quantity by using the Transfer Journal, much like you would change or combine inventory in a bin location.

Combining or Merging Batch Numbers of an Item's Inventory You can also transfer the inventory quantity from one batch number to another when combining batches. Similarly, you can transfer an inventory quantity to a newly created batch number and optionally copy the batch attributes. Combining batches is often termed a batch merge, and a subsequent section provides further explanation about merging batches (Section 25.6).

Batch Tracking on Intercompany Orders When using intercompany orders in a multi-company operation, the batch numbers assigned to the shipped material (on the intercompany sales order) can automatically apply to the received material (on the intercompany purchase order).

Printing Batch Numbers on Documents The batch numbers can be printed on sales and purchase documents based on the form setup policies. For example, the batch numbers can be printed on the sales order packing slip and invoice.

Historical Information About Batch Number Tracking The batch tracking history is automatically maintained based on receipt and issue transactions. This historical information is typically viewed and analyzed using the Item Trace form. It can also be viewed using the Batch form, but the simplified format reflects prior AX versions and does not support the analysis capabilities of the Item Trace form.

You can view historical information about a specified item or batch number, and the on-line inquiry avoids the need for extensive printed reports. In a manufacturing environment, you can view forward or backward trace information using a multilevel indented format that reflects the product structure. Each entry in the indented format indicates a receipt or issue. The batch number for a sales order shipment can be traced backward through the production orders to purchase order receipts. A receipt can also be traced forward.

Batch Tracking and Serial Tracking for an Item Some scenarios require batch and serial tracking for an item. The two tracking numbers represent separate constructs, and a hierarchical relationship does not exist between a batch number and serial numbers for an item.

25.4 Vendor Batch Information

The vendor batch information normally applies to a purchased item, but it can also be used for other items. The information includes a vendor batch number, a field for the vendor-specified manufacturing date, and two fields for capturing country of origin information. It includes additional information about the vendor-specified expiration date for a shelf-life item, and the date can optionally be inherited by the internal batch number. The vendor batch information can be assigned to an item's internal batch number using the Batch Details form, and accessing the Reset Vendor Batch Details form.

Some scenarios assign the vendor batch information when reporting purchase order arrival. It typically involves reporting by the receiving clerk rather than a quality control clerk. This approach requires an additional policy labeled "Vendor Batch Purchase Registration" which is embedded in the Item Model Group assigned to the item.

25.5 Products with Shelf Life

Shelf life information is critical for food products and certain other types of products. It doesn't really apply to most other scenarios, and those readers can skip this section. This section builds on the previous section's explanation about the basics of batch number tracking because shelf life information only applies to batch-controlled items. The previous section explained how to identify a batch-controlled item, the typical inventory transactions requiring assignment of a batch number, picking and moving batch numbers, and the historical information about batch number tracking.

Shelf life information only applies to batch-controlled items with First-Expired-First-Out (FEFO) reservation logic, and these items are commonly called "shelf life items" for short. The FEFO reservation logic helps ensure that inventory will be used prior to expiration and supports other requirements about shelf life. This section includes the following topics.

- Identify a Shelf Life Item
- Different Types of Shelf Life Dates
- Initial Assignment of Shelf Life Dates
- Inheritance of Shelf Life Dates on Batch Orders
- Resetting the Assignment of Shelf Life Dates
- Information About a Batch Number
- Inquiries/Reports About Shelf Life Dates
- Creating a Cycle Count Report for Expired Batches
- Generating Quality Orders for Batches Based on Shelf Life Dates
- Reservation Logic Concerning Shelf Life Dates
- Sales Order Reservation Logic and Customer Requirements About Shelf Life Days
- Shelf Life Dates in Master Scheduling Logic

Identify a Shelf Life Item A shelf life item must be batch-controlled with a FEFO reservation policy. This reservation policy is embedded in the Item Model Group assigned to the item and a related policy indicates whether FEFO logic applies to the expiration date or best-before date. Depending on this date basis, you must define additional setup information about the default value (expressed in days) for the item's "shelf life period" or "best before period." Further explanation focuses on the use of expiration dates and the default value for the item's shelf life period. This default value is used to calculate an expiration date based on the manufactured date for a batch number, or for a planned receipt of the item.

Different Types of Shelf Life Dates For a given batch number, you can assign a manufacturing date (termed the batch date) and three additional dates concerning its expiration date, best before date, and shelf advice date.[2] The various dates are collectively termed shelf life dates. The manufacturing date is

---

[2] The best before date means that the material is good through midnight of the day before. The expiry date means that the material is good through midnight of the specified expiration date.

typically assigned at the time of receipt, and the other dates are initially calculated based on item-specific default values (expressed as a number of calendar days).[3] These dates for a given batch number can be subsequently reset.

The shelf life information for a batch number of purchased material includes two additional dates about the vendor-specified manufacturing and expiration dates. These two dates can be assigned at the time of purchase order arrival, and you typically indicate that the vendor-specified dates should act as the value for the internal batch number. These two dates can also be assigned to a purchase order line item prior to receipt. The dates for a vendor batch can be subsequently reset just like the other shelf life dates.

Initial Assignment of Shelf Life Dates The shelf life dates (and manufacturing date) are typically assigned to a batch number at the time of receipt, such as a purchase order receipt or the finished quantity of a production order. The initial assignment reflects the manufacturing date plus the item-specific default values (expressed in calendar days) for the three shelf life dates. With a purchased item, the initial assignment typically reflects the values for the vendor-specified manufacturing and expiration dates, as noted above.

Inheritance of Shelf Life Dates on Batch Orders When using the inheritance capabilities for a formula line, reporting the finished quantity for a batch order can automatically update its expiration date based on the earliest expiration date for applicable ingredients that have been picked. .

Resetting the Assignment of Shelf Life Dates You can optionally override the dates for a selected batch by accessing the Reset Shelf Life Dates form. It can be accessed from several starting points, including (1) a line on the Purchase Order form, (2) the Batch Order or Production Order form, (3) the Transfer Order form, and (4) the Batch Details form. A basic rule is that the expiration date must be greater than today's date. After changing the expiration date, an infolog provides a prompt to automatically update the best before and shelf advice dates.

A mass-update approach can also be used to override the dates. Three different periodic tasks correspond to changing (1) the expiration date, (2) the best before date, and (3) the shelf advice date to a specified date based on selection criteria such as the batch number, item number, and/or batch date.

---

[3] A basic rule is that the default days for the expiration date must be greater than the defaults for shelf advice and best before.

A manually created batch number may be created without a manufacturing date. When receiving this batch number, an infolog message will prompt the user to update the empty manufacturing date with the current date.

Inquiries/Reports About Shelf Life Dates Three different inquiries display a list of batch numbers based on a comparison between a user-specified date and (1) the expiration date, (2) the best before date, and (3) the shelf advice date that occurs on or before the specified date. For example, the expiration inquiry can display all batch numbers that expire on or before the user-specified date. Each inquiry form displays the current inventory for a batch, and provides access to the Reset Shelf Life Dates form in order to change information. In a typical scenario with an expired batch, you might change the batch disposition code, or scrap the inventory to prevent further usage.

Three different reports (corresponding to the three different dates) can also be generated, where the selection criteria define the basis for the report contents (such as a date criteria of "<01/01/20XX"). The reports contain the same information as the inquiries. One other report displays a list of batches with expiration dates that have already been exceeded.

Creating a Cycle Count Report for Expired Batches You can optionally access the Create Counting Journal of Expired Batches form as part of creating the lines for a cycle count journal. Using this form, you specify selection criteria about the date range for batch expiration dates so that the batches will be included as line items in the cycle count journal.

Generating Quality Orders for Batch Numbers Based on Shelf Life Dates You can manually create a quality order for a batch number in order to perform additional tests. Alternatively, you can use a periodic task as a mass-update approach to generating quality orders for multiple batch numbers. As part of the periodic task, you specify selection criteria such as the batch number, item number, and batch date.

Sales Order Reservation Logic and Customer Requirements About Shelf Life Days The reservation logic for a sales order line considers the delivery date at the customer site, so that batch numbers expiring on or before that date will not be reserved. However, a customer may have requirements about remaining shelf life that need to be enforced on sales orders to the customer. For example, the customer may not accept a batch number with less than 30 days remaining until its expiration date. A customer's specified time horizon can be defined on the Sellable Days by Customer form (accessed from the Customer form). The horizon can be specified for individual item numbers, a group of items (based on the item group) or all items. Batch numbers will only be reserved when they satisfy the customer requirements about sellable days after the delivery date.

If you change a sales order's scheduled delivery date so that it is beyond the expiration date of a reserved batch number, you will receive a prompt to remove the reservation, keep the reservation and allow you to ship the expired batch, or return the date to its previous value.

Shelf Life Dates in Master Scheduling Logic Shelf life dates are considered in master scheduling logic when you specify the shelf life policy for the set of master plan data The calculations assume that inventory will no longer be available after its expiration date. Master scheduling logic considers the expiration dates of existing inventory and of scheduled receipts in suggesting planned orders to satisfy demands. The expiration dates are also considered in capable-to-promise logic for a sales order line, since this generates planned orders that mirror the master scheduling logic. You can view the expired quantity and date of existing inventory and scheduled receipts in the inquiries about net requirements.

25.6 Merging Batches

Some scenarios involve the merging of two or more existing batches of a batch-controlled item, typically with assignment of a new batch number. A typical example involves a tank that has been filled with multiple batches of an item. AX supports two different approaches to merging batches, which can be labeled batch merge and transfers to a different batch.

Batch Merge You use the Batch Merge form to select the item and its existing "source" batches, specify information about the new "merged" batch, and then generate and post the related transactions. These transactions are termed a Batch Merge Journal, and they represent the same functionality as a BOM Journal. That is, the journal contains one line for receiving the new "merged" batch and an additional line for issuing each "source" batch. This approach provides complete batch tracking information.

The complete list of all Batch Merge transactions is displayed on the All Batch Merges form, and you select one to view it on the Batch Merge form. The Batch Merge form provides an easy-to-use approach for merging multiple existing batches into a new batch, and inheriting a batch expiration date based on the source batches. In comparison to the second approach, it forces you to merge the entire quantity of a source batch (rather than a partial quantity), and it does not support inheritance of batch attributes from a selected source batch.

Transfers to a Different Batch You can use Transfer Journal to transfer one or more existing batches to a different batch number, which typically reflects a new batch number for the item. This approach provides complete batch tracking information.

In comparison to the Batch Merge approach, you can transfer a partial quantity of an existing batch (rather than the entire quantity). In addition, you can transfer to a batch number with existing inventory, and optionally identify whether the batch attributes of an existing batch should be copied to the new batch number. The Transfer Journal can also be used to change the batch number for an existing batch, as described in a previous section within this chapter (Section 20.3).

Case 79: Merging Physical Batches into a New Batch

A food products manufacturer used a single batch order to represent the production of multiple physical batches, where the finished quantity of each physical batch (produced in a kettle) was piped into a single tank. The physical batches within the tank were then merged into a new batch, thereby providing correct batch tracking and reporting of test results. The business process is illustrated in Figure 25.1 and described below.

Figure 25.1 Merging Physical Batches into a New Batch

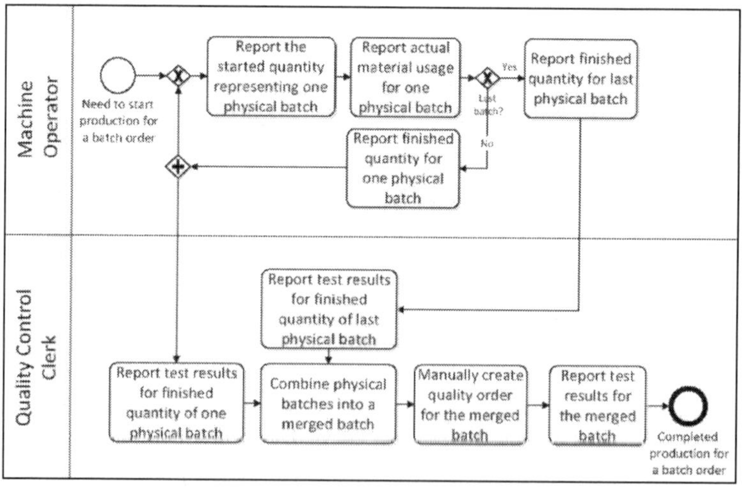

The machine operator (for a given kettle) reported a started quantity for the batch order that represented one physical batch. This step automatically generated a picking list journal for the started quantity, which the machine operator used to report actual material usage. Material had already been placed by the group of kettles based on raw material picking work to a production input location. When the kettle operation was completed, the machine operator reported the finished quantity that was piped into a single tank (based on machine readings). This step automatically generated a quality order, which the quality control clerk used to report test results.

When the last physical batch was completed, the machine operator reported the finished quantity—which generated a quality order and updated order status to *Reported as Finished.* The quality control clerk reported the test results for the last batch, and then performed a batch merge for all physical batches that had been placed in the tank. The quality control clerk also created a new quality order to report test results for the merged batch. The tank and pipes were typically cleaned before being used for a different product.

25.7 Batch Attributes

One or more batch attributes can be assigned to a batch-controlled item, and actual values recorded against the batch numbers for the item. The use of batch attributes requires some setup information, including the definition of batch attributes and assignment of batch attributes to the item. An additional type of batch attribute can identify potency, and it requires additional setup information and considerations about how it will be used. For example, potency can be considered in potency-based formulas and batch balancing for production orders. Further explanation falls outside the book's scope.

Recording Actual Values for Batch Attributes The actual value for an item's batch attribute can be recorded after creation of a batch number. When the batch attribute reflects an integer or fraction, an infolog provides a warning or prevents entry (based on the tolerance policy) when the actual value exceeds the minimum or maximum. The actual value for an item's batch attribute can also be updated by the validated test results for a quality order. The next chapter provides further explanation of quality orders (Section 26.3).

Batch Attribute Searching You can search for an appropriate batch based on actual values of the item's batch attributes. This is termed a batch attribute search. A batch attribute search may be used in the context of finding an ingredient for production, or in the context of order entry. For example, a customer may have specific requirements for the values of batch attributes, so that a batch attribute search (and reservation) can be performed as part of order entry.

25.8 Batch Disposition Codes and Restricted Usage

Batch disposition codes often represent a critical tool in food products and other process manufacturing businesses, especially because the policies associated with a code can selectively enforce restricted usage.[4] Batch disposition codes may also apply to other businesses, and they represent an optional capability for managing inventory of batch-controlled material,

This section describes the setup information for batch disposition codes, and the assignment (and reassignment) of a disposition code to an item's batch. Those scenarios that do not require enforcement of restricted usage can define and use a single disposition code that reflects available material without restricted usage.

Setup Information for Batch Disposition Codes The user-defined batch disposition codes must be set up on the Batch Disposition Master form. One batch disposition code should reflect available material, where the disposition status is designated as available. The number of additional codes will depend on the desired variations in restricted usage, where the disposition status is designated as unavailable. The typical requirements for two additional batch disposition codes include (1) non-nettable with all usage restrictions and (2) nettable with some usage restrictions.

The following policies can be assigned to a batch disposition code with an unavailable disposition status, where the policies indicate aspects of restricted usage:

- *Nettable.* This policy determines whether inventory will be considered available by master scheduling logic.

- *Restricted Usage for Sales Orders.* You can designate one or more of the following policies on restricted usage:

  - Block reservations. This policy prevents reservation of the batch inventory

[4] Batch disposition codes represent a different construct than the RMA disposition codes for handling return orders from customers. They are also different than the "combined disposition code: used in the Advanced WMS approach, which reflects the combination of RMA disposition codes and the values for Inventory Status.

  - Block picking. This policy prevents picking of the batch inventory.

  - Block shipping. This policy prevents posting of the sales order slip of the batch inventory.

- *Restricted Usage for Transfer Orders.* You can designate one or more of the following policies on restricted usage. However, you should not block transfers if you intend to return a purchased batch to the vendor, or move the batch to a different location.

  - Block reservations. This policy prevents reservation of the batch inventory for a transfer order.

  - Block picking. This policy prevents picking of the batch inventory for a transfer order.

  - Block shipping. This policy prevents transfer order shipment of the batch inventory.

- *Restricted Usage for Production Orders.* You can designate one or more of the following policies on restricted usage:

  - Block reservations. This policy prevents reservation of the batch inventory.

  - Block picking. This policy prevents picking of the batch inventory.

Assignment of a Batch Disposition Code to an Item's Batch Number

The initial value of the batch disposition code can be automatically assigned to a batch number based on a default value for the item. You define this default value within the Item Model Group assigned to the item. Otherwise, the batch disposition code can be changed as needed.

The assigned value can also be defined as part of the information for quality orders. One value can be defined for a failed validation and another value can be defined for a passed validation, so that validation will update the batch disposition code to the assigned value.

Once an internal batch number has been created, you can manually override the batch disposition code by accessing the Reset Disposition Code form, or by changing the code via a mobile device transaction. A history of changes to a batch's disposition code is automatically maintained by the system, and viewable on the History of Disposition Inventory form.

Summary of Batch Disposition Codes With an Unavailable Status A summary of batch disposition codes with an unavailable status is shown in Figure 25.2 and described below. An unavailable status provides a form of inventory blocking, and a comparable figure provides a similar analysis of the three Inventory Blocking approaches (Figure 26.1). Batch disposition codes can be used in conjunction with all three approaches to inventory blocking, but is most commonly used with quality orders for updating the batch disposition code based on pass/fail results of validation.

Figure 25.2 Batch Disposition Codes With an Unavailable Status

Considerations	Impacts on Inventory
Create blocking for a specified batch number	Assign a batch disposition code (with an unavailable status) to a batch number
Ability to assign batch disposition code at time of order receipt	Yes
Remove blocking for a batch number	Change the batch disposition code (to one with an available status) for a batch number
Impact of a Batch Disposition code with an unavailable status on master scheduling logic	Nettable or Non-nettable
Allowable transactions for a batch number that has been assigned a batch disposition code with an unavailable status	Restricted usage for sales orders Restricted usage for production orders Restricted usage for transfer order Move Adjustment out Cycle count Return to vendor Create quality order
Additional considerations	Different ways to change the Batch Disposition Code Split the quantity for a batch number to assign different batch disposition codes

A batch disposition code with an unavailable status can be assigned to a batch number at any time, including at the time of order receipt. The associated blocking can be removed by changing the code to one with an available status. The expected outcome for inventory (with a code representing an unavailable status) can be designated as nettable or non-nettable. Some of the allowable transactions are impacted by the restricted usage policies, but many are not impacted such as moves and adjustments.

The batch disposition code can be changed by a quality order or changed directly (via a client or mobile device transaction). The code can be changed via a rework order for the item's inventory. When needed, you can split the quantity for a batch number into two or more batch numbers in order to assign different batch disposition codes. As another option, a subset of a batch number can be blocked via manual assignment of inventory blocking or a blocked value of Inventory Status.

25.9 Additional Case Studies

Case 80: Vendor Batch Numbers A manufacturer used several purchased components that were batch-controlled items. At the time of product receipt, the warehouse workers recorded an internal batch number and the vendor's batch number. A bar-coded label with the internal batch number was affixed to the product receipt, and subsequent transactions referred to the internal batch number.

Case 81: Country of Origin for Purchased Material A manufacturer used several purchased components from other countries. For a given item, the country of origin was specified as part of the foreign trade information for the item. However, some batch-controlled items were sourced from more than one country. They recorded the country of origin as part of the vendor batch details for each batch of these purchased items. Most cases involved a single country of origin, although a few required two different countries. This information was used to support government reporting requirements about country of origin.

25.10 Executive Summary

Some scenarios require tracking of serial numbers or batch numbers for a material item, or both. An item's batch numbers may also involve shelf life information, batch attributes and/or batch disposition codes to indicate restricted usage. This chapter summarized how to setup and use serial numbers and batch numbers for an item.

Several case studies illustrated the use of batch number tracking and serial number tracking. These included RMAs for serialized items (Case 77), deferred assignment for a serialized end-item and its serialized components (Case 78), merging physical batches into a new batch (Case 79), vendor batch numbers (Case 80), and the country of origin for purchased material (Case 81).

Chapter 26

Integration with Quality Management

The concerns of quality management typically extend across every aspect of supply chain management. This broad viewpoint ranges from the definition of item and product structure information through sourcing purchased material, actual production, sales shipments and returns. This chapter focuses on the concerns related to warehouse management activities.

A starting point for the integration of quality management and warehouse management involves the use of inventory blocking. Inventory blocking represents a key tool for quality management, such as preventing usage or indicating the need for inspection. Several variations of an inspection approach can be considered, such as the use of quality orders for updating the Inventory Status of received material. The use of quality orders and product testing represents a cornerstone of quality management, and they apply to many different business processes.

Additional aspects of the integration with quality management include the assignment of a disposition code to customer returns, the impact of holds and stopped flags, the use of nonconformance reports, the management of hazardous materials, and the coordination of quality-related activities. These topics are reflected in the following sections within the chapter.

1. Summary of Inventory Blocking Approaches
2. Variations of Inspection Approach
3. Quality Orders and Product Testing
4. RMA Disposition Codes and the use of Combined Disposition Codes
5. Impact of Holds and Stop Flags on Warehouse Activities
6. Quarantine Orders for the Basic Inventory Approach
7. Nonconformance Reports

8. Coordination of Quality-Related Activities
9. Hazardous Materials and MSDS Documents
10. Additional Case Studies

26.1 Summary of Inventory Blocking Approaches

Inventory blocking represents a key tool for quality management, such as preventing usage and indicating the need for inspection. There are three basic sources or approaches for inventory blocking—labeled Inventory Status, Quality Order and Manual. Each approach results in an entry on the Inventory Blocking form along with information about the source of blocking, and the information can act as a coordination tool for quality management.

One approach employs a blocked value for Inventory Status, as described in a previous chapter (Chapter 4) and in parts of other chapters covering receiving inspection and production inspection for purchase orders and production orders. The second approach employs quality orders, and often works in conjunction with the values of Inventory Status. Quality orders have been mentioned throughout the book, and are further explained in a subsequent section (Section 26.3). The third approach involves manual assignment of inventory blocking, which is introduced in this section. The three approaches differ in how the inventory blocking is created and removed, their impact on master scheduling logic, and their allowable transactions. The three approaches are summarized in Figure 26.1 and described below.

A fourth approach to inventory blocking only applies to batch-controlled items, and it employs the Batch Disposition Codes described in the previous chapter (Section 25.8). It can be used in conjunction with all three of the above-mentioned approaches, but is most commonly used with quality orders for updating the batch disposition code based on test results.

Inventory Blocking Based on a Blocked Value of Inventory Status
This approach reflects a blocked value for Inventory Status which can be assigned at the time of order receipt. The blocking can be viewed on the Inventory Blocking form, and it can only be removed by changing it to a non-blocked value. The inventory is treated as unusable and non-nettable by master scheduling logic. The blocking prevents most inventory transactions with the exception of moves, adjustments, cycle counts, returns to vendor and creation of a quality order. A blocked value can be changed by a quality order or changed directly (via a client or mobile device transaction). A non-blocked value can also be changed via a rework order for the item's inventory. A blocked value can also be assigned to a subset of a batch number or to a specific serial number.

Figure 26.1 Summary of Inventory Blocking Approaches

Considerations about Blocking	Type of Inventory Blocking		
	Inventory Status	Quality Order	Manual
Create blocking for the specified inventory of item	Assign a blocked value for Inventory Status	Create a quality order with full blocking	Manually assign inventory blocking
Ability to assign blocking at time of order receipt	Yes	Yes	No
Remove blocking	Change a blocked value for Inventory Status	Delete or complete the quality order	Delete manual assignment of inventory blocking
Impact of blocked inventory on master scheduling logic	Non-nettable	Nettable on expected date	Non-nettable or Nettable on expected date
Allowable transactions for the blocked inventory	Move, adjustment out Cycle count Return to vendor Create quality order	None	None
Description for blocking	None	Yes	Yes
Note/document for blocking	None	Yes	Yes
Additional considerations	Assign to subset of a batch number Different ways to change value of Inventory Status	Block just sample quantity Impact next steps for order Destructive testing Update Inventory Status or Batch Disposition Code	Assign to subset of a batch number

Inventory Blocking Based on a Quality Order This approach reflects a quality order with "full blocking" as part of the policies for item sampling. A quality order can be manually created for the specified inventory of an item, including inventory that has already been assigned a blocked value for Inventory Status. Alternatively, an item's quality order can be automatically created based on policies defined on the Quality Association form, such as automatic creation as a result of reporting a purchase order arrival or the finished quantity for a production order. Using the Inventory Blocking form, you can optionally define a description and/or notes about blocking related to a quality order.

With full blocking, the inventory associated with a quality order is treated by master scheduling logic as nettable with an expected availability date. This expected outcome is indicated by the automatically-assigned Expected Receipts checkbox, and the expected date inherits the creation date and can be manually changed. However, the blocking prevents all inventory transactions.

Blocking based on a quality order has several additional considerations. For example, blocking can just apply to a small sample quantity; so that blocking does not apply to the rest of the inventory associated with the quality order. A quality order may involve destructive testing. With an automatically generated quality order, the next step(s) for the related order can be prevented until the quality order has been completed, and a validation failure will be identified (via an infolog) when performing the next step. For example, a quality order stemming from a purchase order arrival can prevent posting of the product receipt until the quality order has been completed. Finally, a quality order can be used to update the value of Inventory Status or the Batch Disposition Code.

Inventory Blocking Based on Manual Assignment This approach reflects a manual assignment of inventory blocking to existing inventory. It can only be created and deleted on the Inventory Blocking form, and you can optionally define a description and/or notes about the manual blocking. When you create manual blocking, you can indicate the expected outcome as non-nettable or as nettable with an expected availability date. You indicate the expected outcome via an Expected Receipts checkbox, and the expected date inherits the creation date and can be manually changed. Manual blocking prevents all inventory transactions. For example, the manual blocking must be removed in order to report the inventory as scrapped. Manual blocking can also be assigned to a subset of a batch number or to a specific serial number.

26.2 Variations of Inspection Approach

Different approaches to inspection reflect several factors. Some of these factors include the different values for Inventory Status and/or Batch Disposition Code as part of inspection, and the different roles and ways for reporting a change in value. Other differences reflect the nature of purchased versus manufactured items, the use of a separate QC location, or the two approaches to warehouse management. This section focuses on the variations of inspection using Inventory Status, and summarizes the illustrative case studies from other chapters. It also covers other inspection approaches.

Variations of Inspection Using Inventory Status The value for Inventory Status provides one basis for identifying the results of inspection, as described in a previous chapter and in the next section about quality orders. The value can be assigned by a quality control clerk (based on the test results for a quality order) to purchase order arrivals or production order receipts, including scenarios using a separate QC area for the inventory. However, the value can also be assigned by a non-QC person, such as a receiving clerk (for purchase order arrivals) or a machine operator (for production order receipts). This assigned value can also indicate the need for inspection. Figure 26.2 summarizes these variations and identifies related case studies for both the basic and advanced approaches to warehouse management.

Figure 26.2 Variations of Inspection Approach Using Inventory Status

	Variations of Inspection using the value of Inventory Status	Basic Inventory Approach	Advanced WMS Approach
Purchase Order Arrival	Receiving Clerk reports Inspection	Case 14	Case 58
	Quality Control Clerk reports Inspection via Quality Order	Case 18 ⇨	Same approach
	Quality Control Clerk reports Inspection via Quality Order for inventory located in separate QC Area	Case 22 Putaway after QC	Case 64 Putaway after QC
Production Order Receipt	Machine Operator reports Inspection	Case 39	Case 69
	Quality Control Clerk reports Inspection via Quality Order	Case 40 ⇨	Same approach
	Quality Control Clerk reports Inspection via Quality Order for inventory located in separate QC Area		Case 70 Putaway after QC

Legend: [grey box] = Enter transaction via mobile device

As shown by grey shading in the figure, some transactions can be reported via mobile devices when using the Advanced WMS approach. When using mobile devices, for example, the Inventory Status can be assigned by a receiving clerk (Case 58) or by the machine operator (Case 69), and putaway work can be created and reported for inventory located in a separate QC area (Case 69 and Case 70). Alternatively, when using the Basic Inventory approach, the Inventory Status can be assigned by a receiving clerk using the Arrival Journal form (Case 14) or by the machine operator using the Report as Finished form (Case 39), and putaway after QC can be reported via transfer journals (Case 22).

Transactions related to a quality order—such as reporting test results and validation, or creating a quality order—cannot be reported via mobile devices based on current out-of-the-box capabilities, so reporting will be the same for both approaches (Case 18 and Case 40).

Variations of Inspection Using Batch Disposition Codes The batch disposition code provides one basis for identifying the results of inspection for a batch-controlled item, as described in a previous chapter (Section 25.8) and in the next section about quality orders. The value is typically assigned by a quality control clerk based on the test results for a quality order for purchase order arrivals or production order receipts. The use of batch disposition codes with an unavailable status were previously summarized in a similar figure (Figure 25.2). A previous case study also illustrated an inspection approaches using batch disposition codes (Case 19)..

Variations of Inspection Based on Capturing Quality-Related Data via Mobile Devices The ability to capture quality-related data via mobile devices involves the assignment of an Audit Template ID when defining the mobile device menu item. Each user-defined ID must be defined beforehand, and there are several capabilities associated with the definition of an Audit Template ID. At its simplest, you define one or more data capture questions (and the trigger for asking the questions) as part of an Audit Template ID. In this way, the worker that reports the mobile device transaction will be automatically prompted to answer the questions when reporting the mobile device transaction. Illustrative examples included Case 62 and Case 63.

Variations of Inspection Using Quarantine Orders A quarantine order provides one basis for identifying the results of inspection when using the Basic Inventory approach, as described in a subsequent section (Section 26.6).

Other Variations of Reporting Inspection Results Other variations include reporting of quality order results after putaway (Case 20), reporting delayed test results for a quality order (Case 21), reporting test results during the production process (Case 41), and identifying inspection resources in a routing operation for a manufactured item.

26.3 Quality Orders and Product Testing

Product testing entails the use of quality orders to report test results against a group of predefined tests. The explanation of product testing can be segmented into three areas: the definition of tests and test groups, the use of quality orders for reporting test results, and the rules for automatic generation of quality orders. Quality orders have been previously discussed in the context of inventory blocking (Section 26.1) and variations of inspection approaches (Section 26.2), and they can also be employed in other business processes.

Tests and Test Groups There are two types of predefined tests—quantitative and qualitative—and one or more tests can be assigned to a group of tests.

- *Quantitative Tests.* Each quantitative test must be assigned a testing unit of measure, so that acceptable values can be assigned when it is included in a test group. A pressure test, for example, might use pounds per square (PSI) as the unit of measure. The units of measure must be predefined along with the desired decimal precision.

- *Qualitative Tests.* A qualitative test will have an associated test variable (and its enumerated outcomes) when you assign it to a test group. A taste test, for example, may have one test variable for sweetness (with possible outcomes of sweet, sour and okay) and another test variable for color (with possible outcomes of dark, light and okay). You designate whether an outcome represents a pass or failure of the test.

For both types of tests, you can optionally assign a test instrument and applicable documents that describe the test.

Tests are assigned to a group of tests (termed a *test group*), where the test group has a unique identifier.

- *Test Groups.* For each test group, you assign a sampling plan, an acceptable quality level (AQL), and an indication of whether the tests will require destructive testing of the sample. Destructive testing will result in an inventory reduction of the sample quantity.

- *Sampling Plan.* A sampling plan is used to calculate the sample quantity for a quality order, and it can be expressed as an absolute quantity or as a percentage. For example, a sampling plan of 10% for a purchase order receipt quantity of 500 would result in a sample quantity of 50. The sampling plan can optionally require a different sample for each received batch when receiving multiple batches.

  When a quality order has been generated, it also results in inventory blocking—either for the sample quantity or the entire quantity of related inventory—until the testing results have been validated. The "full blocking" policy within an Item Sampling plan indicates that the entire quantity should be blocked. As described in a previous section, the Inventory Blocking form displays the blocking with a source of quality order,

- *Acceptable Quality Level (AQL).* An acceptable quality level refers to the percentage of tests which must be passed. An AQL of 90%, for example, means that 9 out of 10 tests must be passed, or that 9 out of 10 samples must pass.

- *Tests Within a Test Group.* When assigning a test to a test group, you define the acceptable measurement values for a quantitative test, or the test variable for a qualitative test. Each test can be assigned a sequence number, validity dates, and documents. You can designate which test results should be included in a certificate of analysis report associated with a quality order. An individual test can have its own AQL, referring to the percentage of the sample quantity which must be passed, since test results can be reported for subsets of the sample quantity.

The test group assigned to a quality order provides the initial basis for which tests need to be performed. Tests can be added, deleted, or changed on the quality order.

Use of a Quality Order A quality order defines the tests that need to be performed for an item and a sample quantity of its inventory. It is typically related to a specific order, such as a purchase order, production order or sales order. In addition to communicating the need to perform tests, it provides a mechanism for reporting results against the tests. You can manually create a quality order, or establish quality guidelines within each business process (such as a purchase order receiving process) for automatically creating a quality order. The next subsection explains automatic generation of quality orders.

After reporting the test results for every test within a quality order, you initiate a validation process that assigns a pass or fail status (based on meeting the overall AQL) and closes the quality order. When you try to perform the next step in the business process, an infolog warns you when the quality order has failed or has not yet been closed. In addition, you can optionally reopen the quality order and force the validation process to assign a pass status by accepting any error conditions.

You can view information about a quality order (and its test results) from multiple viewpoints. For example, the quality order can be viewed for the related batch number or from the related sales order, purchase order, production order or quarantine order.

You can optionally generate a certificate of analysis that displays the test results for a quality order. A certificate of analysis, for example, could be printed for a batch of material being shipped to a customer. The printed test results will only be displayed for designated tests within the quality order.

You can optionally create a nonconformance report when a quality order identifies defective material. The nonconformance report provides the basis for further investigation, as described in a subsequent section about nonconformance reports.

Rules for Automatic Generation of a Quality Order You can define rules (termed *quality association records*) for automatic generation of a quality order in different business processes. Each rule defines the set of tests, the acceptable quality level (AQL), and the sampling plan that apply to the automatically generated quality orders. Each rule also defines the event and conditions for automatically generating a quality order within a business process for the item. The business process can be related to purchase orders, sales orders or production orders, but not transfer orders. It can also apply to quarantine orders. The rules for automatic generation of a quality order are summarized in Figure 26.3 and described below.

Figure 26.3 Rules for Automatic Generation of a Quality Order

Business Process Reference Type	Label of the event that triggers a quality order Execution / Document	The actual event that triggers a quality order	Conditions: Site	Conditions: Item	Conditions: Other	Destructive Test Allowed
Purchase order	After registration	Register purchase order arrival	Site-specific or company-wide	Item-specific, quality group-specific, or all items	Vendor or vendor group	Yes
	Before receipts list	Initial attempt to post receipts list				No
	After receipts list	Post the receipts list				No*
	Before product receipt	Initial attempt to post product receipt				No
	After product receipt	Post the product receipt				Yes
Sales order	Before picking process is scheduled	Create picking list or picking work			Customer or Group	Yes
	Before packing slip	Post packing slip for sales order				Yes
Production or Batch order, or Co-product	After registration	Register production order arrival			N/A	No
	Before report as finished	Initial attempt to report as finished				No
	After report as finished	Update the report as finished				Yes
Route operation	Before report as finished	Create batch/production order			Resource or Group Master Operation or Route Group	No
	After report as finished	Report the operation as finished				No
Inventory	None	None			N/A	Yes
Quarantine order	Before report as finished	Initial attempt to report as finished				No
	After report as finished	Report the order as finished				No
	Before end	Initial attempt to report as ended				No
	After end	Report the order as ended				No

The figure summarizes the events and conditions for generating a quality order for various business processes (termed the *reference type*). An event is expressed in terms of the relevant document and execution timing, such as posting the product receipt for a purchase order. These events reflect variations in AX functionality for modeling different business processes. The figure also identifies the actual event that triggers automatic generation of a quality order.

The conditions for generating a quality order can be site-specific or company-wide, and they can apply to a single item, a group of items (based on the quality group assigned to items) or all items. Other conditions depend on the business process, such as vendor-specific conditions for a purchase order or customer-specific conditions for a sales order. A quality order involving destructive tests can only be generated when inventory exists for the event, as shown in the right-hand column of Figure 26.3. The automatic generation of a quality order can be further described for each business process.

- *Purchase Order Process.* The generation of a quality order can occur after registering a purchase order arrival. It can also occur before or after the posting the product receipt for a purchase order. The need for a quality order can reflect a particular site, item or vendor, or a combination of these conditions.

- *Sales Order Process.* The generation of a quality order can occur before or after the posting of a picking list or packing slip for the material being shipped. The need for a quality order can reflect a particular site, item, or customer, or a combination of these conditions.

- *Production Order Process.* The generation of a quality order can occur before or after reporting a finished quantity. The need for a quality order can reflect a particular site or item, or a combination of these conditions.

- *Route Operation for a Production Order.* When a production order contains a routing operation, the quality order can be generated before or after reporting the operation as finished. The need for a quality order can reflect a particular site, item or quality group, or a combination of these conditions. The need for a quality order can also reflect a specific master operation or the route group assigned to operations.

- *Inventory.* A quality order must be manually generated for an item's inventory quantity, and the selected test group determines what tests will be performed. It cannot be generated automatically for an item's existing inventory.

- *Quarantine Order Process.* The generation of a quality order can occur before or after reporting the quarantine order as finished or ended. The need for a quality order can reflect a particular site, item or vendor, or a combination of these conditions.

A rule must be defined for each variation in a business process requiring automatic creation of a quality order. The validity dates for a quality association record enable you to model planned changes in the business process.

26.4 RMA Disposition Codes and the Use of Combined Disposition Codes

RMA processing builds on sales order functionality. Each RMA has an associated sales order (termed the *returned order*) for handling returns, and an optional second sales order (termed the *replacement order*) for handling replacements. Both sales orders have the same order number (but a different order type) with linkage to the originating RMA number. A key aspect of handling an actual return involves the assignment of an RMA disposition code.[1]

This section summarizes the use of various RMA disposition codes, which differs slightly for the two approaches to warehouse management. You can directly assign the RMA disposition code when using the Basic Inventory approach to warehouse management. However, the Advanced WMS approach involves assignment of a "combined disposition code" which reflects the combination of RMA disposition codes and the values for Inventory Status.

RMA Disposition Codes A user-definable RMA disposition code has an assigned action that indicates how to handle a returned item and possible replacement. You can assign an RMA disposition code when registering RMA arrival of the returned items; it can be reassigned as part of the inspection approach. The key point of a RMA disposition code is the assigned action. There are three types of actions that apply to RMA processing (with or without a replacement order):

- *Credit [and Put in Inventory].* This action indicates that inventory balances should be updated by the returned item. For example, you may be able to reuse the item "as is" or refurbish/repair the item to make it usable.

- *Scrap.* This action indicates that inventory balances should not be updated by the returned item.

- *Return.* This action indicates that the inventory balances should be updated so that the returned item can sent back to the customer regardless of its condition.

There are two additional types of actions that only apply to RMA processing when use of a replacement order depends on the disposition of returned items.

---

[1] An RMA disposition code represents a different construct than a batch disposition code, which was described in a previous chapter (Section 25.8).

- *Replace and Scrap.* This action indicates that the inventory balances should not be updated by the returned item, and that a replacement order should be automatically created after the returned item has gone through the arrival/inspection process. You must specify the replacement item after recording arrival/inspection of the returned item. This action is not allowed when a replacement order was created for immediate shipment, since it would result in duplicate replacement efforts.

- *Replace and Credit.* This action indicates that the inventory balances should be updated by the returned item, otherwise it is exactly the same as the return and scrap action.

The limited number of action types (five) means that you may need a minimum of five RMA disposition codes. Symmetry in naming these RMA disposition codes can simplify explanations, so you can avoid saying things like "the disposition code of Scrap and its related action type of Scrap."

Combined Disposition Code for the Advanced WMS Approach The advanced approach involves selection of a "combined disposition code" when reporting purchase order arrival or RMA arrival via mobile device transactions. A "combined disposition code" reflects the combination of one RMA disposition code and one value for Inventory Status.[2] For example, a combined code of *Needs-Rework* could reflect the combination of the RMA disposition code for *Credit [and put in inventory]* and the Inventory Status value for *Needs-Rework.* An additional combined code would be needed for an Inventory Status of *Return-To-Vendor.*

26.5 Impact of Holds and Stop Flags on Warehouse Activities

Warehouse activities can be affected by several factors described in previous sections, such as inventory blocking or restricted inventory usage based on a batch disposition code. This section describes the impact of additional factors related to holds, stop flags and other restrictions.

---

[2] As a confusing issue, the same form name of "Disposition Codes" is used for two different forms. You define the RMA disposition codes on the Disposition Codes form (as part of the sales and marketing setup information for sales order returns), and you define the "combined disposition code" on the Disposition Codes form (as part of warehouse management setup information for mobile devices). This "combined disposition code" can also be displayed on the mobile device transactions for purchase order arrivals and RMA arrivals, and it is labeled just "disposition code."

Impact of a Stop Flag for a Production Order on Picking Activities The Stop flag primarily serves warehouse management purposes and prevents changes in order status until it has been removed. For example, assigning the Stop flag to a scheduled order prevents a change in order status to Released or Started. By preventing a change to a Started status, it indirectly prevents creation of a picking list journal and reporting of actual picked material. Preventing a change to a Released status impacts the Advanced WMS approach, since it indirectly prevents creation and reporting of raw material picking work. The Stop flag has no impact when assigned after a production order has been started.

Impact of a Customer Hold on Sales Order Picking/Shipping The assignment of the hold policy of "all" to a customer will prevent any picking/shipping transactions for the customer until it has been removed or changed. It results in a corresponding infolog when attempting to enter transactions.

Impact of an Order Hold on Sales Order Picking/Shipping The assignment of a Hold Code to a sales order will prevent any picking/shipping transactions until the Hold Code has been cleared. It results in a corresponding infolog when attempting to enter transactions.

Impact of Stopped Sales Activities for an Item The sales order transactions for an item can be stopped, either as a companywide or site-specific policy within the item's default order policies. The stopped flag prevents further transactions for an item's existing sales orders (including picking/shipping transactions) until it has been removed. It results in an infolog when attempting to enter a transaction. A similar stopped flag can be specified for an item's inventory transactions, which also prevents further transactions.

Impact of a Vendor Hold on Purchase Order Receiving The assignment of a vendor hold for "all" transactions will prevent posting of product receipts until it has been changed or removed. It results in a corresponding infolog when attempting to enter transactions. However, it does not prevent registration of purchase order arrivals from the vendor.

Impact of a Stopped Flag for a Purchase Order Line A line item on a purchase order can be flagged as stopped. The stopped flag prevents further transactions for the line item (including registration of arrivals and posting of product receipts) until it has been removed. It results in a corresponding infolog when attempting to enter transactions.

Impact of Stopped Purchasing Activities for an Item The purchase order transactions for an item can be flagged as stopped, either as a companywide or site-specific policy. The stopped flag prevents further transactions for an item's existing purchase orders (including registration of arrivals and posting of product receipts) until it has been removed. It results in a corresponding infolog when attempting to enter transactions. A similar stopped flag can be specified for an item's inventory transactions, which also prevents further transactions.

No Impact of an Item's Approved Vendors on Purchase Order Receiving An item's approved vendor can have an expiration date, so that the vendor is no longer approved at the time of registering purchase order arrivals or posting product receipts for an existing purchase order. However, this has no impact on the ability to finish these transactions.

No Impact of a Nonconformance Report A quality control clerk can create a nonconformance report in order to identify a problem. The nonconformance report can identify the related inventory, purchase order, sales order, or the related vendor or customer. However, a nonconformance report does not prevent warehouse transactions.

26.6 Quarantine Orders for the Basic Inventory Approach

A quarantine order represents one of the inspection approaches, and it only works for the Basic Inventory approach to warehouse management. It involves placement of an item's inventory into a quarantine warehouse and location, which prevents usage until the quarantine order has been ended. Its supports scrap reporting of rejected material. For useable material, it supports an expected availability date and optional putaway to a normal warehouse and location.

A quarantine order can be created using several different approaches. For example, it can be manually created, or automatically created from an arrival journal or for a failed quality order. These different starting points and the typical business process for a quarantine order are illustrated in Figure 26.4 and described below.

The setup information for handling a quarantine order includes the definition of a quarantine warehouse (and associated bin locations), and assignment of this quarantine warehouse to the corresponding main warehouse. The locations within a quarantine warehouse can reflect QC-specific locations when inspection involves a separate QC area. They can also mirror some of the locations in a normal warehouse when inspection of inventory occurs in place.

Figure 26.4 Process a Quarantine Order

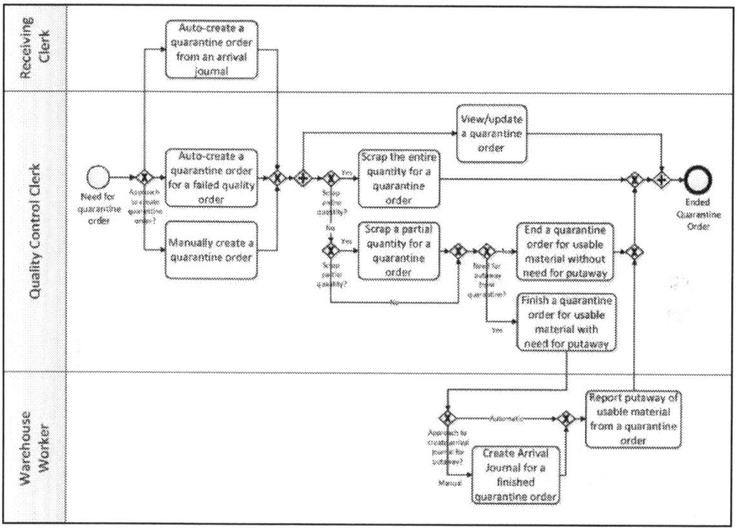

Auto-Create a Quarantine Order From an Arrival Journal When registering purchase order arrival using an arrival journal, the receiving clerk can identify the need for a quarantine order on a journal line. The need for a quarantine order can also be inherited from an item-specific policy (embedded within the Item Model Group assigned to the item).

Auto-Create a Quarantine Order for a Failed Quality Order When reporting validation of test results for a quality order, the quality control clerk can specify that a quarantine order should be automatically created upon validation failure of the test results. This will automatically move the material to the quarantine warehouse and a related bin location, and prevent usage until the quarantine order has been processed.

As part of the setup information, you can define a policy for creating a quarantine order upon validation failure (within the Quality Association information for an item) which acts as the default when validating a quality order.

Manually Create a Quarantine Order The quality control clerk can manually create a quarantine order for an item's inventory.

View/Update a Quarantine Order The quality control clerk can view quarantine orders and their status, and also update the information. For example, the quality control clerk can assign an expected availability date and optionally split the quantity to create an additional quarantine order for reporting different results. The newly-created quarantine order has a status of Created, and requires an additional step for updating the status to Started. Other updates include scrap reporting and possible transfers to putaway locations, as described in subsequent steps.

Scrap the Entire Quantity for a Quarantine Order The quality control clerk determines the item is not usable and scraps the entire quantity, which removes the quantity from inventory and charges the Inventory Loss account. It also updates the quarantine order status to Ended.

Scrap a Partial Quantity for a Quarantine Order The quality control clerk determines that a partial quantity is not usable and must be scrapped, which removes the quantity from inventory and charges the Inventory Loss account.

End a Quarantine Order for Usable Material Without Need for Putaway For usable material that does not require putaway, the quality control clerk reports a quarantine order as Ended. The inventory remains in the same location (within a main warehouse and location) that reflects initial creation of the quarantine order.

Finish a Quarantine Order for Usable Material With Need for Putaway For usable material requiring putaway, the quality control clerk changes the quarantine order status to Reported as Finished and designates the approach for creating an arrival journal to handle putaway. An arrival journal name can be specified (to indicate an automatic creation approach) or left blank (to indicate a manual creation approach).

Create an Arrival Journal for a Finished Quarantine Order The warehouse worker creates an arrival journal for a finished Quarantine Order in order to support putaway of the usable material. This arrival journal can be created manually or created from the Arrival Overview form.

Perform Putaway of Usable Material From a Quarantine Order The warehouse worker uses the arrival journal (associated with the Quarantine Order) to move the material from the quarantine location to the desired put-away location. Posting the arrival journal automatically updates the quarantine order status to Ended.

26.7 Nonconformance Reports

A nonconformance report (termed a *nonconformance* within AX) is typically the responsibility of a quality control specialist. It describes an item that has a quality problem where the descriptive information includes the source and type of problem. The problem source is termed a *nonconformance type*. You assign a problem source and an associated problem type when you create a nonconformance report. This section summarizes the setup and use of nonconformance reports.

Types of Problem Sources for a Nonconformance Report There are five types of problem sources (aka nonconformance types) that can be assigned to a nonconformance report, and each type can have optional source information. For example, the source information about a customer problem can include the customer number or sales order number, while the source information about a production problem can include the production order number.

Problem Types The user-definable problem types provide a classification of quality problems for each nonconformance type. For example, the problem types for service requests could reflect a classification of customer complaints, whereas the problem types for an internal nonconformance could represent a classification of defect codes.

Use of a Nonconformance Report A nonconformance is initially created with an approval status of *new*, indicating that it represents a request for action. You can approve or refuse a nonconformance (which changes the approval status to *approved* or *refused*) to indicate that you will or will not take action on the nonconformance.[3] You can also close a nonconformance (as indicated by a separate check box) to indicate that you are finished with it, or reopen a nonconformance to indicate that further consideration is required.

A printed conformance report and nonconformance tag can be used to assist material disposition.[4] You can selectively generate reports and tags based on selection criteria, such as the nonconformance number, item, customer, vendor, or status that are associated with a nonconformance.

---

[3] A user cannot approve a nonconformance unless the user has been assigned an employee identifier (via the User relations form). The system tracks the nonconformance history in terms of the employees who changed the status.

[4] The printed nonconformance tag and report will display an assigned quarantine zone (along with information about unusable versus restricted usage) to guide handling of defective material. The zones may or may not correspond to inventory locations or resources. Use the Quarantine zones form to define zones that can be assigned to a nonconformance.

- *Nonconformance Report.* The nonconformance report displays identification information, such as the nonconformance number, item, and problem type. The report displays the related notes based on your report setup policies.

- *Nonconformance Tag.* The nonconformance tag displays identification information, such as the nonconformance number and item. The tag displays the related notes based on your report setup policies. The tag also displays the quarantine zone and type (such as restricted usage versus unusable) that you assigned to the nonconformance in order to guide disposition of the defective material.

Additional Options for Nonconformance Reports There are several additional options for handling the business processes pertaining to a nonconformance report, such as corrective actions, the description of work, additional testing, and related nonconformance reports.

26.8 Coordination of Quality-Related Activities

Several tools can help coordinate quality-related activities, such as lists of blocked inventory, quality orders, and nonconformance as well as a production schedule for a quality-related resource.

List of Inventory Blocking The Inventory Blocking form displays an entry for each source of blocked inventory related to Inventory Status, quality orders and manual assignment.

List of Quality Orders The Quality Orders form displays an entry for each quality order and its related order (such as a purchase order or production order) and batch number. For a selected order, it displays the needed tests and the test results reported to-date.

List of Nonconformance Each nonconformance report (termed a nonconformance) describes an item that has a quality problem, where the descriptive information includes the source and type of problem. A related list of corrective actions identifies what type of diagnostic should be performed, who should perform it, and a requested date and a planned date for completing the diagnostic.

Production Schedule for Quality-Related Operations The production schedule and job list identify routing operations to be performed by a resource that represents quality resources. The quality resource may include a labor pool of inspectors, a burn-in area, or other resource under quality management control. This may require time reporting (or unit completions by operation) to correctly reflect progress against the routing, availability for the next operation, auto-deduction of material, and actual costs.

List of Quarantine Orders The Quarantine Orders form displays an entry for each quarantine order and its related order (such as a purchase order or production order) and batch number.

26.9 Hazardous Materials and MSDS Documents

A regulated item requires a Material Data Safety Sheet (MSDS) that can be sent to the customer. The MSDS document for a purchased item may also be received from a vendor. For a selected item, you can define the associated document by accessing the Product Data Safety Sheet form. This form consists of one or more line items uniquely identified by a system-assigned document number. When you add a line item, you define the related information for the item's MSDS document (such as the effective date, expiry date, version number, and an active flag), and use the document handling capabilities to identify the associated file containing the actual descriptive text. The descriptive text for MSDS documents can also be obtained from a subscription service such as Atrion International.[5]

The requirements for sending an item's MSDS document may apply to all countries or to selected countries. This item-specific information must be defined on the Material Regulated Countries form.

When entering a sales order line for the item, an infolog warning can be displayed about sending the latest active MSDS document to the customer. This infolog warning occurs when the customer has not yet received the item's MSDS document, or when a newer version (defined by the document's effective date) needs to be sent.[6] An infolog warning can also be generated when an existing MSDS document is about to expire. You can optionally print the relevant MSDS documents when posting the packing list or invoice for the sales order, and even

---

[5] See www.atrionintl.com/ for additional information about their subscription service.

[6] In the context of sales order entry, the effective date of an MSDS document can be viewed in terms of the sales order delivery date or the current date, as defined by a companywide policy on the Inventory and Warehouse Management Parameters form.

prevent posting when a document's expiry date has been exceeded.[7] The system automatically tracks when an item's MSDS document has been printed for a customer, along with the *last sent date*. The *last sent date* can also be manually entered. The tracking information (about the actual document number, the related sales order number, and the last sent date) can be viewed on the Product Safety Data Sheet Log, accessed from a sales line for the regulated item. The tracking information provides the basis for displaying the infolog warnings described above.

When entering a purchase order for a hazardous material item, you can view the tracking information about the item's MSDS document. The tracking information (about the actual document number, the related purchase order number, and the last received date) can be viewed on the Product Safety Data Sheet Log, accessed from a purchase order line for the regulated item. An infolog warning can also be generated when an existing MSDS document is about to expire.

26.10 Additional Case Studies

Case 82: Certificates of Analysis for Sales Order Shipments A manufacturer enclosed a certificate of analysis with sales order shipments of selected items. The certificate reflected the test results reported for the item, where test results were captured as part of a quality order. The contents of a certificate of analysis reflected each customer's requirements for selected test results.

Case 83: Nonconformance Reports for Purchased Material The quality manager wanted to track problems related to several purchased items. When a problem was identified, a quality specialist created a nonconformance report that identified the problem source by vendor. The specialist also described the problem (via textual comments), assigned a user-definable problem type that provided a classification of the quality problems, and printed a tag that was attached to the material. When the nonconformance report was approved for further action, it was assigned one or more corrective actions that identified what type of diagnostic should be performed, who should perform it, and the requested date for completion. In some cases, a quality order was also created to capture test results about the material. The status of the nonconformance report was changed to closed after work was completed.

[7] These two options are displayed on the Posting Packing Slip and Posting Invoice forms, and the values initial default from the companywide policies defined on the Inventory and Warehouse Management Parameters form.

Case 84: Destructive Testing of Finished Quantities During the ramp up period for production of a new manufactured item, the testing requirements involved destructive tests for a significant sample size of the finished quantity. Several steps were involved in modeling this process. First, the quality manager assigned a destructive test policy to the test group containing the required "destructive test," and the sampling plan indicated the quantity required for destructive testing. Second, the quality manager defined a quality association for automatic generation of a quality order for the new manufactured item. This included the relevant sampling plan and test group for destructive testing, and the validity dates reflected the ramp up period. As a result, when using production orders during the ramp up period, reporting a finished quantity automatically created a quality order, and the inventory quantity associated with destructive testing was initially assigned a *reserved physical* status. Validation of the quality order deducted the destroyed quantity from inventory, and the inventory transaction history identified the quality order that required the destructive test.

26.11 Executive Summary

This chapter covered the integration of quality management and warehouse management. As a starting point, it explained the use of inventory blocking to prevent usage or indicate the need for inspection. It also covered several variations of inspection approaches, especially the use of quality orders. Additional aspects included the assignment of a disposition code to customer returns, the impact of holds and stopped flags, the use of nonconformance reports, the management of hazardous materials, and the coordination of quality-related activities.

Several case studies within the chapter illustrated some of the quality management concerns, such as certificates of analysis for sales order shipments (Case 82), nonconformance reports for purchased material (Case 83), and destructive testing of finished quantities (Case 84). However, numerous case studies throughout the book have covered other aspects of the integration with quality management.

Chapter 27

Summary

This book focused on how Microsoft Dynamics AX provides an integrated ERP system to support warehouse management in manufacturing/distribution firms. It also covered the integration of warehouse management with the larger context of supply chain management, as well as the integration with quality and transportation management. This focus guided the prior research and the scope of book topics that were described at the beginning of the book. In particular, this book covered the basic and advanced approaches to warehouse management, and explained some of the strategic options.

The targeted reader primarily consists of those individuals responsible for warehouse management at manufacturing and distribution firms. In particular, it is intended to assist professionals implementing or considering Dynamics AX as their ERP system as well as those providing consulting assistance. The summary reviews the learning objectives for these targeted readers. These learning objectives and related chapters were described at the beginning of the book.

27.1 Accomplishing Your Learning Objectives

The book contents were segmented to support several categories of targeted readers, so that you can focus on just the relevant chapters for your learning objectives. The various learning objectives are summarized in Figure 27.1 and described below. The suggestions reflect the organization of book chapters into two groupings about the basic versus advanced approach to warehouse management, so it may be helpful to view this information first (Figure 1.2). The underlined words in Figure 27.1 indicate the key differentiator for the learning objective. The last two learning objectives apply to knowledgeable AX users.

Learn the Advanced Approach to Warehouse Management One half of the book covered the functionality and mobile device transactions supported by the advanced approach to warehouse management. These chapters provided a linear sequence of explanation, and built on the chapters covering foundation information about items, batch/serial numbers, and quality management.

Figure 27.1 Summary of Learning Objectives

	Learning Objective	Estimated Pages
	Advanced WMS Approach to warehouse management	200
	Basic Approach to warehouse management	130
	Business Processes related to warehouse management	
	Warehouse management for a Distribution operation	
	Warehouse management for a Manufacturing operation	45
	Integration with Supply Chain Management	
	Integration with Quality Management	20-40
	Integration with Transportation Management	20
For AX Veterans	Incrementally Learn the Advanced WMS Approach	160
For AX Veterans	Confirm/Extend knowledge of the Basic Approach to warehouse management	

The advanced approach represents new functionality in the latest release of Dynamics AX that became available less than a year ago, so that few have extensive implementation experience at this point in time. Many people face a significant learning curve about the extensive functionality, its underlying conceptual models, and the details of designing/using mobile device transactions—especially those unfamiliar with advanced WMS capabilities in other systems. The advanced approach is reflected in the AX user documentation topics about "features in the warehouse management module."

Learn the Basic Approach to Warehouse Management The other half of the book covered the functionality supported by the basic approach to warehouse management. These chapters provided a linear sequence of explanation, and built on the chapters covering foundation information about items, batch/serial numbers, and quality management. The basic approach does not include out-of-the box mobile device transactions, but can employ 3rd-party applications for supporting mobile devices.

Those unfamiliar with AX will likely face a comparatively shorter learning curve about the simpler functionality and its underlying conceptual models. An incremental learning curve would also apply to those using a third-party application for the mobile device transactions.

Learn the Business Processes Related to Warehouse Management Each chapter about a warehouse management transaction started with a simple yet typical business process. A Business Process Modeling (BPM) diagram illustrated the process and identified the key steps and role responsibilities. Subsequent sections identified the key constructs and their related life cycles, the reversing transactions, and the major variations of the business process. The major variations often involved an in-depth explanation and the same explanatory approach—with a BPM diagram and the identification of key constructs, life cycles and reversing transactions. The BPM diagrams primarily served as a learning tool for incremental learning of complex functionality.

For many implementations, the business processes for warehouse management (and the larger context of supply chain management) should reflect the standard AX capabilities as much as possible. Until the project implementation team has a basic understanding of these system capabilities, it is difficult to leverage AX for their business processes except for just asking that the system must do what their current system does today.

Learn Warehouse Management for a Distribution Operation The segmentation of book topics supported a focus on distribution operations, such as purchase orders, sales orders, transfer orders and the fundamentals of modeling a distribution business.

Learn Warehouse Management for a Manufacturing Operation The segmentation of book topics supported a focus on just manufacturing operations, including both internal and subcontracted production.

Learn Integration of Warehouse Management and Supply Chain Management The broader context of a supply chain management (SCM) perspective was embedded throughout the book. Effective use of AX for supply chain management makes life easier for warehouse management.

Learn Integration with Quality Management The integration with quality management is critical in many scenarios. The book included separate chapters about quality management and serial/batch tracking, every chapter included the quality management concerns, and numerous case studies highlighted the integration with quality management.

Learn Integration with Transportation Management Many aspects of transportation require close integration and coordination of warehouse management activities. The book covered the basics of transportations (such as the significance of delivery dates and expected transportation time), and explained how the constructs of loads and shipments are used in the advanced approach to warehouse management. It also covered the incremental TMS capabilities for supporting transportation requirements such as assigning a rate/route to a load.

Incrementally Learn the Advanced WMS Approach The segmentation of book topics was intended to help knowledgeable AX users with incremental learning of the new functionality. The new functionality represents a dramatic change from previous AX versions, especially for the warehouse processes related to sales orders, transfer orders and purchase orders. Many people face a significant learning curve about the extensive functionality, its underlying conceptual models, and the details of designing/using mobile device transactions. The learning curve tends to be more difficult for those unfamiliar with advanced WMS capabilities in other systems. This new functionality is reflected in the AX user documentation topics about "features in the warehouse management module."

Confirm/Extend Knowledge of the Basic Approach to Warehouse Management A knowledgeable AX user will already be familiar with most aspects of the basic approach. However, there are slight changes and several new capabilities for the basic approach in the latest AX release, such as support for wave picking and calculating space utilization for a non-WMS warehouse. This previous functionality is reflected in the AX user documentation topics about "features in the inventory management module."

The topics and chapters about the basic approach essentially represent a check list for assessing your current level of AX knowledge about warehouse management and its integration with supply chain management and quality management. Hence, it can help quantity your learning curve about unfamiliar topics.

27.2 Concluding Remarks

When reviewing or learning any ERP software package, it is important to understand its underlying conceptual models and how it supports variations in business processes. It is easy to get bogged down in the navigational details. This book summarized how Microsoft Dynamics AX can support the warehouse management requirements of manufacturing and distribution businesses, especially in the broader context of supply chain management. It also addressed the learning objectives for those new to AX as well as those already familiar with AX.

Appendix A Summary of Common Functionality

The two approaches to warehouse management share a high degree of common functionality. This section summarizes the common functionality segmented into several topics reflecting chapters within the book, and is primarily geared for knowledgeable AX users.

Definition of an Item The common functionality related to item definition is fully explained in Chapter 24. This includes item identification and descriptions, unit of measure considerations, alternative item identifiers, inventory valuation and financial reporting, and the information about purchased and manufactured items. It also includes the definition of notes and different note types, and the note inheritance capabilities.

The details of standard costing and actual costing fall outside the book's scope. In addition, much of the required information for manufactured items—such as the definition of a bills of material and routing data, and the associated cost calculations—fall outside the book's scope. However, the aspects related to warehouse locations for issuing raw material and receiving finished quantities—based on BOM/routing information—are covered in the chapters about production orders.

Batch Number and Serial Number Tracking The common functionality related to batch and serial numbers is fully explained in Chapter 25. This includes the assignment of serial numbers for serialized items. For batch-controlled items, it includes the assignment of batch numbers and vendor batch information, the use of shelf-life and batch attribute information, the merging of batches, and the use of batch disposition codes for restricting usage of inventory.

Integration with Quality Management The common functionality related to quality management is fully explained in Chapter 26. This includes the variations of inventory blocking and inspection approaches, the use of quality orders, and the impact of various holds and stop flags. It includes the use of nonconformance reports and coordination of quality-related activities.

Use of Inventory Status The common functionality related to Inventory Status was fully explained in Chapter 4. It is also covered as part of the chapters about strategic options (Section 2.1) and quality management (Section 26.2).

Fundamentals of Warehouse Management The common functionality includes activation of the multisite capabilities, inquiries/reports about inventory and transaction history, the calculation of ABC classifications, and counting statistics about inventory accuracy. It includes viewing and updating the reservations about items and orders. The basic inventory transactions within the Basic Inventory Approach—such as quantity adjustments or transfers—can also be performed when using the Advanced WMS approach. Separate chapters covered the fundamentals for the Basic Inventory approach (Chapter 3) and the Advanced WMS approach (Chapter 13), and described common functionality for both approaches.

Fundamentals of Order Processing The common functionality includes the steps to create and process purchase orders and sales orders, and the use of simple inventory transactions to report receipts and shipments. It includes the steps to create transfer orders, and to create and process production orders. It also includes the use of delivery tolerances and safety lead times for purchase receipts, sales shipments, and transfer order shipments and receipts.

Purchase Orders The common functionality includes the significance of posting product receipts and the product receipt journal, the process of purchase order returns, and the vendor performance metrics. It also includes the simple inventory transaction for purchase order receipts.

Sales Orders The common functionality includes the significance of posting the packing slip and the packing slip journal, sales-related backorders, and the performance metrics for on-time delivery and full quantity. It also includes the simple inventory transaction for sales order shipments.

Transfer Orders The common functionality includes the significance of posting a transfer order shipment, which can also be reported as a simple inventory transaction. It includes the definition of transport time between warehouses and viewing in-transit inventory.

Production Orders The common functionality includes the significance of the picking list journal and the alternatives for reporting finished quantities of a production order. It also includes the significance of order status, the use of auto-deduction for reporting material usage, and the definition of BOM/routing information applicable to warehouse transactions.

Subcontracted Production The common functionality includes the definition of BOM/routing information to model subcontracted production, the use of a purchase order for the subcontracted service, and various transactions related to supplied material and production output (especially when stocked at the warehouse representing the subcontractor).

AX User Documentation About Common Functionality The common functionality is not necessarily highlighted in the user documentation from Microsoft. For example, in the user documentation for AX 2012 R3, a mixture of the common and unique functionality for the Basic Inventory approach is covered in the current topics about "Setting Up and Maintaining Inventory Management" and "Working with Inventory Management." My informal analysis indicates that 50% of the current topics cover common functionality and 30% cover the unique functionality of the basic approach. The other 20% primarily covered the "old WMS II" functionality.

Appendix B Comparing Approaches

The two approaches to warehouse management can be compared in several different ways. The amount of functionality provides one way to make a comparison. The amount of functionality associated with an ERP package typically correlates with complexity. It is difficult to measure the complexity of an ERP package, let alone the amount of functionality. However, with respect to the basic versus advanced approaches to warehouse management, one metric for the amount of functionality can be based on a page count analysis of the book's explanations about each approach.[1]

Several perspectives apply to the amount of functionality. First, the two approaches share a high degree of common functionality (as summarized in Appendix A) but have significantly different amounts of unique functionality. The unique functionality in one approach does not apply to the other approach. Second, the amount of applicable functionality for a given company depends on their choice of a strategic option. You can use just the basic approach or just the advanced approach, or you may require both approaches. You may decide to implement a subset of available functionality. Third, the amount of functionality for each approach differs by business process. These considerations are reflected in the following topics within this appendix.

1. Comparing the Amounts of Common versus Unique Functionality
2. Comparing the Amounts of Functionality for Sales Order Picking/Shipping
3. Comparing the Amounts of Functionality by Topic
4. Incremental Learning for Knowledgeable AX Users

[1] This metric for amount of functionality makes an assumption that my explanations are reasonably complete and consistently at the same level, so that page counts provide a reasonable approximation.

Comparing the Amounts of Common versus Unique Functionality

The two approaches for warehouse management share a high degree of common functionality. However, the basic approach has some unique constructs and does not include out-of-the-box support for mobile device transactions. In contrast, the advanced approach has a different set of unique constructs and a much broader scope of functionality which includes out-of-the-box support for mobile device transactions and work orders. The total amount of functionality for each approach, and the relative amount of common versus unique functionality, are illustrated in Figure B.1 and described below. The metrics for amount of functionality reflect a page count analysis for the book's explanations about each approach.

Figure B.1 Comparing the Amounts of Common versus Unique Functionality

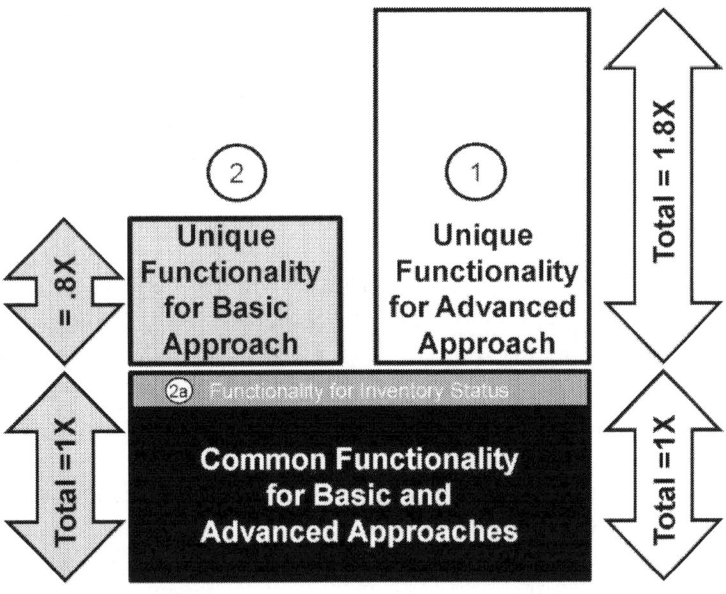

As shown in the left side of the figure, a firm implementing just the Basic Inventory approach will need to learn its unique functionality and the common functionality (which may include the use of Inventory Status). Those readers already familiar with AX will probably know most of this functionality based on their experience with the "old WMS I" capabilities. The amount of common functionality is identified as "1X" (about 100 pages), and the comparative amount of unique functionality represents ".8X."

The right side of the figure applies to firms implementing just the Advanced WMS approach. The comparative amount of unique functionality represents "1.8X" relative to the common functionality, or more than twice that of the basic approach. A firm implementing the advanced approach will not necessarily use all possible capabilities and mobile device transactions, so the aggregate level would be less. A firm can also start simply and evolve to greater sophistication. However, an additional level of complexity (not shown in the figure) involves the detailed design for interactive use of mobile device transactions.

A firm requiring both approaches would need to learn the unique functionality for both. However, they may not use all possible capabilities within each approach, such as using selective transactions for managing inventory at off-site warehouses.

Comparing the Amounts of Functionality for Sales Order Picking/Shipping The amount of functionality for each approach differs at the aggregate level; it also differs by business process. An illustrative example involves the process for sales order picking/shipping, and the relative amounts of common and unique functionality. Figure B.2 summarizes the comparison via three different yardsticks. The yardsticks indicate the advanced approach has "2.5X" the amount of functionality compared to the basic approach, and the yardstick is even longer when using both approaches.

Figure B.2 Comparing the Amounts of Functionality for Sales Order Picking/Shipping

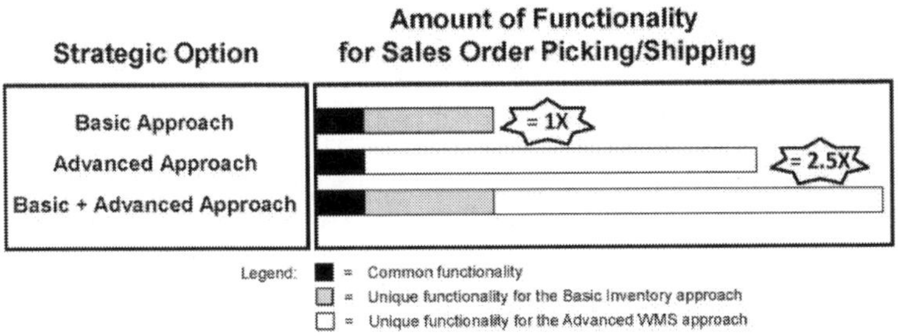

Comparing the Amounts of Functionality by Topic The differences in aggregate functionality can vary by business process, as previously illustrated for sales order picking/shipping in Figure B.2. A similar analysis for all of the book topics is shown in Figure B.3. As you can see by the yardsticks, the magnitude of common functionality and unique functionality varies by topic. The basic approach involves a smaller amount of unique functionality for most topics, whereas the advanced approach often involves a large amount (or the only amount) of unique functionality. As a specific example, the advanced approach provides the largest amount of unique functionality for sales order picking/shipping. Many of these capabilities also apply to the business process for transfer order picking/shipping. Companies using both approaches may need to understand the cumulative functionality represented by both yardsticks for a topic.

Figure B.3 Comparing Amounts of Functionality by Topic for Incremental Learning of Advanced Approach

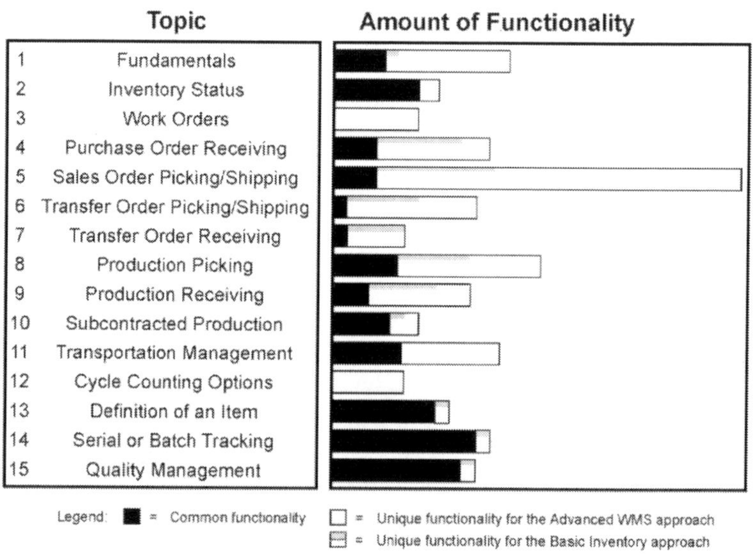

Incremental Learning for Knowledgeable AX Users The amount of functionality in each approach is also relevant for those trying to plan and quantify their learning, not only for new users but also for those already familiar with previous versions of AX. A comparison of the aggregate functionality for each approach provides a starting point for the amount of incremental learning. The graphics in Figure B.3 are primarily oriented to the incremental learning for the advanced approach to warehouse management.

Appendix C Comparing Conceptual Models

The two approaches to warehouse management can be compared in several different ways. The differences in conceptual models provide one way to make a comparison. The conceptual models within the two approaches reflect different levels of complexity. It is best illustrated by comparing the two approaches for a simple yet typical business process involving order-based picking for sales orders. This provides the basis for an apples-to-apples comparison. For each approach, the analysis covers the comparable steps in the business process, a comparison of the key constructs and their life cycles, and the number of major variations supported by the approach. These considerations are reflected in the following topics within this appendix.

1. Comparable Steps for Order-Based Picking of Sales Orders
2. Comparing Constructs and Life Cycles for Order-Based Picking
3. Comparing the Number of Major Variations Supported by Each Approach

This apples-to-apples comparison draws on the book's explanations about a simple yet typical process for sales order picking/shipping using the basic and advanced approaches. The abbreviated versions of an apples-to-apples comparison are provided for each type of warehouse transaction. These abbreviated versions cover purchase order receiving (Section 15.10), sales order picking/shipping (Section 16.17), transfer order picking/shipping (Section 17.13), transfer order receiving (Sections 18.7), production order picking (Section 19.9), and production order receiving (Section 20.9). The advanced approach employs several unique constructs where an apples-to-apples comparison is not easily made, including license plates (Section 13.2), the definition of bin locations (Section 13.15), and the use of work orders (Chapter 14).

Comparable Steps for Order-Based Picking of Sales Orders The comparable steps for order-based picking are summarized in Figure C.1 and described below. These steps also represent the minimum number of touch points within the business process for updating status. In summary, the comparable steps indicate differences in the starting point and in subsequent transactions; although both approaches require a final step of posting the sales order packing slip to update financial information. The starting point differs significantly between the basic approach (which generates picking lists for selected orders using the Release Sales Order Picking form) and the advanced approach (which releases selected orders to the warehouse using the Release to Warehouse form). The advanced approach also employs a mobile device transaction for reporting picking work (shown with grey shading in the figure). It also requires an additional step to confirm the outbound shipment—either before or after posting the packing slip—which can update the associated freight costs for sales orders within the shipment/load.

Figure C.1 Comparing Approaches for Sales Order Picking/Shipping

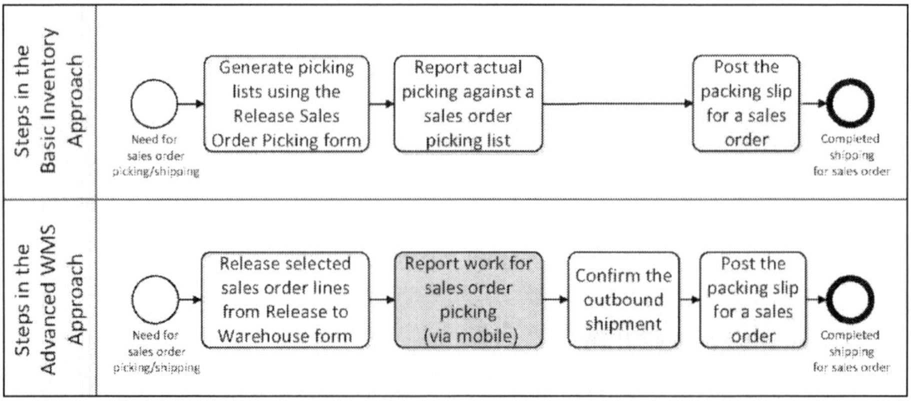

- *Steps in the Basic Approach.* The shipping clerk typically uses the Release Sales Order Picking form to review and select open sales order lines that require picking/shipping, and to generate the picking lists for selected orders. The generation of a picking list will reserve the inventory for each sales line (if not already reserved).

  The warehouse worker reviews the printed picking list and reports actual picking against the picking list. The shipping clerk reports actual shipment and updates financial information by posting the sales order packing slip for picked items.

- *Steps in the Advanced Approach.* The shipping clerk uses the Release To Warehouse form to review and select open sales order lines that require picking/shipping, and to release the selected orders to the warehouse. Inventory for each sales line must be reserved prior to the release-to-warehouse step. In this scenario of order-based picking, the release-to-warehouse step automatically creates a shipment, load and a released shipment wave for a sales order based on wave template policies. The shipping clerk can review the shipments and loads in a waved status.

  The warehouse worker reviews the picking work for the released shipment wave, and uses the mobile device to report work for each pick (from stocking locations) and the put to an outbound dock location. At that point, the shipping clerk can review loads and shipments that are ready to ship. The shipping clerk confirms the outbound shipment after the goods have actually left, and then posts the packing slip against the relevant sales order. The shipping clerk can confirm the shipment before or after posting the packing slip.

Comparing Constructs and Life Cycles for Order-Based Picking The different conceptual models are most easily identified by comparing the constructs and life cycles involved in each type of warehouse transaction. In the context of order-based picking, Figures C.2 and C.3 summarize this information for the basic and advanced approaches, and each figure has a separate explanation.

Figure C.2 Life Cycles Related to Basic Inventory Approach for Sales Order Picking/Shipping

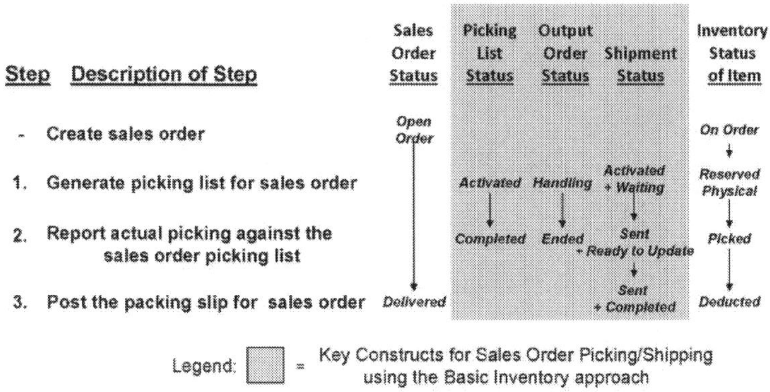

◆ *Life Cycles Related to the Basic Inventory Approach.* The Basic Inventory approach to order-based picking involves several related constructs, where the status for each construct reflects various steps in the process. Figure C.2 summarizes this information and only displays those steps representing the minimum number of touch points for updating status. Grey shading highlights the key constructs of a picking list, output order and shipment.

With order-based picking, the first step will create a picking list (with line items reflecting output orders) and a corresponding shipment. It should be noted that the status for a shipment is identified by the combination of two fields termed the Shipment Status and the Physical Update Status. For example, the combination of *Activated* + *Waiting* indicates the shipment has been created. Subsequent steps will update status when you report actual picking and post the packing slip for the sales order. The right side of figure shows the inventory status for an item on a sales order line. For example, various steps will change this status from *on order* to *reserved physical*, *picked* and *deducted*. You can reverse transactions after initially generating a picking list, after reporting actual picking and after posting the packing slip for the sales order.

Figure C.3 Life Cycles Related to Advanced WMS Approach for Sales Order Picking/Shipping

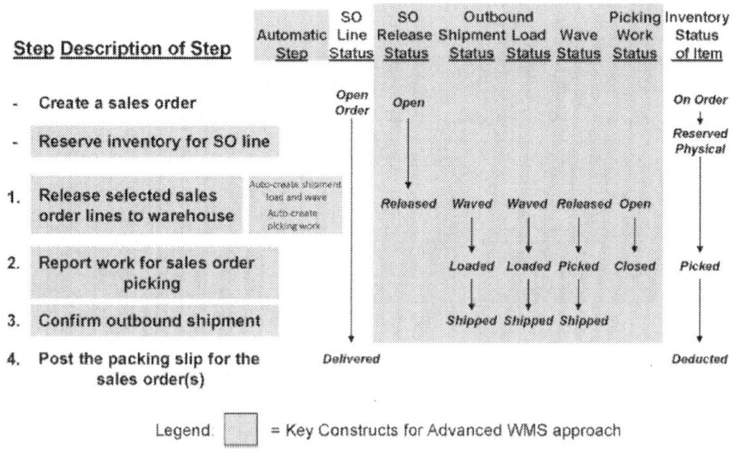

◆ *Life Cycles Related to the Advanced WMS Approach.* The Advanced WMS approach to order-based picking of a sales order involves several related constructs, where the status for each construct reflects various steps in the process. Figure C.3 summarizes this information and only displays those

steps representing the minimum number of touch points for updating status. Grey shading highlights the key constructs about the release status of a sales order, and the related shipment, load, wave and picking work.

The first step (using the Release to Warehouse form) only works when inventory has already been reserved for sales lines, but other variations of the release-to-warehouse step do not. With order-based picking, the release to warehouse step automatically creates a shipment and corresponding load for each sales order, and automatically creates and releases the corresponding wave (as reflected in a waved status for the shipment and load). The released wave also results in the automatic creation of picking work for the wave.

Subsequent steps will update status when you report picking work, confirm the outbound shipment, and post the packing slip for the sales order. You can reverse transactions after initially creating the picking work for the released wave, after reporting picking work, and after posting the packing slip for the sales order.

Comparing the Number of Major Variations for Sales Order Picking/Shipping The basic approach supports very few major variations sales order picking/shipping. The advanced approach supports many variations. However, one major variation applies to both approaches, where you employ a simple inventory transaction to bypass use of related constructs.

The comparative number of major variations can be illustrated for warehouse transactions related to sales order picking/shipping, as summarized below. The major variations for other types of warehouse transactions are identified and explained in each chapter.

- *Simple Inventory Transaction for Both Approaches.* A simple inventory transaction applies to both approaches, where you report actual picking when posting the packing slip for a sales order. In this way, you can bypass the use of picking lists and shipments when using the basic approach. You can also bypass the use of loads, shipments, waves and work when using the advanced approach. The applicable "simple inventory transaction" is identified for every business process covered in the book.

- *Limited Variations Supported by the Basic Approach.* The only major variation involves wave picking based on use of the Picking Workbench form, where picking lists can be grouped together under a separate identifier termed a picking batch.

- *Multiple Variations Supported by the Advanced Approach.* The advanced approach supports multiple variations, including load planning for outbound loads, wave picking, manual or automated packing, replenishment of picking locations, staging and loading steps prior to shipment, and several alternatives for the release to warehouse step. A subset of these capabilities also apply to transfer order picking/shipping.

  These variations typically involve different steps and life cycles of the key constructs (for shipments, loads, waves and work orders), and corresponding differences in reversing transactions. Some of the variations involve a new construct (such as containers for manual or automated packing) or different types of work orders (such as replenishment work and counting work).

List of Figures

Advanced WMS Approach

List of Cases

Advanced WMS Approach

Chapter 13: Fundamentals of Advanced WMS Approach

Chapter 14: Overview of Work Orders

Chapter 15: Purchase Order Receiving

Chapter 16: Sales Order Picking/Shipping

Chapter 20: Production Order Receiving

Chapter 21: Subcontracted Production

Chapter 23: Integration with Advanced Transportation Management

Common Foundation

Chapter 24: Definition of an Item

Chapter 25: Batch Number and Serial Number Tracking

Chapter 26: Integration With Quality Management

About the Author

Scott Hamilton has specialized in SCM/ERP information systems for three decades and consulted globally with several hundred manufacturing/distribution companies. His publications include multiple books about SCM using Dynamics AX as well as two textbooks about SCM/ERP, and his books have been translated into Russian and Chinese. His regular column "The AX Solution Architect" is published in MSDynamicsWorld.com. Scott has been a frequent speaker at Microsoft and AXUG events around the world, and a multi-year winner of the rarely-given Microsoft MVP award for AX. He earned a doctorate in information systems specializing in manufacturing and taught SCM/ERP as an MBA professor at several leading universities in North America, Europe and the Pacific Rim. He lives in Minnesota, a place where people still build ice castles.

About UXC Eclipse

Scott Hamilton has become the "go to" authority on Microsoft Dynamics AX in the manufacturing space. His books provide valuable insights into the market place we serve, which gives us all the opportunity to expand our thinking and see beyond the software features and functions.

UXC Eclipse is widely recognized as a global leader in industry solutions built on the Dynamics AX platform. We have a depth of experience across the horizontal global ERP market with specific focus on industry solutions for Retail, Wholesale and Distribution, Manufacturing and the surrounding supply chain.

We help organizations streamline their business and operational processes to bring the best from their organizational experience to the best of our Dynamics AX solutions; the result is 'win-win'. From their Dynamics AX solutions, our customers realize operational efficiencies, improve business performance and heighten their supply chain collaboration. At UXC Eclipse we use a combination of old-fashioned service with ISO-9001 accredited quality systems and controls to ensure our implementations deliver to our customers' expectations – on time and on budget. Our happy customers are the true indication of our success. With a global team of over 650 people, some 2,700 customer sites rely on UXC Eclipse for their project implementation services and everyday support.

We trust you find this book to be a useful insight into Microsoft Dynamics AX. If UXC Eclipse can be of service on your supply chain journey, then please get in touch with us at *www.uxceclipse.com*

Bradley Stroop
Chief Executive Officer
UXC Eclipse Group

43611076R00269

Made in the USA
San Bernardino, CA
21 December 2016